# ONE NATION
# UNDER GOLD

## OTHER BOOKS BY JAMES LEDBETTER

*Unwarranted Influence: Dwight D. Eisenhower
and the Military-Industrial Complex*

*The Great Depression: A Diary* (coeditor)

*Dispatches for the New York* Tribune: *Selected
Journalism of Karl Marx*

*Made Possible By . . . : The Death of Public
Broadcasting in the United States*

*Starving to Death on $200 Million: The Short,
Absurd Life of the Industry Standard*

# ONE NATION UNDER GOLD

How One Precious Metal
Has Dominated the American Imagination
for Four Centuries

# JAMES LEDBETTER

Liveright Publishing Corporation
A division of W. W. Norton
*Independent Publishers Since 1923*
New York • London

For information about permission to reproduce selections from this book,
write to Permissions, Liveright Publishing Corporation,
a division of  W. W. Norton & Company, Inc.,
500 Fifth Avenue, New York, NY 10110

For information about special discounts for bulk purchases, please contact
W. W. Norton Special Sales at specialsales@wwnorton.com or 800-233-4830

Manufacturing by Berryville Graphics
Book design by Lisa Buckley
Production manager: Anna Oler

ISBN 978-0-87140-683-5

Liveright Publishing Corporation
500 Fifth Avenue, New York, N.Y. 10110
www.wwnorton.com

W. W. Norton & Company Ltd.
15 Carlisle Street, London  W1D 3BS

1 2 3 4 5 6 7 8 9 0

*To Henry, who reminds me that gold is very rare.*

# CONTENTS

# TIME LINE *of* EVENTS

―――――――――――――――○――――――――――――――

## 1700s

**1788**  US Constitution is ratified. Article I, section 10 stipulates that no state shall coin money, or "make any Thing but gold and silver Coin a Tender in Payment of Debts."

**1792**  The Coinage Act creates a bimetallic, silver-gold standard in the United States. The US dollar is defined as equivalent to 24.75 grains of fine gold and 371.25 grains of fine silver, a silver-to-gold ratio of 15 to 1. Due to global market fluctuations in the gold-silver price ratio, gold is used primarily for transactions abroad, and silver primarily for domestic transactions.

**1799**  A twelve-year-old boy in Cabarrus County, North Carolina, discovers a 17-pound gold nugget, setting off the Carolina Gold Rush.

## 1800s

**1804–1828**  North Carolina supplies all the gold for domestic coinage from the US Mint in Philadelphia.

**1812**  For the first time, Treasury issues notes (not legal tender) that promise to pay gold or silver at a future date.

**1816**  Great Britain puts the pound sterling on a gold standard.

**1834**  Congress changes the silver-to-gold ratio to 16 to 1, thereby restoring gold coins to domestic use.

**1848**  Gold is found at Sutter's Mill near Sacramento, ushering in the California Gold Rush.

**1859**  Comstock Lode of gold and silver struck in Nevada.

1862    Congress passes the Legal Tender Acts, creating for the first time paper money ("greenbacks") that is not convertible to gold or silver. A dollar-gold market immediately emerges.

1868    Gold is discovered in South Africa.

1869    A ring of investors attempts to corner the gold market, which crashes on "Black Friday" after the US Treasury announces a sale of gold.

1873    Silver is demonetized, putting the United States on an informal gold standard.

1896    William Jennings Bryan "Cross of Gold" speech at the Democratic convention in Chicago.

1898    Gold is discovered in Klondike, Alaska, creating an Alaska Gold Rush.

## 1900s

1900    The Gold Standard Act formally places the United States on a gold standard.

1913    The Federal Reserve system is established, requiring that Treasury notes be backed 40 percent by gold.

1914–1919    Most countries (though not the United States) abandon a gold standard to pay for World War I.

1925    Great Britain restores a "gold bullion" standard, with money redeemable for gold but no circulating gold coins.

1931    Great Britain defaults on gold payments and abandons gold standard.

1933    United States leaves the gold standard and makes individual ownership of gold coins and bullion illegal. The Roosevelt administration begins day-to-day management of the price of gold.

1934    The Gold Reserve Act devalues the dollar and returns the United States to a gold bullion standard, setting the price of gold at $35 an ounce.

1939    War in Europe forces the London gold market to close.

1942    World War II brings about the closure of all US gold mines.

1944    The world's major economies meet at the Bretton Woods conference in New Hampshire to create a new international monetary system, based on a dollar convertible to gold.

1954    London gold market reopens.

1960    Gold market spikes, pushing prices above $35 an ounce and indicating a US balance-of-payments crisis.

1961    Major central banks form "Gold Pool" to control private market transactions. American citizens are prohibited from owning gold abroad as well as at home.

1965    American government officials begin secret plans for "Operation Goldfinger" to dramatically increase US gold production.

1967    South Africa produces the first Krugerrand coin. UK devalues the pound sterling, causing large outflows of gold from the United States.

1968    Congress narrowly votes to lift the "gold cover" for US currency. The United States stops buying and selling gold with individuals. The world's largest economies agree to a "two-tier" market, with one value for privately traded gold and a fixed value for transactions between central banks. The London gold market closes for two weeks.

1971    Richard Nixon "closes the gold window," devaluing the dollar by making it no longer redeemable for gold.

1974    On December 31, it becomes legal for Americans to buy and own gold for the first time in forty years.

1975    Krugerrand becomes available for purchase in the United States.

1980    US Republican Party platform calls for a "dependable monetary standard—that is, an end to inflation," inter-

preted as the first pro–gold standard party pledge in
decades.

1981  US Gold Commission, chaired by Treasury Secretary
Donald Regan, convenes to study gold's role in the US
monetary system.

1986  US Mint introduces American Eagle Gold Bullion Coin,
minted with gold mined in the United States.

1990  After a decade of remarkable growth, the US gold industry becomes the second-largest producer in the world
after South Africa.

## 2000s

2007  China surpasses South Africa as the world's largest gold
producer.

2012  US Republican Party platform invokes 1981 Gold Commission and proposes a similar commission to investigate
possible ways to set a fixed value for the dollar. The
party's 2016 platform repeats the same pledge.

# PREFACE

NO ONE TRYING TO UNDERSTAND the United States would be so careless as to avoid an examination of its money. The country that produced the wealthiest society in the world, the seat of the largest stock and bond markets, the granddaddy of the consumer society that has enveloped much of the planet—at home and abroad, America is synonymous with its dollar and the unabashed pursuit of it.

As powerful and ubiquitous as the dollar may be, however, America's relationship to its own currency has throughout its history been uneasy, rocky, and divisive nearly to the point of insurrection. What is the dollar worth, according to whom, and how should that value be measured? These seemingly fundamental questions have never been settled to universal satisfaction even through four centuries of American financial history. From the very origins of the nation in eighteenth-century political fervor to the twenty-first century's presidential debates, we continue to argue about the dollar with the often implicit understanding that far more than a piece of paper is at stake. The question of American money is wrapped up in patriotism, in the nation's self-worth, and in America's standing in the world, a standing that never feels as confident or sturdy as the imperial reach of the dollar and the American military machine might imply. In modern America the dollar is a way of projecting strength into the world, and therefore many Americans insist that the dollar must stand for something besides itself; the dollar ought to guarantee an enduring promise;

the dollar should be, as President John F. Kennedy first said (and many after him), as good as gold.

The idea of money "as good as gold" is simple, immediately grasped, and quintessentially human; gold coins became a standard of exchange at least as far back as 1500 BC, and the United States, like most nations, used gold and silver coins as money for much of its early commerce. Gold has many qualities that one would hope to associate with money: it is indestructible, it is rare, and it is beautiful to behold.

And yet, gold for Americans is anything but simple. From the very beginnings of our national life, it has seemed impossible for Americans to look at gold dispassionately. The metal—and its seductive hint of boundless wealth—tap into a psychological wellspring that reaches beyond any purely physical qualities. Gold brings with it a spiritual dimension, a nonrational totem that stands for strength, control, and even adoration. We seek the immutable characteristics of gold in the same way that religions posit the divine and everlasting qualities of God and an afterlife, as if gold can somehow connect us to eternity and protect us from the vagaries of actual human existence.

The problem is that monetary gold can't do those things. Fixing our money to gold and amassing great stacks of it is no more a guarantor of sustained economic health than a witch doctor's potions. And, as with religion, what gold believers do can often resemble, in the eyes of the less devout, madness and destruction. From the earliest days of the American republic, gold blinded men from seeing the financial realities around them. And it brought with it all manner of fraud and false hope, gold by-products that are still with us today.

To slice through the hype of gold, we need to see our own history clearly. It is not enough to evoke the past, because gold mania carries its own nostalgic historical hues. Yes, gold can make Americans spectacularly wealthy, and the twentieth century's restrictions on owning it were justly fought and overturned. Beyond that, however, lie many prejudices about gold, some debatable and some dangerous. To avoid gold's false paths, we need to argue with the past, to test the assumptions that are too often and too casually passed uncritically. This book, I hope, is that argument.

# ONE NATION
# UNDER GOLD

# INTRODUCTION

———————————————○———————————————

**THERE WERE FEW OBVIOUS REASONS** for cheer when James K. Polk delivered his fourth and final presidential message to Congress on December 5, 1848. Although Polk had been the youngest man to assume the American presidency, his term had taken a physical toll; he was visibly unhealthy and within a few months would die of cholera. The recently ended war with Mexico had cost thousands of lives and a then-exorbitant $100 million. Although the war with its jingoistic rallying cries had brought some benefits to an adolescent nation, it had exacerbated the tension over slavery that would soon erupt into the Civil War, with millions of Americans agreeing with Abraham Lincoln that the war had been "unnecessarily and unconstitutionally commenced."

And yet, there was one unequivocally bright portion of Polk's speech that united his political allies and foes in jubilation. Among the prizes won in the rusty skirmish with Mexico was California, a geographical gem with tantalizing proximity to Russia, China, and South America, a territory that Polk predicted would become "a great emporium." Better still, Polk reminded his audience of the reports that California contained mines of precious metals. "Recent discoveries render it probable that these mines are more extensive and valuable than was anticipated," he intoned. "The accounts of the abundance of gold in that territory are of such an extraordinary character as would scarcely command belief were they not corroborated by the authentic reports of officers in the public service who have visited the mineral district and derived the facts which they detail from personal observation." With this speech, Polk also presented the War Department's report and announced that a new Treasury mint would imminently open in San Francisco, to more "speedily and fully avail ourselves of the undeveloped wealth of these mines."[1]

In the American nation's sixty-odd years of existence, no presidential speech had ever created as much fervor and euphoria. The fantasies of unlimited wealth emanating from the ground that had propelled Cortez and Pizarro to conquer the New World seemed now to be realized or even surpassed. The *Albany Argus* said that based on the government's accounts, "the fabled El Dorado is as nothing, compared to the gold regions of Alta California."[2] To many Americans, the passion for California's gold not only invoked religious fervor, it surpassed it; one weekly newspaper declared, "the coming of the Messiah, or the dawn of the Millennium would not have excited anything like the interest" in Polk's pronouncements.

Indeed, it was common in nineteenth-century America, which was on the cusp of the Third Great Awakening, to interpret world events as a reflection of divine will—and the discovery of gold confirmed for many that God had tremendous plans for the United States. "Our country seems destined, in the coming age, to be the new historical centre of the earth," wrote *The American Review*, a monthly magazine associated with Edgar Allan Poe and the Whig Party (Polk's rivals, who took over the White House in 1849). "God intends to give here, on this continent, a scope for human energies of thought and will, such as never yet been seen since the days before the flood . . . in overcoming and annihilating the old limitations of human endeavor; in unfolding the physical resources of the earth; in the creation of boundless wealth and a boundless sphere for action and enjoyment."[3] It was as if gold had reversed the curse of Eden, restoring mankind to a state of laborless wealth, at least in the United States.


Not everyone, however, viewed California's gold in a positive light. References to gold "mania" and gold "disease" were common, and pulpits across America warned about excess, idolatry, and a loss of traditional values. The reality on the ground seemed to bear out their concerns, as California fast became a magnet for outcasts, charlatans, fugitives, and desperation. Two historians concluded, "The gold rush was the product of a kind of mass hysteria, and it set a tone for California and created a state of mind in which greed predominated and disorder and violence were all too frequent."[4]

But for better and worse, the California Gold Rush made clear that America's so-called manifest destiny was now intertwined with the precious yellow metal that has entranced mankind throughout human civilization. Gold did not, of course, spring up genie-like in the nineteenth century but had already been enshrined in the US Constitution. Article I, section 10 says that no state shall "make any Thing but gold and silver Coin a Tender in Payment of Debts," although the meaning of that simple-seeming assertion, as this book demonstrates, has been hotly contested through the centuries. Gold has been at the center of American political debate as far back as the Constitutional Convention and right through to the most recent presidential campaigns. The 2012 and 2016 Republican platforms, for example, mentioned "a metallic basis for U.S. currency" and anachronistically proposed a commission "to investigate possible ways to set a fixed value for the dollar." In 2016, Donald Trump became the first major-party nominee in more than half a century to advocate a return to a gold standard. "Bringing back the gold standard would be very hard to do, but, boy, would it be wonderful," Trump said. "We'd have a standard on which to base our money." Decades after the major economies of the world moved to a floating currency, there is no other developed nation in the world in which a major political party proposes returning the country's currency to a gold standard.[5]

Obviously, part of gold's appeal is universal, and not exclusively American. Gold ties us to ancient civilizations and religions, and it connects us to countless cultural guideposts, from the Bible to Shakespeare to Kanye West. Gold is suffused in our language and our lives: our best athletes win gold medals; our best-selling musical recordings are (these days, only metaphorically) cast in gold; we speak of anything best in its class as a "gold standard." Our everyday references—from Oz's yellow brick road to the gold-toothed "grills" favored by hip-hop stars—are forged in the yellow metal. Even if we could overnight strip the role of gold from the international monetary system—a goal of many an economist and late twentieth-century American policymaker—our language and our need to think in symbols of perfection and indelibility would still be suffused with gold.

And yet for Americans, gold's appeal is more specific, more grounded in the national experience. Gold carries for Americans a sense of national pride and birthright. Gold mining on the American continent goes back at least as far as four thousand years, and from the very first encounters with European explorers and conquistadors the metal was the object of fascination and desire. When Christopher Columbus landed in the Bahamas in 1492, he noticed that the inhabitants wore small pieces of gold in pierced nose holes, and his early communication with them was an attempt to discover where he might find a greater supply.[6] This finding seemed natural enough, since he had set out to find a route to gold-rich Asia, and his discoveries encouraged a wave of Spanish and Portuguese expeditions in the early sixteenth century in search of gold and other riches. Ponce de Leon, for example, reported finding a cache of gold in Florida in 1513.

Not long after the United States became an independent nation, in 1799, gold was discovered by accident. A twelve-year-old boy in Cabarrus County, North Carolina, was shooting fish with a bow and arrow on a Sunday afternoon when he found an unusually marbled 16-pound rock "the size of a small smoothing iron" and took it home to use as a doorstop in his family's farmhouse. Three years later, a Fayetteville jeweler identified the rock as gold, and mining began in North Carolina. Soon thereafter gold was unearthed in Georgia, and a genuine gold rush set in. Tens of thousands of men worked the mines, and tens of millions of dollars' worth of gold were mined and refined in the early nineteenth century in this region; prior to 1829, all the gold mined in the United States and coined in the Philadelphia Mint came from North Carolina.[7] The Carolina Gold Rush foreshadowed the "Gold Fever" that would spread over California and other western states beginning in the late 1840s.

This sense of gold as an American birthright is more than just symbolic. The booming gold industry led to massive westward migration and the development of mining towns, and crowned California as a genuine global economic power. Gold was also a wellspring of economic expansion and innovation. From the earliest days of placer mining in California, gold mining has provided a laboratory for technological and business-model breakthroughs. In addition, the need to ship gold was a major reason for railroad expansion and overexpansion. This innovation did not end with the nineteenth century; gold would go on to play a critical role in many of the high-tech industries that helped define the second half of the twentieth century, from the early transistor to the space program.

It is unsurprising, then, that so many Americans, from the highest public officials to the field and factory workers, would look to gold as a creator and protector of wealth. For most of the United States' existence, the public and private stockpiling of gold has been a powerful, if sometimes deceptive, symbol for American strength and prosperity. The sudden and sizable additions of gold to the US economy in the nineteenth century, from the early North Carolina discoveries through the California Gold Rush to the Klondike discoveries at the turn of the century, were rungs in a ladder that culminated in America's economic domination of the globe. Alas, an enviable gold pile never provided the protection against economic contraction that governments and bankers hoped it would. But amassing quantities of gold was hardly an irrational strategy for much of America's existence, and in the shaky global finances of the nineteenth century, it certainly helped establish a fledgling republic as a creditworthy nation.

Similarly, for much of America's history, gold literally was money—and therefore ignited some of the most contentious political battles the nation has ever seen. The metallic basis for the dollar was one of the most heated issues in nineteenth-century politics. A reliance on monetary gold was, for example, the defining basis of Andrew Jackson's Democratic Party. When the Northern states needed to fund the Civil War, they issued for the first time nationally sanctioned money that had no value in gold or silver; to this day, some Americans believe that these "greenbacks" were unconstitutional. Throughout the twentieth century, the role of gold as a basis for American money has diminished, to the point in 1971 when the dollar "floated" against other currencies. Nonetheless, millions of Americans today still argue that the country's economy would be better off if we returned to a gold standard.

Economic reliance on gold has its bleaker consequences, one of which is that all major American wars have been tied up with America's gold supply and have frequently forced a decisive break with the monetary status quo. It is not quite the case that the United States of America has ever gone to war over gold mines—which, by contrast, the Boers and the British arguably did in South Africa at the turn of the twentieth century. Nonetheless, the ties between American wars and gold are profound and complex, pulling the nation apart and together sometimes simultaneously. The discovery of gold in California in 1848 took place just as the United States was acquiring that territory at the end of its war with Mexico. The American Civil War and the states' rights versus federal republic battle had direct analogues centered on the role of money, and indeed the North financed its war efforts by issuing, for the first time, a national paper currency not backed by gold. The ensuing market for gold owed its very existence to war, and gold speculators monitoring their investments were sometimes better informed of battlefield developments than the White House. Liberty bonds to pay for America's participation in World War I were backed by gold. And the seemingly bottomless costs of the Vietnam War were a critical factor in the United States finally going off the gold standard in 1971.

All of those attachments to gold are centuries old. There is one further, very potent American attachment to gold that is of more recent vintage for all but the wealthiest Americans: gold as an investment. And it is impossible to understand the economics of buying gold in today's America without understanding the political and historical forces that stretch back to the founding of the republic. Through the end of the nineteenth century, the overwhelming majority of Americans were not able to afford investments of any kind—and given that day-to-day money for many years was made out of or exchangeable for gold, it's far from obvious that gold would also be the preferred investment even for those who could afford it. Then, beginning in 1933, it was illegal for Americans to own gold in any significant quantity for forty years. Even today, the percentage of Americans who own gold as an investment is likely quite small, and the ancillary fees for investing in it can be prohibitively high.

Nonetheless, a sizable percentage of Americans would presumably like to own gold. Gallup annually surveys Americans on their perceptions about investments. In 2011, when gold prices were relatively high, gold was deemed the best long-term investment with 34 percent preferring it (real estate was next at 19 percent).[8] But as gold prices subsided, the percentage naming gold as the best long-term investment fell behind real estate and, in 2014, tied with stocks and mutual funds. Significantly, Republicans and independents have greater faith in gold's investment power than do Democrats. In addition, the higher an American's household income is, the less likely he or she is to pick gold as the best long-term investment—and the more likely to choose real estate or stocks and mutual funds. Gold, it seems, is the preferred investment vehicle for those who can't afford it.

Harder to measure by any poll is the undeniable fact that gold can theoretically make you rich, even when—perhaps especially when—there are few other viable options available. Beginning in 2008, Americans went on an investors' roller-coaster ride—mostly downhill—with the collapse of the housing market and the onset of the Great Recession. For the next several years, virtually every personal investment strategy once deemed prudent and reliable was shown wanting, leaving tens of millions of Americans feeling lost if not outright cheated. For a significant period of time, the only ones consistently smiling were those who invested in gold; its value increased sixfold between 2001 and 2011. During that period, there was effectively no legal, popularly traded investment asset class—not oil, not other commodities, not stocks, not bonds, not "emerging markets"—that even came close to gold's performance.

Of course, as with any investment, what goes up will almost always go down. Those who bought gold in 2011 or 2012 saw their investments worth less five years later. For better or worse, however, the unfortunate reality of investment timing doesn't appear to deter Americans from investing in gold (or real estate or stocks), and there's little reason to think that future generations will behave differently.

In the 1950s and 1960s, those Americans who advocated gold ownership operated as renegades at the outskirts of the law, some with more than a tinge of paranoia. Even with gold ownership now legal for decades, the fear has not entirely dissipated; for some, the fear that economic collapse will lead the American government to confiscate or outlaw investment in gold—as occurred in the 1930s—remains a real, if distant, possibility. Such views may represent an extreme minority, but they are rarely far from the surface in American gold investment circles and are sometimes incorporated as a sales pitch. And thus while a small—even tiny—percentage of Americans actually own gold, the freedom to own it has a strong political resonance, akin to the freedom to own a gun.

The gun comparison is not as far off as it may seem; after all, not all American associations with gold are positive. For many Christians in the middle of the nineteenth century, the mass migrations of would-be gold miners represented mayhem, a sign of a coming apocalypse. "Oh this lust of gold! What unforeseen miseries it is destined to bring!" wailed the *New York Herald* in 1849.[9] Those who were rushing to California were not seeking an honest living, the paper insisted. "It is to grasp the shining metal, which, for past ages, has been the fruitful cause of untold murders, and the massacres and crimes which have stained the annals of every nation on God's earth, that ever possessed mines—gold mines." It might sound overwrought, but the basic point is echoed today by economists and political scientists who speak of a "resource curse."

And while the California gold mines unquestionably enhanced the American economy, the domination of gold was far from universally applauded. Half a century after the California Gold Rush, the populists of the South and West denounced gold as the principal instrument of economic oppression. The naturalist writer Frank Norris depicted in his novel *McTeague* a bleak parable in which lust for gold ends in a Death Valley stalemate, in which a live man is handcuffed to a dead one, finally in possession of a gold stash he will never be able to spend. And an unhealthy, desperate attachment to gold's unique qualities has caused even government officials with state-of-the-art technology to abandon common sense in a twentieth-century alchemy quest.

Whether Americans see in gold the country's salvation or its damnation, it has always represented a struggle with modernity, a symbol of timeless strength yet an accelerant of economic progress. It also symbolizes the divisions that progress brings: between city and farm, between technology and tradition, and between haves and have-nots. Such struggles with modernity lead many nations to political extremes and civil wars. For the most part, American political institutions have been able to resist such dire outcomes. But our understanding of those institutions is incomplete without understanding how gold itself has shaped them, and how they continue to shape gold.

# CHAPTER 1

# El Dorado Comes True

GEORGE WASHINGTON WAS NOT an especially successful farmer or businessman—but he was a meticulous bookkeeper. In 1779, encamped in Middle Brook for months after the stalemated battle of Monmouth, New Jersey, the Revolutionary War general unleashed his financial frustrations in a letter to his nephew. Much of the wealth he had inherited through marriage was, once the war began, loaned out to Virginia neighbors and merchants. The trouble was that by the time the borrowers paid him back, the money they used was worth a fraction of its earlier value. "I am now receiving a shilling in the pound in discharge of Bonds which ought to have been paid me, and would have been realized before I left Virginia, but for my indulgence to the debtors," Washington complained. At twenty shillings to the pound, this implied a loss of 95 percent. Washington said in the same letter that his losses exceeded ten thousand pounds; according to one biographer's estimate, that was approximately a year's worth of his farm's income.

Continuing his tirade, Washington wrote, "It is most devoutly to be wished that the several States would adopt some vigorous measures for

At this sawmill near Coloma, California, James Marshall found gold flakes in January 1848. While it was not the first gold discovery in the United States, it altered the nation's economic and political landscape more than any other. *Courtesy Library of Congress* the purpose of giving credit to the paper currency and punishment of speculators, forestallers and others who are preying upon the vitals of this great Country and putting every thing to the utmost hazard." By the time the war ended, Washington was so disabused of worthless paper currency that he "paid his manager in produce, not money."[1]

It is almost impossible to overstate the dislike that most of the Founding Fathers, and indeed most of the American ruling class, had for paper money in the late eighteenth and early nineteenth centuries. The currencies issued by most states depreciated to the point of being worthless. One historian has gone so far as to argue that the colonies themselves were so tapped out by their own useless money that they embraced the idea of a federal government just to unburden themselves of their debt: "Paper money, therefore, or rather the reaction from it, helped to secure the adoption of the federal constitution."

With the crucial exception of slavery, no issue tormented nineteenth-century America longer or more passionately than the question of what our money should be. The money question gouged deep wounds into every major public policy concern of the era: the structure of government; economic growth and the expansion of national land; the concentration of wealth, geographically and individually; the conduct of wars, and the debt and inflation they created; and the very meaning of the Constitution, including the amendments that ended slavery itself.

As hated as paper money might have been, there were no universal alternatives. Commerce in the regions that would form the United States was for more than its first century conducted in a hodgepodge of currencies. Gold was the most enduring and in some ways the most powerful of these currencies: until the twentieth century there was never a point when gold could not be used to pay most debts, and some specific types of debt required gold. But any currency based on a physical substance will inevitably be subject to limitations, and gold—a bulky metal that must be mined, refined, measured, stamped for purity, and heavily guarded against theft—is especially limiting. In this sense, gold as a means of currency is overqualified: Because there is only so much gold in a country at a given time, how can economic activity—and, especially, economic growth—take place if no one wants to part with his share?

The answer, much of the time, is that it cannot. And thus, an abundance of alternative, sometimes exotic currencies, official and unofficial, sprang up. Silver coins were officially minted through the early nineteenth century, and were widely used until the mid-1830s, but at many points their use was rarer than their imprimatur might suggest. Market discrepancies between the prices of gold and silver meant the silver coins were often more valuable if melted down. One government official estimated that at the outbreak of the Civil War in 1861 there were, for example, probably fewer than one thousand silver dollars in circulation in the entire country.[2]

At various points in the eighteenth and nineteenth century, Spanish coins were widely and reliably enough circulated to constitute a semi-official currency; indeed, Spain's "pieces of eight" were legal tender in the United States until 1857. British, French, Russian, Portuguese, and Dutch coins—representing countries all jousting to be colonial powers—could also be found. In many parts of the country, Mexican coins circulated as money, albeit "debased and worn," as one observer put it.[3] Washington himself recorded a list of the money he took with him on a single trip to Philadelphia: "6 joes, 67 half joes, 2 one-eighteenth joes, 3 doubloons, 1 pistole, 2 moidores, 1 half moidore, 2 double Louis d'or, 3 single Louis d'or, 80 guineas, 7 half guineas, besides silver and bank-notes"—this being currency from Portugal, Spain, France, and Britain.

Despite the prevalence of coins, paper money was abundant from the colonial period onward. Most states had a banking system that could issue its own notes, often theoretically redeemable for a given amount of gold, but in practice more useful as paper, even if at a discount from face value. During what was known as the

"Free Banking Era"—from the fall of the Second Bank of the United States in 1837 until the passage of the National Banking Act in 1863—hundreds of loosely supervised banks were launched that printed paper money known as "shinplasters," "stump tails," "red dogs," "smooth monkeys," and "sick Indians."[4] In some regions individual cities and companies issued certificates for paying state dues that circulated as money; in the West some railroads even created reusable train "tickets" that functioned as currency. And the Civil War, of course, created Confederate money that circulated in the South and "greenbacks"—money printed by the Union government without being redeemable for gold or silver—in the North.

Some early American leaders accepted that nonmetallic money would be necessary and actively advocated its use. Benjamin Franklin, a visionary in so many diverse fields, argued that America should have a paper currency precisely because it had no native supplies of gold or silver. Others, particularly those stung by the inflationary experience of paper money in the late eighteenth and early nineteenth centuries, held different views. The patrician landowner Thomas Jefferson feared paper money as issued by private financiers; he warned that "bank notes will be as oak leaves" but advocated the issuance of paper money backed by the government.[5] Alexander Hamilton, for all his disagreements with Jefferson, on this matter concurred. Of course, to many eighteenth- and nineteenth-century thinkers, the idea of the national government legitimizing a particular currency—regardless of the physical medium—represented an uncomfortable mixture of state and financial power. In the early days of the American republic, an argument about what constitutes money quickly became an argument about what type and size of government one favored. The most vigorous objections to a national currency and a national banking system came from Whig populist Andrew Jackson and what would become the Democratic Party.

And so while modern-day gold-standard advocates sometimes downplay the complexity of currency in the eighteenth and nineteenth centuries, the unstable crazy quilt of early American money could make any sensible person yearn for an immutable yardstick of value. Against the backdrop of monetary chaos, gold took on for early Americans a sense of psychological security. In a nation that embraced revolutionary change in political matters, gold was a vital tie to the ancient world. Gold meant self-reliance: it could not be destroyed and its value—compared, say, to that of paper money— could not easily be manipulated. Just as important, the more gold Americans possessed, the more they could decrease dependence on European (and in particular, British) financiers, an economic condition that long persisted even after the founding of the American republic and that especially vexed the likes of James Madison.[6]

It may seem astonishing that by the middle of the nineteenth century an economy the size of the United States had not adopted a uniform paper currency, and yet to a considerable degree this was by design. In the popular mind, paper money was equated with fraud and failure, even if in some instances bad financial management was mostly to blame. Banknotes in the early colonies often resulted in rapid and disastrous inflation; in Rhode Island, bills issued in the 1730s were worth no more than 4 percent of their face value by 1750. Throughout the early 1800s, bank failures were rife, and the experience of holding worthless paper money issued by a dissolved bank was all too common. One businessman and publisher wrote of his experience with paper money in the early 1800s: "Such was the state of the currency, that in New Jersey, I met with an instance where a one dollar note I had taken in change, which was current on one side of a turnpike gate, would not pass at an hundred yards distance on the other side!"[7]

Even where paper money had been a relative boon— Pennsylvania is usually cited—it ran against the historical grain. The size and structure of the US government had been conceived by men with a strong desire to undo the taxation and government interference of British colonization. Under the original Articles of Confederation, for example, Congress was given no authority to levy taxes; only the states had that power, and many failed or declined to collect what was ostensibly owed to them. The Constitution did not create a central bank, and for more than half a century after the Constitution was ratified, many powerful Americans—notably Andrew Jackson—maintained that the document explicitly prohibited a national bank. That the Supreme Court in 1819 unanimously upheld the constitutionality of a national bank in *McCulloch v. Maryland* barely dented Jackson's certitude that it was unconstitutional.[8] Thus, for those who advocated a small federal government with limited power, the use of gold as currency not merely was deemed to be the only legally allowable nationwide currency but also served a specific political agenda: gold prevented any mechanism by which a federal government could grow, thus helping to guarantee the states' rights ideal.

This could be seen clearly in Jackson's war against a central bank. During the relatively brief lifetime of the First (established in 1791) and Second (1816–1836) Banks of the United States, their managers did not help their cause with the American people through blatant use of bank funds for political purposes, or monetary policy that was at times destructive. But at its core, Jackson's crusade was over a vision of government—whether the United States would mimic larger European nations with a central bank and a national paper currency, or whether it would remain a federation of states whose size and strength could be kept in check through a metallic-based currency.

Jackson's view on the Bank bordered on obsessive, but his distrust of a national bank and the political power that could adhere to it was widespread, and reflected an agrarian view that the concentration of businesses and financial power in the Northeast was probably corrupt and at a minimum rigged against the South and the West. (Not surprisingly, when the original law passed in 1791 to authorize the First Bank of the United States, only one member of Congress north of Maryland opposed it and only three south of Maryland favored it.)[9] Even after Jackson left the White House, a strong notion prevailed in American law that government had to be kept separate from banks, and that the federal government could make its payments only in gold.[10]

After engineering the 1832 presidential election as a referendum on the Bank, Jackson's cunning and decisive blow came when he withdrew the government's deposits from the central bank and placed the funds in a selected series of "pet" banks.[11] He frequently couched his view not in economic terms, but in absolute moral ones; his opponents were misguided banking idolaters while he pursued the one true monetary path. In a somewhat inverted but nonetheless searing metaphor, Jackson declared, "Were all the worshippers of the golden Calf to memorialise me and request a restoration of the Deposits, I would cut my right hand from my body before I would do such an act. The golden calf may be worshipped by others but as for myself I will serve the Lord."[12]

This move to the pet banks destroyed the central bank; its charter expired in 1836. Politically, Jackson's victory was total, and the Democratic Party became strongly identified for decades with a hard-money standard and a bias against any kind of centralized banking system. Nonetheless, Jackson's war against the Bank made any efforts to rationalize the nation's banking system extremely difficult. His successor, the more urbane Martin Van Buren, established an independent Treasury system, whereby the government had neither a central bank nor a set of favored private banks; instead, it simply kept its money in its own vaults. Most commercial banking was then conducted in state-chartered banks. These institutions were often barely regulated and all too keen to engage in land speculation, reckless railway expansion, and other dubious financial practices. Almost immediately after the Bank's fate was sealed, the Panic of 1837 set in, and America entered a severe recession that lasted well into the next decade.[13]

Within Jackson's idealization of hard money can be glimpsed the ultimate American monetary argument—namely, that God wanted currency to be metallic, especially in America. As gold's devotees throughout history have noted, the yellow metal has been associated with divinity and religious worship for as long as history has been recorded. Despite fairly explicit biblical condemnations of materialism in general and gold in particular, the dominant Christian ideology of America's first century had little trouble equating gold and God's will. Hugh McCulloch, treasury secretary in October 1865, declared in a speech in Fort Wayne: "By common consent of all nations, gold and silver are the only true measure of value . . . I have myself no more doubt that these metals were prepared by the Almighty for this very purpose, than I have that iron and coal were prepared for the very purposes for which they are being used."[14]

The idea that gold and silver reflect God's will is probably easier to accept in a nation where they are found in relative abundance, and McCulloch's straightforward assertion reflects the fact that the discovery of gold in California in 1848 had transformed the United States like nothing else the relatively young nation had before seen. People throughout California—from newspaper editors to army soldiers—abandoned their jobs en masse to pan in rivers. It upended the nation's population, as tens of thousands flocked west in search of rapid wealth. The French consul in California remitted to a colleague, "Never, I think, has there been such excitement in any country of the world."[15]

And the boom was not only domestic: would-be miners came from Ireland, Scotland, Spain, China, Chile—what one transplanted southerner called a "heterogeneous comminglement of living souls . . . persons from almost all civilized parts of earth, judging from their acts, some from the uncivilized portions."[16] By 1860, a phenomenal 14 percent of California's population was from Germany. The rush created a center of financial and political clout in the West that had not before existed. California's population exploded from about 14,000 people in 1848 to nearly 100,000 by the end of 1849, then 223,000 by the end of 1852. San Francisco, with a population of under 1,000 residents as 1848 began, became the undisputed capital of this nation within a nation: as late as 1900, one out of every five people living between the Rocky Mountains and the Pacific Coast lived in the San Francisco–Oakland area. Sometimes overlooked are the secondary industries the gold rush created. In a very short period of time California became one of the largest grain producers in the world, thanks largely to wheat grown in the San Joaquin and Sacramento Valleys to feed those who had come west.

And of course American gold transformed the nation's—and the globe's—economy. The United States went from being a negligible producer of gold in 1848 to, between the years 1851 and 1855, producing 45 percent of the world's supply. The rapid and substantial increase in the amount of gold in circulation created worldwide economic ripples. San Francisco's stock exchange quickly became the second-largest in the country (and briefly in the 1870s surpassed New York's).[17]

Yet as with many mass phenomena, it is important to separate out the effects. Accounts of the gold rush, then as now, understandably focus on the extraordinary luck and unimaginable riches of the early arrivers. In July 1848, mere months after the initial discovery of gold at Sutter's Mill, an army colonel reported that "upwards of 4000 men were working in the gold district, of whom more than one-half were Indians, and that from 30,000 to 50,000 dollars' worth of gold, if not more, were daily obtained."[18] Moreover, the fact that men with no resources or specialized skills could in minutes produce a month's or year's worth of wages led many contemporary commentators to proclaim that a new era of industrial relations had been born, one that upended the workingman's long-standing dependency on wealthy landlords or lenders. A California newspaper declared, "From the fact that no capital is necessary, a fair competition in labor without the influence of capital, men who were only able to procure one month's provisions, have now thousands of dollars of the precious metal. The laboring class have now become the capitalists of the country."[19] Decades later, some theorists would lump California's Gold Rush in with other New World discoveries and credit them with the very development of the modern Western economy.

Such sweeping claims have fueled the mythology that surrounds the gold rush to this day, but they are in need of perspective. Perhaps even more impressive than the extent of the vast wealth unearthed in the middle of the century was just how evanescent its riches were. It is the nature of mineral discovery that a great deal is discovered early on, and then the rate of increase slows down; in many cases commodities are entirely depleted in a matter of months or years. Thus, overall gold production in California rose rapidly until it peaked in 1852 or 1853, and then began declining steadily into the Civil War period. Extremely high wages were even more fragile; while of course a handful of pioneering prospectors could make fortunes well through the 1850s (particularly if they branched out beyond California), the average gold worker after 1848 never made as much per day as during those first heady months. And while average wages of about $3 a day in the late 1850s were still higher than those on the East Coast, the cost of living in a place where the basic stuff of life had to be imported over great distances was about twice as high. Equally important for those who celebrated the gold rush as a triumph of the individual laborer is that the maturation of the mining industry meant that, by the mid-1850s, very few solo prospectors could succeed on their own; the gold readily available to surface miners was gone, and what remained required complex machinery—and therefore substantial capital—to profitably extract.

Moreover, the discovery of valuable resources in an otherwise underdeveloped part of the country created a complex and often contradictory relationship between mineral wealth and the American state. Nearly all the gold discovered in California (and, later, other western territories) existed by default on land that belonged to the government. In theory, the riches discovered in this public space could have been allocated to benefit all Americans. And yet in the late 1840s and early 1850s, the idea that the United States had the authority, the resources, or the government infrastructure to take advantage of the gold windfall—let alone to distribute that wealth for the benefit of those outside the gold rush—was simply fanciful. Richard Barnes Mason, a military man dispatched to report on the gold mines, hit on the dilemma within a few months of the Sutter's Mill discovery: "It was a matter of serious reflection to me, how I could secure to the Government certain rents or fees for the privilege of securing this gold." But given the large expanse of land being mined, the character of the people who would need to be policed, and the nearly nonexistent forces available to the government, Mason decided not even to try. So new and feeble were public institutions in the American West before the Civil War that the resolution of fierce disputes among miners often determined the systems of law (by community consensus, and sometimes by lynch mob) rather than the other way around. It is understandable how "frontier justice" created a western-based political mindset that was resistant or even hostile to conceptions of government that prevailed in the East. At the same time, as the United States incorporated mineral-rich states like California (1850), Nevada (1864), and Colorado (1876), the politicians who represented mining wealth were hardly shy about demanding their slice of the federal pie.[20]

It is also irresponsible to examine the effects of the gold rush without considering what historian Kevin Starr labels its *"noir* dimension." For example, from the very beginning of the gold rush, Chinese immigrant miners were denied access to the more productive lodes; or hounded out of camps when they appeared to be prospering; or simply lynched in a quasi-legal fashion. In 1848, for example, miners in Mariposa County passed a resolution allowing that "Any Chinaman who tries to mine must leave on twenty-four hours notice, otherwise the miners will inflict such punishment as they deem proper." Such incidents formed the basis for institutional discrimination in California later in the century.[21] Hundreds of Chinese, Native American, and Mexican women were forced into prostitution to service the miners who had left women and children at home (the population of California measured in 1850 was 92 percent male; in mining towns it was 98 percent). Mining destroyed game and fish in El Dorado County, and with it the livelihood of Native Americans there. Debris from mining towns destroyed the drainage system of the lower Sacramento Valley, causing massive floods almost annually in the 1870s. The tremendous demand that mining placed on water and timber caused vast and irreversible environmental damage. Mercury was used to recover gold from the ground in such huge volume—hundreds of liquid pounds for a single sluice—that it was found contaminating water and fish more than 150 years later in both California and Nevada.[22]

Yet these sobering truths do little to tarnish gold's place in the American mythical self-image. The nineteenth century established and deepened a psychological identity between Americans and gold. No one would assert that every American would get rich quick; by the 1850s many of those who set out west in covered wagons with signs like "Pikes Peak or Bust" could attest to the sad prevalence of the latter option. But it was not wrong to think that, under the right circumstances, anyone *could* get rich, and it almost automatically followed that nearly everyone should want to do so. This was something new in the American psyche, a motivation for wealth quite apart from Calvinist notions of austerity, or that financial success could come only from sustained hard work and spiritual devotion. In the concise formulation of H. W. Brands, the new ideal held that "El Dorado, not some Puritan city on a hill, was the proper abode of the American people."[23] To the American conception of freedom, the possibility of instant wealth through gold added a new dimension, one that was philosophically not merely negative (such as the freedom from oppression, from government interference with speech or religion) but on its surface positive: the boundlessness of riches.

The embrace of material wealth acquired with minimum suffering appears at odds with Christian teaching, and there were some who believed that the temptations of western metals led America down the wrong path. Certainly for nineteenth-century Christians who believed that gambling, alcohol, and prostitution were grave offenses to God, the early gold settlements of the West readily looked like epicenters of sin. Yet for most Americans, the material wealth associated with the gold rush was not cause to abandon any sense of being God's chosen nation. On the contrary, it implied that gold and silver were a national birthright, at once proof that America is a divinely promised land—and the very means to realize the promise. It may sound strange to a modern secular ear, but Americans in the Third Great Awakening believed that gold and silver were deliberately placed beneath the Earth's surface by a benevolent God. Many believed that the fact that precious mineral resources are located in some places—say, the Rocky Mountains—and not others was a form of divine choosing; it of course followed from that premise that mining and using those riches to create American wealth was part of His plan that Americans had an obligation to fulfill. And with God and gold on their side, many Americans in the 1850s felt blessed to the point of invulnerability. The sense of invulnerability did not last long.

For the first half of the 1850s, America's prosperity expanded and seemed indomitable. Gold production was most prominent among many other factors, including immigration (due in part to the Irish Potato Famine), railroad construction, and export growth thanks to the reduction of British import duties. And because the gold rush was completely unprecedented, it was easy to assume that daily infusions of domestic gold constituted a new normal.

The logistical reality was far more complicated. Most or all of the economic boosters were subject to cyclical overreach: the financing of railroads, for example, could easily outpace the timetable of actually building them, leaving some investors in the lurch. And the heady advantage of a continual supply of domestic gold could be deceiving. One of the gold rush's strangest side effects was to provide a rational justification for an endeavor that on its face seems anything but rational: the speculative long-distance sea voyage. In 1849 alone, more than five hundred sailing vessels left the East Coast seeking to land on the West, and the majority of these planned to sail around the perilous waters of Cape Horn—a journey of some 15,000 miles that would take at best five months and often quite longer. The ships were crowded, fetid, floating disease wards, on which seasickness, dysentery, and scurvy were common. The journals of those who survived tell stories of spoiled food and despotic captains commandeering leaky ships; some passengers went insane mid-voyage and had to be shackled in confinement. It is not coincidence that the first psychiatric hospital in California—dubbed the Insane Asylum of California at Stockton—was founded in 1853 after existing hospital facilities became overwhelmed with mentally ill gold seekers.

A significant innovation involved using the Isthmus of Panama; would-be argonauts could sail down the Atlantic Coast, usually stopping in Havana or Kingston, and land on the east coast of Panama. There they would cross the 47 miles or so of the isthmus (after 1855, via railroad), and sail in a different ship up the Pacific side to San Francisco, with the whole journey typically requiring little more than one month. The trip was neither cheap (a steerage class ticket cost $200, plus a $30 fee for crossing the isthmus) nor easy: the Panamanian terrain was punishing, and the jungles were filled with mosquitoes and disease. But the thirst for gold had to be quenched, and by 1850 the Pacific Mail Company was providing trips every other week, with each steamship carrying hundreds of passengers.[24] These steamships also carried tens of thousands of letters and, because the navy was interested in converting from sail power to steam, the carriers also received a subsidy from the federal government. In addition to the Pacific's main rival, the United

States Mail Steamship Company, a dozen competitors would soon emerge, including a line run by Cornelius Vanderbilt.

The frequency and relative speed of these journeys gave them, in the days before railroads reached the West, a significant economic impact—less because of the thousands of potential miners headed west, and more because the return trips were usually filled with the fortunes of those who'd struck it rich. The discovery of plentiful West Coast gold had fundamentally transformed the US economy, and much of the Western world's as well. Through the 1830s, global production of gold usually averaged around $13 million annually; it hit $155 million in 1853. This bounty was reflected in an explosion in the US financial sector. After the Second Bank of the United States was liquidated in 1841, most businesses relied on state-chartered banks. Throughout the 1840s the number of these banks in the United States remained constant at a little more than 700; by 1856, that number had nearly doubled to about 1,400, and the amount of loans and notes in circulation more than doubled.[25] An economic journal noted in 1852: "Every portion of the country is teeming with new undertakings requiring a heavy outlay of capital and labor, and indicating rapid strides in wealth and prosperity." The effects were international as well. By increasing the overall amount of gold in money markets, California (and, after 1852, Australian) gold raised prices everywhere, which was especially a boon to British manufacturing and exports.[26]

Yet the economic boom made the shipping of gold neither easier nor intrinsically reliable. In September 1857, the USS *Central America*, part of the United States Mail Steamship Line, left Havana for New York with 572 people aboard.[27] The ship encountered a major hurricane a few days later, about a hundred miles off the coast of Georgia. The *Central America* took on water fast, and a night of bailing was unable to keep the ship's pumps and engines working. The captain ordered lifeboat evacuation of all female and child passengers, almost all of whom were eventually rescued by other vessels. The ship, however, sank with the captain, and more than four hundred of the passengers and crew lost their lives. Newspaper accounts called the event "one of the most fearful marine disasters ever known" and "the greatest single ship disaster of a commercial vessel attributable to a hurricane."

The *Central America* sinking carried an extra dimension of public fascination that would last more than a century because so many of its passengers were returning east with large quantities of gold. As they scrambled to fill lifeboats, many had to choose between their quickly gained fortunes—the very reason they were on the ship to begin with—and their lives. Satchels of gold dust and suitcases of gold coins were left unattended or scattered about the ship. One passenger had strapped himself with twenty pounds of gold dust and was knocked overboard before the ship sank (and although the metal weighed him down, he was eventually rescued). The total value of gold that went down with the ship was estimated at about $1.3 million; this was some 30,000 pounds of gold and said to equal approximately 20 percent of the gold held in New York banks at the time. Beginning in the late 1980s, a team of marine explorers located the wreckage and recovered substantial amounts of gold (although that mission led to a major battle between its financiers and its chief salvager, Tommy Thompson, who disappeared several years after the gold was recovered).

It has become common in popular recollections to assert that the *Central America* sinking caused or contributed significantly to the economic downturn known as the Panic of 1857; one historian said, "the loss of its golden cargo helped strike a crippling blow to the American economy."[28] The Panic saw a wave of bank failures—particularly in New York, Ohio, Pennsylvania, and Rhode Island—as well as the collapse of several railroad stocks. Rapid layoffs in shipbuilding, manufacturing, and cigar-making brought a financial-sector crisis into the mainstream, and at the Panic's peak in October, mobs of thousands of New Yorkers assembled outside of the city's banks, almost all of which were forced to close their doors.[29]

The economic impact of the *Central America*'s demise was easy and natural to exaggerate, given the accident's human toll and its proximity to the worst economic bust since the gold rush had begun. This was also one of the first sensational news events of the telegraph age, combining public fascination over mass death with the timeless mystery of fortunes lost at sea. And there can be no question that the overall economy had stretched into perilous territory; the growth associated with the discovery of gold had created rapid expansion and widespread stock speculation. In particular, bank and railroad stocks in the second half of 1857 were highly volatile and sensitive to any unexpected loss. Significantly, however, the gold on board the ship that belonged to banks and businesses—though probably not that belonging to individuals—was insured, and the insurers (mostly in London) agreed to remit payments immediately. Moreover, the economy on the East Coast had already shown signs of sputtering before the *Central America* had even set sail. The US stock market, troubled by rising interest rates in Britain and France following the Crimean War, showed weakness in the summer. Falling grain prices, overcapacity in railroads, and concern about the state of slavery and rebellion (the *Dred Scott* decision was handed down in March 1857) might well have caused a recession even without a sunken gold steamer. And in August, when Ohio's largest bank went under, largely because the man running its New York office was an embezzler, the Panic had already begun.

Nonetheless, the incident made plain the pitfalls of what had become, in a few short years, a financial system unhealthily dependent on gold. The western states' bounty had created the semblance of an easy and endless supply of gold, and the illusion of an economy that only went up. Rapid expansion of credit to meet the economic opportunities created by the gold rush turned the largest East Coast banks into a kind of just-in-time financial system. As soon as the gold came in the door, it went out again in the form of expanded credit—and there was no easy way to reverse the process if the supply were disturbed. One contemporary banker summarized the Panic this way: "The immediate cause of the revulsion was the violent course of the Banks in the city of New York, who . . . expanded their loans in July from 117 to 122 millions of dollars, and then becoming alarmed by the loss of gold, endeavoured to see how quickly they could contract to 100 millions."[30] The discovery of plentiful, world-changing gold on American soil may, in the minds of millions, have represented divine will and the rise of El Dorado, but it was not enough to prevent the vagaries of human economic activity and the inevitability of recession.

And if the dictates of the business cycle disturb the harmony among gold, currency, and the American economy, war typically shatters it outright. War creates urgent, often unanticipated needs for new spending, which are usually paid for through tariffs and taxation, which can cause damage well after fighting stops. War shifts capital and manpower away from productive economic activity—such as farming and manufacturing—into destructive activity. And war can threaten every link in the chain of any economy (in the form of blockades, boycotts, or other barriers to supply and distribution). By 1860 the United States had experienced multiple wars, at least two of which—the War of 1812 and the Mexican-American War (1846–1848)—had long-lasting economic consequences.

One of the enduring arguments for hard money is that it keeps an absolute check on the size and expansion of government; the dawn of the Civil War put that truism into starker relief than any previous time in the Republic's history. The outbreak of the Civil War provoked a dramatic shortfall in government's spending capability and led to a fundamental restructuring of the relationship among the American government, its people, and its money. And while the currency saga of the Civil War may lack the pathos of hundreds of thousands of war dead and the emancipation of American slaves, its effects have been just as long-lasting.

In the years leading up to the Civil War, the finances of the US government were in unusually bad shape. The Panic of 1857 and the debt built up by the Buchanan administration had taken a heavy toll, and although few could have understood that gold production in the western states had peaked, the numbers had already begun to decline. At the time of Abraham Lincoln's first election in 1860, the coffers of the federal government were empty; there was, according to a treasury secretary of the era, "not enough money even to pay Members of Congress."[31] And thus when the Fort Sumter raid occurred a few months later and the Union government was faced with mass deployment and mobilization of troops, there was an urgent need for hundreds of millions of dollars to be raised and spent quickly. No person in the world had any plausible idea of where—in the absence of some radical change—the necessary funds would come from. From across the Atlantic, *The Economist* stated definitively: "It is utterly out of the question, in our judgment, that the Americans can obtain, either at home or in Europe, anything like the extravagant sums they are asking for: Europe won't lend them; America cannot."[32]

Warring parties before and since have found ways to meet their financial needs, and Lincoln's cabinet and Congress did in fairly short order avail themselves of the usual methods: taxation, tariffs, and borrowing. But these techniques were neither fast enough, nor anywhere near large enough, to fund the needs of a fighting force of over two million. When Congress met in special session in July 1861, Treasury Secretary Salmon Chase provided his estimate for the first year's war expenditures, which came to just over $318.5 million. For perspective, the entire gross national product of the United States at the time was an estimated $4.3 billion, and compared to annual government spending, the figure was astronomical; the Buchanan administration had raised eyebrows (and deficits) by borrowing some $10 or $20 million a year. Another yardstick of comparison is that during the three years that included the Mexican War (April 1846 to April 1849), the entire spending of the War Department amounted to $80 million.

Indeed, Chase had asked for more money to be spent on the first year of fighting the Confederacy than there was gold and silver currency in circulation—about $250 million worth—in both North and South at the time. That gap doesn't represent a paucity of gold holdings—quite the contrary, gold was flowing into US banks at a record rate. Rather, it represents the massive cost of mobilizing for war. Moreover, the existing hard currency was not meaningfully available to the federal government. Even if all of that metal could easily be collected, such confiscation couldn't be done without wrecking the state banks, since their laws required them to hold a certain percentage of gold reserves against their various loans and bonds.

For a few months in the second half of 1861, Chase tried to cobble together war funds using traditional methods. The government issued bonds and Treasury notes (though because of the country's volatile state the interest rates were very high, when the notes could be sold at all) and arranged with northern banks to loan the government money. The loan plan was convoluted and probably doomed; among other hurdles, the law dating to 1846 stipulated that the federal government could only accept and make payments in gold and silver; even states' banknotes were not permissible as payment. In November, when a US naval captain arrested two Confederate envoys aboard a neutral British mail ship, causing a major diplomatic flap—this was dubbed "The Trent Affair"—the nation looked perilously close to being at war with Britain as well as with itself, and Chase's delicate scheme unraveled. The stock market panicked and forced nearly every bank in the country to suspend payments of specie in late December. Most of the notes that Treasury had issued that year were suddenly orphaned, and it became obvious that more drastic measures were required, and immediately.[33]

These were the dire circumstances behind the introduction of the United States' first legal-tender act. On the same day that the New York banks announced their suspension of payments, a bill was introduced in Congress to create a paper currency, legally tender for all debts but not redeemable for any kind of metal. It was not entirely without precedent—many European countries already had paper currency issued by central banks, and prior to the Revolutionary War, several colonies issued paper currencies that were legal tender. Some, such as Virginia's, were deemed successful, particularly if they covered a stated loan for a stated period of time. But for many in the commercial and political class, paper currency was synonymous with ruin; the Continental Congress, for example, had issued paper currency, which depreciated rapidly and led to the popular phrase "not worth a Continental." That experience had contributed directly to the Constitution's insistence that "no state shall . . . make anything but gold and silver coin a tender in payment of debts."

And thus creating a nationwide paper currency, with nothing but government fiat behind it, that also carried the force of legal tender, was wholly outside the American experience. The very notion assumed and asserted a government financial sovereignty that had been highly controversial since the days of Alexander Hamilton and that paralleled the very states-versus-federal tension behind the Civil War itself. The legal-tender bill was created by Congressman Elbridge Spaulding of New York, a Republican former banker who called it "a war measure." Whether he was expedient or sincere, Spaulding was unambiguous in his justification; he repeatedly said that the bill's ends—"we were never in greater peril than at this moment"—justified its unusual means.

It borders on unthinkable today that such a revolutionary overhaul of the nation's currency—especially in wartime—could take place without the total support of the executive branch. Yet it is conspicuous in contemporary accounts that Lincoln's view of the greenback question is scarcely even referred to, let alone trumpeted or denounced; the few details sometimes discussed are dubious.[34] The central figure outside of Congress was Chase, who portrayed his personal position on the bill as reluctant acquiescence. Chase's economic experience prior to Treasury had been minimal, though he shared the Jacksonian view on the importance of hard money. He had offered two alternative plans at the end of 1861 that Spaulding and his Ways and Means committee had deemed insufficient to the urgent tasks of funding the army and navy (he estimated the cost at $1.6 million a day). Pressed by Congress to offer his opinion on the question of paper notes, Chase agreed that they had become "indispensably necessary." Yet even here he felt the need to distinguish his personal view from practicality; he said that his preference would be not to make the notes legal tender, but because some companies and individuals would refuse to use them they needed to be made universally acceptable. It is emblematic of American hostility toward paper currency that this use-case argument—as opposed, say, to the constitutional issues at stake—was so widespread and seemingly persuasive. The apparent lack of coordination between Treasury and Congress partly reflected the hands-off approach of the independent Treasury system created in the 1840s and may have reflected tensions between Chase and Spaulding; the politically ambitious Chase, as we shall see in the next chapter, may well have had his eye on the future. Regardless, as one commentator put it, "no more striking illustration of the unsympathetic relations of a cabinet minister with the legislative branch can be found in the range of fiscal history."[35]

Predictably, most of the powerful American banks initially opposed Spaulding's bill; legal-tender paper currency would both threaten the value of their existing assets and provide them competition that carried a government imprimatur. Congressional opponents were even more vehement. They pointed with obvious justification to the constitutional prohibition against anything but silver and gold. Not only, these opponents held, did the Constitution's framers explicitly deny the federal government the power to issue money, but they had done so deliberately; "it was intentionally left out of the Constitution, because it was designed that the power should not reside in the Federal Government."[36] They argued that to make greenbacks legal tender (and thus applicable to all debts) was to undermine existing contracts, because the paper money was sure to depreciate and all creditors would be getting less than they'd bargained for.

Because the debate concerned paying for a devastating war, it evolved into posturing about national pride and public morality. Some maintained that paying soldiers with paper money was both destructive and a kind of fraud. Assuming the intrinsic failure of paper currency, Congressman Justin Morrill rejected the very premise of a wartime justification: "If this paper money is a war measure, it is not waged against the enemy, but one that may well make him grin with delight. I would as soon provide Chinese wooden guns for the army as paper money alone for the army." Others considered greenbacks an admission of failed virtue. "The bill says to the world that we are bankrupt, and we are not only weak, but we are not honest," said V. B. Horton of Ohio.[37] Even when discussing the practical aspects of legal-tender paper money—e.g., predicting that it would cause financial ruin, create runaway inflation, drive out legitimate money, and encourage the issuance of paper money forever—the bill's opponents conjured up an image of a dark Satanic paper-money mill, a monetary reflection of the Industrial Revolution's failed morality. "Cheap in materials, easy of issue, worked by steam, signed by machinery, there would be no end to the legion of paper devils which shall pour forth from the loins of the Secretary," warned one congressman.[38]

Spaulding and his allies argued that the Constitution's prohibition against any nongold or nonsilver money applied only to states, not the federal government. Moreover, the Constitution also gave Congress power to coin money and "regulate the value thereof." The American government had long regulated the value of metallic money (including, importantly, defining how pure the metal had to be and what the exchange ratio between gold and silver was); Spaulding maintained that his bill would simply transfer this power of regulation to paper money. Massachusetts senator Charles Sumner allowed that while of course the Constitution may not explicitly give the government the power to issue paper money, it also doesn't give it the right to issue Treasury notes, the legal sanction of which had been unquestioned since the War of 1812. Proponents also rejected the assumption that paper currency would inevitably fail; the British, as a result of the Napoleonic Wars, had effectively moved to a "paper pound" standard between 1797 and 1821 without economic disaster.

The constitutional debate was at times fascinating and arcane (much energy was expended on determining the correct meaning of the word *necessary*), but it could never be finally resolved outside of court review. The urgency of fighting the South trumped any philosophical or even practical monetary views; as Spaulding put it, "Our army and navy must have what is more valuable to them than gold and silver. They must have food, clothing, and the material of war." The Senate approved the legal-tender bill (with some seemingly modest modifications that would soon be roundly attacked) on February 13 by a vote of 30 to 7; the House and president approved a final version on February 25.

By that time, the case for legally tender paper money had become almost indistinguishable from the case supporting the Union in the war. It was an argument in favor of a strong, centralized federal government, an acknowledgment that the Industrial Revolution and its affiliated social effects had strained the limits of the American socioeconomic contract to a point where the arguable letter of the Constitution (not merely the gold and silver clause but also the Tenth Amendment's limitation on the powers of the federal government) had to give. The move to a nationally authorized paper currency was a blow against Jacksonian economics, not only because it broke money out of its metallic cocoon, but because it acknowledged officially that debt is not something in all instances to be feared but rather is an essential part of national growth. Legal-tender paper currency also forced the North to choose among a set of values that had become collectively untenable. That is, while protecting the Union, fighting slavery, and holding on to hard money might all be worthwhile goals, it was no longer possible to maintain all of them; setting a pattern for the future, when fundamental national goals would come into direct conflict with a strict insistence on hard currency, hard currency lost. Moreover, as will become especially pointed in the next chapter, paper currency signaled to the world that monetary value is not God-given and thereby fixed, but is fluid, variable, and subject to manmade assessments and vagaries. The financial historian Bray Hammond elevated the legal-tender debate to a realm of political metaphysics. "As an exercise of sovereignty," Hammond wrote, greenbacks "advanced the national government's powers far beyond what had ever been ascribed to it before. They lifted federal powers . . . to a mystical level where . . . the nature of a thing could be changed by giving it, through legislative enactment, a new name."[39]

The flip side is equally true: the arguments in favor of asserting gold and silver as the only possible backing for currency became increasingly indistinguishable from those favoring states' rights, secession, and slaveholding. They were an argument for a government both formally limited in power (in the sense of not having the authority to print paper money) and practically limited in size (in the sense of being forced to live within its means). They were an argument to default to states' rights on questions where the Constitution did not explicitly give the federal government authority. Given the country's geographic concentration of financial power, the agrarian identification with metallic money—already strong from the days of Jackson—deepened, while the industrial cities became more identified with paper currency. And because legal-tender paper currency represented a novel monetary wave, gold-standard advocates found themselves implicitly arguing in favor of tradition and against modernity. And yet, even while these battling categories represented the full passions of the Civil War, they would not withstand the convulsions that were to come.

# BLACK FRIDAY.

This is a Photograph ... Bulletin Board in the Gold ...
at N.Y. Sept. 24, 1870 the Black ...
of the Gold Panic — It was produc...
before the Committee of Banking & Curren...

## CHAPTER 2

# A Crash, a Clash, and a "Crime"

IN MID-JUNE 1869, President Ulysses S. Grant was traveling with his family through the Northeast. He attended the commencement at his alma mater, the United States Military Academy at West Point, where his son was a cadet in the third class. Also on his agenda was the National Peace Jubilee, a massive, three-day music festival in Boston featuring tens of thousands of performers. Between the two events, Grant and his wife visited the president's newly wed sister in her mansion on West 27th Street in Manhattan. Grant's sister Virginia had lived a quiet life with her parents in Ohio and reached the age of 37 with few marital prospects. This changed with her brother's political ascendance, and Virginia had caught the eye of a 61-year-old financier named Abel Corbin; they married within two months of Grant's March inauguration.

Grant's Manhattan visit was a brief encounter of a few hours but, unbeknownst to him, a group of calculating businessmen—including his brother-in-law—used it to gain access to the president as part of a scheme that would, in just a few weeks, create perhaps the greatest gold panic in the history of the United States.[1] Waiting at the home

This chalkboard was used to record the wild price swings in the price of gold on "Black Friday," September 24, 1869. The market crash erased fortunes and shattered confidence in gold as a protector of the American economy. *Courtesy Library of Congress* of Grant's sister and brother-in-law was Jay Gould, a 33-year-old financier already notorious for successfully battling with the Vanderbilt brothers for control of the Erie Railroad. A year before, Gould and his buccaneering partner Jim Fisk had been threatened with arrest if they set foot in New York State; now they were about to meet the president of the United States in a family setting. Gould knew Grant's son-in-law Corbin through a real estate transaction that the two men had conducted in New Jersey. Gould had convinced Corbin to allow him to meet the president in order to try and persuade him to pursue a particular policy path regarding gold and agricultural prices. Not coincidentally, Gould had been speculating on the still new, and effectively unregulated, gold market in New York—and had a plan to corner it. He had recently purchased some $7 million in gold at a price of $131 per $100 of gold coin. At the time this was, remarkably, nearly half of all the gold in circulation in the New York market.

When the two men met, Gould suggested to the president that the most pleasant way to travel to Boston would be on a steamship to Fall River, Massachusetts, and to take a train from there. Grant, who enjoyed the company of wealthy men, agreed, and Gould arranged for a military escort for the president and his party downtown to a pier on Chambers Street. The steamship *Providence* was docked there, decorated lavishly for the president's visit, which the owner and captain—Gould's Wall Street partner Jim Fisk—knew in advance to expect. A brass band on the wharf played "See the Conquering Hero Comes" as the president approached; cigars, champagne, and liquor were passed along; and each of the ship's 125 rooms came with its own caged canary.

Dinner began at about 9 p.m., and Grant found himself smoking cigars with an incestuous ring of businessmen—including Cyrus Field, who earlier that decade had dramatically laid the first trans-Atlantic telegraph cable and was now in the railroad business with Gould; and the once-powerful stockbroker William Marston, who was in the shipping business with Fisk—who were keen to learn his views on gold, money, and the economy. Grant, perhaps aware of the sleazy reputation of his hosts, was taciturn and non-committal. At the time, Grant favored the "contraction" policy that he had inherited from the beleaguered Andrew Johnson admin-istration. The idea was to take the greenbacks out of circulation, a process that had begun almost as soon as the war ended; when greenbacks came in as tax revenue, Treasury would literally destroy the paper. Congress approved of this action although it wanted to put constraints on it; in 1866 it authorized the destruction of as many as $4 million per month, a rate that would have removed all greenbacks from circulation by the mid-'70s. Greenbacks were viewed as a once-necessary evil that should now be purged. Echo-ing the view of many of the nation's founders, the Treasury Depart-ment's official position was that paper money brought shame to the United States if it was not convertible to gold: "It is not supposed that it was the intention of Congress . . . to perpetuate the discredit which must attach to a great nation which dishonors its own obli-gations by unnecessarily keeping in circulation an unredeemable paper currency."[2]

Grant shared this view and wanted ultimately to restore money backed by gold—and he equated that cause with the honor and morality of the Civil War that he had won. In his inaugural address in 1869, Grant declared that "to protect the national honor, every dollar of Government indebtedness should be paid in gold, unless otherwise expressly stipulated in the contract." Within two weeks of this pledge, Congress passed the Public Credit Act—mostly on party lines, with Grant's Republicans supporting and most Dem-ocrats opposing—which required the government to pay back all bondholders who funded the Civil War in gold. This was the most concrete action since the war ended indicating that the government intended to return to money backed by gold (and it corresponded to a low point in the price of gold, right around the level at which Gould was snapping the metal up).

Grant's inaugural address had taken the point a step further.

He argued that the very timing of the discovery of gold and silver on American soil suggested it was God's will that they be used to pay the country's war debt. "It looks as though Providence had bestowed upon us a strong box in the precious metals locked up in the sterile mountains of the far West, and which we are now forging the key to unlock, to meet the very contingency that is now upon us," said Grant.[3]

The logical next steps for contraction policy, naturally, involved the government selling into the private market as much of the gold stock it had acquired during the war—estimated at about $100 million—as practical, in preparation for "reentry" into a gold-backed currency. After all, if banks were to issue gold-backed currency as they had in the past, they would need to restock their vaults. Accordingly, Treasury had sold $1 million of gold into the market in April and $6 million in May, and that June would sell $8 million. These large government sales hurt Gould and his cronies by suppressing the value of gold that they were sitting on. Gould adopted the position that, as a railroad magnate, he had special insight into the importance of a high gold price and freely circulating greenbacks to being able to move the country's crops in the fall and to secure a market abroad for them—the nation's interests and his interests were perfectly and conveniently aligned. Thus, aboard the *Providence*, Gould offered a rebuttal to Grant's implied plans to put more gold into the market. "I remarked that I thought if that policy was carried out, it would produce great distress, and almost lead to civil war; it would produce strikes among the workmen, and the workshops, to a great extent, would have to be closed; the manufactories would have to stop," Gould later told Congress.[4]

Gould's implication that financial ruin in the country's farmlands could have revived armed rebellion might have been alarmist and self-serving, but it wasn't entirely off base. The reintegration of the United States following the Civil War is one of the most complex tasks ever undertaken by the federal government, and it took place under conditions so contentious that they often resembled wartime.

Most people today recall the Fourteenth Amendment for outlawing slavery and giving America's former male slaves citizenship and the right to vote—but this was a sea change in American economics as much as it was in civil rights. Slaves were property, and emancipating them meant taking property away from existing slaveholders. The text of the amendment explicitly prevents any state or the federal government from paying for "any claim for the loss or emancipation of any slave."

How America valued its currency, therefore, was one of several issues that threatened to reopen the issue of secession and rebellion. Not only did the South on the whole decline to repay its war debts, but it would have been severely challenged if it wanted to, given that the war and greenback system greatly weakened the state banking system on which the South had relied.[5] Many, probably most, southern property owners expected that part of the conditions for rejoining the United States was that the government would compensate their war losses. A US Army general who had been stationed in Alabama since Lee's surrender said, "They talk very freely in regard to an effort being made by their members, once in Congress, to get pay for all the negroes they have lost, or that have been freed under the President's proclamation."[6] Closely related to this was southerners' expectation that their real estate damage would be compensated, and that they would seek to have the members of Congress not pay the northern war debts if these conditions weren't met. What Andrew Johnson's government had faced, then, was a very real threat that if the South were allowed to reenter the Union largely under the conditions of the status quo antebellum, they might combine forces with northern democrats and essentially refight the Civil War. Thus the Fourteenth Amendment contains a sweeping (and to this day much-debated) section, which Grant's inaugural invoked less than a year after it had been ratified: "The validity of the public debt of the United States, authorized by law, including debts incurred for payment of pensions and bounties for services in suppressing insurrection or rebellion, shall not be questioned." For Grant and many leaders of the national Republican Party in the 1860s, returning to the gold standard was the only honorable and creditworthy way to retire the country's staggering war debt (estimated at more than $2 billion—far higher than the total amount of currency in circulation in the country, and not including the $428 million in greenbacks which were supposed to be removed from circulation). To suggest otherwise was to question the validity of the horrible war's outcome, although putting the brakes on gold's return was precisely what many in the South and West wanted, and what Gould was advocating.

The steamship encounter was, as Gould later put it, a "wet blanket" over his gold-market plans. But he, Fisk, and Corbin had many other plans of attack. The position of being the president's brother-in-law carried considerable unwritten influence. Corbin had tried to get his first wife's son-in-law appointed as deputy treasury secretary, a position responsible for monitoring the gold market. When the man found out that he would be expected to signal Corbin in code in advance of any government gold sales, he withdrew from consideration. Corbin's next choice was Daniel Butterfield, a family friend who had been a Civil War general and was the son of the founder of American Express. Butterfield had also raised the money that Grant used to buy a house in Washington, DC—from Corbin. Shortly after Butterfield took the job, he met Gould, who gave him a check for $10,000—which was higher than his annual government salary—seemingly with no strings attached. Through his new friends, Butterfield maintained active trading accounts in the very gold market he was supposed to be overseeing.

The next step was to create the public impression that the government was going to slow or cease its gold sales. The price of gold that summer had dropped from its onetime high, thanks to the government sales and capital inflows from abroad. Gould and a few other Wall Street associates formed a "bull pool" to buy up gold wherever possible, and before the end of August the pool held more than $10 million in gold. In the meantime, Gould and Corbin drafted an appraisal of Grant's monetary intentions and managed to convince the pro-Grant *New York Times* to publish it as an unsigned editorial. The paper praised Grant's sound thinking and predicted, true to Gould's desired scenario, that "until the crops are moved, it is not likely Treasury gold will be sold for currency to be locked up."[7] In fact, the opposite was true; Treasury Secretary Boutwell was planning for September to be the biggest month for government gold sales since Grant took office. But Gould almost certainly knew that it would be irresponsible of Boutwell to publicly confirm or refute the assertion, and thus the editorial had its desired effect: the gold price began to creep back up. To enhance the illusion that the government was officially in cahoots with the Gold Ring, Fisk created a special account at Gould's brokerage called the National Gold Account.

At this stage, Gould seemed to have fallen victim to his own propaganda. Nearly everything he saw confirmed his hope that the government would stop selling gold. On Wednesday, September 1, Grant stopped in at his sister's Manhattan home after several days' vacation in upstate Saratoga and had breakfast with his brother-in-law, Corbin. Over breakfast, Grant effectively declared that he had converted to Gould's theory that gold should be scarce and expensive. The harvest looked strong and farmers deserved the government's support; Grant told his brother-in-law that he had written a letter to Boutwell telling him to cancel the government's plan to sell gold in September.

What happened next is so absurd that it seems lifted from the script of a drawing-room comedy. Unbeknownst to the president of the United States, the largest gold speculator in the country was just down the hall in the living room. Corbin excused himself from the president, shut the door, and went down the hall to tell Jay Gould that Grant would now abstain from gold sales for the foreseeable future. With this ultimate insider's tidbit, Gould slipped out of the house and scurried downtown to buy more gold. Corbin then went back to the kitchen to resume his breakfast with the president.

Is it possible the breakfast meeting was a trap? Grant's conversation with his brother-in-law seems, by today's standards, impossibly indiscreet, although at this point Grant's promiscuity with the Gold Ring, willing or unwilling, was hardly shocking. The apparent absence of the Grant-Boutwell gold "cancellation order" is another anomaly.[8]

If it was a trap, it was about to catch its prey and ensnare many others in a multimillion-dollar disaster. Confident that he now had the inside track, Gould that day bought another $3 million in gold, much of which was on behalf of Corbin and the president's sister, as well as in the trading account of assistant treasury secretary Butterfield. Within days, Gould's gold pool controlled more than $18 million in gold—with prices continuing to rise, banks and other gold holders could not resist selling.

For all his cockiness, Gould worried that rival financiers might persuade Grant to change his mind. Gould persuaded Corbin to write a long letter to the president, detailing Gould's crop theory of the virtues of abundant money and scarce gold. The letter was too delicate to be entrusted to a normal courier, so Gould's partner Fisk provided an Erie Railroad functionary for the occasion. The letter reached Grant while he was on one of his many vacations in 1869 (the White House was being renovated that year) in Washington, Pennsylvania, not far from Pittsburgh. In fact, the president was playing croquet with a close assistant whom Gould had tried to bribe with a half-a-million-dollar gold account. Grant read the letter, and the courier went to the nearest telegraph office to send Gould and Fisk a wire: "Letter delivered all right."

But all was not right. After a summer of mingling with Wall Street fixers, Grant finally seemed to understand that he was being played. Grant instructed his wife to write a letter to his sister telling her that she should tell Corbin to remove himself from the Gold Ring. When the letter arrived on Wednesday, September 22,

Corbin showed it to Gould and demanded that his share in the Gold Ring be liquidated immediately. Gould, acting like a cornered animal, tried to argue his way out; he offered Corbin $100,000 in cash on the spot. Corbin considered this overnight, but was adamant the next day that he wanted out. Gould left his house pleading that Corbin keep quiet, saying, "If the contents of Mrs. Grant's letter is known, I am a ruined man."

Meanwhile, anyone who had been paying attention to the gold market knew that an attempted corner was in progress. On Monday, September 20, the *Sun* publicly named "notorious Erie speculators"—Gould and Fisk—as part of a "conspiracy to raise the price of gold," and labeled it "one of the most immoral and pernicious conspiracies ever concocted in Wall Street." This only increased the trading frenzy. The "official" location of American gold trading was a high-ceilinged chamber adjacent to the New York Stock Exchange known as the "Gold Room." Its main feature was a circular iron railing around a bronze fountain statue of Cupid and a dolphin, at the bottom of which was a goldfish pond. Buyers and sellers congregated around the rail and stared up at a new invention: an electronic gold price indicator, which flashed the latest gold-trading price to every trader in the room, as well as on a sign outside and to various trading offices in the city via telegraph. The operator was a 22-year-old tinkerer who already had some telegraph patents to his name: Thomas Alva Edison. His job consisted of turning several wheels with numbers on them, including one wheel with fractions.

The Gold Room was dominated by a few Wall Street firms, and most of them were now working with Gould's unspoken corner on the market. Rumors of a bull pool caused sales to spike; daily gold-trading volume roughly doubled to $160 million a day every day from September 4 to 10, and then to $200 million for the next two days. New York banks reported that their gold reserves had begun to deplete. And all the while the price crept higher—on Wednesday, September 22, gold closed at $141, and on Thursday at $144¼, with five times the normal volume of trading. These prices were pure speculative energy; nothing in the supply of gold or other economic fundamentals justified them. On the floor it was rumored that Grant himself had an interest in gold going up. And the speculation knew few bounds. The gold trade was still new and loose enough that there were still unofficial venues to buy and sell gold, notably "Gallagher's evening exchange," which took place in hotel rooms in Manhattan even after it had theoretically been shut down in 1865. That night in the Fifth Avenue hotel market, gold traded at more than $180.

Outside of the small ring who owned the gold, these prices were ruinous. Imports and exports froze, because no one could afford the gold necessary to pay in foreign currencies. Wheat, cotton, and corn prices all dropped. On Thursday, Grant relented to his treasury secretary; the gold price at more than $144 was "unnatural," and the government should intervene if things got worse. The next morning the price topped a phenomenal $150. Boutwell and Grant decided to sell $4 million in gold, and the sell signal was to go out over two different telegraph lines, suggesting that they knew Butterfield was tainted. The telegram arrived in New York at 11:57 in the morning, minutes after gold had passed the $160 mark.

Within ten minutes, the gold price had dropped $20, or 12.5 percent. On that day, Gould was himself discreetly selling gold while aggressively claiming the price was going to continue to rise. Trading became so frantic and complicated that Gould's brokers had to be careful not to sell to brokers who they knew would soon be bankrupted by their indebtedness to Fisk and Gould. Men screamed in desperation, and threatened brokers on the gold floor with stabbing or worse. Many had not settled their trades from the day before, and so what they had thought were profits were now losses. Within minutes angry crowds spilled out of the Exchange and descended on Jay Gould's office, where he and Fisk had locked themselves in a small room. When night fell they were able to escape to an opera house on 23rd Street that Fisk owned, with guards posted at every entrance. Dozens of brokers were wiped off Wall Street, and hundreds went bankrupt, though Fisk and Gould, thanks to a friendly judge, were never made to pay back the millions they owed.

The Black Friday incident is instructive for many reasons. The first is that a country valuing two forms of money will quickly create an arbitrage market between them, and that market will almost inevitably swing violently to the point of political or social impact. To proponents of "sound money," Black Friday was the most powerful lesson imaginable that severing the value of American money from gold would lead to disaster. For Grant and his presidential successors (mostly Republican but including Democrat Grover Cleveland), the chaos of Black Friday was an argument that only a gold standard could maintain a stable American economy. A second lesson is that American financial markets were, through the latter nineteenth century and beyond, stunningly exposed to profound and easy corruption. The very idea that a high-ranking Treasury official in charge of monitoring the gold market could himself be making massive gold investments—let alone that he was colluding with the largest gold-market manipulators—would today drive nearly all legitimate investors away from any such market. For all the laissez-faire rhetoric that circulates about gold as a monetary instrument, Black Friday proves that an unregulated market will quickly become politically corrupt and financially disastrous. The idea of a president, even one not financially tied to the gold trade, making buy-or-sell decisions based on a market price ought to give pause to those who advocate gold standards and limited government power.

The country as a whole, however, derived a different lesson, which only deepened the political tensions of the Jackson period. To many, Black Friday proved that the nation's economy was too easily manipulated by East Coast elites for results that harmed the rest of the country. "Confidence had been severely shaken," one financial historian wrote. "Markets were far more susceptible to declines on bad news than they had previously been."⁹ And this mistrust pushed the population in a monetary direction completely opposite of Grant's. Jay Gould was a cynical, self-interested, manipulative East Coast railroad baron, but the monetary policy he advocated—keeping gold scarce while allowing other forms of money to circulate to points in the marketplace where they would help businesses like railroads and the telegraph to continue to thrive— had many passionate adherents who, like Gould, valued growth over party loyalty. That audience would continue to grow and to reshape American politics.

As if Black Friday were not convulsive enough, within a few months the country would face the most bizarre monetary legal decision during its century of existence. Despite Grant's intention to restore a full gold standard, it became clear even before he took office that greenbacks would remain on the economic landscape for some time to come. "Contracting" the economy by taking greenbacks out of circulation might have seemed like responsible economic policy in places like New York and Washington. After all, the depreciation of the tender notes so despised by their opponents was very real; in the late 1860s it typically took between $1.20 and $1.40 worth of paper money to buy a dollar's worth of gold. But in the South and West, that contraction would involve genuine economic pain, and thus the political pressure to retain paper money was strong. The bigger problem with greenbacks was that their constitutionality had never been resolved, and where one stood on this delicate question depended largely on whether one identified with the creditor class or debtor class, and with the Republican or Democratic Party. Between 1863 and 1870 at least sixteen lawsuits were filed at the state level questioning the constitutionality of the legal-tender clauses. Democratic judges, reflecting the old Jacksonian prejudice against anything but gold, almost always deemed greenbacks unconstitutional, while their Republican opponents, eager not to interfere with the Republican financing of the war, usually approved of them.

The case that finally came before the Supreme Court, *Hepburn v. Griswold*, was a seemingly straightforward dispute over a contract signed in 1860 and due in February of 1862, five days before Congress created the first greenbacks. The debtor (Mrs. Hepburn) repaid in 1864, using paper money for the amount owed plus interest to her creditor (Mr. Griswold). Griswold refused payment, and after some legal back-and-forth Hepburn took the case to the Supreme Court.

What was not straightforward was what had happened to the Court. In late 1864, the chief justice of the Supreme Court, Roger Taney, died and Salmon Chase, who had been trying to resign from the Lincoln cabinet, was named to replace him. Chase, of course, had been treasury secretary when the greenbacks were established, and had argued at that time, albeit reluctantly, for their constitutionality. Lincoln and his successors might well have assumed that Chase would maintain his position or perhaps—given the obvious conflict of a man who pushed through a piece of legislation later deciding on its constitutionality—recuse himself. The case was argued and reargued; one legal scholar asserted, "it is probable that never in the history of the Court has any question been more thoroughly considered."[10] The justices were initially split, 4 votes apiece—with Chief Justice Chase now coming out against the constitutionality of legal paper money. Later, Justice Robert Grier, who was 75 years old and not able to walk by himself, changed his mind, and the vote was 5 to 3.

Although the votes were taken in November 1869, the announcement of the verdict was postponed until February 7, 1870—after the aging Grier had already stepped down. Chase was said to be "almost wholly inaudible" as he delivered the verdict.[11] Without referring directly to his own reversal, he blamed the war. "The time was not favorable to considerate reflection upon the constitutional limits of legislative or executive authority," Chase said.

"Many who doubted yielded their doubts; many who did not doubt were silent. Some who were strongly averse to making government notes a legal tender felt themselves constrained to acquiesce in the views of the advocates of the measure. Not a few who then insisted upon its necessity, or acquiesced in that view, have, since the return of peace and under the influence of the calmer time, reconsidered their conclusions, and now concur in those which we have just announced."[12]

In important ways, the *Hepburn* decision was limited in its scope; the Court said merely that the Legal Tender Act could not be enforced for debts incurred prior to its passage, of which there were believed to be relatively few anyway. Nonetheless, Chase's decision framed the issue as one of foundational freedom—here was a plain instance of Congress stretching the meaning of the Constitution to interfere with a private contract between two citizens. To allow it to stand "would completely change the nature of American government," Chase wrote. "It would convert the government, which the people ordained as a government of limited powers, into a government of unlimited powers." For a country that had within the last decade been plagued by a cataclysmic civil war and the assassination of a president followed by the impeachment of his successor, to say that paper money was not merely unconstitutional but a step toward tyranny was a provocative challenge. The political overtones of the decision were heightened by the fact that all the votes to reject greenbacks came from Democrats (Chase had switched party affiliation after the war) and all the votes to uphold the law came from Republicans. A *New York Times* editorial chided Chase bluntly: "If these views had then prevailed the rebellion would have been successful, probably to the extent of imposing its own authority over the entire Union." For their part, many conservative scholars and advocates to this day argue that the original *Hepburn* decision repudiating greenbacks was constitutionally correct.[13]

The initial market response to the decision was subdued, yet the drama was far from over. The battle over Andrew Johnson's impeachment had left the Court scarred and polarized. In 1866, Congress passed a law reducing the total number of Supreme Court justices from ten to seven. Then, in 1869, with Johnson out of office, Congress brought the number back up to nine, one chief and eight associates. By the time the Hepburn decision was released to the public, Justice Grier had resigned, meaning that there were two vacancies on the Court. One of Grant's nominees was blocked, and another died four days after his confirmation. Thus, when the *Hepburn* decision was released, the four votes in its favor did not constitute a majority of the whole membership of the Court authorized by Congress.

It was obvious that another decision would be necessary, to deal with the debts incurred after the law's passage. Such cases were already in the lower courts, and the administration was key to having a judgment, especially with new Republican justices whom Grant appointed on the very day that the *Hepburn* decision was announced. (Although Grant partisans denied at the time that Grant had "packed" the Court with judges he knew would reverse the decision, subsequent scholarship makes a compelling case that he did precisely that.)[14] Chase tried to keep new cases off the Court's calendar; a rival justice charged that Chase "resorted to all the stratagems of the lowest political trickery to prevent their being heard."[15]

Strong asserted that Congress's constitutional power "to coin money and regulate the value thereof" clearly included the right to define money as it saw fit. After all, the Coinage Act of 1834—an example designed to stymie his opponents, as it had been championed by Democrat Andrew Jackson—changed the relationship among gold, silver, and the dollar. Strong categorized this as part of "that general power over the currency which has always been an acknowledged attribute of sovereignty in every other civilized nation than our own." An additional, more practical argument came from one of the newer justices, reflecting the value that greenbacks brought to the broader economy: "If relief were not afforded, universal bankruptcy would ensue, and industry would be stopped and government would be paralyzed in the paralysis of the people."

And thus, while the Court's 1872 rulings in the *Knox* and *Parker* cases were the last word legally about the validity of inconvertible paper money, the political resentment over paper money and its raw assertion of government power never quieted and would continue to echo through the twentieth. Both sides could point to the Court's highly unusual and contradictory actions as proof that an injustice had occurred. Little wonder that a twentieth-century chief justice would classify the Legal Tender cases, along with the *Dred Scott* decision and the 1895 income tax decision, as one of "three notable instances [in which] the Court has suffered severely from self-inflicted wounds."[16]

And the political gap between governmental monetary policy and popular opinion was about to get wider. A seemingly innocuous passage in the US Coinage Act of 1873 would, as the century wore on, be blamed for any number of economic ills and vilified as the "Crime of 1873." The law's goal seemed straightforward: to move the country's money back onto a metallic standard. The act provided for various official changes to the role of a mint within Treasury and also spelled out specifically the denominations for both gold and silver coins. In an omission that was largely ignored at the time, the bill's text did not refer to any role for a traditional silver dollar, but only half-dollars, quarter-dollars, and ten-cent pieces.[17] Congress also put a $5 limit on the legal-tender status of any payment made with silver coins.

These steps were not accidental: many congressional leaders and the Grant administration were deliberately trying to restore a gold standard and thereby demonetize silver. Partly they feared that the recent discovery of the Comstock Lode in Colorado would flood the country's monetary supply with silver. In addition, many of the world's most important economies in 1871—

notably Germany—were also making a monetary shift from silver to gold. And neither was the legislation passed in haste or in secret: the Coinage Act was drafted, redrafted, and submitted widely for comment over a period of three years before it was passed, and there was ample time for any concerned legislators or other parties to express dissatisfaction. Few did, and indeed those who would later decry the Coinage Act were part of the robust majorities that voted for it; the act passed by a vote of 110 to 13 in the House and 36 to 14 in the Senate.[18]

If the Coinage Act's details seem minor, it's because on paper they were. Nothing in the 1873 law made it illegal to forge silver coins, and in fact through the mid-1870s Treasury was minting millions of dollars' worth of silver coins every month. The disappearance of the obsolete silver dollar, which had scarcely been minted since 1853, would hardly have been noticed by most Americans; as a financial journalist later put it, "Not one man in ten of mature years had ever seen one."

However, there were parts of the country where the demonetization was indeed noticeable: silver mines and the local economies that depended on them. Another overlooked omission in the 1873 act was that it did not mandate that Treasury mint coins for anyone who brought it silver bullion, as had been common earlier in the century when silver coins were still in circulation. By 1876, for example, the San Francisco Mint was telling silver miners along the Owhyee River in Idaho that it was six months to a year behind in its operations and could not promise to mint coins at all by any firm date—which was ruinous to miners who needed to cover expenses. "This dilatory policy on the part of the Government in coining the precious metal," an Idaho newspaper scolded, "is ruinous beyond calculation."[19]

As similar complaints mounted, western legislators and their journalistic allies began portraying the Coinage Act as a massive financial fraud perpetrated on the public. In 1876, Nevada senator John P. Jones, a doctrinaire advocate of the silver standard, called the law a "grave wrong." It was difficult, however, for members of Congress to explain why they had so overwhelmingly passed such a terrible law. The first, and reasonably plausible, excuse was that they didn't know what they were voting on. One after another, congressmen and senators lined up to profess their ignorance of what the act did to silver. Senator Allen Thurman was typical: "There is not a single man in the Senate . . . who had the slightest idea that it was even a squint toward demonetization." Even President Grant, according to some widely distributed but rarely attributed accounts, declared, "I did not know that the act of 1873 demonetized silver. I was deceived in the matter."

Another supposed culprit was shadowy foreign influence. A tale emerged about a British economist and author named Ernest Seyd who, it was said, had raised $500,000 from various European bondholding interests and come to the United States to bribe members of Congress to demonetize silver. Newspapers and magazines (particularly, though not limited to, those favorable to the Democratic Party) peddled versions of this "fake news" story, some of which contained doctored quotations and made-up publications. These were offered as proof that "European money kings" had "hoodwinked" both houses of Congress into demonetizing silver. The plan, charged Ohio Democrat Thomas Ewing, was that "they wanted to have the United States, and the other nations whose bonds they held, to demonetize silver and pay their bonds in gold."[20]

As an assessment of European financial interests, this view had some basis in fact, although at the time Ewing spoke the United States was actually a net importer of gold. The Seyd bribery tale, however, was garbled to a nearly comical degree. Seyd was a distinguished, careful author who had indeed provided counsel on the Coinage Act. But he was also a renowned advocate of bimetallism, and his lengthy 1872 letter to the House argued forcefully *in favor* of keeping the silver dollar.[21] Despite the flimsiness of such claims, popular anger, especially strong in midwestern and western states, continued to boil, and by the late 1870s it was very common for

Democrats and western Republicans to blame the "Crime of 1873" for the nation's recurring economic woes.

Part of the argument from silver advocates was simple economics: they claimed the supply of gold was simply insufficient to carry the nation's economic burdens. In 1877, it was deemed to be only about half as large as it had been in 1852 "and is always so fitful and irregular from the manner of its production that no metal is so ill-suited to be a sole measure of values," as a congressional report put it. (The flip side of this argument, of course, is that the silver boom that was well under way—global silver production from 1850 to 1900 was four times what it had been from 1800 to 1850—introduced its own potential monetary distortions.)

Especially given the reliance on false tales and even forged documents, it is clear that the fervent movement that began in the late 1870s to remonetize silver was motivated by forces beyond mere economic reasoning. In some ways, the silver movement and the related greenback movement—the Greenback Party had launched in midwestern states in the middle of the decade—represented a restaging of Jacksonian populism with different metallic costumes. Because silver was plentiful and associated with western states where it was produced, it was treated as the currency of the common rural farming man. With gold increasingly scarce (for the time being) and used largely in international transactions, it was associated with wealthy, eastern banking and industrial interests. As one mining executive asserted, "There can be no question as to silver being the money of the poor man, for where there is one man carrying $5 in gold there are twenty who carry the less amount in silver."[22] Such class differentiators extended even to the tonsorial. Richard Bensel notes that pro-gold eastern Democrats were usually clean-shaven, "allowing at most a mustache and sideburns to adorn their face." The pro-silver Democrats from the South and West cultivated "long, unkempt" beards.[23] These identities were more symbolic than fixed, but as the century moved on they would grow and harden into the Populist movement—and reshape American politics largely along the question of what combination of metal or paper should constitute a dollar.

Despite many attempted legislative fixes, the government in the last quarter of the nineteenth century could find no way to maintain a stable system of metal-backed currency. In 1875, Congress set the stage for returning the United States closer to a full gold standard by passing the Specie Resumption Act, which required Treasury to redeem the greenbacks "for coin" beginning in 1879. As a result, Treasury began accumulating a gold reserve. Yet during the same period, political pressure from western states also made sure that silver would maintain some role in the monetary system.

A bimetallic system was difficult to maintain both economically and politically. As part of a broad economic compromise that included the nation's first antitrust laws and a higher tariff, the Republican-controlled Congress passed the Sherman Silver Purchase Act in 1890. It mandated Treasury to buy a much higher amount of silver than in the past—4.5 million ounces a month, essentially all the silver being produced in the country—and to issue legal-tender notes in exchange that could be redeemed for gold. The act, which was urged by the silver and greenback "inflationist" forces, also required the government to maintain gold and silver "on parity with each other." Almost immediately the law was a disaster. Gold and silver might have had equal legal status but given a choice, nearly everyone took gold. Domestically, just about anyone who had to pay custom duties chose to do so in silver or greenbacks. In 1890, 95 percent of custom duties were paid in gold; three years later, it shrank to 5 percent.[24] Outside the United States and particularly in Britain, where the pound was fixed on a gold standard, many of those who held bonds or other American securities that could be cashed in for gold did so; gold-packed steamships pushed out of New York harbor every day. According to one estimate, 10 percent of the $3 billion in US securities held abroad were redeemed between 1890 and 1894.[25]

As a result, the US Treasury experienced what would be a recurring problem during gold-standard periods: there was no way to keep the gold supply from migrating into private hands at home and abroad. Cleveland pointed to the legal requirement for Treasury to put greenbacks back into circulation after they had been redeemed for gold as an "endless chain" that would drain Treasury's gold, and indeed, the early 1890s witnessed the fastest reduction of gold from US reserves in the country's history. At the beginning of the decade, the United States held approximately $190 million worth of gold in reserve; by 1895 nearly two-thirds of that gold had gone elsewhere.[26] In 1895, there was more coined American gold in the vaults of the Bank of England than in the US Treasury. The law on the books said that Treasury had to keep $100 million in reserves to back up the currency (although there was some disagreement between Democrats and Republicans about whether those funds could be tapped for other purposes).[27] But both Benjamin Harrison and Grover Cleveland, who took office for a second time in January 1893 with a Congress that was heavily pro-silver, were powerless to stop the outflow of gold and stood in open violation of the law.

Nonetheless, 1892 had been a year of economic expansion following a mild recession in 1890 and 1891. But 1893 began ominously; the railroad business had expanded haphazardly and with shaky financing, and several prominent railroads declared bankruptcy in February. Then in early May, the National Cordage Company—which imported hemp and manufactured rope— went bankrupt and caused a stock market sell-off as multiple brokerage firms went under. The Panic of 1893 had begun, and it would become the worst and longest economic depression the United States had ever seen. At the lowest point, as many as 20 percent of American workers were jobless, and more than eight hundred banks closed between 1893 and 1897. In June 1893 alone, twenty-five national banks closed, the largest monthly number that had ever been recorded. Banks became protective of their own gold stashes, and began inserting clauses into mortgages and other contracts that they be repaid in gold. More than one hundred railroads went bankrupt by 1894, and the breakneck pace at which the West was being settled slowed down.[28] The infamous Pullman Strike, in which union firebrand Eugene Debs led nearly 100,000 men to shut down huge portions of the country's rail commerce and the US mail, exacerbated the effects, and as the financial crisis on the East Coast spread west, it encountered failing farms and families pushed toward desperation. Amidst a global drop in prices for grains and food, farmers dumped their grain into the street rather than accept the low prices that they were being offered. Reports of families on the brink of starvation began to fill the newspapers. In Seward County, Kansas, for example, bonds had been issued just a few years earlier to build schoolhouses worth $30,000, but now dozens of families were going without food for days on end.[29]

These desperate financial conditions found their political expression in silver versus gold. Cleveland held firm in his belief that the gold standard would protect the nation's credit standing and thus its ability to borrow and trade abroad. This stance led to his total political isolation, as even members of his own party became converts to greenbacks and silver-based currency. In a sense, western and southern legislators were working in tandem with foreign financiers to squeeze the Treasury, in hopes of forcing Cleveland to impose a silver standard. The country's largest trading partners were on a gold standard and thus were unwilling to accept silver or paper as payment. Yet the law required the government to maintain two metals at parity. Every time Congress proposed a move in the direction of a silver standard, Cleveland vetoed it; every time Cleveland tried to issue bonds that would help protect the nation's gold reserves, Congress refused to approve it. With the country in a deep recession and completely split on the currency question, the Democratic Party was demolished in the 1894 congressional elections. In the House of Representatives, the Democrats went from a majority of 220 to 124 to a minority of 93 to 254—the single largest shift in a midterm election in US history.

In early 1895 the country's gold reserves, already well below the $100 million level required by law, came perilously close to disappearing altogether. Once again, Cleveland tried and failed to pass legislation that would allow him to issue bonds payable in gold and to stop the circulation of greenbacks and silver certificates. Cleveland and his cabinet were desperate. In late January, even before the bill met its inevitable demise, Cleveland sent Assistant Treasury Secretary W. E. Curtis to New York to meet with Wall Street financiers in search of a solution that was eluding Washington. Curtis met with August Belmont—son of a Democratic railroad magnate who inherited his father's business, and who also built New York's race track Belmont Park—and with J. Pierpont Morgan, typically considered the most powerful man on Wall Street. Morgan was not unknown to the president; between his two terms in the White House, Cleveland worked for a law firm that handled much of J. P. Morgan's business, and Morgan had also generously supported Cleveland's presidential campaign.

The bull-headed Morgan proposed that the government issue $100 million in bonds, but instead of selling them through open bids—the tactic that had failed the year before—they would be sold to a syndicate that he would coordinate with Belmont, who represented the interest of the Rothschild banks. Cleveland could not help but be attracted to a deal that would not only offer him gold but the means to protect it as well.[30] Morgan pressed the point that the nation's gold reserves had nearly evaporated. He told Cleveland he'd heard that a single party was owed $10 million in gold. "If that $10 million draft is presented, you can't meet it. It will all be over before 3 o'clock," Morgan said. Morgan proposed a deal in which his syndicate would pay the government 3.5 million ounces in gold, at least half of which would come from Europe. He also pledged that he could keep anyone from redeeming securities for gold, so that this amount would stay in Treasury for the foreseeable future. In return, the syndicate would receive $65 million in thirty-year 4 percent gold bonds at 104½. In addition, Morgan wanted his syndicate to have first dibs on any future such bonds the government would issue. The president wondered aloud if the arrangement was even legal, and Morgan reminded him of a little-known statute passed during the Civil War that allowed the president in an emergency to issue "coin bonds" to buy gold. And so the deal was struck, an odd public-private pact that some historians label a "reverse bailout."[31] The deal also, as Cleveland biographer Alyn Brodsky put it, "amounted to an agreement to temporarily rig the gold market."[32]

The gold rig worked as planned. Promises of gold came rushing in; in New York the bonds sold out in twenty-two minutes. Gold exports stopped immediately; the week that the contract was signed, a $7 million shipment of gold that had been withdrawn from the Treasury and packed for export was taken off a steamship before it sailed and returned back to Treasury. By the end of June, Treasury's reserves were back over the $100 million mark (although they would fall well below that before the end of the year).[33] Morgan also apparently made a handsome profit, although he declined in a Senate hearing to say for what price he had sold the bonds.

Never before—not even during wartime—had the US government had to turn so cravenly to Wall Street to keep itself alive financially, certainly not under conditions so nakedly favorable to the country's richest bankers. It set a low-water mark for public confidence in banks and financial authority and also set a dangerous precedent. Nonetheless, many Cleveland biographers and other economic historians give Cleveland credit for finding a way out of a seemingly hopeless plight. After all, the country had no central banking system or means of international appeal, and Congress was dead set against anything the administration wanted to do.

The contemporary reception, however, was vicious. The paranoia and nativism that had boiled up to denounce the "Crime of 1873" gave way to open hatred and, in particular, to anti-Semitism. The *New York World* called the bond syndicate deal the work of "bloodsucking Jews and aliens." And in Congress, William Jennings Bryan of Nebraska asked the clerk to read into the congressional record Shylock's speech from *The Merchant of Venice*. The populist revolt against East Coast gold and its power was about to reach its apogee.

*" You ought to be ashamed of yourself!"*

# CHAPTER 3

# The Dangers of the Yellow Brick Road

WHEN GROVER CLEVELAND was cutting a desperate deal with J. P. Morgan to bail out the government of the United States in 1895, William Jennings Bryan was at best semi-employed. His congressional career had been reasonably accomplished for someone who served only two terms; he ran for Senate in 1894, but in the anti-Democratic tidal wave of that year, the seat went to a Republican. In April, what was arguably his biggest political accomplishment to date—an income tax amendment to a tariff bill—was struck down as unconstitutional. He drew a small salary editing and writing for the *Omaha World-Herald*, and could command decent sums for his pro-silver speeches, which sometimes went on as long as three hours. With the "Cleveland Depression" in full swing, Bryan's trained orator's voice found a receptive (and often unemployed) audience for a message about the moral superiority of silver over gold, and specifically that the nation's economic woes could be solved by monetizing silver at the ratio of 16 ounces to 1 ounce of gold.

Although there was talk of Bryan as a presidential candidate for 1896, and he himself never lacked confidence, he was far from

First published in 1900, L. Frank Baum's fanciful novel *The Wonderful Wizard of Oz* can be read as a parable of the monetary debates at the end of the nineteenth century, specifically over the role of gold and silver.

an obvious choice. At 36, he was barely old enough to constitutionally qualify as president, and no one from Nebraska had ever been
elected president before (or since).[1] And while the cause of silver
was championed in the West, the main powers within the party,
still shakily led by President Grover Cleveland, favored gold. As
the spring of 1896 unfolded, however, the degree of silver support
within the party became more and more evident (the Republican Party, too, carried a strong pro-silver faction; when the GOP
adopted a pro-gold platform at its convention in June, a significant
group of delegates walked out in protest). Beginning with Oregon
in April, each state Democratic Party had held a convention and
declared itself for gold or silver. The largest state delegations—those
from New York and Pennsylvania—favored gold. But right behind
those were Illinois, Ohio, and Missouri, all of which supported
silver.[2] In Ohio's state convention in June, a delegate called for the
removal of a portrait of Cleveland, complaining that "looking down
on this convention is that arch-traitor, that Benedict Arnold of the
Democratic party, Grover Cleveland."[3] Most states bound their delegates by those choices, so it was clear weeks before the July convention that one or many pro-silver candidates would have powerful
support.

To the extent that there was a front-runner in what was a broad
and unruly group, it was Richard "Silver Dick" Bland, a US representative from Missouri whose nickname reflected his commitment to the populist metal. Bland had been the coauthor of the
important Bland-Allison Act of 1878, which required the US government to buy millions of dollars' worth of silver every month,
to be minted and circulated as coins. He had not lost his passion
for the cause of silver; in March he had referred to Cleveland's gold
standard as "a stench in the nostrils of the plain people." Bland's
chances for the presidency, however, were slim; he was considered,
at nearly 61 years of age, too old for the job. Out of arrogance or
indifference, Bland chose not to attend the Chicago convention in

early July, staying instead on his farm in Lebanon, Missouri, and communicating with his well-organized team via telegraph.

Bryan's plan could not have been more different. He traveled from Lincoln with the feisty Nevada Democrats in a multi-railcar convoy, festooned with banners reading "Nebraska First to Declare 16 to 1" and "The William Jennings Bryan Club." The convention was held in the Chicago Coliseum, at the time the largest permanent exhibition space in the world, with a floor of five-and-a-half acres and seating capacity for 20,000 people.

For years, the silver forces had been gaining steam and appealing to a mass audience. A colleague of Bryan's had produced a pamphlet called *Coin's Financial School*, which leaned heavily on the "Crime of '73" and depicted European bankers ("The Rothschilds") as an octopus that ruled the world by owning half of all its gold and enforcing a gold standard; it sold over a million copies. The pamphlet spawned several sequels and imitators, making the 1890s a kind of "silver age" for pot-stirring, populist mass literature, much of which depicted the behavior of eastern bankers as a plot against farmers and workers, and some of which spilled over into anti-Semitic stereotypes.[4]

For all the silver movement's prominence, the raucous, radical environment in Chicago startled the gold men. When William C. Whitney—one of the wealthiest men in America, who had managed Cleveland's 1892 campaign and was considered a viable pro-gold candidate for '96—arrived in Chicago, the ceaseless carnival of silver hats and banners made him dispatch a team to take the temperature of the crowd as he hunkered down in his hotel suite. Upon return, one of his men said, "For the first time I can understand the scenes of the French Revolution!" The influence of the would-be Jacobins was everywhere. Even the choice of the convention's temporary chairman—normally a formality—was subject to the silver-gold litmus test, and the silverites won the battle.

In the maelstrom, Bryan could see a chance to seize the nomination, or perhaps a cabinet seat or the vice-presidential slot. But one man whose blessing he needed, Illinois governor John Altgeld, proved difficult to persuade. Weeks before the convention, Bryan showed Altgeld his sample speeches and asked for comment and support. Altgeld's response typified the reaction that many Democrats had to Bryan: "You are young yet. Let Bland have the nomination this time. Your time will come."

The pro-gold forces seemed to know that they were licked. Defense of gold at the convention was not especially robust, and was notably practical rather than passionate or moral. On the third day of the convention, July 9, David Bennett Hill, a New York senator who supported bimetallism in theory but aligned himself with Cleveland politically, spoke for the East Coast gold supporters, declaring himself "a Democrat, not a revolutionist." The issue of a monetary standard, Hill asserted, was simply not one that Americans were capable of solving on their own. "We should not attempt the experiment of the free and unlimited coinage of silver without cooperation of other great nations," Hill said. "It is not a question of patriotism, it is not a question of courage, it is not a question of loyalty. It is a question of finance. It is a question of economics. It is not a question which men, ever so brave, can solve." International bimetallism might be the best course, Hill said, but without cooperation from the rest of the world, a single gold standard was best. "I know that it is said by enthusiastic friends that America can mark out a course for herself. I know that that idea appeals to the pride of the average American, but I beg to remind you that if that suggestion be carried out to its legitimate conclusion, you might as well do away with our international treaties."[5] Leaving aside the economic merits of this internationalist argument, its most fascinating aspect is that it would be rejuvenated throughout the twentieth century—but as an argument *against* the gold standard and in favor of some more expedient monetary regime.

Although tepid, Hill's speech and those of his colleagues were better received than the defenses of silver, which failed to ignite most of the sympathetic crowd. Bryan had maneuvered to be the last speaker on the main topic. He had been practicing versions of the speech for years; some of the best-known metaphors had even been delivered on the floor of Congress. But this was a combustible combination of speaker and audience. Bryan's speech was a masterpiece of Americana, an appeal for a vital if nostalgic vision of the nation's past wrapped in a plea for inclusivity. The trouble with the "gold men," Bryan argued, was that they had defined the interest of the businessman too narrowly. "The farmer who goes forth in the morning and toils all day—and who begins in the spring and toils all summer—and who by the application of brain and muscle to the natural resources of the country created wealth, is as much a business man as the man who goes upon the board of trade and bets upon the price of grain," Bryan said. Here was a class distinction and a theory of value to warm the hearts of any socialist—the ruling class makes its money from speculation on the backs of the workers. The agrarian man is virtuous and creates true value, the urban dweller is speculative and parasitic. The latter scores his victory with piles of gold, while the former demands justice in silver.

And lest there be any doubt what happens when the classes conflict, Bryan offered an almost Biblical prophecy: "You come to us and tell us that the great cities are in favor of the gold standard. I tell you that the great cities rest upon these broad and fertile prairies. Burn down your cities and leave our farms, and your cities will spring up again as if by magic. But destroy our farms and the grass will grow in the streets of every city in the country." It is worth remembering that the primary targets for this tirade were Bryan's fellow Democrats.

Bryan's themes hit precisely the contours of historian Richard Hofstadter's definition of progressivism as "the effort to restore a type of economic individualism and political democracy that was widely believed to have existed earlier in America and to have been destroyed by the great corporation and the corrupt political machine, and with that restoration to bring back a kind of morality and civic purity that was also believed to have been lost."[6] What Bryan achieved was to fuse this sentiment to a monetary policy: gold was the corrupting modern influence that could be defeated only by virtuous silver.

As Bryan built to his conclusion, he invoked one of the giants of the Democratic Party: "What we need is an Andrew Jackson to stand, as Jackson stood, against the encroachments of organized wealth." Jackson, of course, had been a steadfast supporter of gold, but Bryan managed to borrow Jackson's energy while switching his signature metal. "If they dare to come out in the open field and defend the gold standard as a good thing, we shall fight them to the uttermost, having behind us the producing masses of the nation and the world. Having behind us the commercial interests and the laboring interests and all the toiling masses, we shall answer their demands for a gold standard by saying to them, you shall not press down upon the brow of labor this crown of thorns. You shall not crucify mankind upon a cross of gold."

With these final lines, Bryan pressed his fingers against his temples to illustrate a crown of thorns, and stretched his arms out perpendicular to illustrate a crucifixion—a pose he held for a full five seconds. After a moment of stunned silence, the hall exploded with cheers. Bryan's political club had been given red bandanas that morning, and now they were enthusiastically swirling them in the air to the sounds of whooping and chanting. As Bryan walked through the hall past the Nebraska delegation, he "was caught in the whirlwind of frenzied enthusiasm and lifted high on the shoulder of delegates."[7]

Whomever the delegates would end up nominating, the Democratic Party of Andrew Jackson, with its moralistic insistence that gold was the only true money and all forms of debt and paper currency were sins, seemed to be dead. That cause, going forward, would now be championed by the Republicans, who themselves were not entirely ready to embrace it uniformly. For his part, Bryan felt himself like a great conductor of men. "The audience seemed to rise and sit down as one man," Bryan recalled in a memoir. They "acted like a trained choir—in fact, I thought of a choir as I noted how instantaneously and in unison they responded to each point I made."[8]

The political reality, however, was less harmonious. Despite the acclaim the speech brought, it took five ballots before Bryan won the nomination. The Democrats were hopelessly factionalized; if they had been more united, even in favor of silver, it seems unlikely that Bryan would have been the nominee. In order to balance the ticket, Bryan added a millionaire shipbuilder and railroad executive, an odd choice for the candidate of the working class. Outside the Chicago hall, some heard in the silverite rhetoric the stirrings of secession; others felt that for a national party to stray so far from the true path of gold was disastrous. "The Chicago platform invites us to establish a currency which will enable a man to pay his debts with half as much property as he would have to use in order to pay them now," scolded Charles Dana, the influential editor of the *New York Sun*, who had been one of Grover Cleveland's most loyal supporters. "This proposition is dishonest." "The Democratic party has simply committed suicide," lamented the *Minneapolis Tribune*. The paper predicted that a sizable group of Democrats would vote for Republican William McKinley "as the most effectual mode of defeating the most unblushing and dangerous conspiracy against the public credit and the faith and honor of the country that was ever organized into a political movement."[9]

The *Tribune* was correct; almost immediately after Bryan's nomination, a group of more conservative, pro-gold Democrats hastily formed a "National Democratic Party." While its chosen presidential candidate did not win a single state, the party was nonetheless able to run in all but seven states and to field congressional candidates in twenty states—a remarkable feat given the severe time constraints. In addition, the short-lived party attracted the support of many in the Democrats' more conservative wing, including a Princeton professor named Woodrow Wilson.[10]

The turnout was high and the election was reasonably close— McKinley won about 600,000 more votes than Bryan, and the state count was 23 to 22—but more importantly, for the first time since 1872 the victorious candidate had actually won a popular and electoral majority. There were reports of bosses pressuring workers to vote Republican, and allegations of fraud, though it is difficult to know whether these phenomena were more pronounced in 1896 than in an "average" presidential election. The voices of silver had spoken with the most eloquent tongue available, but had still not captured most Americans. The country reacted in a time of high factionalism, akin to wartime patriotism, by rallying around gold.

From the very beginning of McKinley's presidency, he made it clear that "hard money" was his priority. In his inaugural, McKinley restated the old prejudices against nonmetallic money: "The several forms of our paper money offer, in my judgment, a constant embarrassment to the Government." And yet, despite the gold-fueled Republican victory at the polls, a full-on embrace of a unimetallic standard was not quickly accomplished. One crucial factor was support from the business and financial community. The Morgan coziness with Grover Cleveland's Democratic administration did not extend to the Bryan wing of the party. Throughout the 1890s, bankers and business owners waged an unprecedented campaign to convince at least part of Bryan's potential audience to support "sound money." This effort included a multiday monetary convention in Indianapolis and the funding of several magazines and pamphlets designed to compete with *Coin's Financial School* and similar silverite publications. This clash of ideas represented the first time that both major political parties acknowledged that an urban, industrialized nation of working and middle classes was a permanent feature of American society, and the battlefield on which future campaigns would be fought.[11]

Yet the most decisive factor in moving the United States to a gold-only standard was the discovery of new troves of gold in both North America and South Africa. Indeed a second gold rush, even more improbable and treacherous than the first, began in the late 1890s. A month after Bryan's speech, an American prospector discovered gold in Rabbit Creek, a tributary of the Klondike River in the Yukon Territory of Canada. Starting the next year, an estimated 100,000 people in both Canada and the United States set off for the Yukon territory in what was known as the "Klondike Stampede." "The image of rivers filled with gold was, in the uncertain and difficult economic times of the late nineteenth century, a compelling one, sure to attract endless interest among the continent's legions of unemployed and disillusioned."[12] Men worked in temperatures as low as 50 degrees below zero, with scarce food and expensive sled dogs. And those were the ones who made it—most never got to the goldfields, and most of those who did never found gold. Gold was flowing from South Africa as well. Not in half a century had the monetary stock of the nation increased so rapidly. On the day that Bryan delivered the cross of gold speech, there was just over $500 million in monetary gold in the United States; three years later it was $859 million, a staggering increase of 70 percent.[13]

Especially after the Senate elections of 1898, which gave the Republicans a powerful legislative majority, the conditions were ripe to move away decisively from a bimetal standard. When the new Congress convened, it took up a currency act that confirmed gold as the basis for US money, a position the Republicans largely backed. The Bryan element remained; several pro-silver legislators argued that to demonetize silver officially would take money out of the hands of farmers and laborers. William V. Allen, a one-term Nebraska senator from the Populist Party, said, "The bill is one of spoliation and confiscation, and to increase and perpetuate the national debt." The Senate vote of 44 to 26 was almost entirely along party lines.

The bill became known as the Gold Standard Act of 1900. It made silver officially a subsidiary currency and allowed for the remaining greenbacks to be fully redeemed for gold. When specie payments had resumed in 1879, there had been no dedicated gold fund to pay for the notes; an important provision of the new law was that Treasury was to maintain a fund of $150 million in gold coin and bullion to be used to redeem US and Treasury notes. Using a more complicated version of the Bank of England's practice, the act provided that the reserve fund would be replenished with gold from Treasury's general fund, and that if the reserve dipped below $100 million, Treasury would be authorized to use bonds to buy gold back from the public. President McKinley signed the bill into law using a brand-new gold pen, furnished to him by Jesse Overstreet, the Indiana congressman who had introduced the bill.

When twenty-first-century advocates talk of returning to a gold standard, they are generally referring to a system akin to what passed in 1900: gold is convertible to paper money, and a minimum amount of gold is required to back up the currency. And faith in such a system hearkens back to the doubt-free pronouncements that allowed Republicans to dominate the early part of the century. The McKinley administration and the financial interests pushing sound money believed that they had scientifically solved a problem that eluded most of human civilization. Two months after the Gold Standard Act became law, Treasury Secretary Ellis Roberts gave a speech to a banking group in which he was nothing short of triumphant. "On the face of all our money, paper and coin, white and yellow; on all our bonds, all wages, all trade, all banking, all business, it brands deep and sure, the pledge of gold."[14] American credit was the best in the world, and the "endless chain" problem that had plagued Cleveland had been solved, because no gold could leave Treasury unless it was replaced by gold. And thanks to recent mining discoveries at home and abroad, Americans were practically swimming in the stuff. "For three years, more than ever before has the yellow metal been thrusting itself into our markets, our vaults, into the pockets of the people." The country was adding gold in circulation at a rate of some $100 million a year. "Our Government commands unlimited treasure at rates unknown to finance and astounding to all the bourses from London and Berlin to Hong Kong," Roberts boasted. "The Treasury of the United States is thus richer in gold than any other nation or any corporation or combination."

That same month—May 1900—bookstores began stocking a fanciful new work from a Chicago-based author who described his book as "written solely to pleasure children of today." *The Wonderful Wizard of Oz* was written by L. Frank Baum, a playwright and journalist who had paid close attention to the presidential campaign of 1896. The book features a Kansas girl whose home is ripped from its moorings by a cyclone, who finds that she has landed in a strange land called Oz, where she is given silver shoes to walk on a road made of golden bricks to reach the Emerald City. The book, with its prodigious sales—some three million copies were sold by the time the book entered public domain in 1956—and the MGM movie version released in 1939 and featuring Judy Garland in a career-making role, has become one of the most recognizably classic tales in all of American history. Although the film was not a blockbuster hit in its original theatrical release, it found its true home on television beginning in 1956; many critics and scholars believe that the Wizard of Oz is the most-watched television movie of all time, with a viewership that probably extends to the billions.

In 1964, a high school English teacher in Mount Vernon, New York, named Henry Littlefield published an article in *American Quarterly* magazine in which he offered an irresistible reading of the story as an allegory for the political and currency battles of the late nineteenth and early twentieth centuries. "In the form of a subtle parable," Littlefield wrote, "Baum delineated a Midwesterner's vibrant and ironic portrait of this country as it entered the twentieth century."[15]

In Littlefield's view, the symbolism in *The Wonderful Wizard of Oz* was remarkably specific and reproduced aspects of the worldview of Bryan and the prairie populists, if only to satirize them. For example, Littlefield notes that the Witch of the East had cast a spell on the Woodman that caused him to chop off his body parts with every swing of his axe, and eventually turned him through overwork to tin. "In this way Eastern witchcraft dehumanized a simple laborer so that the faster and better he worked the more quickly he became a kind of machine," Littlefield wrote. "Here is a Populist view of evil Eastern influences on honest labor which could hardly be more pointed."

Littlefield's thesis set off a kind of multigenerational parlor game in which subsequent historians and economists extended the symbolism and analogies.[16] In these readings, the Cowardly Lion is Bryan (Bryan rhymes with Lion, and both Bryan and the Populist Party were often depicted in political cartoons as lions in the 1890s); the cyclone is the free silver movement; the yellow brick road is a gold standard (remember that in the book version, the footwear that Dorothy inherits is not ruby slippers but "silver shoes with pointed toes"); Oz is the abbreviation for ounce, implying a metallic money; the scarecrow represents the unlettered farmers; the Wicked Witch of the East is most likely the banking industry;

the Wicked Witch of the West could be the populist Mary Elizabeth Lease (or, alternatively, the Witch of the East was Grover
Cleveland and the Witch of the West was McKinley); Dorothy's dog
Toto (a play on "teetotaler") represents the Prohibitionist movement; et cetera. At some point the interpretations surely reach a
level that Baum would not have sanctioned, but that is beside the
point; as Littlefield himself said, "the relationships and analogies
outlined above are admittedly theoretical." The endurance of a
debate about the correct monetary symbolism in *The Wonderful
Wizard of Oz* well more than a century after its publication demonstrates that the passions and politics of the Populist period are still
very much alive.

In the opening years of the twentieth century, the yellow brick
road seemed like a prosperous place to be. The period saw dramatic consolidation and mergers in a number of major industries—
including agricultural machines, automobiles, oil, and steel. This
was followed by an unprecedented antimonopoly movement led by
Theodore Roosevelt; it saw giants, including Northern Securities
and Standard Oil, broken up. After some initial fright, the owners
of large trusts, including Morgan and Rockefeller, made their
peace with government regulation. The stock market applauded
the moves; between the first quarters of 1904 and 1906 the Dow
Jones average doubled. And thanks to healthy gold production in
the United States and the end of the Boer War in South Africa,
the world was comparatively swimming in gold. In June 1905, US
treasurer Ellis Roberts proudly announced that approximately
one-quarter of all the world's gold now resided in the United States.
The credit of the United States was excellent; for a nation that had
to be bailed out by Morgan a decade before, this could be scored a
vast improvement.

And yet nearly everyone who looked closely at the US monetary system could see that it was deeply flawed. The fundamental problem had not changed since the days of Black Friday, nor had the political fault lines changed much since the rise of agrarian populists. Breakneck expansion of farmland in the Midwest and West pushed the prices of crops downward, while making it hard for farmers to borrow money or meet mortgage payments. The bulk of the nation's metallic wealth sat in eastern banks or in the big national banks. Each summer, large quantities of money needed to be shipped to the Midwest and West—usually in very small denominations—in order to get crops out of the field and dispersed. If, as often happened, there were hurdles in this predictable process, the credit market would tighten; at the end of 1905, interest rates as high as 125 percent were being charged for bank loans, because money was so tight. With the United States on a gold standard, there were strict limits on how much currency could be printed or even redeemed; the "inelastic" currency was widely criticized at the time. The agrarian populist response to this was to advocate expanding the money supply with silver and paper; the establishment hoped to muddle through with a gold standard and the virtues of "sound money."

In early 1906, Jacob Schiff, a prominent German-born Wall Street financier who funded railroads and floated bonds for the Japanese government to fight Russia, delivered an assault on the nation's monetary system, calling it "nothing less than a disgrace to any civilized country." The problem, Schiff insisted, was not that the country was facing hard times. On the contrary; "wherever you look, there is prosperity—prosperity as we never had it before." The problem was that there was not enough circulating money to meet the demands of legitimate businesses. Too much was being locked up in bank vaults or siphoned off by speculators. "If this condition of affairs is not changed, and changed soon, we will get a panic in this country compared with which the three which have preceded it would be only child's play."

Then in April came the calamitous San Francisco earthquake and fire, which leveled most of the city and killed thousands of residents. About half of all the city's private and commercial insurance policies were underwritten by British firms, and within days massive amounts of gold were leaving London for San Francisco—first a shipment of $30 million in April and then $35 million in September. This represented a 14 percent decline in the amount of gold held by the Bank of England, the largest drop between 1900 and the outbreak of the Great War.[17] Within the United States, too, the gold was flowing westward in desperately needed relief, and by winter the nation was facing a serious credit crunch.

New York was in no condition to fight the financial fire that was about to hit. Like Jim Fisk and Jay Gould a half-century before, the barrel-chested Fritz Heinze had made his name and fortune by taking on the established powers of the business world. Through creative exploitation of Montana's mining regulations, he had managed to challenge the Rockefeller copper powerhouse, and he then turned his eyes to Wall Street. He bought a bank and made partnerships with some sharp New York financiers, spreading the stock of his copper company far and wide. One October morning in 1907 he discovered that there were more shares trading than actually existed. He and his associates attempted a squeeze and a corner on the copper market—again, akin to what Fisk and Gould tried with gold in 1869, minus the presidential manipulation, and with similarly grim results. Heinze's brother's brokerage house failed in late October, bringing down with it the Knickerbocker Trust, a novel type of financial institution, performing many of the same functions as a bank but regulated less strictly, and thus able to hold certain types of securities that most traditional banks could not.

The disease spread within days to smaller banks, then to the companies that relied on them, then to larger banks and eventually to the top of the country's food chain—the point where Morgan and Carnegie needed to get involved. By the end of the month, New York City couldn't pay its employees and needed at least $20 million to avoid insolvency. There was so little money to go around that a streetcar company in Omaha resorted to paying its employees with 600,000 nickels from the cars' fare boxes.

The federal government was by turns ignorant of what was going on—President Theodore Roosevelt was hunting in Louisiana as the panic unfolded—and powerless to stop it. Less than a decade before, the United States had boasted that the country had built the largest stockpile of gold in the history of mankind; now it was clear that the supply was nowhere near what was needed. The country needed another gold bailout, and this time Morgan's money and influence was not enough, because his interests were too tied to the banks that were teetering or had already collapsed. On one Saturday night in early November, Morgan locked several bank presidents in his library and refused to let them leave until they signed an agreement to loan money to the Trust Company of America, a kind of firewall against further destruction.

In the meantime, emergency gold came in from Argentina, France, and Great Britain. On November 8, a shipment of $12.4 million arrived when the Cunard liner *Lusitania* landed on a Manhattan dock. The metal had traveled on a special train from London to Liverpool and took nearly a week to cross the ocean. This was, apparently, the single largest cargo of wealth ever to travel the Atlantic on one ship. The gold was removed—all 334 boxes of it— one container at a time, with two longshoremen carrying each box out of the ship's steel-lined hull.[18]

Although the Panic of 1907 would, within a generation, be overshadowed by the Great Depression, it was one of the worst financial calamities in American history, by some measures worse than that in 1893 (though shorter-lived). It was obvious that whatever virtues a formal gold standard might have, they were insufficient to stave off rapid economic disaster. Something had to be done to make the American financial system more stable. During this time the United States had an absolute glut of commercial banks. In 1912, there were an estimated 80,000 banks in the United States, of which approximately 28,000 were partly or entirely commercial. This meant that the reserves were so scattered as to be ineffective in emergencies, as was demonstrated in the Panic; each bank wanted to hoard its meager supply of gold, making the aggregated gold of little use to anyone. In addition, thanks to the Jackson-era resistance to mixing government operations with banking, the Treasury's own reserves were distributed in nine sub-treasuries and with as many as 1,500 national banks. The Panic of 1907 widely exposed the problems; as one historian has written, the Panic "crystallized reform sentiment and gave it a strong popular base, making a basic overhaul of currency and banking arrangements virtually inevitable."[19]

The ensuing attempts to rationalize the system entailed an extremely delicate balance between banking interests, regional pressure, legislative prerogatives, and radical objections. A congressionally appointed committee produced a daunting twenty-three-volume study of banking. The chances of the whole effort turning into a logjam were high. Treasury Secretary William McAdoo later recalled, "As I look back on that ardent summer of 1913, I wonder how the Federal Reserve Act ever struggled into existence."

Conservative Democrats had their own objections and pet projects; Carter Glass of Virginia referred to "that imperialistic scheme to seize the banking business of the United States."[20] Republican Elihu Root, who had been Teddy Roosevelt's secretary of war and rarely addressed the Senate floor, delivered a tirade in which he predicted that the federal reserve system would create inflated money and drive gold out of the country. "Long before we wake up from our dream of prosperity upon inflated currency, the sources from which the gold will have to come to keep us from catastrophe will have lost their confidence, so that no rate of interest will bring the money but a rate so high as to ruin American business."[21] One of the biggest potential obstacles was the still-stinging opposition from populists, who were wary of concentrating central banking power, particularly on the East Coast. Yet William Jennings Bryan was no longer the ferocious force he had been in the previous century; the Democratic Party, which won the White House in 1912, had managed to tame him. Woodrow Wilson, having once been violently opposed to the Bryanite wing of the Democratic Party, had managed to skillfully cultivate them for his own gain. During the 1912 party convention, for example, the delegates had no candidate after forty-five ballots—until Bryan threw his support behind Wilson. As a reward, Wilson appointed Bryan as his secretary of state, although this didn't guarantee his support for something as momentous as a national banking system. Bryan still symbolically led the populist faction, and he insisted on a prominent role for greenbacks. Eventually, however, Bryan produced a letter urging the pro-silver and inflationist Democrats "to stand by the president and assist him in securing the passage of this bill at the earliest possible moment."

Throughout the debate, some in the Treasury and in banking circles watched anxiously as gold began to flee America's vaults. The pending war in Europe caused those jittery nations who could afford it—including Argentina, Canada, France, and Germany—to stockpile gold; within the first few weeks of 1913, some $23 million in gold was drained from US coffers.

The Federal Reserve Act became law just before Christmas 1913. A new national currency—Federal Reserve notes, issued by the Reserve banks—was designed to adjust to trade, and thereby solve the issue of money's "inelasticity." That money in turn was to be backed by gold reserves worth no less than 40 percent of the value of currency in circulation. The act also gave the Reserve banks the authority to buy and sell gold in open markets, and envisioned for the Fed a role in maintaining the country's gold supply (which had previously been the responsibility of the Treasury).

The Federal Reserve system left the gold-based dollar untouched, yet gave the United States for the first time a set of tools to manage an economic downturn. In its early years, the fledgling institution lacked political clout and was almost immediately overtaken by armed conflict in Europe. Nonetheless, the Fed board believed that it had greatly improved the flow of capital across the country, largely through the introduction of a "gold settlement fund," which systematized and streamlined transactions between banks. Indeed, the Fed board was so pleased with its innovation that it foresaw a time in which a world at peace might establish an "international gold exchange fund." The Fed's 1918 annual report acknowledged that little could be accomplished until a stable peace was widespread. Still, an internationally shared fund could have benefits. "The gold deposited in a government bank or banks should be in the nature of a special or trust fund, and all nations participating should deposit their proper proportions of gold," the report explained.[22] And the "saving of loss and expense incident to abrasion and transportation charges and interest on gold transferred will be enormous, and the advantage to the commerce of the world will be incalculable," the report gushed.

Alas, the monetary paradise was not to come about, at least not after the Great War. Nonetheless the war, like many major conflicts before and after it, brought a wholesale change in the world's monetary system. The belligerent nations were forced to abandon a gold standard in order to pay their massive war bills; the United States, having only officially joined the war in 1917, remained on a gold standard, although for a time it restricted gold exports. Abandoned with that standard was the relative price stability and ease of foreign investment that the world's prewar economy had enjoyed. Getting back to a gold standard was widely prescribed but difficult to accomplish. Wartime production created destructive bouts of inflation, particularly in Britain, and countries such as France and Italy found it politically difficult to cut the government spending that a return to gold required.

By the late 1920s, however, most of the world's major economies had restored a gold standard. And throughout the period, the United States continued to increase the amount of gold it held, roughly in line with the growth in its economy. Over the same period, thanks in large part to Great War expenditures, the gold stockpiles of Britain, France, and Germany declined (the latter precipitously). Once again, the United States became the undisputed gold center of the world.

The late 1920s also saw the ascension to power of Herbert Hoover, one of the most ardent pro-gold presidents in modern times; he referred to the gold standard as "little short of a sacred formula." Herbert Hoover has the peculiar distinction of being the only man to occupy the White House who had a deep, firsthand knowledge of the mining industry. Indeed, one of Hoover's singular achievements was that he and his wife translated from Latin one of the most important books in gold mining, a sixteenth-century textbook written by Georgius Agricola called *De Re Metallica*. "Of all ways whereby great wealth is acquired by good and honest means, none is more advantageous than mining," Hoover's translation of the book advises.

Hoover's experience undoubtedly influenced his steadfast adherence to the ideal of a gold standard, with which his party had already been identified since the beginning of the century. But it did little to prepare him for the economic avalanche that hit the nation. By the summer of 1929, output and employment in the United States began to fall. When the stock market crashed in October, as two economists later put it, "the decline turned into a catastrophic rout."

The bare economics of what became the Great Depression

were dismal enough. Its effects were exaggerated by a withering succession of events, many beyond the influence of any president or government institution. In 1930 "the most severe drought in the climatological history of the United States" struck, devastating the farming areas of the South and West. Judge John Barton Payne, chairman of the American National Red Cross, said, "in all of its experience of more than a thousand emergencies the Red Cross has never been confronted by a disaster of larger proportions." As crops died in the field, a financial chain of pain spread through the land; as one observer put it, "The farmer owes the merchant, unable to pay his obligations; the merchant owes the small bank, unable to pay his obligations; the small banks unhesitatingly state they were unable to meet their obligations to the City banks."

Hoover's fellow Republicans and the private sector's "sound money" advocates were pushed into ideological irrelevance by tumbling prices and failing banks. Their worldview could barely incorporate the idea that such an economic catastrophe could happen in a country on the gold standard. Today, it is often understood that the gold standard was the problem. As two prominent economic historians have written: "There now exists agreement among most economists that the gold standard was a key element—if not the key element—in the collapse of the world economy."[23]

Regardless of what caused the Depression, the overwhelming experience of the early 1930s was that nothing seemed to work to reverse the process: not the gold standard, not Fed market operations, not the Resolution Finance Corporation. For all its unprecedented power, the Federal Reserve seemed incapable in 1931 and 1932 of making anything happen; it was far better at debating and making administrative changes than at anything resembling effective action.[24] An exasperated Treasury Secretary Mills told the board, "For a great central banking system to stand by with a 70% gold reserve without taking active steps in such a situation was almost inconceivable and almost unforgivable." The independence of the Federal Reserve—so important to its integrity—became a quality to regret or even mock. In a hearing with Fed chair Eugene Meyer, a congressman threatened him: "Your careful policy may be the very means of Congress passing out some other kind of a command to the Treasury to do something to take the place of the inactivity of the Federal Reserve Board."[25] Of course, the Federal Reserve was not the only institution prone to inaction. Congress itself was an obstacle, particularly Senator Carter Glass, one of the principal architects of the Federal Reserve system, who was loath to make new changes. More than fifty bills to increase money and prices were introduced in the 72nd Congress, but none became law.

If there was a single event most likely to force change upon a shell-shocked system it was in September 1931, when Great Britain went off the gold standard. A run on the dollar ensued, and that fall, gold began to leave the United States at a pace similar to that in the 1890s. In the last two weeks of September, the US gold stock fell by $275 million. In October it decreased by an additional $400 million. The gold cupboard, once so impressive, was nearly bare. At the height of the 1932 presidential election, Hoover told an audience of Iowa farmers that the shortage of gold earlier that year had pushed the country to within two weeks of abandoning the gold standard, because it would not have been able to pay gold to those who demanded it. A Hoover aide later asserted that "it was almost a matter of hours."[26]

The country's gloom perhaps guaranteed that the White House would change hands in the 1932 election. And yet, in their party platform that summer, the Democrats gave little hint of a dramatic change: "We advocate a sound currency to be preserved at all hazards and an international monetary conference called on the invitation of our government to consider the rehabilitation of silver and related questions." Even the perfunctory hat tip to the silver states was identical to what the Republicans proposed. In his campaign speeches, Franklin Roosevelt tended to depict the drain on the US gold supply as a disastrous result of the administration's high-tariff policy, rather than a systemic monetary obstacle. And yet, even before Roosevelt took office, it had become clear that he and a handful of close advisers were deadly serious about removing the gold standard.

# UNDER EXECUTIVE ORDER OF THE PRESIDENT

### issued April 5, 1933

## all persons are required to deliver

# ON OR BEFORE MAY 1, 1933

## all GOLD COIN, GOLD BULLION, AND GOLD CERTIFICATES now owned by them to a Federal Reserve Bank, branch or agency, or to any member bank of the Federal Reserve System.

### Executive Order

FORBIDDING THE HOARDING OF GOLD COIN, GOLD BULLION AND GOLD CERTIFICATES.

By virtue of the authority vested in me by Section 5(b) of the Act of October 6, 1917, as amended by Section 2 of the Act of March 9, 1933, entitled "An Act to provide relief in the existing national emergency in banking, and for other purposes", in which amendatory Act Congress declared that a serious emergency exists, I, Franklin D. Roosevelt, President of the United States of America, do declare that said national emergency still continues to exist and pursuant to said section do hereby prohibit the hoarding of gold coin, gold bullion, and gold certificates within the continental United States by individuals, partnerships, associations and corporations and hereby prescribe the following regulations for carrying out the purposes of this order:

Section 1. For the purposes of this regulation, the term "hoarding" means the withdrawal and withholding of gold coin, gold bullion or gold certificates from the recognized and customary channels of trade. The term "person" means any individual, partnership, association or corporation.

Section 2. All persons are hereby required to deliver on or before May 1, 1933, to a Federal reserve bank or a branch or agency thereof or to any member bank of the Federal Reserve System all gold coin, gold bullion and gold certificates now owned by them or coming into their ownership on or before April 28, 1933, except the following:

(a) Such amount of gold as may be required for legitimate and customary use in industry, profession or art within a reasonable time, including gold prior to refining and stocks of gold in reasonable amounts for the usual trade requirements of owners mining and refining such gold.

(b) Gold coin and gold certificates in an amount not exceeding in the aggregate $100.00 belonging to any one person; and gold coins having a recognized special value to collectors of rare and unusual coins.

(c) Gold coin and gold bullion earmarked or held in trust for a recognized foreign government or foreign central bank or the Bank for International Settlements.

(d) Gold coin and gold bullion licensed for other proper transactions (not involving hoarding) including gold coin and bullion imported for reexport or held pending action on applications for export licenses.

Section 3. Until otherwise ordered any person becoming the owner of any gold coin, gold bullion, or gold certificates after April 28, 1933, shall, within three days after receipt thereof, deliver the same in the manner prescribed in Section 2; unless such gold coin, gold bullion or gold certificates are held for any of the purposes specified in paragraphs (a), (b) or (c) of Section 2; or unless such gold coin or gold bullion is held for purposes specified in paragraph (d) of Section 2 and the person holding it is, with respect to such gold coin or bullion, a licensee or applicant for license pending action thereon.

Section 4. Upon receipt of gold coin, gold bullion or gold certificates delivered to it in accordance with Sections 2 or 3, the Federal reserve bank or member bank will pay therefor an equivalent amount of any other form of coin or currency coined or issued under the laws of the United States.

Section 5. Member banks shall deliver all gold coin, gold bullion and gold certificates owned or received by them (other than as exempted under the provisions of Section 2) to the Federal reserve banks of their respective districts and receive credit or payment therefor.

Section 6. The Secretary of the Treasury, out of the sum made available to the President by Section 501 of the Act of March 9, 1933, will in all proper cases pay the reasonable costs of transportation of gold coin, gold bullion or gold certificates delivered to a member bank or Federal reserve bank in accordance with Sections 2, 3, or 5 hereof, including the cost of insurance, protection, and such other incidental costs as may be necessary, upon production of satisfactory evidence of such costs. Voucher forms for this purpose may be procured from Federal reserve banks.

Section 7. In cases where the delivery of gold coin, gold bullion or gold certificates by the owner thereof within the time set forth above will involve extraordinary hardship or difficulty, the Secretary of the Treasury may, in his discretion, extend the time within which such delivery must be made. Applications for such extension must be made in writing under oath, addressed to the Secretary of the Treasury and filed with a Federal reserve bank. Each application must state the date to which the extension is desired, the amount and location of the gold coin, gold bullion and gold certificates in respect of which such application is made and the facts showing extension to be necessary to avoid extraordinary hardship or difficulty.

Section 8. The Secretary of the Treasury is hereby authorized and empowered to issue such further regulations as he may deem necessary to carry out the purposes of this order and to issue licenses thereunder, through such officers or agencies as he may designate, including licenses permitting the Federal reserve banks and member banks of the Federal Reserve System, in return for an equivalent amount of other coin, currency or credit, to deliver, earmark or hold in trust gold coin and bullion to or for persons showing the need for the same for any of the purposes specified in paragraphs (a), (c) and (d) of Section 2 of these regulations.

Section 9. Whoever willfully violates any provision of this Executive Order or of these regulations or of any rule, regulation or license issued thereunder may be fined not more than $10,000, or, if a natural person, may be imprisoned for not more than ten years, or both; and any officer, director, or agent of any corporation who knowingly participates in any such violation may be punished by a like fine, imprisonment, or both.

This order and these regulations may be modified or revoked at any time.

FRANKLIN D ROOSEVELT

THE WHITE HOUSE
April 5, 1933.

### For Further Information Consult Your Local Bank

**GOLD CERTIFICATES** may be identified by the words "GOLD CERTIFICATE" appearing thereon. The serial number and the Treasury seal on the face of a GOLD CERTIFICATE are printed in YELLOW. Be careful not to confuse GOLD CERTIFICATES with other issues which are redeemable in gold but which are not GOLD CERTIFICATES. Federal Reserve Notes and United States Notes are "redeemable in gold" but are not "GOLD CERTIFICATES" and are not required to be surrendered

### Special attention is directed to the exceptions allowed under Section 2 of the Executive Order

## CRIMINAL PENALTIES FOR VIOLATION OF EXECUTIVE ORDER
### $10,000 fine or 10 years imprisonment, or both, as provided in Section 9 of the order

Secretary of the Treasury.

CHAPTER 4

# FDR Bids Good-bye to Gold

PRIOR TO THE PASSAGE OF the Twentieth Amendment, presidential inaugurations took place in March, turning the nearly half-year period following a November election into a purgatory of agony and boredom for the outgoing administration. In the case of 1932–1933, it was also economically the worst winter in the history of the United States. Banks, like dominoes, began closing and falling throughout the country, while one in four in the American workforce was unemployed. In the final hopeless days of the Hoover administration, the exhausted president was laboring furiously and having almost no impact whatsoever. He was sleeping perhaps three hours a night, and working "at an almost killing pace."[1]

FDR offered the shiny opposite: decisive action, which he could make look easy. And in some ways, taking the United States off the gold standard was a remarkably simple action—so simple that it seems obvious that Roosevelt had planned it before his inauguration on Saturday, March 4, 1933, in which he had promised the American people "an adequate but sound currency." The following evening, top FDR confidant

These posters were hung in post offices to help enforce Franklin Roosevelt's Executive Order 6102, which required US citizens to turn in their gold and gold certificates, to be reimbursed at $35 per ounce. Most Americans complied. *Courtesy of the U.S. Government Printing Office*

Henry Morgenthau had dinner with George Warren, an agricultural economist who had flown from Cornell University in upstate New York to Washington to advise the new administration. Few were hit as hard by the Great Depression as those who lived in America's farmland; on average, farm incomes dropped by nearly two-thirds in the beginning of the 1930s. Farmers and their communities were at least as desperate and as politically enraged as they had been during the days of William Jennings Bryan; when banks foreclosed on farms, angry mobs of farmers often showed up to auctions to prevent bidding on the assets—to the point where Iowa, Minnesota, and other farming states created moratoriums on foreclosures. Dairy farmers dumped countless gallons of milk into the street rather than accept a penny a quart. Warren ardently believed that the most effective way to raise the depressed crop prices was to take the country off the gold standard and inflate the value of the dollar artificially. For months Roosevelt and his circle had been meeting with experts, advocates, and businessmen who made similar arguments, although of course the Hoover administration and nearly all of the country's financial establishment wanted to keep the gold standard that the Republicans had upheld since the turn of the century.

Morgenthau let Warren know over dinner that the president, whom Warren had met as the governor of New York State, agreed with his views. When their meal was finished, Warren joined the newly appointed secretary of state Cordell Hull, FDR's adviser Raymond Moley, and the president himself. Roosevelt told the group that Hull's first two acts would be to call a special session of Congress later that week, and to issue a presidential mandate to close the banks and outlaw the hoarding of gold and silver. At 1 a.m. Monday morning—the president deliberately waited until after midnight, lest religious Americans complain that he had signed crucial legislation on a Sunday—Roosevelt issued a proclamation to close every one of the nation's 18,000 banks. That, however, was not the part of the bill that intrigued Roosevelt and his circle; the bank closure and refinancing details were handled almost entirely by Hoover aides who stayed on. FDR had his eye on the gold. Warren wrote in his diary that FDR told the group, "We are now off the gold standard," adding that the president exuded "a great deal of glee."[2]

But of course, it was not that simple—either procedurally or politically. Abolishing a long-held monetary standard was enormously complex, and there were few if any legal or political guideposts. FDR recognized this, teasing reporters in his first presidential press conference: "As long as nobody asks me whether we are off the gold standard or gold basis, that is all right, because nobody knows what the gold basis or gold standard really is." As it happened, taking the United States off the gold standard required more than a dozen steps of legislation and executive orders, few of which had been apparent to FDR's "brain trust" on Inauguration Day. At a neck-snapping pace, the Roosevelt administration moved from forbidding banks to pay out or export gold, to abrogating gold clauses in private and public contracts, to outright nationalizing and confiscating gold. In conjunction with other actions, these moves helped the United States emerge from the global Depression. Today's mainstream economists tend to agree with the assertion from Ben Bernanke—the bearded Stanford and Princeton economist who became the chairman of the Federal Reserve—that "to an overwhelming degree, the evidence shows that countries that left the gold standard recovered from the Depression more quickly than countries that remained on gold."[3]

For all the high drama and seemingly decisive action, however, many of the administration's steps were improvised or clumsily handled—and the political cost was high. Roosevelt would end up bitterly dividing his administration in the crucial first year of the New Deal, and he very nearly brought the country to a constitutional crisis over court cases pertaining to the use of gold in commercial contracts. He created a permanent political coalition deeply opposed to his view of the federal government, using gold as its central symbol and occasionally veering into the politics of conspiracy and hate. Moreover, while Roosevelt famously and successfully campaigned to repeal the prohibition of alcohol, his unprecedented monetary action enacted a prohibition against gold ownership that would last forty years.

The financial legislation that Congress passed during Roosevelt's first week in office was breathtaking. It had two massive goals, both unprecedented even during wartime: first, it outlawed operating a bank without the permission of the treasury secretary, and created a system whereby the nation's 18,000 banks—closed since Monday morning, March 6—could be examined for health and allowed to reopen or recapitalize. And second, it authorized the treasury secretary to confiscate "any or all gold coin, gold bullion, and gold certificates owned by . . . individuals, partnerships, associations and corporations." The president asserted the authority for both these sweeping actions by invoking the Trading With the Enemy Act, a wartime provision passed during World War I that gave the president the power, among other things, to regulate the trade and hoarding of gold and silver.

From a monetary perspective, the prohibition against gold ownership was logical. The frightening run on banks that had taken place over the previous months demonstrated that the Federal Reserve had no genuine control over the nation's banking system. Either the government had to control the supply of money, or no one would. To close the banks but to continue to allow commercial transactions to occur in gold carried multiple risks, including moving much of the nation's gold supply out of bank vaults and into private hands, or indeed out of the country, from which it might never return. The latter concern was very real; during this period, war-scarred France was obsessed with stockpiling gold, raising its share of gold worldwide from 7 percent in 1927 to 27 percent in 1932.

And of course, the nation was desperate. Bankruptcies were rampant and many communities functioned only through hastily created "scrip" money or even personal bankbooks that traded at a discount to their face value. Voters had elected Roosevelt and a heavily Democratic Congress—the electoral vote was a lopsided 472 to 59—out of a sense that almost any change had to be for the better. Yet as a matter of public policy, the Emergency Banking Act ought to have been widely resisted or at least contested. Using the Trading With the Enemy Act to justify a peacetime bank holiday seems on its face suspect; the language of the 1917 act refers repeatedly to "war" and "enemies," neither of which were apparent in 1933. In his inaugural address, FDR declared that if Congress would not cooperate with his plans, "I shall ask the Congress for the one remaining instrument to meet the crisis—broad Executive power to wage a war against the emergency, as great as the power that would be given to me if we were in fact invaded by a foreign foe"—but introducing new government powers on the basis of martial metaphors seems at least worthy of scrutiny.

After all, there was already a track record of caution and resistance around using the Trading With the Enemy Act to control the nation's finances. Hoover's Treasury Department as far back as 1932 had considered invoking the act for both a bank holiday and to fight gold hoarding; an aide had even drawn up presidential proclamations similar to those that FDR would later issue. (Indeed, Milton Elliott, the first general counsel of the Federal Reserve, and Paul Warburg, a Federal Reserve Board member, deliberately added wording to the Trading With the Enemy Act that authorized the president to investigate, regulate, or prohibit certain gold and silver transactions even during peacetime—precisely because "at some future time the government might desire to place an embargo upon the export of gold.") Hoover, however, consulted with the Federal Reserve Board and found its majority unwilling to support the measure.[4]

Neither did Roosevelt or his advisers have a clear, shared idea of what their gold policy was. During Roosevelt's first week, he strongly hinted to reporters—off the record—that the country was now off the gold standard. Yet Treasury Secretary William Woodin that same week publicly insisted on the opposite: "It is ridiculous and misleading to say that we have gone off the gold standard, anymore than we have gone off the currency standard. We are definitely on the gold standard. Gold merely cannot be obtained for several days." Then, once it was established that the country was indeed off the gold standard, the public had no way to know whether it should understand the situation as permanent or temporary. In an April press conference, Roosevelt was asked, "Is it still the desire of the United States to go back on the international gold standard?" He replied, "Absolutely; one of the things we hope to do is to get the world as a whole back on some form of gold standard," a remark which was misleading at best.[5]

Similarly, in those early days, Roosevelt and his circle seemed unsure whether they wanted to confiscate Americans' gold—or if they even needed to. The initial version of the Emergency Banking Act originally submitted to Capitol Hill, for example, did not require individuals to relinquish their gold to the government, nor did it give the power of rounding up gold and monitoring its future use to the executive branch. Rather, the first draft allowed that if the Federal Reserve Board deemed it necessary, member banks of the Federal Reserve could be required to turn in their gold and accept payment from the Fed's board. Even this relatively modest board power could only be exercised, the draft bill said, "upon the affirmative vote of five of its members."[6] Putting the Federal Reserve in charge of the gold was consistent with a request that the Fed board made on March 8, asking all Federal Reserve banks to compile a list of anyone who had withdrawn gold since February 1 but not returned it by March 13.

But when Congress was called into special session on March 9, the legislation was changed; the gold-hoarding protections were apparently the section that was most heavily edited in the office of Senator Carter Glass of Virginia. There were few on Capitol Hill with more financial savvy and legislative experience than the self-educated and

territorial former journalist Glass. He had been instrumental in passing the Federal Reserve bill a generation earlier; in the twenty-first
century he is still occasionally invoked as one-half the name of the
long-standing Glass-Steagall Act. Glass, who had turned down FDR's
request to become his treasury secretary and would go on to oppose
much of the New Deal, was being advised by several members of the
Federal Reserve staff. In Glass's office the bill was rewritten to apply
to individuals, partnerships, and corporations; moreover, the new
draft made future oversight of all gold transactions a responsibility
of the treasury secretary rather than the Federal Reserve.[7] According to Walter Wyatt, who was advising the Federal Reserve Board,
"That morning, when we were in Senator Glass's office, somebody
asked us to change that provision and invest the power in the Secretary of the Treasury to require gold to be paid in to the Treasury
Department."[8] No one seems to have kept any record of who the
"somebody" was or why the change was made.

The lack of communication between the major institutional
players about the most effective ways to handle gold hoarding or
the devaluation of the dollar was downright dysfunctional. When
the Treasury Department asked the New York Federal Reserve
for its opinion about the gold-hoarding legislation, its president
George Harrison said that while it was now too late, he would
have preferred that gold bullion be exempted, "partly because there
is an insignificant amount of gold bullion now hoarded, and partly
because we have felt that the fewer the restrictions that may be
made now the easier it will be later to determine the country's
gold policy." A month later, Harrison could make neither head nor
tail of the administration's dollar devaluation, and wrote confidentially to Treasury Secretary Woodin demanding that he explain it.[9]
(Woodin was probably not the best equipped man in the administration to ask.)

This was typical of the harried, slapdash approach to one of the
most important pieces of financial legislation in American history.
FDR's adviser Moley noted in a memoir that "the decisions made

and actions in Washington were crowded into so few days, the individuals directly concerned were so few and so hidden from public notice at the time, and the Congressional action was so swift and so lacking in debate that the record tends to be speculative and sketchy."[10] If anyone in the US Congress felt that the government was overextending its power, or that a different approach would have been better, it left little trace on the official record. Congress acted more like a body in a parliamentary system than a check on executive power. The House of Representatives was denied the ability to amend the bill. There were no committee hearings and next to no debate, and indeed the bill passed without even a roll call taken. Then again, it would have been difficult for members of Congress to discuss a bill they hadn't read. Reportedly, Alabama representative Henry Steagall was the only member of Congress given a copy of the bill, and that version contained penciled markups; for the rest it was read aloud into the record. The House minority leader, Bertrand Snell of New York, complained that "it is entirely out of the ordinary to pass legislation in this House that, as far as I know, is not even in print at the time it is offered," although he ended up supporting the bill.[11] According to Moley, the bill "was represented by a folded newspaper in the House because there had not been time to print copies of it."[12] Within a matter of hours, both houses of Congress had approved the bill on March 9 and the president had signed it. The front page of the next day's *New York Times* referred to the government's newfound "dictatorship over gold."

As dictatorships go, however, FDR's over gold does not appear to have been the most forceful. Once the banking law and its various amendments and extensions were in place, and as banks began reopening in the spring, the federal government and the banks began the enormous, almost comical task of rounding up all the gold in private American hands in a matter of weeks. The modern record of governments attempting to prohibit and confiscate material that the population deems useful or enjoyable is far from stellar. Just a few years earlier, as part of a broader attack on jazz music's supposedly decadent and subversive powers, the Soviet government had tried to ban all use, manufacture, and imports of saxophones. This effort did not succeed. It is difficult to assess whether the United States' effort to combat gold hoarding—both in Hoover's later months and in the first several months of the Roosevelt administration—was any more effective.

To this day, no historians have assigned an unimpeachable figure for how much gold was actually in the hands of Americans in the early 1930s. Most Americans, of course, could not afford to own gold as an investment during the Depression. Many who owned gold coins had probably acquired them recently; gold withdrawals rose sharply after the Bank of England had been forced to abandon the gold standard in September 1931. In January 1932 the Hoover administration had estimated that between $1.3 and $1.4 billion in "hidden money" was being hoarded in private hands; that represented about 30 percent of the amount that the US government held in reserve.[13] If American hoarders had been a central bank, their reserves would have been more than twice the amount of reserves in the Bank of England, larger than those of any central bank in the world besides France and the United States.[14] Hoover created a special task force to recover hoarded gold, headed by Colonel Frank Knox, who had been the publisher of the *Chicago Daily News*. It warned economically depressed Americans that "a dollar hoarded not only ceases to perform its function as currency but destroys $5 to $10 in potential credit."[15] At least in the minds of the federal government, the problem of gold flowing to private owners was severe and had nearly forced the country off the gold standard involuntarily. In a speech at the height of the 1932 presidential election, Hoover criticized nineteenth-century greenbacks as a Democratic "panacea," while also disclosing that his own treasury secretary had told him the country came within two weeks of abandoning the gold standard, which would have created "chaos." A Hoover aide later said that "it was almost a matter of hours."[16]

Hoover's anti-hoarding measures were mildly effective for a

few months, but the problem was too sprawling for a domestic task force alone to solve, especially because hoarding was probably not the chief cause of domestic gold shortages. Most of the world had gone off the gold standard; by mid-1933, among the world's largest economies, only France, Switzerland, Belgium, and Holland remained on the gold standard. For a variety of reasons these countries had begun exercising the right to cash in financial obligations in gold rather than US currency. In the spring of 1932, for example, France alone had taken some $700 million of gold out of the United States—a significant sum, considering that all of the US Federal Reserve banks held only a little more than $2.5 billion in gold at the time, and the law required 40 percent of the nation's currency value to be backed up by gold. In an apt metaphor Hoover declared that "a mass of gold dashing hither and yon from one nation to another has acted like a cannon loose on the deck of the world in a storm."[17]

Now, however, the government had some means to tie the cannon down, and many Americans did appear to comply with the new law. Larger gold "hoarders" were no doubt fearful of public exposure and fines; those with smaller stashes of gold were probably caught up in the great national desire to support Roosevelt's recovery program, whether or not they agreed with it or understood it. When the president's first orders went out, streams of people showed up at banks with sacks of gold to be redeemed; some $200 million in gold was said to be recovered in the first week. On March 11, Treasury issued a chipper statement: "Already from every quarter of the Nation is reported a large and steady current of gold flowing back to the banks." A seven-year-old girl in Chicago, channeling the can-do spirit of that era's heroine Shirley Temple, sent a single gold dime to the White House, saying she did "not want to be a hoarder."[18]

Those with larger supplies were watched closely by Treasury and the Justice Department. Officials unearthed some clear efforts to mislead the government; evidently some five hundred people had

withdrawn gold under fictitious names. Nonetheless, actual prosecutions were uncommon. In the fall of 1933, a New York lawyer
named F. B. Campbell was indicted after he tried to recover some
$200,000 in gold bars that he had been keeping at Chase National
Bank in violation of the law. Campbell argued in court that the
Emergency Banking Act was unconstitutional, but the judge did
not agree. Campbell's case was an exception, however. All told, the
attorney general's office by the end of 1933 knew of fewer than two
dozen complaints or indictments.[19]

It is nearly impossible to declare whether the confiscation of
gold beginning in 1933 was a success. In part this is because the
Roosevelt administration gave contradictory accounts of the gold
confiscation program, both internally and externally. The lack of
significant prosecutions could be interpreted as a sign of widespread compliance, but the administration at times made it clear
that it was impractical to legally chase after anything but the largest gold stashes. When a former US senator from Colorado taunted
the government to come after him for $120 worth of gold he held,
$20 over the legal threshold, Attorney General Homer Cummings
assured him that such small sums were not worth the effort to
collect. Yet in May, Treasury estimated that approximately $700
million in gold and gold certificates remained in circulation, and it
was never clear if such amounts could be recovered by going after
the biggest hoards.[20] In early June, Justice said it was investigat-
ing 10,000 possible hoarders, a number that quickly rose to 15,000.
Cummings took a tough stance: "All of these will be run down
and not one person who can be located will escape investigation.
I am so thoroughly committed to the necessity that all gold be
returned to the Treasury that I have not patience with those who
hold it out in defiance of their government, and I brand them as
slackers." Then in August, the attorney general said that there were
only forty known hoarders of gold who refused to turn in their
metal without explanation, and that their holdings were worth
only $400,000.[21] In response to the criticism that he made threats

that he could not follow up, Cummings reportedly said, "Hell, I was looking for gold, not for victims."[22]

A bigger problem—one that the American government would continue to encounter through subsequent decades—was that gold is exceedingly difficult to count reliably. Many historians have been taken in by a bit of sly official bookkeeping. Looking at the official statistics today, the amount of gold coin in circulation did drop dramatically, from $284 million in February 1933 to $24 million by the end of the year—a 91.5 percent reduction. But those figures are wildly misleading. Originally, the government count in January 1934 showed $287 million of gold coins still in circulation. But Treasury and the Federal Reserve decided that because gold ownership by 1934 was illegal, it no longer made sense to include that figure at all. So they dropped the $287 million in January 1934 to zero, and subtracted $287 million from all earlier calculations going back to 1913. Using the original figures, gold coins went from $571 million in February 1933 to $311 million in December—or a percentage drop of 45.5 percent.[23]

Why the change? "This was done primarily because private holdings had become illegal," a Federal Reserve publication later explained, "but there was also reason to believe that much of the *computed* amount of gold coin in private hands had in fact been lost or taken out of the country by travelers."[24] Explaining the apparent overstatement of gold coins in circulation in previous years, the Federal Reserve's annual report said: "Results of official efforts during [World War I] to concentrate gold and more recently, since March 6, 1933, to secure its return from private hoards, have indicated that the overstatement was large." So Hoover and Roosevelt may have been chasing after tens or hundreds of millions of dollars' worth of hoarded gold that simply wasn't there, or perhaps the efforts to chase it down drove the gold out of the country or caused it to be "lost." For their part, Milton Friedman and Anna Schwartz's monumental monetary history concluded that the bulk of the missing $287 million in gold coin "was retained illegally in private hands."[25]

One crucial question is whether FDR and his circle intended the value of the American dollar to be managed by the government indefinitely, and—as a corollary—for the private possession of gold to be prohibited to the vast majority of Americans forever. By invoking the Trading With the Enemy Act to ban the flow of gold, FDR effectively declared a national economic emergency that was equivalent to war. Typically, however, emergencies pass; most of the nation's banks, for example, were reopened a few days or weeks after the "holiday" ended.

But the confiscation of Americans' gold was a prerequisite to the program that the administration began moving toward: the nationalization of all American gold and the day-to-day management of the US dollar. A series of steps taken over the spring and summer set the stage for near-absolute control over gold by the executive branch. Gold exports were explicitly prohibited without a license, and the government announced that no new licenses would be issued. Non-hoarding use of gold, such as for industrial and artistic use, would now require approval from Treasury. By a joint resolution of Congress, clauses in contracts that required repayment in gold were declared void, a move with potentially shattering ramifications. All domestic production of gold—which in 1932 had been about 2.1 million fine ounces—now had to be sold to the secretary of treasury at a price that Treasury would determine. And most crucially, the Thomas Amendment to the Agricultural Amendment Act gave the president the power to fix the value of the dollar to gold and silver as he saw fit, up to 50 percent inflation. Nothing like this total monetary control had ever existed in the United States. With the passage of the Thomas Amendment on May 12, a top pro-gold Roosevelt aide declared the "end of civilization."[26]

Somewhat perversely, these supplementary measures drew greater attention and deliberation from Congress than the far more sweeping March 9 legislation they were designed to implement. Even so, relatively little of the debate focused on the removal of gold from the American monetary system. One exception was Louis McFadden, a Pennsylvania Republican, who introduced articles of impeachment against many members of the Roosevelt administration as well as the Federal Reserve Board for, among many other sins, "having deprived the people of the United States of their lawful circulating medium of exchange."[27] (McFadden was a perennial gadfly, who had also unsuccessfully attempted to impeach Hoover and who charged that a cabal of Jewish Wall Street bankers had aided the Soviet revolution.) If anything, especially among inflation advocates in the West, the spirit of William Jennings Bryan was still alive; among these partisans, the measures to remove gold from American financial life were seen as great steps of human progress. During the debate on gold clauses in contracts, Congressman Martin Smith, a Washington Democrat, said, "The enactment of this law is another emancipation proclamation, declaring liberty for 120 million Americans from the thralldom and cruel yoke of gold which has enslaved the human race."

Collectively, these measures represented a unique and high-risk experiment in the history of monetary policy in the United States. One economic historian calls the period between Roosevelt's inauguration and January 1934 "in many ways one of the most complex and baffling in twentieth-century United States monetary history."[28] And throughout the period, Roosevelt had little support from traditional quarters. The Federal Reserve Board, especially under chairman Eugene Meyer, opposed nearly all aspects of Roosevelt's first-year monetary actions, although it did little to undermine them. Roosevelt's own economic team, which included several holdovers from the Hoover administration, grew increasingly distant from the president, particularly after Roosevelt made it clear to a world monetary conference in July that he was rejecting "old fetishes of so-called international bankers" and that the dollar's relationship to commodities was more important to him than its relationship to currencies abroad.

Roosevelt's plan centered on a "managed currency," in which the dollar's gold value would change frequently to a price set by the administration. This concept was more than controversial; it became, as historian Eric Rauchway put it, "the principal article in the Roosevelt administration's profession of faith." James Warburg, a longtime ally of Roosevelt's who never formally joined the administration, could not abide the idea of a dollar permanently untethered from gold. He sought allies with whom he hoped he could persuade the president. One was Dean Acheson, the brilliant, headstrong lawyer who was undersecretary of treasury (and would become, after World War II, secretary of state). In August, Acheson told Warburg that the president had given him a "penciled note" that asked him to try his hand at purchasing newly minted gold at $28.00 an ounce—meaning thereby a substantially weaker dollar. Acheson was appalled; he could not accept the principle behind the Thomas Amendment granting the president the power to dictate the dollar's value. Acheson believed that Treasury could only buy gold at the price that had been established in the nineteenth century, $20.67 an ounce.

Acheson thought he had the law on his side, as well as the opinion of the attorney general. He was not merely resistant to change; Treasury was about to complete a sale of Liberty Bonds to the public, and Acheson feared that devaluing the dollar would violate the government's obligation to its bondholders. For the president, however, this was not useful; as an Acheson biographer put it, "what FDR wanted was to be told how he could do it, not that it was impossible to do."[29] And indeed the objections of Acheson, Warburg, and the Federal Reserve did little to impede Roosevelt. On August 29 he signed an executive order authorizing Treasury to buy gold mined in the United States, which could then be sold to authorized users or abroad. The price would be "equal to the

best price obtainable in the free gold markets of the world." To
the press, "high Treasury officials" insisted that this soft nationalization of gold had nothing to do with cutting the gold value of
the dollar, and indeed it would help gold producers by allowing
them to obtain a higher price.[30] The market agreed; in an otherwise
unspectacular period of trading, gold-mining stocks shot up.

On September 7, gold producers delivered an estimated 10,000
ounces of newly mined metal to government offices in New York
and San Francisco, and the following day the purchase price was
announced: $29.62 an ounce, or nearly $9 an ounce more than Treasury paid to coin gold. Of course, this did not constitute a return to
the Civil War–era gold market; only gold producers were allowed
to sell, and Treasury was the only buyer, reselling only to authorized industrial or artistic users or to foreign buyers. Nonetheless,
for the first time in decades, the United States had a gold market,
and its prices were unlikely ever to return to the $20.67-per-ounce
level at which the dollar had officially been defined. As a *New York
Times* editorial noted, this development was little understood "in
the somewhat perplexed mind of the general public." But if Roosevelt's currency policy ever had a point of no return, this was
it; domestic gold producers would not lightly accept a return to
an export ban, and the downward trajectory of the dollar's value
seemed indelibly linked to a widely appreciated pickup in business.

This, however, was merely the first phase of gold buying. By late
September, Roosevelt, along with Morgenthau and his staff, had
cooked up a clever, if convoluted, plan whereby the Reconstruction
Finance Corporation—the agency Hoover had set up to aid troubled banks—would issue short-term debt in order to buy gold, and
that debt in turn would be bought by Treasury. With the economy
beginning to show more strength than it had in years, Roosevelt
knew he could sell this novel, even radical idea to the public. In
his fourth "fireside chat," on October 22, Roosevelt told listeners
that it "may be necessary from time to time to control the gold
value of our own dollar at home." He continued, "I am authorizing

the Reconstruction Finance Corporation (RFC) to buy gold newly mined in the United States at prices to be determined from time to time after consultation with the Secretary of the Treasury and the President." The administration had hoped to begin gold purchases the following day but still couldn't agree on details. The plan was also deliberately secretive and vague; there was no target value set for the dollar; nor any commitment to buy gold on any given day; nor an announced endpoint of the purchasing program.

Although Roosevelt had told the country that he would set the gold purchase price with the secretary of treasury, in reality Woodin, who was in poor health, had nothing to do with it and was generally opposed to the program. The decisions were made with Morgenthau (who by mid-November would take over at Treasury), RFC chairman Jesse Jones, and occasionally members of the Federal Reserve, with a pricing method that was less than scientific. "I believe it was on Friday that we raised the price 21 cents," Morgenthau wrote in his diary, "and the President said, 'It is a lucky number because it is three times seven.' If anybody ever knew how we really set the gold price through a combination of lucky numbers, etc., I think that they really would be frightened."[31]

Initially, the policy had little impact, and the administration was clearly out of its element. On October 25, the government began buying domestic gold at the price of $31.36 an ounce, or about 27 cents above the world market price, and implying a gold price of the dollar of 66 cents. But the value of the dollar on the currency market actually went up—the opposite of what they'd planned. One misstep was the initial decision to buy only domestic gold. The prices of American farm products were set in international markets, where they were purchased with foreign currencies. Thus, buying only gold mined in the United States would not affect the market price because Treasury's purchases wouldn't affect the price of gold abroad.

Roosevelt and his advisers recognized almost immediately that the policy of buying only domestic gold was ineffective, and they began seeking ways to buy foreign gold as well. This policy met resistance from the Federal Reserve; George Harrison from the New York bank cautioned the president that having the US government buy gold in the open marketplace could create trouble abroad. He also told the president that the policy would not achieve the aims he sought. Roosevelt persisted, and on October 30, Harrison phoned the whiskered Bank of England governor Montagu Norman, who "hit the ceiling" over the idea. "It would be an outrageous thing," Norman contended, "for a Government to go into another country's market to buy gold which it did not want, and at the risk of chaos in the exchange markets, deliberately to depreciate its currency."[32] The differences were soon smoothed over, and the administration publicly announced that it would buy foreign gold (which ended up being a much larger portion of RFC purchases than domestic gold). Still, much or all of the conflict with the Federal Reserve and other central banks could have been avoided if the White House had consulted genuine experts beforehand. Even Roosevelt supporters found the efforts amateurish. Walter S. Salant, a Keynesian economist who was loyal enough to Roosevelt to stay in the administration through World War II, remarked in an oral history: "I think the most interesting aspect of gold policy was the casting about for people who knew something, and the complete inability of the President or anybody very close to him to distinguish somebody who knew something from somebody who knew nothing."[33]

During the three-month life of the gold purchase program, the RFC bought 695,000 ounces of gold in the US at a total cost of $23 million, and 3.3 million ounces of foreign gold at a cost of $108 million. Because the specific goals of the RFC gold-buying program were so vague, it is difficult to assess if it achieved its objectives. In a recent appraisal, Federal Reserve official Kenneth Garbade calls the program "ineptly executed," noting several weaknesses.[34] First, reflating prices presumably required an actual increase in the money supply, but the RFC was not a central bank; it had to fund its gold purchases by issuing short-term debt. Second, the administration kept raising the price it would pay for gold almost every business day. Few actual markets move only in one direction, and this anomaly caused anxiety in the markets—first abroad, where the fear was that American inflation would grow out of control, and then in November in the domestic bond market. Arthur Schlesinger, in his generally sympathetic account of the early days of the New Deal, wrote: "To what extent did the President really think that he could raise the price of commodities by raising the price of gold? The answer is, not very much."[35]

But for Roosevelt and his most loyal advisers, any shortcomings in the currency management program were preferable to the cost of inaction. That fall, tens of thousands of agricultural and cotton workers had gone on strike in California; in Wisconsin, creameries and cheese factories where workers picketed were bombed and one dairy farmer was shot to death. On a somber Sunday afternoon on October 29, Roosevelt told a White House group: "Gentlemen, if we continued a week or two longer without my having made this move on gold, we would have had an agrarian revolution in this country."[36]

Nonetheless, the idea of setting a new price every day was not sustainable, and the administration began to look for a more realistic solution. They hit upon the idea of reducing the gold content of the dollar and then restoring it to a "gold bullion standard"—meaning that the dollar would be convertible to gold at a fixed rate, but that gold would not be available in a hoardable form to anyone but the extremely wealthy. When the new year arrived, this notion had taken the form of legislation. In late January, Congress passed the Gold Reserve Act, which formalized the arrangements that had been put in place the previous year. Under its terms, all gold had to be turned in to the federal government, to be reimbursed at $35 an ounce, a 59 percent premium over the price that had been established in 1900. Most Republicans and bankers fought it all the way, but they had already been rendered impotent by the prior year's emergency actions. Throughout the period, Roosevelt retained a strong, if somewhat dark sense of American economic history. Just as he had thundered in his inaugural address against the "practices of the unscrupulous money changers [who] stand indicted in the court of public opinion, rejected by the hearts and minds of men," he saw his gold dictatorship as an assault on the banking class, in great Democratic tradition. "A financial element in the larger centers has owned the government ever since the days of Andrew Jackson," he wrote to the diplomat Colonel House. "The country is going through a repetition of Jackson's fight with the Bank of the United States—only on a far bigger and broader basis."[37]

As cataclysmic and unprecedented as the financial overhaul of 1933 and 1934 was, and despite the insistence in financial circles that Americans preferred "sound money," most Americans settled in to the new gold order without excess fuss. Will Rogers, the everyman humorist of the era, published several columns in 1933 and 1934 that supported going off the gold standard while managing to poke fun at it. "We been on a gold basis since the boys started digging it out of the creeks, and the girls started digging it out of the boys, yet I doubt if we got a boy or a girl in this country under twenty that ever saw one of our gold coins," Rogers wrote. "Our paper money said, 'Payable in gold,' but it should have had under it in small letters, 'Can't you take a joke?' "[38] And law enforcement soon realized that gold prohibition provided them with an effective new tool. When Charles Lindbergh's infant son was kidnapped in 1932, it gripped the nation in what was called the "crime of the century." A $50,000 ransom was paid in gold certificates that would become illegal to possess a few months after the money changed hands in a graveyard. In September 1934, police were tipped off after kidnapper Bruno Hauptmann pumped his Dodge sedan with gas at a filling station at Lexington Avenue and 127th Street in Manhattan—and paid with a now-contraband $10 gold certificate.

One effect of the gold-buying program, unanticipated by the administration but probably welcome, is that the higher dollar value of gold gave a boost to the American gold-mining industry. In 1934 domestic gold production jumped 21 percent to nearly 2.8 million ounces, and by 1937 was more than 4.1 million ounces. Throughout the West, gold and silver mines that had been left to gather dust became active again, sometimes by organized companies and sometimes by individuals striking out on their own.[39] Beginning in the early 1930s, many amateur miners with no better employment prospects would drive to old placer mines to try their luck, leading some to label the era "the automobile gold rush."[40] Encouraged by often sensational newspaper headlines of freak gold discoveries, plenty of hard-strapped Americans wanted to believe that gold could be their salvation, as they imagined it had been for their grandparents. In California, Arizona, and Georgia, among other places, at least 100,000 Americans in 1933 alone rushed to once-productive placer mines, hoping that the ground could provide them with the wealth that the American economy could not. Alas, like the nineteenth-century gold rushes, the supply could not keep up with the demand. A government report estimated that there were twenty would-be "automobile gold rush" miners for every one who actually found gold, and that the payouts even for the successful were modest.[41] "Disillusionment was rapid," concluded the report.

Disillusionment overtook parts of the administration as well; the fallout from Roosevelt's gold actions was bitter and long-lasting. A large number of top officials and advisers parted ways with the White House, and a kind of permanent opposition to Roosevelt formed, with gold as its organizing principle.

The opposition had three chief (and in some ways overlapping) components, each of which created a political thrust that outlasted the Roosevelt presidency. The first was essentially partisan in nature, using the opposition to Roosevelt's gold policy as the centerpiece of a broader attack on the New Deal and an attempt to reelect Hoover or another Republican as president. Beginning in the fall of 1933, Hoover and onetime Roosevelt ally James Warburg set up in Chicago to assemble a group of businessmen—including representatives of Quaker Oats, Montgomery Ward, International Harvester, and Frank Knox, the publisher of the *Chicago Daily News*, who also had headed up the gold antihoarding task force for Hoover—to propagate anti-inflation, anti-Roosevelt ideas to influence Congress and public opinion.[42]

The second group represented the economic orthodoxy, which included most of the American banking industry as well as economists who believed as a matter of principle that the economy would run best on a gold standard. They were the inheritors of the "hard money" legacy from the nineteenth century, but Roosevelt's decisive split from gold gave their arguments new focus and urgency. In some instances, this stance was also associated with the development of theories about the business cycle and inflation, and there were several economics associations that sprung up at this time—such as the American Institute for Economic Research in Massachusetts, founded in 1933—that advocated a return to a gold standard as part of a broader conservative economic policy.

The third group reached into the darker recesses of American politics. During the Populist period, arguments against eastern banking elites had sometimes elided into explicit hatred for Europeans and Jews. And while Roosevelt's inflationist policy to a considerable degree was meant to accommodate the western populists, the forces of paranoia and hate were not placated and made Roosevelt their target, often using the same pro-gold, anti–New Deal arguments as the Republicans and orthodox economists. In some cases these were just angry individuals who managed to build sizable followings by offering extreme anti-Roosevelt rhetoric. For example, James True was a onetime *Chicago Tribune* advertising employee and freelance writer who began selling a weekly newsletter in July 1933 called *Industrial Control Report*. In addition, he published a seventy-six-page book in 1938 called *Gold Manipulations and Depressions.*[43] He was also a vicious anti-Semite; he spoke of the "Jew Communism which the New Deal is trying to force on America" and claimed to have applied for a patent on a heavy-duty policeman-style club he called a "Kike Killer."

In a sense, this tendency represented a continuity of the most despicable and least viable parts of the Populist legacy—and significantly without the mass support that William Jennings Bryan enjoyed. Nonetheless, political identification with gold became synonymous with opposition to Roosevelt, including the extremist (and, especially later, isolationist) opposition. And the Supreme Court was about to hand that opposition one of the most powerful rhetorical weapons available.

# CHAPTER 5

○

# The Arsenal of Gold

**THERE WERE FEW DAYS** in FDR's first term that his attorney general would have considered relaxing. Yet on the evening of January 10, 1935, Homer Cummings, who had originally only taken the attorney general job on a temporary basis when Roosevelt's initial nominee died, was feeling especially troubled. Cummings and his colleagues had spent three punishing days arguing multiple cases before a feisty Supreme Court, and he was nervous about the outcome. In the context of the New Deal, with its sweeping overhaul of so many institutions of everyday life, these cases—known informally as the "gold clause" cases—were not particularly well known or understood. Compared, say, to the National Recovery Act, which the Court would unanimously strike down as unconstitutional a few months later, the gold-clause cases were a major concern for only a small number of people, almost all of whom were quite wealthy.

To house the gold that the federal government began confiscating in 1933, the Treasury Department constructed a massive bullion depository inside Fort Knox in Kentucky. The billions of dollars of gold bullion and the legendary security around them have excited the American imagination for decades. *Courtesy Library of Congress*

And yet Cummings knew that if the Court decided against his position, the economic consequences could be devastating, quite likely catapulting the United States into another period of severe economic contraction like that which began in 1929 and from which the country was still slowly recovering. For this reason, Cummings decided for the first time since he'd taken the office to make the oral arguments to the Supreme Court himself. Worse still, to lose the gold-clause cases would almost certainly drain the US Treasury of unprecedented billions of dollars, leaving the government without the stimulus resources that had been the only source of hope after the Depression had hit. By Cummings's own calculation, if the Court upheld the validity of gold clauses in contracts, it would add nearly $70 billion to the country's already formidable public and private debts. (Later, some economists estimated the damage higher still.) This was an almost unimaginable figure; the entire gross domestic product of the United States at the time was roughly $100 billion. Never before had such a towering sum been directly at risk over the votes of nine justices.

Despite the high stakes, the administration had been conspicuously unprepared to handle the issue of gold clauses; they largely ignored it when they first moved to take the dollar off gold, even though it had been much debated by experts. And now, Cummings and his allies were paying the price for being unprepared. The questions from the Court's justices had been not merely skeptical but, as one newspaper put it, "savage."

And thus, when Cummings returned to the White House that evening, he relayed the news to Roosevelt and Treasury Secretary Henry Morgenthau, who were discussing tax policy along with Robert Jackson, a fast-rising Treasury attorney who, within a few years, would join the very Court that was now vexing his colleagues. Roosevelt expressed deep concern about the consequences of losing the cases, "and was quite determined that he just could not accept an adverse decision," Jackson later recalled.[1] The president spoke openly about whether it was possible to defy the Court's ruling; within a few weeks, Roosevelt would go so far as to draw up a radio address explaining to the nation why his administration had to ignore the ruling of the highest court in the land.

Jackson, a cunning, politically seasoned lawyer who had never graduated from law school, then spoke up. He noted that he had recently read an article by economic historian Sidney Ratner, which made a persuasive argument that President Grant had appointed two additional justices to fill vacancies in order to reverse the Court's decision in the Legal Tender cases. The two men discussed the possibility of expanding the Court, and the topic surfaced again at the next day's cabinet meeting. Harold Ickes, Roosevelt's hard-driving liberal interior secretary, wrote approvingly in his diary: "The Attorney General went so far as to say that if the Court went against the Government, the number of justices should be increased at once so as to give a favorable majority."[2] At least as far back as his 1932 campaign, Roosevelt had railed against the Republican leanings of the Court, and there had been loose talk about appointing additional justices, but this was the first time that a true plan was being laid out. To get his way, Roosevelt would seek congressional approval, appeal directly to the people, and even shut down the stock market if he had to. If the Court wanted a constitutional crisis over gold clauses that would likely throw the country into bankruptcy, Roosevelt and his administration were prepared to deliver one.

There is no flattering explanation for why the Roosevelt administration was late to realize the massive problem that gold clauses represented. The clauses themselves had been in use at least as far back as the Civil War. Indeed, the introduction of greenbacks raised the question of whether contracts demanding payment in gold or silver were enforceable; the Supreme Court had ruled in 1868 that they were.[3] The concept was simple: a debtor agreed to pay a creditor the amount owed in gold if asked. This was a hedge against any devaluation of currency. The rise of agrarian populism, inflationists, and silver advocacy in the final third of the nineteenth century caused many individuals and businesses to seek a way to protect themselves from possible disruptions in the value of currency in the event that, say, a William Jennings Bryan should be elected president and fulfill the promise to change the value of money.

By the 1930s, gold clauses had become more or less standard in home mortgages and big businesses. Railroads in particular almost universally wrote gold clauses into bonds; the $11 billion worth of debt owed by railroad companies in the early 1930s was nearly all secured by gold-clause contracts. Gold clauses were also used in many corporate bonds; bonds that contained gold clauses were considered less risky and thus tended to sell at a lower cost than those that did not. After the Panic of 1893, gold clauses became an important component of the "sound money" system championed by Grover Cleveland and the Republican Party; it has been argued that in the depressed 1890s there would have been no buyers of American bonds without the gold clause.

The federal government itself used gold clauses. In 1910, the government began requiring that all future government bonds issued "shall be payable in principal and interest in United States gold coin." The Liberty Bonds that funded World War I were payable in gold, cementing a connection between gold and patriotism. As with the gold standard itself, gold clauses in contracts tapped a place in American psychology where the monetary realm met moral and psychological realms. One historian has written that gold-backed money and the support represented by gold clauses in contracts "had become deeply embedded in American thought, business practices and popular psychology. It was thought of as sacred, absolutely essential to the proper functioning of business and commerce."[4]

When the Depression hit, many gold bondholders and legislators began to worry what would happen to gold clauses if the United States followed the lead of other countries and went off the gold standard; recall that Herbert Hoover told an audience in October 1932 that earlier in the year the Treasury came within two weeks of depleting its gold supply. It was clear to some observers that if the value of the dollar was going to be depreciated, the status of gold clauses in contracts would quickly fall into legal limbo. Either creditors would lose out because they would be forced to accept payment in a depreciated currency, or debtors would lose out because they would have to pay a gold premium on top of the nominal amount owed—but no one would know which until a definitive ruling was made. At the corporate level, as one economist put it, "it would be impossible to know absolutely whether it would be better to own stocks or bonds."[5] Such fundamental uncertainty would be sure to slow business activity, especially if the cases took years to resolve legally.

Some commentators foresaw far thornier, even dire, consequences. While few predicted that personal ownership of gold would be prohibited, it was obvious that if a currency devaluation was going to happen it would make gold scarce. Already in 1931 and 1932, demand for gold had hit unprecedented levels, and the metal was disappearing from the country, as we have seen, faster than the government could count it. Thus, if gold clauses were upheld as valid, private corporations would very likely not be able to get enough gold to meet their contractual debts, which would trigger a massive wave of foreclosures. Imagine, too, the complexity that could arise at the state level; at least five states at the turn of the century passed contradictory laws about the ability or inability of private parties to demand payment of a contract in a specific type of money. And finally, there was the question of gold clauses in government bonds held abroad. If foreign bondholders in countries not on the gold standard were not required to make interest payments in gold, what would prevent them from making payment in a local currency that was possibly even more devalued than the dollar? And if the US government repaid its bond debt in depreciated dollars, would bondholders have the right to sue—and in which nation's courts?

In the summer of 1932, James Truslow Adams, one of America's best-known historians—he coined the phrase *the American dream*—warned that a government failure to uphold the gold clause would represent "a great breach of faith." As part of an in-depth exchange in the financial weekly *Barron's*, Adams foresaw the crisis that evidently eluded Roosevelt's team as it plotted its early steps on gold. "If we went off gold and Congress ruled either that the gold clauses were valid or invalid, suit would be brought by interested parties on one side or the other, rising eventually to the United States Supreme Court."[6] Adams continued, "In view of the enormous property value at stake, and the fact that such a decision would transfer that property from one mass of citizens to another mass, the decision would be the most fateful, perhaps, in the history of the Court."

Some legislators tried to treat the gold-clause issue with the gravity it merited. In February 1933—that is, a month before Roosevelt was inaugurated and the emergency banking legislation was passed—an Iowa congressman introduced a bill to nullify gold clauses.[7] Nonetheless, congressional leaders were unwilling to devote much time to the gold-clause issue, in part because they doubted that nullifying the clauses was constitutional. By contrast, Roosevelt and most of his advisers do not appear ever to have discussed the issue of gold clauses until April 1933—more than a month after Roosevelt declared, at least to his intimates, that the country had left the gold standard and Congress had already prohibited private gold ownership. One exception was an outside adviser named Alexander Sachs, a Lithuanian-born Lehman Brothers economist, who drafted a memo in February about the "serious legal complications" that could arise from devaluing the dollar; it is unclear how widely read or considered Sachs's memo was.[8]

When the Thomas Amendment to the agriculture relief law passed in May, it gave the president the power to regulate the value of the currency, and made US currency legal tender for all debts public and private. But the amendment had at least two holes: it failed to address whether currency could now be used to pay debts in existing gold-clause contracts, and whether gold-clause contracts would be valid in the future. (Bizarrely, the Thomas Amendment may also unintentionally have made coins from the Philippines legal tender in the United States.) In an effort to fill these holes, a resolution was introduced into both houses of Congress on May 26 to abrogate existing gold clauses and prevent their use in the future. The resolution declared gold clauses to be contrary to public policy and declared them null. The Senate report supporting the resolution made the issue sound both matter-of-fact and urgent: "The Government should have specific authority to control its gold resources." It also clearly took a side in the creditor versus debtor debate: "Private debtors with gold clause obligations are entitled to protection and a prompt and clear definition of their legal position."[9]

These assertions were vigorously interrogated and denounced in the ensuing Senate debate. Faced with the proposition that the United States would try to wiggle out of its debt obligations by substituting paper money for gold, Republican senator David A. Reed of Pennsylvania used the same insult his nineteenth-century counterparts had; the bill was "repudiation" and a blow to the American character: "This is the most serious question of national dishonor since I entered the Senate," Reed declared. "We are saying to the peoples of foreign countries that the sacred promise of this country is merely a scrap of paper. The national honor is about to receive a stain we cannot erase for 100 years. . . . for generations to come Americans will grow red around the ears when they think of what this Congress did."[10] The legislation, he and several colleagues argued, was unconstitutional.

The resolution passed and, as predicted, lawsuits quickly ensued. Several of these made it to the Supreme Court in 1934, and the cases were consolidated into three categories: those dealing with railroad bonds, grouped under *Norman v. Baltimore & Ohio Railroad Company*; a case over the gold clause in US Treasury gold certificates, *Nortz v. United States*; and a case concerning the gold clause in Liberty Bonds, *Perry v. United States*.

The oral arguments began on January 8, 1935. Cummings did his best to re-create the desperation that reigned when the Roosevelt administration took office in March 1933, when the economic situation in the United States and much of the world was teetering between chaos and disaster. Banks were closing daily. Prices were plummeting. Bankruptcies were mounting. Millions were out of work. International trade had all but dried up. Cummings told the Court justices that in 1933 "our people were slipping to a lower level of civilization."[11]

This invocation was meant not only to explain the expediency of the government's initial policies but to warn what could recur if, overnight, an additional $69 billion were to be added to the public and private debts of the nation. "The stupendous catastrophe envisaged by this conservative statement is such as to stagger the imagination. It would not be a case of 'back to the Constitution.' It would be a case of 'back to chaos,'" Cummings intoned.

In contrast to the president's soothing fireside reassurances, Cummings's opening argument was one of the few instances in which the Roosevelt administration publicly acknowledged the radical change it had made to the nation's historical idea of money. "Gold is not an ordinary commodity," Cummings told the Court, peering through his rimless eyeglasses. "It is a thing apart, and upon it rests, under our form of civilization, the whole structure of our finance and the welfare of our people." His point was that gold was separate from money, gold was a powerful tool to measure the value of money—but that the federal government had the constitutional authority to regulate money. Nonetheless, his invocation of gold's unique historic financial role must have pushed at least some of his listeners in the opposite direction from what he intended. Cummings also elaborated on a concept that had been central in the second Legal Tender case: that the ability to regulate the value of currency is a fundamental aspect of sovereignty.

This, he insisted, was the clear intent of the Constitution's framers, who "took pains to see that this power, just like the power of the sword, this great attribute of sovereignty, should reside in one single authority."

All of the justices seemed uncomfortable with the issues at stake. Justice Harlan Stone, a Republican World War I veteran, vowed that he would personally never again purchase securities from a government "so faithless to its obligations." Chief Justice Charles Hughes, who was generally in favor of government regulation and not blindly opposed to the New Deal, brought up the instance of a war bond, designed to raise money for the military. It contains a promise to pay a certain amount of gold at a prescribed degree of weight and fineness. "What is the power in the contract to alter it to the detriment of the one who bought the bond?" Assistant Solicitor General Angus MacLean answered that Congress had the right to decide what the money in the contract should be. Hughes, who sported an immense walrus-like white mustache and beard, demanded, "Where does Congress get that right?" MacLean's answer: "From its constitutional power to coin money and regulate the value thereof."[12] It was the same right that the government invoked in defending the constitutionality of greenbacks not backed by gold—but it was as hotly contested in 1935 as it had been in 1869. Once again, the idea of money that was worth only what the government says it is worth was not merely offensive but deemed to be immoral.

The following day, in front of a packed courtroom with half a dozen US senators in attendance, the justices burst out laughing at the government's argument, a rare lapse in manners. Pierce Butler threw questions and statements at government attorney Stanley Reed that one newspaper labeled "savage." Butler thundered: "Under that theory Congress could stamp the word dollar on a dime and make it legal tender for the discharge of gold obligations. What were the words put there for? There can be no confusion of meaning. It was intended to pay so much gold."[13]

Justice Louis Brandeis, generally a critic of big business and one of the Court's liberals, conspicuously asked no questions in the oral arguments over three days. Shortly thereafter, Harvard law professor Felix Frankfurter, a friend of Brandeis's and an adviser to Roosevelt, met with Brandeis and asked him about his silence. He responded that he knew already what his legal conclusions were, and that he was "so completely out of sympathy on matters of policy with what [the government] did that I thought it best to say nothing." He added that while he found the economics of the case "doubtful at best," he thought its "morals were plain and most important. I don't know whether we shall recover."[14]

The fear created by the Court's treatment is what led the White House to consider, on January 10 and 11, expanding the number of justices on the Court. Not long after, the idea began to surface prominently in the press, in what read as calculated shots across the Court's bow. The *New York Times* on January 13 ran a front-page Associated Press story revealing that "Some Congressional inflationists were studying the possibility of increasing the membership of the Supreme Court from nine to eleven or twelve." While that was deemed a last resort, the story said, "all were agreed that certainly President Roosevelt would leave nothing undone to offset a decision which would destroy the new monetary system built up by the administration."[15] For its part, the *Chicago Tribune* noted that "talk of packing the court has been heard in the corridors of the capitol, the treasury and other government buildings since the opening of the gold clause cases last Tuesday." Few would speak on the record, the *Tribune* noted, because "the possibility of a citation for contempt for such talk during the pendency of a case was obvious." Nonetheless, Senator Elmer Thomas averred for the paper that "undoubtedly there will be a program" to pack the Court if the decision were to go against the government.[16]

Roosevelt had an additional, Machiavellian tactic in mind: roil the markets. After lunch with Morgenthau on January 14, the president called Attorney General Cummings to join them, which began what Morgenthau called "one of the most unpleasant hours I have had since I have been in Washington."[17] Roosevelt asked Morgenthau to use the newfound powers of the Exchange Stabilization Fund—an emergency Treasury reserve created by the 1934 Gold Reserve Act—to create as much discord in the markets as possible until the Court made its decision. "I want bonds to move up and down," Roosevelt said. "The only way that the man in a taxicab can become interested in the gold case is if we kept the story on the front page." The president continually turned for support to Cummings, who agreed with everything he said. Morgenthau "argued harder and more intensely than I have ever before in my life." Not only did Morgenthau object to the president's suggestions as a matter of conscience, he saw them as destructive: "Mr. President, you know how difficult it is to get this country out of a depression and if we let the financial markets of this country become frightened for the next month it may take us eight months to recover the lost ground." Morgenthau, realizing he would have to resign if asked to manipulate markets this way, pointed his finger at Roosevelt and said: "Mr. President, don't ask me to do this." Roosevelt responded, "Henry, you have simply given this thing snap judgment. Think it over." Morgenthau returned to his office, steaming. "I felt that the President was making a terrific mistake and that I did not know whether my advice or influence would prevail."

As it happened, the markets were already jittery over the uncertain outcome of the gold-clause cases. On that very day, January 14, the *New York Times* had published a front-page story reporting that "Federal experts" were discussing whether an adverse Court decision would cause Congress to restore the gold value of the dollar to its earlier level. On the next day, the foreign exchange markets had a vigorous session of trading, and the dollar unexpectedly shot up in value while stocks and commodities declined. Traders were nervous and Morgenthau, already struggling with his boss, was as furious with the banks as he was with the Court. "Now what the hell has the Supreme Court got to do with the price of gold?" he asked a colleague in frustration. The weaknesses in the operation of the Exchange Stabilization Fund were beginning to show; while Treasury relied on international banks to buy and sell gold and dollars to protect the value of the dollar, there was nothing Treasury could do to keep the banks from betting in the other direction. Morgenthau was incensed. "This demonstrates to me that when the United States Government is in difficulty the international speculator sells its government short in order to make a penny and when there's a little doubt and they just don't know—they're scared and they're yellow," Morgenthau fumed. "They haven't got any guts, they haven't got any backbone and they haven't got any flag that they follow."

A few days later, Treasury drew up an action plan in case the Supreme Court restored the clauses.[18] There would be an immediate embargo on export and import of gold. The administration might not be able to avoid the Court's order that contracts be paid in gold, but it could make it all but impossible to do so by taking all the gold. Treasury proposed to "make gold practically contraband, so that even in the unlikely event that the Supreme Court granted specific performance in gold of a gold clause obligation, the gold paid out could be simultaneously seized and returned to the Treasury."

A domestic stock market crash was obviously also a concern. On January 21, Morgenthau phoned SEC commissioner James Landis, and asked "whether he would cooperate with him in closing all the exchanges should the Supreme Court render an adverse opinion and, therefore, the stock market go to pieces."[19] Landis agreed, and Morgenthau even arranged to have an additional telephone installed in the cabinet room so that he could have direct access to Landis's office if the exchanges were closed. Within a few days, unnamed sources were reminding the press that the SEC and the president had the legal authority to shut down the stock exchanges for up to ninety days if they felt they had to—which seemed like a direct message to the Court justices.[20]

The administration was faced with a delicate task—it wanted to convey to the Court that, one way or another, a path around an unfavorable decision could be found. At the same time, too much pressure could be counterproductive. Alexander Sachs, a Wall Street adviser who played various roles within the administration, tried to dissuade the White House from using tactics that were too heavy-handed. He wrote to a presidential aide: "It seems to me that there should be a certain discouragement of the talk of how an adverse decision could be nullified. For obviously it does not improve the atmosphere in which a conscientious quest by members of the Court is proceeding. They are fully aware of the long and checkered fight on the Legal Tender cases, in which the Government was finally upheld, and so they realize that Governments do find ways of getting their position vindicated."[21]

If, however, the government were to lose the cases, there would be no room for subtlety, and very little time to act. Roosevelt would have to speak to the public directly and explain why his government was willing to provoke a constitutional crisis by defying the Court. Roosevelt's draft speech is fascinating in part because it represents a heroic effort to explain complicated, abstract financial ideas to a mass audience. He offered a hypothetical case in which an investor bought a railroad bond for $1,000, and now, because of the Court striking down Congress's abrogation of gold clauses, would be able to collect $1,690 from the railroad. "Not only is it unconscionable for the individual investor to make an unexpected, unearned profit of that kind, but . . . a letter of the law enforcement of this decision will automatically throw every railroad of the United States into bankruptcy."[22] And not only private companies would be stricken: many towns, counties, and states would also be forced to default.

Still closer to home, Roosevelt noted that most mortgages contained a gold clause. If that clause could now be enforced, then most homeowners would now have an immediate 69 percent hike in their monthly mortgage payments, and would owe 69 percent above the monthly price in back payments for nearly two years. Finally, Roosevelt pointed out the ultimate absurdity: there was simply no way that $169 billion in contracts could all be paid off in gold—the Earth did not possess anywhere near enough of the stuff. "There exists in the United States a total of about eight and one half billion dollars of gold and in all the rest of the world— Europe, Asia, Africa, Australasia and the Americas—there is not more than twelve billions of dollars of gold." Roosevelt appealed to authorities presumably greater than the Supreme Court: "I want every individual or corporation, public or private, to pay back substantially what they borrowed. That would seem to be a decision more in accordance with the Golden Rule, with the precepts of the Scriptures and the dictates of common sense."

The speech was never needed, although when it was leaked to the *New York Times*, the paper's Washington bureau chief wrote: "It would have marked the most sensational and historic episode in the constitutional history of the United States since Andrew Jackson said of a Supreme Court ruling: 'John Marshall has made this decision; now let him enforce it.'"

The rulings handed down on February 18 did not create economic havoc, but were not a vindication of the administration's policy or arguments, either. The *Perry* decision was a harsh reprimand for Congress's action and the administration's legal argument. If the government could borrow money and later reject the method of payment in the bond, the Court reasoned, it could equally reject the amount it owed. "The contention necessarily imports that the Congress can disregard the obligations of the government at its discretion, and that, when the government borrows money, the credit of the United States is an illusory pledge," Hughes's decision said.[23] The Court ruled clearly that Congress's abrogation of gold clauses "went beyond the congressional power." And yet, the Court also found that the plaintiff was entitled to no damages, because he hadn't lost anything via the bond that he would not have lost if he held the equivalent amount of gold (which, relevantly, he could no longer legally hold anyway). Even legal scholars who were content with the outcome could not endorse the opinion's logic. Thomas Reed Powell said the decision "well nigh passes comprehension." The well-respected Harvard Law professor Henry Hart pronounced it "baffling." Many commentators, beginning with newspaper columnist Walter Lippmann, concluded that Hughes knew full well that if the Court tried to restore or enforce gold clauses, Congress and the administration would be compelled to find some other, possibly more damaging way to achieve the necessary end. Lippmann, a hardened realist who was close to FDR's circle but often enraged them, reasoned that the Court realized its own legitimacy was on the line. "Any other decision by the Supreme Court would have created an almost impossible situation," Lippmann wrote. "Congress would have been compelled to take measures to circumvent the court's decision. This would seriously have impaired the court's authority."[24]

Unsurprisingly, the dissent was harsher still. Chief Justice Hughes slammed the "confiscation of property rights and repudiation of national obligations." Dissenters declared Congress's goal with the abrogation of gold clauses to be illegitimate, that its "real purpose was not 'to assure uniform value to the coins and currencies of the United States,' but to destroy certain valuable contract rights." McReynolds departed from his text and delivered an extemporaneous speech "bristling with scorn and indignation." The crowd gasped as he mocked the logic of the decision. "The Treasury of a great nation says, 'Take this depreciated dollar. Congress made it unlawful for you to accept what is due to you.' And since it is unlawful there is no damage." He invoked Nero and concluded, "It seems impossible to overestimate the result of what has been done here today. The Constitution as many of us have understood it has gone."[25]

In the White House, however, they were jubilant. The telephone relay system set up to shut down the stock market if necessary did not need to be used. As a kind of mock celebration,

Roosevelt read his drafted radio address to a few close advisers; after lunch he announced that he was going to sleep for four days. Roosevelt wrote to Joe Kennedy: "How fortunate it is that [the] Exchanges will never know how close they came to being closed up by the stroke of the pen of one 'J.P.K.' Likewise, the Nation will never know what a great treat it missed in not hearing the marvelous radio address that the 'Pres' had prepared for delivery to the Nation Monday night if the cases had gone the other way."[26]

Within a matter of months, the gold-clause cases would be subsumed by Court rejections of New Deal policies. On monetary policy, Roosevelt and a congressional majority had achieved nearly all of what they had hoped for. Some scholars have pointed to unfortunate consequences of inflating the dollar; it had a protectionist effect of automatically raising trade tariffs, for example.[27] Yet Roosevelt, however clumsily or peremptorily, had squared a circle that had utterly eluded his predecessor and Congress. The administration's monetary policies were among the few viable options available to any government that wanted to restore confidence in the American economy without giving in to more radical demands for inflation and silver coinage that came from western members of Congress, the radical farmers' lobby, and populist agitators like Father Coughlin.

Politically, however, a wall had now been erected, separating not only those who advocated gold-based money from those who opposed it, but also separating those who believed in a role for gold in the private economic lives of Americans from the government and monetary institutions that would come to dominate life in the twentieth century. "Goldbugs" may or may not have represented a majority of Americans, but over time their inability to exercise the benign-seeming right of buying a gold coin or ingot pushed them into the legal and political margins while tapping Populist-era frustration at governing systems—and the Supreme Court pronouncements in the gold-clause cases legitimated their grief.

Beginning in the late 1930s a tremendous metallic gulf also opened up in America and across the world. Although American citizens could not own gold, the American government was amassing the largest stockpile of gold in human history. The devaluation of the dollar boosted the value of the federal government's gold holdings; at the same time, the rise of the Nazi Party in Germany and jitters about imminent European war created an unprecedented flow of gold into the United States. Under other circumstances, European nations might have seen it as desirable to hang on to gold in case of war. The prospect of defeat, however, made it seem safer to store the gold in the United States, in return for gold certificates that could always be redeemed once the war fears subsided. Even France, which alone among the world's major economies maintained a currency pegged to gold, gave up substantial amounts of gold in the mid- to late 1930s; many of its wealthier citizens worried about the future monetary policies of left-wing governments. In 1934 and 1935 alone, the value of gold held by the US government increased by more than $6 billion, a little less than half of which was attributable to raising the price of gold to $35 an ounce. By 1936, the US gold stock was worth more than $11 billion, more than half the world's total supply.

Although there were obvious benefits to increasing the amount of gold inside America's borders, the inflow also created its own set of economic problems. In 1940 two economists published an influential book called *Golden Avalanche*, arguing that the gold glut was hurting the American economy; expending so much energy and capital to acquire a metal that created no economic benefit took away from more productive activity. More specifically, too much gold created at least three significant headaches. One was that because gold was once again synonymous with money (if somewhat indirectly), the sudden increase in money supply could potentially create inflation. To stave this off, the Federal Reserve enacted a policy whereby the incoming gold and new domestic gold production was "sterilized," or kept outside the money supply, starting at the end of 1936. Sterilization, however, created its own economic problems, and many economists believe that it contributed to the economic downturn—the second phase of the Depression—beginning in the spring of 1937.[28]

The second problem was logistical. Especially given the prospect of war, Morgenthau and others recognized that this massive haul of gold needed to be stored somewhere securely; coastal cities such as New York and San Francisco were vulnerable to attack. And thus, in yet another tie between gold and the US military, Treasury took control of a military facility in Kentucky that had once housed the cavalry—Fort Knox—and began rush construction of an impregnable gold vault there, some thirty-one miles west of Louisville, nestled safely between the Rockies and the Appalachians. The government began shipping billions of dollars' worth of gold bullion, particularly from San Francisco, to Kentucky in 1935, and the Fort became operational in 1937.

The third problem was global and much harder to solve. The gushing inflow of gold to the United States was perforce an outflow of gold from other places, mostly Western Europe. Even though most countries were no longer on a gold standard, draining their coffers of gold meant that they had less and less capital—at a time when war against Germany and Italy looked more and more likely. The Roosevelt administration struggled to support Britain, France, and other allies within the confines of the various Neutrality Acts that Congress passed beginning in 1935. Congressional isolationists resisted support for Britain, and to try to appease them Roosevelt made a show of seizing British assets and liquidating British securities held in the United States. This put a strain on Anglo-American relations at a critical time. Throughout 1940, British officials told Morgenthau's Treasury Department that they had barely enough gold to meet the statutory requirement to back up their currency.

The conflict came to a head in December, the month that Roosevelt warned Americans that Britain's war was their war, too. "We must produce arms and ships with every energy and resource we can command," Roosevelt proclaimed in one of his most famous fireside chats. "We must be the great arsenal of democracy."

But building the arsenal of democracy required money that Britain no longer had. Roosevelt was willing to give the British whatever they needed but they had to pay for it. When they couldn't, improvisations were needed, such as a swap of rusty American destroyer ships in return for access to British bases. And sometimes the United States simply had to take what it was owed. A week before the "arsenal of democracy" speech, Roosevelt ordered the USS *Tuscaloosa* cruiser to sail to South Africa to pick up $50 million worth of Britain's gold; Morgenthau even wanted the British to pick up the insurance tab. This was too humiliating for Britain. Prime Minister Winston Churchill wanted to tell Roosevelt that he was behaving like " a sheriff collecting the last assets of a helpless debtor," although he thought better of sending that note. In a more measured letter written on New Year's Eve, with the ship already en route, Churchill implored Roosevelt to reconsider. To stock a US warship with British gold in a dock in Cape Town, Churchill pleaded, "will disturb public opinion here and throughout the Dominions and encourage the enemy, who will proclaim that you are sending for our last reserves."[29] The tension eased somewhat when Congress passed the Lend-Lease Act in March 1941, the law that allowed the United States to support allied countries with materiel and supplies on the condition that it be repaid in kind. Churchill dubbed the law "the most unsordid act in the history of any nation," and it carried the Allies through until the United States formally entered the war after Pearl Harbor was bombed.

These wartime realities—the gaping imbalance between the United States' gold supply and the rest of the world's, and the war debts that the Allies would find difficult to repay—would profoundly affect the role that gold would play in the world's money when the war ended. Toward the end of World War II the United States became something like the world's gold monopolist and policeman; the United States found itself reprimanding other nations for buying gold from the "wrong" sources. The Axis powers would typically seize gold and other valuable assets from countries that they had conquered, and that gold became an important form of international currency as the war drew to a close. In 1944 Morgenthau declared that the United States would not recognize the title transfer of looted gold, and he urged other nations to take similar actions.

Nearly four dozen nations participated in the conference in Bretton Woods, New Hampshire, in July 1944, to forge a new international monetary order out of the wartime chaos. There were many visions of such a world, including that offered by the Federal Reserve at the end of the previous war for an international gold exchange. John Maynard Keynes, probably the twentieth century's most influential economist, had envisioned a world in which currencies could be valued based on the strength of the economies that issued them and a centralized global bank would control credit and issue a global currency called the "bancor." American negotiators at Bretton Woods, led by Harry White, envisioned a system in which gold would still play a central role, as would the dollar.[30] While in many respects Keynes's plan was probably superior, there were two large obstacles to implementing it. One was that it would require the world's central banks to give up much or all of their gold to a central authority, which they were understandably reluctant to do (the Soviet Union—a major if secretive gold producer—was especially unlikely to agree to such a provision). And second, there were few advocates for Keynes's system who had the international leverage to bring it about; the allied countries were broke and, to a greater or lesser degree, in debt to the United States. If depression had created a need for flexibility and inflation, protracted and expensive war created a need for stability and growth. The world had little choice but to turn to the United States monetarily just as it had done militarily.

The Bretton Woods system was not technically a gold standard; it is usually referred to as a gold-exchange standard or gold convertibility standard. At its core, the dollar was fully convertible to gold at the same rate as in 1934: $35 an ounce. Each other major currency was assigned a par value from which it could deviate up to 1 percent; larger revaluations required permission from the International Monetary Fund, one of the two major institutions (along with the World Bank) established by the Bretton Woods agreement. The United States was not expected to intervene in foreign exchange markets, and the Fund would lend or sell gold and currencies to member countries that were in deficit. This system had its flaws, as will be discussed in the next chapter. But for a decade or so it worked remarkably well as an engine of stable expansion. Western European countries and Japan experienced year upon year of hefty growth, without breakneck inflation or punishing boom-and-bust cycles. In 1985, forty years after the Bretton Woods agreement (and after its most fundamental building blocks had been removed), one economist wrote: "The real commodity output of the world has increased fourfold since World War II; the real commodity trade of the world, sixfold. Even though the population of the world has more than doubled—from approximately 2.2 billion in 1950 to 4.5 billion today—living standards have risen substantially on the average."[31]

Within the United States, however, the politics of gold and the international monetary system were not always widely appreciated or even understood, any more than they had been in the late nineteenth century. Most Americans prospered in the postwar period, but a disgruntled minority—largely but not exclusively within the Republican Party, which was outside the White House from 1933 until 1953—believed that the growth was illusory, created by "war expenditures, waste and extravagance, planned emergencies, and war crises."[32] Fighting World War II had vastly expanded the size and expense of the federal government; this continued in the form of the Marshall Plan, the GI Bill, and soon enough the expense of the Korean War. Deficits and debts ballooned to numbers that seemed staggering by pre-Depression standards. The fiscal conservatism of balanced budgets and sound money preached by Hoover was by the mid-1940s so long in the past that many feared it was gone forever. It seemed to this group a supreme folly for a country that could not handle its own money to turn over control of the world's money to nations that were poorer still.

But while the issues of debt, deficits, and the size of government were paramount for Republicans and conservatives in the 1940s, the definition of money had ceased to be the red-hot cause it had been at the turn of the century. Father Coughlin continued his advocacy for monetary silver through the late 1930s, but his influence waned when his radio show stopped airing once America entered World War II. In Washington, federal laws requiring the purchase of prescribed amounts of silver had largely placated western members of Congress. As for gold, it was difficult to gain much political traction advocating a return to a gold standard because Roosevelt had put the country back on a kind of gold standard, albeit with a devalued dollar—which became the bigger object of conservative ire. The 1944 Republican Party platform made vague promises to "maintain the value of the American dollar" and to "repeal existing legislation which gives the President unnecessary powers over our currency," but omitted any mention of gold. The metal itself, for all its symbolic power, became less and less familiar to Americans. The United States shut down all of its gold mines—more than eight thousand mines—between October 1942 and July 1945. During that period, some mines caved in or filled with water, and mining equipment deteriorated, and so even when production resumed it was at a fraction of its prewar level. A mining official lamented near the end of the war, "If the citizen is deprived of the personal protection of gold as money, if he only knows of it as being in national treasuries or central banks, how can he help losing his present viewpoint of its high psychological value?"[33]

Yet by the late 1940s, the philosophy espoused by Justice McReynolds began to harden into a new form of populism. Like the populism of the 1890s, its appeal was largely in the Midwest and West, in farming areas. But unlike the populism of the 1890s, it did not preach inflation as a solution; instead, inflation was now deemed the enemy. Roosevelt, by inflating the dollar, had made it "worthless." On this issue, the men running Wall Street and many big businesses as well as the men speaking for midwestern farmers could unite against a common enemy: the abstract global economic order. And accordingly, gold was not the source of evil as it had been for Bryan; gold was the solution.

One such dissident was Howard Buffett, a three-term congressman from Nebraska, whose district bordered the one that was represented a half-century before by William Jennings Bryan. In the tradition of isolationist prairie populists long skeptical of European money masters and wars, Buffett (the father of billionaire Berkshire Hathaway chairman Warren Buffett) viewed the Bretton Woods agreements as an encroachment on American autonomy. In opposing the 1945 legislation, he and a colleague wrote of the IMF and World Bank: "This world-embracing corporate body would usurp the social and private function of carrying on international trade and commerce and substitute therefor authoritarian domination over such pursuits." Among other objections, Buffett and Ohio's Frederick Smith maintained that the United States under Bretton Woods would be handing over to other countries "the power to manipulate the price of gold." This, they insisted, "seems to be a clear violation of the Constitution."[34] These were, to be sure, minority views, but they resonated with millions of Americans and they also conspicuously matched the perspective of the financial community—much of which fought Bretton Woods and wished to return to a domestic version of a gold standard.

Buffett expressed the frustration many felt that gold was no longer something American citizens could hold in their hands and spend as money—the huge supply of metal seemed to exist merely to make foreign countries happy. In a 1948 magazine article that is still often cited in the twenty-first century, Buffett wrote: "Even though there is a lot of gold buried down at Fort Knox, that gold is not subject to demand by American citizens. It could all be shipped out of this country without the people having any chance to prevent it." Pat McCarran, an influential Democratic senator from Nevada who was also a Communist-chasing ally of Joe McCarthy, echoed Buffett's sense of mistrust about the nation's gold hoard: "We do not know what the treasury proposes to do with this enormous mass of precious metal. It has never stated its intentions and, so far as I know, no policy with respect to this gold has ever been formulated."[35]

Just as earlier expressions of gold populism invoked the values and fears of their eras—the belief that paper money represents the Devil, say, or that inflation is bound to be ruinous—Buffett and his allies in the late 1940s framed their arguments for the new and terrifying Cold War. Unless the United States restored economic order and returned to a gold standard, Buffett argued, it would be engulfed by its enemies. "The surest way to bring communism is to get printing press money started," Buffett said in 1949.[36] Paper money, Buffett declared on another occasion, "is an enemy much more to be feared than Soviet military power, real or fancied."

These were not simply words: Buffett believed in practical solutions. In 1948, Buffett introduced a bill into Congress to put the United States back on a gold standard. It sought to "restore the right of American citizens to freely own gold and gold coins; to return control over the public purse to the people; to restrain further deterioration of our currency."[37] Daniel A. Reed of New York and Robert Hale of Maine also introduced related bills around the same time. Buffett also lent his support to a nonlegislative effort to return to a gold currency. When Congress passed the Gold Reserve

Act in 1934, it left open some obscure loopholes. One of these involved gold in its "natural state"—that is, gold recovered from natural sources that "has not been melted, smelted, or refined or otherwise treated by heating or by a chemical or electrical process." When Treasury issued regulations to enforce the act, it allowed this natural gold to be acquired and transported.[38] Not only was it legal to possess gold in this form, but also Treasury was barred from purchasing gold in this state, as the African American author and activist W. E. B. DuBois learned when he unsuccessfully tried to sell a West African gold nugget to Treasury in 1934.[39] This also meant that the $35 an ounce statutory gold price did not apply; natural gold could trade for whatever price a buyer and seller could agree upon.

In the late 1940s, a Reno-based company called Gold Corporation of America announced a novel, ostensibly legal system to create money around this type of gold. The company took out advertisements in major newspapers offering to sell such gold at a price of $51 an ounce; after several such sales the price was lowered to $42 an ounce. But the business of shipping gold nuggets proved cumbersome; one Pennsylvania buyer who purchased 1,000 ounces of gold had to travel across the country to take personal possession of the metal. The company's founder, E. L. Cleveland, then devised a plan through which sellers would place the gold in a warehouse, which in turn would issue a receipt for the gold. That paper could then function as money effectively backed by gold, though not convertible to it. "The receipt may not be legal tender," Cleveland told a reporter. "But any groceryman who refused it would be a darn fool."

Buffett—the son, after all, of an Omaha grocer who had vocally opposed a third term for FDR[40]—agreed. He praised the company for discovering a "twilight zone" in which a gold-backed paper currency could legally function. Moreover, Buffett thought the experiment with gold pricing was also valuable, because inflation of the dollar would inevitably make the fixed $35 an ounce price obsolete. "There is a large body of expert opinion that inflation has gone too far to permit operation on the $35 an ounce price," Buffett said in 1948. "I think there is a 50–50 chance that we can still operate at that price, and that's why I put such a provision in the bill. But that point may have to be changed, and the gold content of the dollar lowered."[41]

The Gold Corporation of America and other companies seem to have had some modest success in the late '40s. Treasury undertook a special canvas of gold sellers in 1948 and 1949 to determine how much gold was being sold in this form at a premium price. Estimates were between 25,000 and 30,000 ounces a year, out of the typical 2 million or so ounces mined in the United States every year; most of the natural gold came from Alaska.[42] Although Cleveland seemed primarily motivated by profit—he collected a $1 per ounce broker's fee on every sale—he also wanted to restore a gold market in the United States (a common position among gold-mining executives). He hoped that if a Republican was elected president in 1948, his warehouse receipt plan might be used to springboard a return to a day-to-day, gold-based monetary system.

The late '40s cluster of gold-standard activity, however, had little sympathy in the White House. In July 1948, a reporter at a press conference asked President Truman about legislative efforts to return the United States to a gold standard "as a means of combating inflation." Truman replied, inaccurately, that the country "has been on the gold standard all the time." He continued, "We own more gold than any other government in the history of the world." The reporter persisted, "I can't turn in a dollar for it, though, sir." Truman responded, "No, you can't; but then your dollar is backed by that gold backing. That's what makes it good."[43]

In 1949, a gold legalization bill introduced by Senator McCarran got as far as the hearings stage. The gold-mining industry, battered by the wartime shutdown and slow to recover, made its position clear. To them, the newly active "natural gold" market represented an opening that ought to be expanded. Fred Searls Jr., the president of Newmont Mining Corporation, pointed out in testimony the contradiction between a natural gold market in which any agreed-upon price could be paid, versus the official market in which gold could only be sold to the US government at the increasingly hard-to-maintain price of $35 an ounce.[44] To illustrate his point, he brought to the committee table "100 ounces of fine gold in its natural state," for which he said he had paid $4,100. He estimated that he had sold perhaps 10,000 ounces of gold in this form, but was unable to sell more because "the buyers—and there are a good many of them—are afraid that the Treasury will change the rules again."[45]

Searls and his buyers were absolutely right. In June 1950, Treasury clarified its regulations: natural gold could only be sold by someone who had physically mined it. Any secondary transactions were illegal. This effectively put Gold Corporation of America and related companies out of that business.

Clearly, any efforts to restore legal gold would require support from the executive branch, and there were efforts to make gold an issue in presidential campaigns. Buffett's disdain for big government and militarism was not confined to Democrats. In 1952 he called Dwight Eisenhower "the most militaristic man who has ever been suggested for President" and said that Eisenhower's nomination "would mean the destruction of the Republican Party." Specifically, Buffett charged Eisenhower with enabling Soviet concentration camps. "Eisenhower, months after the war ended approved and signed an order that sent uncounted hundreds of thousands of German civilians into Russia for slave labor," Buffett wrote in the spring of 1952.[46] "This one ruthless action alone, duly exposed, would lose enough normal Republican votes to insure Republican defeat in November. This is only one of the hidden blots on the Eisenhower record."

Buffett worked on the campaign of Eisenhower's rival Robert Taft, whose defeat that year represented to many in the party's conservative wing that "Eisenhower and Dewey were traitorous liberals who had compromised the party's values simply to win elections." The Taft-Eisenhower battle and its fallout, one recent historian has argued, "set the stage for the conservative takeover of the GOP that begin in earnest in 1964 and continued in fits and starts through the end of the twentieth century."[47]

And yet gold was not yet the dividing line between the two camps that it would later become. Curiously, the most outspoken advocate of a gold standard in the 1952 presidential race was a relative liberal—Harold Stassen, the onetime governor of Minnesota who became a perpetual presidential candidate in the middle of the twentieth century. His 1952 platform called for "A Modern Gold Standard for a Solid American Dollar," and he argued in speeches that a gold standard would serve as a check on excessive government spending and inflation. "If the people insist that they should have the right, whenever they want to, to change their paper money to gold coins, and change gold coins back to paper money, they thereby make their government keep their paper money in sound shape," Stassen said. But Stassen's following was never large enough to force this as an issue.

Eisenhower, as will be shown in the next chapter, had little use for gold in economics. For his part, Taft was sympathetic to a gold-backed dollar and would have found some support for it among his voters. However, his political sense was that the issue was too risky for whatever it might gain. Taft had, for example, declined requests—even from Wall Street—to insert a gold-standard plank in the 1944 Republican Party platform. His economic reasoning was that "there are several different forms of the Gold Standard and we could not very well stop to explain which one we meant or at what figure we would fix the value of the dollar." And his political conclusion was, "it is not of much importance because very few people understand anything about the subject."[48]

It was tempting and none too difficult in the late 1940s and 1950s to dismiss Buffett and those with similar views as gadflies and cranks. Buffett was not well liked in official Washington circles; when he lost his seat in 1948, the Washington columnist Drew Pearson called him "a bedrock reactionary who shot off his mouth once too often." Buffett knew that his gold crusade was lonely. "I'm like a man selling lawn mowers in Omaha in January," he often said. And to the extent that a return to a gold-coin standard was promised as a solution to any economic ills, such dismissal could have been warranted. But Buffett and other critics were right about at least one thing: the Bretton Woods framework was, in the medium to long term, unstable, and when it began to topple, all the gold in Fort Knox wouldn't be able to prop it up.

# CHAPTER 6

# Out of Balance

THROUGH THE EARLY SUMMER of 1960, as Cold War tensions between the United States and the Soviet Union escalated, the London gold market was a place where quite reliably not much happened. In important respects the trading of gold on the London market had not changed significantly since its beginnings in the seventeenth century (World War II forced the shutdown of the London gold market but it began operations again in March 1954). Many markets in developed capitals featured shouting and gesticulating traders, and some had already introduced electronic tickers, but the London gold market still had the aura of a staid private gentleman's club. The venue was a wood-paneled chamber lined with oil paintings, the "fixing room" in the offices of N. M. Rothschild, on a narrow medieval lane in the City of London, named for a ninth-century Saxon bishop and one building away from the Bank of England itself. Every weekday morning at precisely 10:30 a.m., five men from various banks and mining firms determined that day's price of gold for most of the world's legitimate market.

Given that the world's largest holder of gold—the US government—was known to buy gold at $34.9125 an ounce and sell it

This 14-pound statue of a rooster was designed by artist Frank Polk and cast in solid gold in 1958 to promote a Nevada casino. The federal government—desperate to enforce gold prohibition in the wake of a balance-of-payments crisis—seized, incarcerated, and eventually released the bird.
*Courtesy the Coeur d'Alene Art Auction*

at $35.0875, price movement was minimal, with day-to-day fluctuations usually measured in pennies or smaller units: "The chairman suggest[s] a price, in terms of shillings and pence down to a farthing . . . chosen at the level where it is thought that buyers and sellers are likely to be prepared to do business."[1] The five representatives would then announce their intention to buy or sell, and conduct their business for the rest of the day. At the moment of "fixing," 90 percent of the day's total transactions might be conducted immediately on some days; on other days, 10 percent. The atmosphere was, in the most British of ways, collegial to a point of collusion; there was not even a required method for dealing with an imbalance of buyers and sellers. If, for example, there was a desire to buy one hundred bars but only fifty were offered up for sale on a given day, the fifty bars might be divvied up equally among the buyers, or the price might be raised—it all depended on what the people sitting in the room wanted. And while orders could be taken over telephone and telex for those inside and outside the country, bars and coins did physically change hands right in the Rothschild offices; the London market prided itself on the fact that two of its five participants actually engaged in the melting and refining of gold.

This orderly, almost sleepy ritual had repeated itself daily since 1954 with little disturbance. The continuity was understandable, since not much money was directly at stake. Most of any given day's trade involved central banks from various countries or large commercial banks pushing their metal back and forth; the market for privately held gold was growing, but still modest. While the London gold market was larger than any of its counterparts, the actual amount of money changing hands remained very small compared to what went on in any significant stock or bond market. In fact, through the first half of 1960, daily transactions of the London gold market were estimated at a few million dollars.

But that summer, something happened to disrupt a quaint system that had prevailed for centuries: an unusually high number of people wanted to buy gold. The dollar price for gold on the

London market hit $35.13 on August 24, and the trading volume was its highest since the market had reopened in 1954. The upward crawl continued, and by mid-September the price hit $35.24. At that price, someone sitting in, say, Zurich might arguably have been better off buying gold from the United States at the statutory $35.0875 price and paying to have it shipped, instead of buying it in London. That threshold of just a few cents was dangerous for the US government and for the world economic order.

What caused the sudden jump in gold's price? One of the driving ideas behind markets is that they create transparency by giving all players as much information as possible. In the postwar London gold market, however, almost no participants could know for certain everyone who was buying, everyone who was selling, or why. Some of the increased demand was structural and represented increasingly prosperous European governments using part of their growing foreign reserve funds to buy gold (often under legal obligation). Recent changes in Swiss banking regulations might also have encouraged some buyers to purchase gold in London to save on commissions. On the supply side, the spike might have been enhanced by the Soviet Union and South Africa, both of which had been selling gold on the market but stopped in the late summer. Yet it was also clear that some gold buyers were making a pessimistic bet on the American economy, which had officially entered a recession that spring, the last full year of Eisenhower's presidency. While it was illegal for Americans to own gold at home, there had been no such prohibition against buying and owning it abroad. In the worried corridors of Washington, some estimated that as much as 70 percent of the heightened gold market activity came from Americans, whether those living abroad or those living at home and purchasing the gold overseas.[2]

Closely linked to that observation was the idea that the market movement—especially the murky American component—sprang from politics. In the context of a hotly contested presidential race in the United States, the gold price movement quickly took on an electoral hue. The fear was that a new president, hoping to jolt the sluggish economy, might take the drastic action of revaluing the dollar's relationship to the price of gold, which could have made an ounce bought in the summer of 1960 more valuable a year or so later. There's not much to suggest that then-senator John F. Kennedy or his campaign ever intended such a policy, but Democrats had groused about high interest rates and in theory Kennedy's expansive rhetoric implied greater government spending, which could in turn force a gold repricing. And in the swirling of cause and effect that markets sometimes create, the idea—spurious or not—began to take hold and prices continued to rise. Kennedy, for his part, privately told colleagues he believed that hostile banking forces deliberately planted the gold rumor to harm his campaign.[3]

Why would a few extra dollars tacked onto the price of a gold bar moving across a table in London matter in a presidential campaign thousands of miles away? The answer is that even though in the late 1950s and early 1960s the US government held far more gold than any other entity in the world, it didn't, for contemporary purposes, have enough. The higher the price rose, the greater the possibility that the United States would run out of gold it could use. And while the White House had not, prior to the summer of 1960, paid close attention to the ups and downs of London's gold prices, it was well aware of the high stakes. The Eisenhower administration had identified a "balance-of-payments deficit" at least as far back as 1956. The issue through the middle part of the decade hadn't been that the United States was physically losing a great deal of gold; the country's gold stock remained relatively stable through Eisenhower's first term at between $20 billion and $22 billion. But as the United States imported more goods and services in the postwar boom, governments and companies outside the country rapidly increased their holdings in dollars and US securities, and those holdings represented potential gold redemptions, payable immediately. This category of claims rose from about $8 billion in 1949 to $12.7 billion at the end of 1953, and then to nearly $16.5 billion by the end of 1956. Because federal law required about half of the gold stock to be held in reserve to shore up the dollar, that meant that if all the foreign claims were redeemed at once for gold, the United States would not be able to make all the payments—a scenario that was universally considered an economic doomsday.

And now, with the market price rising and no one apparently able to stem it, what had been a worrying but manageable trickle of gold outflow from the United States was looking more like a flood. In 1958, actual gold outflows had already topped $2 billion, a number that startled Washington. But the London market explosion made 1958 look benign. In one week in mid-September 1960, America's monetary gold stock dipped by more than $180 million, the biggest weekly drop since the early days of the Great Depression.[4] In November, the outflow of gold would hit just under half a billion dollars for the month; on a single day in early December, the United Kingdom would submit a claim for $50 million.

American officials watched the upward ratcheting of the price of gold with increasing, and fairly helpless, anxiety. On October 19, only three weeks before the presidential election, trading was so frantic during what one dealer called "a pretty wild market" that no one could say for certain what the top price had been; it was estimated at $35.60. The following day, the volume of London gold transactions swooned to between $20 and $25 million—four or five times the already high volume of the late summer. On that day the price hit an unprecedented $40.60 an ounce, fueling still more speculative buying. By the time the staff showed up that morning in the office of the New York Federal Reserve—where the bulk of America's monetary gold resided—"all the alarm bells were clanging away."[5] Frantic Wall Street bankers were phoning the treasury secretary and Fed chair, demanding that the strength of the dollar be upheld. The Bank of England, which normally preferred to stay out of the private market, felt the need to intervene. The Bank sold millions of dollars' worth of gold—both newly mined from South Africa and from its reserves—in hopes of pushing the price down.

The US government might have wanted to do the same, but of course even if selling the gold in its coffers stabilized the market price, the loss in metal would make the nation's situation worse. And at least initially, US officials were unable to obtain even basic information about the Bank of England's gold sales (the volume of sales, how much South African gold remained for future sales if planned, etc.). The Bank politely informed Fed officials that—just as with its competitors, the famously secretive Swiss banks—it kept such information strictly confidential; Parliament itself was not entitled to know. Even months later, after the United States had formally endorsed the Bank of England's gold-market interventions, the Federal Reserve received its data about the London gold market from a renegade Bank of England official who leaked the information in daily telephone conversations conducted in secret code.[6]

On October 25, with the price of gold still above $37, Treasury Secretary Robert Anderson convened a high-level meeting with the president and the chairman of the Federal Reserve Board. Briefed on the state of the market, Eisenhower suggested that since Germany owed the United States a favor, perhaps it could be persuaded to sell gold in London, and he asked that the matter be taken up when two top Treasury officials made a planned visit that fall (although this proposed solution, too, had messy complications).[7] The meeting did not resolve the stated fear that the "psychological effects" of the rising gold price would force the United States to pay out huge quantities of gold.

Yet even as they wrung their hands, Republicans saw a possibility that the run on gold might help them electorally in what appeared to be a tight race. There were Eisenhower Treasury officials who were involved in both gold strategy meetings and in actively advising Vice President Nixon's presidential camp,[8] and thus the issue bubbled up in the late days of the campaign. On the very day that gold soared above $40 an ounce, Nixon warned an audience of economists that "cheap money dogmatists coming to high public office" could create "a totally stupid and, in my opinion, unnecessary gold crisis . . . which could be disastrous not only for America, but for the entire free world." In response, Kennedy joked that Nixon "blames me for the increase in the cost of gold on the London market. Mr. Nixon, if you are listening, I did not do it, I promise you."[9]

Even the president, whose overall enthusiasm for the Nixon campaign was muted, tried to spin the gold crisis into Republican votes. In a late October campaign appearance for the Nixon ticket, Eisenhower told a Philadelphia crowd that the European press blamed the gold price hike on "a growing fear of the cheap money and radical spending" that the Democrats' platform offered.[10] "If these promises should be carried out," Eisenhower continued, "the impact on our economic position, and on the free world, could be catastrophic. . . . [L]et them understand that they and their party assume not only full responsibility for the present dangerous speculation in gold, but also for the developing fear about the future worth of the American dollar."


On November 9, the day after Kennedy eked out a victory, Anderson gave Eisenhower some sobering figures: US gold holdings were about to dip below $18 billion for the first time in many years; $12 billion of that was required to cover the currency, and there were $9.5 billion in external demands that could theoretically come in at any time. Reading a list of twenty small countries now asking to cash in claims, Anderson told Eisenhower bluntly: "We have almost a gold panic situation."[11]

In truth, despite the genuine anxiety many in financial circles felt about gold and the balance-of-payments crisis, the outcome of the election was unlikely to alter much. After all, Kennedy had issued a firm statement that "if elected President I shall not devalue the dollar from the present rate," thereby reassuring the markets and limiting any political fallout. Still, the issue was potent enough that, even with the election over, some in the Eisenhower White

House interpreted the situation in partisan political terms, evoking memories of Hoover being eclipsed by FDR. Defense Secretary Gates expressed "worry over the President's personal position. Should this directive turn out to create a major issue, Senator Kennedy will consider the issue a great advantage to himself." Gates compared this situation to the bank holiday of 1933 and said "the Democrats could ride this white horse for the next twenty years. They will point out how Democrats had had to straighten out the errors of this Administration."[12]

For his part, Eisenhower appeared detached from the political urgency. The topic of gold had been around a long time, and it seemed to make him world-weary about any prospects for change. In an October 1957 National Security Council meeting, for example, Eisenhower recalled that shortly after he'd taken office in 1953, he'd convened some economic experts to advise him on the convertibility of gold, but had found their answers wanting. "All that they had to say," Eisenhower recalled, "was that the President should pray that no one ever really woke up to the fact that in essence gold is valueless—you can't eat it, you can't build things with it, or fire it in guns."[13] Now in the waning days of his presidency, he seemed more curious about utopian fixes. In November 1960, he offered to a group of advisers that since the United States was sitting on about $21 billion worth of refined uranium and plutonium, perhaps these valuable elements could be used as a gold substitute.[14] This proposal was met with polite dismissal.

As outlandish as the idea of using radioactive material as a currency reserve might seem, the administration did feel the need to take bold action. Prior to the election, having no public reaction to the gold market's tumult might have made sense, but the longer the gold price remained significantly above $35 an ounce, the more risk there was in doing nothing; it could undermine confidence in the dollar and force a run on gold. Something had to be done, and to some degree, it didn't matter what. In a never-before-disclosed confidential meeting in December 1960, a Treasury official told colleagues: "Six months ago we could say, if we don't talk about it, no one will notice. Now it is front page news and the only thing that will restore confidence in the world today is a firm feeling that somehow we are going to do something about the problem. And anything that is done is good psychologically."[15]

However, many of the short-term fixes under consideration had either already been tried, or risked worsening the crisis, or both. For example, preventing this type of disaster was part of the mission of the International Monetary Fund, a Bretton Woods institution that, in the 1950s, was still ramping up operations. The IMF's funds were available for precisely such emergencies and, indeed, the Eisenhower administration had very quietly already tapped the IMF for substantial gold "loans"—twice. In early 1956, the Treasury Department had arranged to purchase $200 million worth of gold from the Fund.[16] This transaction had been little noticed by Congress or the press—or financial markets, where it could easily have set off a dollar-weakening storm. Treasury went back again to the IMF for an additional $300 million in September and October 1959. That summer, the IMF was in the process of increasing the quotas that each member country contributed to the Fund's whole; this required the United States to submit $344 million from its gold stock in June, which had to be approved by Congress. But the Treasury was wary of parting with this much precious metal, so it arranged for the IMF to buy $300 million worth of gold back, being careful to make it look as if the idea originated with the IMF, for purposes of increasing its investment funds. Now at the end of 1960, with the presidential race finished, the IMF discreetly arranged to sell the US Treasury another $300 million of its gold.

There were longer-term policies that could address the balance-of-payments problem. One obvious proposal was to reduce or remove the requirement that 25 percent of the currency be backed up by gold; this idea had vocal support on Wall Street, notably from Henry C. Alexander, chairman of the Morgan Guaranty Trust, a banker whose views were closely followed in Washington. Another ambitious plan was to scale back the massive military presence abroad (particularly in Germany and Japan), which was a legacy from World War II. Stationing hundreds of thousands of troops and their families abroad contributed heavily to the balance-of-payments problem, because it involved spending billions of dollars outside the country's borders. And of course, broader economic strategies— such as attracting more tourists to the United States (and getting them to spend dollars here) and increasing exports—would also help. But these were big-picture items that would require time to implement, as well as working with Congress, and the Eisenhower administration's days were coming to an end.

However, two relatively easy fixes did present themselves as 1960 came to a close. One was to create an informal "gentlemen's under-standing" between the United States and other large economies to try and prevent violent swings in the London market. Initially, this took the form of an Anglo-American agreement in late October that the Bank of England would intervene in the London gold market as necessary to keep prices down, and the United States would reim-burse it with its own gold. Around the same time, several central banks agreed that they would not buy gold in the London market above a certain price (the US dollar selling price plus shipping cost, or approximately $35.25), thereby not adding fuel to any speculative sparks that might arise.

These steps stabilized the London market somewhat; one of the London gold market companies noted in its 1960 annual report that central bank buying at the tail end of that year "virtually ceased."[17] But from the perspective of the US gold stock, that didn't solve the outflow problem; after all, it did not affect the fundamental reasons why central banks were purchasing gold in the first place. At best, it simply shifted where the gold was purchased—from the London market to the US Treasury's so-called gold window. In early 1961, when both Germany and the Netherlands revalued their curren-cies, a currency war created a rush to buy gold that drained some $500 million from the US gold stock in a week.[18]

Stricter measures were needed. After months of negotiation, an informal multilateral pact took effect in late 1961, whereby six other nations with major gold holdings agreed to join the US-UK agreement. They committed to provide the Bank of England with a backstop of between $10 million and $30 million each to sell gold into the market to keep the price below the $35.25 danger point.

This founding of the "London Gold Pool" was remarkable for at least two reasons. First, as the economist Susan Strange has noted, it transformed the presumed nature of the London market. What had been the world's largest place for privately held gold to be traded was now a market that was effectively controlled by the Bank of England (and one in which the Bank could also make a tidy profit, at least for a time). Second, as inconceivable as it seems, the agreement was never written down. There were no official signatories to the Gold Pool because there was nothing to sign—not a treaty, not an executive agreement, nothing. Indeed, the central bankers who'd agreed to the Pool's terms initially hoped that the existence of the agreement would be kept a secret. This radical informality no doubt reflected the difficulty that individual governments would have found obtaining speedy political consensus for the Pool's terms. But political expediency is a double-edged sword; an informal agreement that makes entry easy also makes exit easy, and indeed the "spirit" of the Gold Pool would find itself threatened not long after it began.

Of all the short-term tactics that the outgoing Eisenhower administration considered to address the balance-of-payments crisis, none seemed easier or more effective than closing the biggest loophole that gold prohibition had left open: the ability of American citizens to buy and hold gold abroad. Just as the original gold prohibition of 1933 had not been a particular aim of FDR's, there is no indication that forcing Americans to sell gold held outside the United States was a priority for Eisenhower himself. But in late 1960, top officials from Treasury and the Federal Reserve—including Fed chair William McChesney Martin—debated this measure with lively disagreement, as well as a conspicuous lack of reliable information. Fundamental questions presumably central to policy-making—How many Americans owned gold outside the United States? Of that group, how many lived inside the United States, as opposed to overseas? What percentage of the London market swings could be attributed to these groups? What was the total value of their holdings?—were unanswerable.

At one crucial meeting, for example, a Treasury official asserted that one of the London gold market participants had estimated that between 30 and 40 percent of the market activity came from Americans—especially among those in Milwaukee, California, and Texas. One of his colleagues countered that his research made him doubt that American participation in the gold market was "anything more than a nominal one," though he hedged by saying that if the 30–40 percent figure was accurate, then it must represent orders coming in through opaque Swiss banks. A third official said that 70 percent of the London gold market went to Americans living outside the United States (a figure that seemed to surprise his boss, Treasury Secretary Anderson). Others worried that Americans were borrowing on huge margins in Canada, then buying and holding gold in that country; such a plan was being promoted, perhaps in part for personal gain, by a right-wing Texan newsletter writer named Dan Smoot. (Smoot was a former FBI agent whose activities for some years were bankrolled by H. L. Hunt, and thus he probably attracted outsized attention from White House officials.)

The combined inability of top officials from the Eisenhower Treasury Department, the Federal Reserve, and the International Monetary Fund to produce a trustworthy figure for how much gold Americans owned abroad, pointed to a major potential policy problem—enforceability. Policing domestic gold ownership was hard enough, and for some it seemed especially odd that a Republican administration would go down a path that even the Roosevelt administration had considered unwise. Frank Southard, an IMF economist who'd worked for Treasury under Roosevelt and had been involved in the Bretton Woods negotiations, pleaded with the administration to reject the idea of prohibiting gold ownership abroad: "The New Deal, in its bravest days, did not say this should be done, knowing you can't enforce the law—you can't proceed against the people if you can't find the evidence."

A related concern was that in a country like the United States— which by design had relatively few controls on how its citizens invested their money or how noncitizens invested in the United States—singling out one asset for overseas prohibition seemed arbitrary and morally hazardous, in the economic sense. If an American citizen or company wished to use dollars to buy stocks in the London stock market, open a Swiss bank account, or invest in real estate in South America, there would be no problem, but to move those same funds into gold bars held in those countries would be illegal—that scenario made little sense to economists.

Because the people formulating the policy were primarily concerned with international monetary stability, comparatively little consideration was given to the question of encroaching on Americans' rights. One Treasury official said, "we ought not forget this is an additional abridgement of personal liberties," but then added that "perhaps only wealthy Texans are involved." Even the *Wall Street Journal* editorial page, which opposed the extension of gold prohibition, framed its argument in terms of financial discipline and signals to international markets, rather than as an issue of the American citizen's right to own gold.[19]

On January 14, 1961, President Eisenhower signed an executive order, making it illegal after June 1 for the vast majority of Americans to own gold as an investment, whether at home or overseas. Everyone, including those who supported the executive order, recognized that the broader issues would need to be tackled by a new administration. "We hope President-elect Kennedy has this problem high on his agenda," said a *New York Times* editorial applauding Eisenhower for "Plugging a Gold Leak."[20]

Not everyone, however, in the incoming administration shared the view that gold and the balance of payments should have been a top priority. An adviser to Vice President-elect Lyndon Johnson complained that Eisenhower officials were still meddling in several areas that were better left until the transfer of power had taken place; he noted in particular that Treasury Secretary Anderson had "seemed to be almost obsessed over the gold outflow situation."[21] But within weeks, the Kennedy White House would become consumed with the same obsession, and at the highest level.

Indeed much of the country seemed obsessed with gold in the late 1950s and early 1960s; arguably, the more the US government fretted publicly about the gold supply and moved to extend gold prohibition, the more fascinated the public became. In the fall of 1958, the Hughes Tool Company of Houston sought to celebrate its fiftieth anniversary by creating a life-sized, solid-gold replica of the first rock bit used by Howard Hughes Sr. to drill for oil. The sculpture required 2,400 ounces of gold, but the request to Treasury to construct it—which came through the office of Texas senator Lyndon Johnson—was denied.

Gold took on a special place in marketing and popular culture as well. In 1954, an advertising agency working for Quaker Oats hit on an unusual method to promote puffed rice and wheat cereals. To help sponsor the transfer of a popular radio show about Yukon adventures to television, the company purchased 19 acres of land in the Yukon territory for $1,000, near where the turn-of-the-century Klondike Stampede had attracted tens of thousands of would-be miners. With every box of puffed rice or wheat cereal, a customer would receive a "deed of land" to one square inch of land, and presumably to any gold wealth that lay beneath it. Quaker Oats did not anticipate the wild demand or the expense of actually registering 21 million deeds; the "Klondike Big Inch" company went bankrupt and the land was reclaimed by Canada. In the early '60s, the A&P

grocery store chain experimented with two Golden Key drive-in restaurants in New Jersey, each featuring a gold-shingled roof that shimmered in the sunshine. In the spring of 1960, when Floyd Patterson became the first boxer in history to regain the heavy-weight championship, his manager Cus D'Amato rewarded him with a crown made of gold and studded with jewels, supposedly worth $35,000. Patterson's crown seems to have inspired two representatives of the US Mint to survey the fanciest jewelry stores in Manhattan; officials at Tiffany and Van Cleef rattled off examples of expensive gold coffee sets and cigarette cases they had crafted by special request. In one case Cartier confessed to constructing a woman's handbag containing 40 ounces of gold, but the customer never picked it up.[22]

The fascination with gold was more than merely anecdotal. As the increased demand on the London market suggested, nongovernmental gold consumption in the '50s and early '60s was growing dramatically. In the late 1950s, an official source put the value of private gold holdings internationally at between $10 billion and $12 billion, with perhaps half of that sum held in Western Europe and nearly a third of it in France alone (although one prominent economist scoffed at the figures, saying "such estimates can only be pulled from a magician's hat").[23] And the fastest-growing location was the United States, where the estimated private absorption of gold during this period grew at an average of 15 percent per year. Much of that was industrial—the burgeoning electronics and aerospace businesses used plenty of gold—but collectible gold and gold jewelry were also increasingly popular.

The rapid growth in private gold consumption presented a tremendous challenge to federal law enforcement and to the very policy of gold prohibition. It seems axiomatic that the more gold that was bought, sold, held, or used in private hands, the more blatantly illegal activity there would be. A common scheme in the 1950s was for an individual or company to obtain a license to handle gold legally, buy gold through the Treasury or other means, and then find ways to divert the gold onto the black market (which usually involved smuggling the gold out of the country, because officially there was no market for domestically owned gold). One prominent and colorful example was Salvatore Sollazzo, a licensed jewelry manufacturer who was convicted for fixing college basketball games. In 1951, he was also charged with gold smuggling. An associate of his was trying to ship a two-door Buick out of the country on the *Queen Elizabeth* when an official noticed that its back end was sagging onto the ground; stuffed inside the car body was $200,000 worth of gold. Some prosecutors in the 1950s charged that hundreds of millions of dollars' worth of gold were seeping out of the country every year, although Treasury never confirmed such a figure.

While smuggling per se rarely has outright advocates, some in the 1950s were more or less openly flouting the law as a form of financial civil disobedience. The prohibition against individual American gold ownership enacted in 1933 was never conceived as a long-term policy, and in the relative prosperity of the postwar world it seemed anachronistic at best. And of course, the ability to own gold held out the possibility that it could make its retail owners rich, an extra incentive to turn a blind eye to legal barriers. One popular character was a publisher and financial adviser named Franz Pick, dubbed by the *Saturday Evening Post* as "The Black Marketeers' Best Friend." Pick was frequently cited in monetary articles throughout the 1950s. His authority stemmed from the fact that he published monthly and annual almanacs showing in painstaking detail the trading value of dozens of currencies, including many— such as those behind the Iron Curtain—whose worth was opaque. He spouted data about global gold holdings that the IMF couldn't confirm and were perhaps dubious; one Treasury memo warned that Pick was "generally regarded as an unreliable source." At the same time, Pick claimed to have the ear of prominent bankers and businessmen throughout the world.

Pick cultivated an aura of whimsy tinged with doom; the walls of his two-room office in lower Manhattan were covered with paper bills that had become worthless, a fate he implied that all paper money would eventually meet. He claimed that he'd convinced the landlord of his apartment on Manhattan's Upper East Side to accept rent payments in collectible gold coins. Pick presented gold as a kind of moral monetary campaign; he dedicated one edition of his *Black Market Yearbook* to "the legislators of sixty countries who, in order to maintain the fictional values of paper money, government bonds and gold, are the real promoters of black markets."[24]

Some Americans were clearly seduced by such messages, and the increasing ease of international commercial transactions made it possible for them to find ways around the law. While there may have been no way to know how much gold sold on the London market was to or from American hands, the Eisenhower administration was not wrong to focus on Canada, a close neighbor which in the late 1950s was second only to South Africa in annual gold production. Canada had legalized the buying and selling of gold in 1956, and Canadian banks began a sideline business in buying and storing gold bullion for clients. By 1958, two market innovations were introduced that caught the attention of some wealthy Americans. One came from the Bank of Nova Scotia, which began selling "paper gold"—negotiable certificates for bars of gold that were kept in the Bank's vaults—that was far simpler for non-Canadians to hold than the metal itself. Still more enticing was a scheme, hatched by a brokerage firm called Doherty, Roadhouse & Co., allowing customers to buy gold using an installment plan. With a down payment of as little as $34, plus annual payments of $63, buyers could purchase a 1-kilogram bar of gold worth about $1,100, which could be kept in a Doherty vault for a fee. Although an investor would actually lose money (through interest payments) as long as the value of gold remained the same, the installment plan was an instant hit. Doherty took orders for 4,000 ounces of gold on the first day, a majority of which came from the United States. As word of the unique offer spread—the *New York Times*, *Time* magazine, and

*U.S. News & World Report* all covered it—more US citizens snapped up the bars; by mid-1959, it was estimated that between $3 and $4 million of these Canadian gold bars had been sold to American citizens (who, it turned out, would legally be required to liquidate those holdings two years later).

The very idea that a significant number of Americans would be buying and holding gold abroad was so novel that it's not surprising that some of those responsible for it skirted the law. Doherty, Roadhouse, for example, was an important firm on the Toronto Stock Exchange; one of the company's principals, D'Arcy M. Doherty, had been the president of the Exchange in the early 1950s and sat on its Board of Governors after that. Nonetheless, the firm's ties to Canada's mining interests had drawn the wrath of Canadian regulators. In 1957, the Toronto Stock Exchange discovered Doherty had failed to disclose that he had accepted stock options in a mining firm at the time it began trading on the Exchange. A flurry of trading several months after the firm—Aconic Mining Corporation, which had gold as well as other mining claims and projects—went public had caused the stock to plummet and its executive director to declare bankruptcy. The Stock Exchange's Board of Governors declared Doherty "guilty of conduct detrimental to the interests of the Exchange and unbecoming a member," and suspended him from the Exchange for three months.[25]

The chances are strong, however, that most Americans buying gold bars on 3 percent margin from Doherty, Roadhouse neither knew nor cared much about the firm's other activities. Some were speculators betting that sooner or later the dollar-gold exchange rate would change in their favor; some wanted an ultraconservative investment, perhaps balancing out a portfolio with more aggressive holdings; some may have seen gold as insurance against a semi-apocalyptic crash of governments and finance predicted by right-wing newsletters since the Roosevelt days. Regardless of motivation, the gold buyers of the late 1950s represented the adventurous edge of a population that was beginning to romanticize gold ownership, and indeed advocate it. In contrast to those during the Depression, with its emergency atmosphere that gave rise to earlier gold prohibitions and a largely cooperative populace, the new generation treated gold ownership as a cornerstone of American citizenship—a fundamental right that trumped government abstractions like the balance of payments.

Even Treasury and law enforcement officials seemed to question whether every instance of private gold ownership would genuinely cause the world's financial sky to fall. It was almost comical to hear international monetary justifications for chasing down gold peddlers—as if enforcing the written law was somehow insufficient rationale. For example, in 1962, undercover Treasury agents and the New York City police arrested two men in a Manhattan apartment after they had offered to sell up to 200 ounces of gold for $45 an ounce. (The men also hinted that they had access to far more gold near their hometown in Phoenix.) Trumpeting this arrest for what was, in the end, three bars of gold—a small fraction of what was sold legally in London every weekday—an assistant US attorney declared: "The government regards this as a most serious offense, particularly in view of the very serious situation this country faces regarding the gold situation."[26]

In other instances Treasury officials openly acknowledged that their task bordered on the absurd. For decades, the government fought with an order of nuns in Indianapolis known as the Carmelite sisters. These nuns had proposed in the late 1920s to collect scrap gold—rings, bracelets, old coins—from the faithful and melt it down to create a sacred vessel called a monstrance. Treasury officials blocked their efforts, but the sisters, ever hopeful that the government would one day change its mind, continued to plead their case through the 1960s, all the while amassing gold in small amounts. When they finally relented—in 1970—Treasury authorized a firm to buy the 6 pounds of gold they had collected. An exasperated department veteran explained to his newly appointed boss: "After years of fruitless (and ridiculous) attempts to persuade the nuns to give up their project, the Treasury's General Counsel made an informal decision to drop the whole matter. All of those originally involved are long since dead. In view of the Treasury's past dilatory actions, I do not think it either just or politically wise to assess a $1200 penalty on these people at this late stage. They have already lost more than that in foregone interest."[27]

But by far the most extreme example of the crackdown on private gold ownership—a case that required tens of thousands of man-hours from the Treasury and Justice Departments—originated in the Nevada desert. On a blazing hot afternoon in July 1960, three armed US marshals raided a casino lobby and proceeded to seize a golden statue of a rooster. Invited onlookers jeered and hissed as the agents confiscated the statue, whose attorney decried a "colossal miscarriage of justice."

The renegade fowl in question was a nine-and-a-half-inch-tall, 14-pound bird made of solid 18-karat gold. Prior to his arrest, his preferred roost had been in a lighted glass display case at the Nugget Casino in Sparks, Nevada, where he had taken up residence in 1958, helping to promote The Golden Rooster Room, a newly opened restaurant at the fast-growing Nugget, which served fried chicken as its signature dish.

The golden rooster had been hatched by Richard L. Graves, a street-smart Nevada entrepreneur who loved publicity stunts. Graves began his career in Idaho with restaurants that also featured slot machines, but when Idaho banned slots in the early 1950s, Graves moved his operations south to Nevada. In 1955, when he'd opened the Sparks Nugget, he offered a prize of up to $10,000 for anyone who could sit on top of a flagpole across from his casino for up to a year. Graves constructed a 65-foot pole with a 7-foot-by-7-foot platform on top in the shape of a golden nugget. A self-described professional pole-sitter named "Happy Bill" Howard took up the casino's challenge and managed to stay aloft for 204 days, fortified by an unlimited supply of the casino's celebrated "Awful Awful burgers."

Such gimmicks were designed to lure travelers off Nevada's Highway 40 to come spend some time and money at the Nugget. Today, the Nugget is a full-fledged resort with 1,500 guest rooms, but in the late '50s it was, in the words of John Ascuaga, who worked with Graves and eventually bought the business, "more of a diner with slot machines." With the golden rooster, Graves and the Nugget team got a little more publicity than they bargained for. Even before he was manufactured, the rooster's legal status was tenuous. Initially, Graves and his attorney had reached out to Newman's Silver Shop, a jeweler in Reno, Nevada, to build the bird. They produced a wooden model of the rooster and decided to contact the director of the mint in Washington, DC, because the statue was designed to be far heavier than the 50-ounce gold limit that Newman's was licensed to cast.

The director of the mint, however, quashed the idea of sculpting the rooster. The Mint's reasoning was straightforward and consistent with many previous rulings: it was illegal for the vast majority of Americans to own that much gold, whether in the shape of a rooster or in more traditional forms. The exceptions to the law—primarily for a product in which the craftsmanship provided some significant value beyond the value of the metal it contained, and for "customary industrial, professional or artistic uses" of gold—did not seem to apply. In considering the Nugget's proposed sculpture, the Department of the Mint took the position that forming gold into the shape of a rooster was not customary, even if it might be artistic. Moreover, the Mint expressed fear that approving the statue would only set a precedent "which. . . . could be used by unscrupulous persons as a method of hoarding gold."[28] Hoping to appeal, Graves's team reached out to Nevada's two US senators. Even an appeal to Treasury Secretary Robert Anderson—who felt more than anyone else that the country's gold supply was dangerously precarious—could not change the Mint's position.

For most people, when a department of the federal government says "no," that's the end of the project. But Dick Graves was not most people, and so he tried to find someone else to craft his shiny bird. With an eye toward the law's exception for artistic use, he commissioned Frank Polk, a thick-eyebrowed cowboy-turned-artist, to model the rooster. Polk had made a name for himself with bronze sculptures of bucking broncos and other western scenes, but was best known among casino crowds for kitschy slot machines that rendered literal the nickname "one-armed bandits": life-sized statues of a black-hatted desperado with a pistol-holding arm, which gamblers pulled down to make the wheels on the bandit's chest spin.[29] Not terribly enthusiastic about the rooster project—Polk quipped, "all I ever did with chickens was eat 'em"—Polk charged only $50 for the design, a few days' work. Graves had neglected to tell him that the final statue would be solid gold.

To cast the statue, Graves now turned to a downtown San Francisco jeweler called Shreve & Company, a firm with a past rooted in California's Gold Rush, a place where nineteenth-century prospectors had brought in fresh nuggets in exchange for cash or diamond engagement rings. In contrast with its Nevada counterpart, Shreve told Graves that it would have no problem producing the sculpture, as its license allowed it to cast up to 300 ounces of gold. And indeed, a Shreve official sought and received permission from the superintendent of the San Francisco Mint to cast the casino's prized rooster.

Thus did the rooster move to the Nugget in May 1958, to much public acclaim. But before the year was over, the Secret Service contacted Graves and informed him that his rooster violated the 1934 Gold Reserve Act. They demanded a same-day meeting in the US Attorney's office and suggested that Graves bring an attorney. Graves chose Paul Laxalt, an up-and-coming lawyer whose parents had been born in the French Basque country, and who married the daughter of a prominent Carson City lawyer and Republican activist. Laxalt's own political career had already begun to take shape; four years earlier, he'd been elected district attorney of the county surrounding Carson City, and by the time the rooster saga was complete, was well on his way to being elected Nevada's lieutenant governor. From early days, Laxalt's political identity reflected the western states' infatuation with gold. One of his campaign television spots featured a miner panning for gold at the side of a river; he turned to the camera to show the phrase "Laxalt for Lt. Governor" shimmering at the bottom of his pan.[30]

Laxalt and Graves explained to the Treasury officials that Shreve & Co. had obtained permission to make the rooster and considered the matter closed. But eighteen months later, in July 1960, the US government, which at the time was tussling with Nevada's gaming industry as well as watching the outflow of gold, let its disapproval be known. The Treasury Department filed a complaint in federal court in Carson City, entitled *United States of America v. One Solid Gold Object in Form of a Rooster.* They issued a warrant for the rooster's arrest, and that was when the US marshals arrived at the Nugget. The rooster was confiscated and transferred to a federal bank vault in California. Laxalt swiftly applied for bail for the statue, but was denied; the rooster had to stay incarcerated until trial. Graves, never one to miss a publicity opportunity, placed a bronze replica of the rooster in the case outside the restaurant—dressed in prison stripes.

The golden bird stayed locked up for nearly two years, until his trial by jury began in March 1962. If the government prevailed, the rooster would pay the ultimate price: he would be melted down and stored with the rest of the federal government's gold reserves. Much of the trial testimony focused on the question of whether or not the Golden Rooster qualified as a work of art, not usually considered an area of Treasury's expertise. Technically the government conceded that it was art, but maintained that because it was being used for advertising purposes, the rooster was primarily an instrument of commerce. Art critics from Denver and New York were flown into Carson City to meditate on the nature of statuary, and whether emphasizing the gold content of a statue enhanced or detracted from its customary, artistic value. During the trial one critic deemed the bird "exquisite," while the government's attorney, Thomas Wilson, got into an argument with the judge about whether it was more common for statues to be solid or hollow.[31]

Wilson also contended that the metal bird was a threat to the American economy, and even to law and order. He told the jury that Graves's end run around the federal government's explicit rejection of his initial sculpture plan "makes a mockery of both the law and the country's attempt to control the gold problem and preserve our monetary basis." Lest the jury doubt the severity of the Golden Rooster precedent, Wilson spelled it out in his closing argument, using some foreboding (and, at this stage in the trial, hard-to-verify) mathematics. "Our gold reserves have to be 25% of the amount of money outstanding if our money is going to have any stability at all," he warned. "If one out of 180 people is entitled to make a gold object like that, it brings the gold down below the 25% requirement—and the result of that is economic chaos."

Ignoring the unlikely scenario of a million golden roosters glimmering across America, Laxalt framed the tale of the Golden Rooster as a retelling of David and Goliath, with the role of Goliath played by a large and bumbling federal government. Yes, the rooster was a work of art created at considerable expense, but he maintained there was a "symbolic value," which he spelled out: "It is rewarding to feel, people, that any one of us, whether we are big, small, important, unimportant, still have the right under our Constitution, under our laws, to disagree with a Government official." He made it sound as if it was a Nevadan's birthright to own and work with gold, and flattered the local jurors' wisdom and ability to send a message back east. "It is refreshing to me," Laxalt said, "to see people like Dick Graves who will say to themselves, 'I still have rights under the Constitution, under the law a Government official can still be wrong, and I can have this problem resolved by a jury, not by some group in Washington who don't know me or anything about me or the manner in which I live or the manner in which Nevadans live, not by them, but twelve people such as yourselves who live in our area, know the customs of the people and the people involved, and who will come up with a good decision.'" As if to demonstrate the unfeeling nature of the federal government, Laxalt encouraged the jury to consider the fate of the innocent statue should the jury find for his opponent: "It would be a terrible shame to see this rooster confiscated, melted down and put into the gold stocks at Fort Knox."

Laxalt's persuasive powers with Nevadans won the day. The jury deliberated for an afternoon and evening, came back the next day and delivered a unanimous verdict in favor of the rooster—and seven months later, Laxalt was elected Nevada's lieutenant governor—and not long thereafter, governor, and then US senator. Laxalt's rise represented a new era of American politicians—more conservative, more western-oriented, and with a free gold market at the top of their agenda.

# CHAPTER 7

○

# Operation Goldfinger

IN THE SPRING OF 1965, when Treasury official Joe Barr agreed to meet with a group of western members of Congress led by Alaska's senator Ernest Gruening, he knew just what to expect. Barr knew his way around Capitol Hill; the Indiana Democrat holds the distinction of being the first-ever member of Congress with a graduate degree in economics. Although Barr served but a single term, almost immediately after he left office in 1961, President Kennedy appointed him as the chief liaison between Congress and the Treasury, and so he spent his days buttonholing congressmen and listening to their gripes. After a stint as the head of the Federal Deposit Insurance Corporation (FDIC), Barr went right back to Treasury for the Johnson administration, again responsible for talking to the Hill.

Presidential science and technology adviser Donald Hornig, left, with President Johnson and one of his beagles on Johnson's ranch in Texas, in December 1964. Beginning in 1965, Hornig and allies in the Treasury Department convinced the president to back "Operation Goldfinger," which sought to increase dramatically the nation's gold supply by seeking the metal in unusual places. *Courtesy LBJ Presidential Library, photograph by Yoichi Okamoto*

Gruening's home state of Alaska had not been a state for very long, but it was not shy about making demands. Very high on the group's agenda was a plea that the federal government do something—anything—to revive America's stagnant gold-mining industry. Worldwide demand for gold was booming, and yet US mines—once the epicenter of global gold production—were largely missing the party. Fixing the price of gold at $35 an ounce for more than a quarter century had predictably depressed the US mining industry, even as the demand for private gold shot up. The more easily obtained sources of gold had become depleted over the years, while harder-to-reach sources became more difficult to mine profitably, given the static price. Foreign competition—chiefly from Canada and South Africa—was far more intense by 1960 than it had been when Roosevelt set the price of gold. Rather than attempt to compete, many mines simply shut down. US gold production had never strongly recovered from the World War II slowdown; South Africa by this time was producing three-quarters of the world's gold. The United States was a distant third in gold production (fourth, if consensus estimates of secret Soviet gold production were accurate).[1] Gruening's home state was faring the worst; Alaska had achieved international renown in the late nineteenth century because gold seemed to be everywhere in the state, but by the mid-1960s the industry had nearly disappeared. From a peak of almost 700,000 ounces produced in 1940, Alaskan gold production plummeted some 95 percent. In 1966 the volume of gold mined in Alaska was its lowest since 1886, and the value fell to under $1 million.[2] Gold-mining companies had begun to portray themselves as unique victims of an outdated government policy. Edward "Bob" Bartlett—the chief architect of Alaska's statehood and its first senator—said in 1962: "No other industry has thus been discriminated against."[3]

The industry argued that the price of gold needed to go up, or else mining should have a subsidy or a tax incentive to produce more gold; the western senators were drafting legislation for it. After all, the domestic silver industry was subsidized, and at least some gold-producing nations—notably Canada—subsidized their gold industry. To Barr, this was a nonstarter. For years, Treasury had reflexively opposed all versions of this proposal, fearing that any government policy that implied a change in the price of gold

might—regardless of any salutary effects on US production—
have a disastrous effect on the dollar or the government's gold
stock or both. The very discussion was one of those Capitol Hill
rituals in which both sides pretend to engage debate—and both
sides know that neither will budge. But Barr tried to find a small
patch of common ground. While increasing the price of gold or
directly subsidizing the industry were definitely off the table, Barr
did allow that if there were a government-sponsored plan to aid
research in the domestic gold industry, that ought not to interfere
with the delicate role that gold played in the international monetary sphere.

This concession did not placate the western congressmen; if anything, it may have spurred them to attack. That August, Gruening
and seventeen fellow senators—including influential Democrats
such as Frank Church, Henry "Scoop" Jackson, Warren Magnuson,
and George McGovern—signed a blunt letter to President Johnson
accusing him of letting America's gold industry die. Gold, they said,
"is the only commodity held down to a price established 31 years
ago and compelled to sell only to the imposer of this strangling
restriction—the Federal government." Badly needed reform, they
added, was being blocked by Treasury's "negative attitude."[4] This
was just short of a threat that the senators would take action on
gold with or without the administration's support. Previous Con-
gresses had considered, though not passed, legislation to aid the
gold industry, but the landslide Democratic victory in 1964 had
produced "supermajorities" in both houses of Congress, and the
Johnson White House could not afford to alienate western-state
Democrats whose votes it needed for other legislation. And thus
did Barr trek back to Capitol Hill in September, with his Treasury
colleague Fred Deming, to meet again with the western congressmen in an atmosphere Barr described as "more heated than usual."
Fearful of being stuck in the same place, Barr had "a stroke of inspi-
ration and suggested that possibly the Government could assist

in this area by some sort of an R&D approach in the discovery of deposits and in the extraction process." This pleased the members of Congress, and Barr and Deming promised to report back in early 1966.

Barr and a colleague from the US Mint then went to see Johnson's science and technology adviser Donald Hornig, one of the most accomplished American scientists ever to occupy a position of political power. Hornig had worked on the Manhattan Project, babysitting the original test bomb in a shed atop a 100-foot tower; he worked on the space program and became an expert in ocean desalination technology; and he would become president of Brown University. Responding to this Treasury inquiry about gold research, Hornig asked the Geological Survey and the Bureau of Mines for a study, and word came back that, yes, "there is indeed an opportunity to secure significant quantities of additional gold production in the United States within the $35 an ounce price limitation." The solution seemed simple enough: deploy state-of-the-art technology to detect gold and to extract it. Barr described himself as "thunderstruck" and began drawing up potential budget numbers, along with several far-reaching policy and economic questions, many reflecting the fear that applied modern science might be too effective: "At what level of production would the price of gold collapse?"

And so began one of the strangest untold episodes in modern American history. In the mid-to-late 1960s, as gold's role in the international monetary system was about to implode, a handful of top Johnson administration officials, a few sympathetic members of Congress, and hundreds of government-paid scientists set off on a nuclear-age alchemy quest. Perhaps inevitably for a top-secret project of the 1960s, Barr gave it the code name Operation Goldfinger. Under the aegis of the program, the government would end up looking for gold in the oddest places: seawater, meteorites, even plants. And in an era that wanted badly to believe in the peaceful use of subatomic energy, serious plans were drawn up to use nuclear explosives to extract gold deep inside the Earth, and even to use particle accelerators to try to change base metals into gold.

In a sense, Operation Goldfinger represented the logical culmination of what became in the 1960s a government obsession with not having enough gold. No president had ever been as concerned with gold and the international balance of payments as John Kennedy—to a fault, in the eyes of many of his colleagues. Especially given the more visceral geopolitical developments of the period—Fidel Castro's revolution and the Bay of Pigs invasion, the Cuban missile crisis, early escalation of US involvement in the Vietnam War, the Berlin crisis, and the construction of the Berlin Wall—Kennedy's deep concern with the balance-of-payments issue seemed, to many of his advisers, extreme. Kennedy constantly told people around him that the most dangerous and intractable problems the nation faced were (depending on the retelling) either Cuba or the prospect of nuclear war—and the balance of payments. Kennedy's close adviser Theodore Sorenson wrote: "Almost to a man, Kennedy's associates in the administration thought he was excessively concerned about the [balance-of-payments] problem." George Ball, who was Kennedy's undersecretary of state, called him "absolutely obsessed with the balance of payments."[5] C. Douglas Dillon, a Republican from the Eisenhower administration whom Kennedy appointed as his first treasury secretary, said Kennedy "had this almost phobia about gold."[6]

When the price of gold spiked in the London market during the 1960 presidential campaign (see previous chapter), Kennedy tried in public to make light of the predicament. But he believed that the issue was fundamental to the global economic order. Less than a month after he took office, Kennedy delivered a special address on gold and the balance of payments. "This loss of gold is naturally important to us, but it also concerns the whole free world," he told

Congress. "We are the principal banker of the free world and any potential weakness in our dollar spells trouble, not only for us but also for our friends and allies who rely on the dollar to finance a substantial portion of their trade." In a private 1962 conversation with the chairman of the Federal Reserve, Kennedy hit the point more urgently: "My God, this is the time . . . if everyone wants gold we're all going to be ruined because there is not enough gold to go around."[7] Kennedy also seems to have been the first president to use a phrase that would be recycled thousands of times by presidential successors and contenders: he pledged that the American dollar "should be as good as gold." Some who were close to Kennedy attribute his outsized concern for gold and the balance of payments to the influence of his father. Nonetheless, his successor quickly reached a similar view; Johnson told Senate minority leader Everett Dirksen, "The biggest problem I've got outside of Vietnam is balance of payments."[8]

While those around him may have found Kennedy's "obsession" to be distorted, the balance-of-payments issue was in several ways closely tied to that decade's geopolitical tensions (and particularly, as we shall see, to the Vietnam War). Partly, that connection existed because Kennedy built his budgetary oversight in a manner that explicitly linked gold with national security spending. The Kennedy administration aimed at spreading American wealth throughout the world, partly out of a belief that America's economic interests were served by enriching its friends, and partly as a bulwark against Communist intrusion in places like Latin America and Africa. In a 1962 address, Kennedy called foreign aid "a method by which the U.S. maintains a position of influence and control around the world and sustains a good many countries which would definitely collapse or pass into the communist bloc."[9] And thus substantial sums were committed to programs like the Agency for International Development, the Alliance for Progress, and the Peace Corps.

Even assuming, however, that America had sufficient wealth to be able to send it abroad for no tangible goods in return, and that these programs were essential to maintaining a capitalist system in the face of global Communist intrusion, such aid intrinsically strained the balance-of-payments problem—the very fact of having so many dollars abroad threatened the stability of the currency, and thus of the international economic order. Kennedy hoped to have it both ways; in August 1961, he sent a "national security action memorandum" to his treasury secretary, asking to be regularly provided with "an up-to-date study of our gold position." Responding to this concern, the following year the administration introduced a "gold budget," in which the impact of every spending program had to be evaluated on the basis of how it affected the country's gold supply. This program factionalized Kennedy's cabinet by making the Treasury and Budget office seem like unwanted supervisors over State and Defense. It also had the effect of pretending that the nation's gold stock could somehow provide an objective basis for decisions that were intrinsically political; who, after all, but the president could adjudicate whether one abstract goal (creating global military and economic security to stem Communist influence) should take precedence over another (preserving the balance of payments to prevent a dollar crisis)?

The second tie between gold and national security was that, assuming the views of American officials could be taken at face value, America was remarkably defenseless in the face of even modest fluctuations in the gold market. The 1960 spike in gold prices represented a genuine crisis for the American and global economies, albeit one in which only a handful of officials knew the full extent of the problem. Yet by all credible accounts, the crisis came about spontaneously. It was therefore not hard to imagine one or more foreign governments threatening the global economic order simply by manipulating the price of gold or demanding all at once that dollars held in reserve be converted. The Soviet

Union (a significant gold producer, though in amounts that were secret and much debated) would have been an obvious such adversary. Although the threat remained largely theoretical, it was not far-fetched. Barr, who became treasury secretary in 1968, later recalled: "The only time we could see much interference from Moscow was perhaps in the gold operations. It did look to us as though they were playing the gold markets. . . . I can't say that we did take into account much what the bloc countries were doing."[10] But the threat could also come from a strategic ally, perhaps one that elected a left-wing government or had come to resent America's dominance of the world economy. After all, through the mid-1960s Japan and most European governments deliberately held the bulk of their reserves in dollars, rather than cash them in for gold at the US Treasury window. This was done in deference to the United States and its protective nuclear umbrella. One Treasury official in 1969 defined America's genuine dollar-gold convertibility policy: "We do not formally turn anyone down when he asks for gold, but we make very clear we are unhappy if he asks."[11] And thus there was little to prevent governments from changing their minds.

Indeed, a rush to convert dollar holdings to gold might occur even in reaction to an event beyond the control of the United States itself, such as a sudden drawing on the IMF's reserves or a jolting revaluation of the British pound or other major currency. Take, for example, Germany, a long-standing source of balance-of-payments concerns for the United States. The cost of maintaining hundreds of thousands of American troops in Germany became harder and harder to justify with every year. Getting Germany to pay its postwar debts, and to agree to make payments to "offset" the US military presence, helped. But when pushed too far, such measures could force the Germans to revalue the deutschmark, which they did in 1961, creating turmoil in both markets and diplomacy. The United States' need to steer Germany's economy to ease America's balance of payments very explicitly clashed throughout the 1960s with the need to keep Germany as a NATO ally and check against expansion of Soviet influence.

More straightforwardly, countries might simply demand gold from the US Treasury. For years the White House worried about how seemingly arbitrary gold withdrawals could upset the global balance of power. In a 1960 National Security Council discussion about the difficulty of getting NATO countries to share the burden of military spending, for example, Treasury Secretary Robert Anderson groused that two years earlier, the Italian Parliament had ordered its central bank to remove $2.5 billion in gold from the United States, making a significant dent in the country's reserves.[12] And in early 1965, Charles de Gaulle's government formalized a long-standing French preference for a return to a genuine international gold standard; France announced that it would redeem $300 million in dollar holdings from the United States into gold, and make further gold purchases from Treasury every month. The risk that other countries would follow France's lead on gold was very real, and could have easily dissolved the transatlantic alliance at a time when the US military was particularly exposed; the gold–national security link was strong enough that some executive discussions about gold and balance of payments remain classified even more than half a century later.

That the US economy was so vulnerable to a gold-currency crisis in the 1960s was deeply ironic. The military and economic aid programs that the United States undertook starting in the immediate postwar period had been so successful in lifting up its allies that they threatened America's position at the system's center. The rules of the international monetary game imposed by Bretton Woods had been instituted largely at the United States' urging; now many in the United States saw those rules as handcuffs keeping the United States from being able to act. The most far-seeing critic of these limitations was the economist Robert Triffin, who had been an outsider in the late 1950s when he wrote his seminal critique *Gold and the Dollar Crisis* but whom the Kennedy administration brought in as an adviser. "The Triffin dilemma" pointed to the instability of the world's monetary system; as the global economy grew, there were more and more US dollars and interest-paying US Treasury bills held outside the United States. All of these were theoretically redeemable for gold, but even with the United States owning the lion's share of the world's monetary gold, the time would come, as Kennedy put it, when "there is not enough gold to go around." Only a few outcomes were possible: global growth would need to slow; a global devaluation would need to occur; some kind of gold-dollar convertibility crisis would erupt; or the rules would need to change (which might involve its own crisis).

The perception of a government gold shortage was heightened by an international gold system that was taking on a shape in the mid-1960s never before seen. While the world continued to produce more gold every year, the amount available for monetary use by the world's largest economies was not growing by much. Instead, the 1960s witnessed a rapid increase in the amount of gold used for purposes other than propping up currencies and central banks. As governments in Canada and elsewhere relaxed their wartime-era prohibitions against ownership, more and more gold found its way into private hands. By 1967, the South African Chamber of Mines had already begun minting the Krugerrand, an easily tradable one-ounce gold coin that, within a few years, would propel private gold ownership to previously unknown levels.

Industrial and artistic uses of gold also rose.[13] With the price of gold held artificially at $35 an ounce, the metal was especially attractive for industrial applications that were already defining the second half of the twentieth century. The first transistor had been created in 1947 at AT&T Bell Labs, using two pieces of gold foil wedged into a block of germanium; by the mid-1960s tens of millions of transistors were being produced every year and the number would continue to explode for decades. Another Bell Labs innovation was the laser, first developed in 1960 using gold-coated mirrors. Most iconic of all was the space program; rocket engines were coated in gold to act as a heat shield, while the visors worn by the first American astronauts were covered with a thin film of gold to block out the sun's rays. By the end of the decade many tons of gold were being used annually in the space, military, and electronics fields, far surpassing the amount used in gold fillings for teeth. Gold jewelry, coins, and medallions too became increasingly popular. With incomes rising in most of the developed world in the 1950s and 1960s, capping gold at $35 an ounce had the effect of making gold items look comparatively cheap. One institution estimated in 1966 that internationally, such personal gold consumption had tripled in the previous ten years.[14]

Collectively these uses of gold were gaining ground against global monetary gold. The International Monetary Fund estimated that in 1965 alone, gold "absorption" by private holders, industrial use, and artistic use amounted to $1.6 billion, approximately $500 million more than the year before.[15] The next year, 1966, for the first time since the end of World War II, the world did not add any gold to its monetary stock; on the contrary, the world's monetary stock lost $40 million worth of gold. Not coincidentally, the silver market went through similar changes in the mid-1960s, prompting the Johnson administration to eliminate all silver from quarters and dimes, and reduce the silver content of half-dollars.[16]

Inextricably connected to the gold and balance-of-payments issue were the domestic budget deficit (in 1964 it hit a worrisome $2.8 billion) and the fact that the dollar was overvalued; Johnson's economists could see no simple way to unwind these knots. Most in the administration favored a tax increase, which would curb consumption and send a signal of fiscal discipline to central banks abroad, increasing the likelihood that they would not trade their dollar reserves for gold. However, at least through 1967, a tax hike was considered politically impractical. A onetime devaluation of the dollar would be effective, but seemed bound to provoke other countries to respond in kind, in addition to roiling global capital markets and harming consumers. Johnson had created a cabinet committee on balance of payments that identified many issues— curbing US banks' loans abroad, speeding up payment of debts from foreign countries, stimulating exports—that were theoretically manageable through policy shifts, though often slowly.

But much of the problem seemed beyond the administration's control. Everywhere Johnson's advisers looked, they saw balance-of-payments demons—even in seemingly trivial places. For example, more and more Americans were vacationing and doing business abroad, where they spent US dollars. Not only were Americans wealthier, but technology improved—the transatlantic jet had debuted in 1958, making it far easier for millions of Americans to travel to Europe and the Mediterranean with their dollars every year (the Caribbean and Central America were the second-favorite destinations). One Johnson White House official asserted that travel abroad by Americans was increasing by a hefty 10 percent every year; in the years 1964–1966 that estimate was probably low. In 1960, US tourists spent about $2.3 billion abroad, and by 1967 the figure was over $4 billion. The situation was mitigated by travel in the opposite direction—that is, tourism to the United States—but even so, in 1967, what the White House called the "tourist gap" was over $2 billion. For years the Johnson administration debated whether to increase passport fees, reduce customs exemptions, or even impose an outright travel tax. Officials knew, however, that such measures would be opposed by the State Department, the travel industry, and the general public.

And, of course, there was the war in Vietnam, which was growing, not shrinking, and contributing to the balance-of-payments problem in multiple ways. Most of the money spent on the war, aside from the cost of domestically made munitions, was a direct expenditure on supplies and services—literally shipping US dollars to Southeast Asia. The war also required importing raw materials and other goods needed to create military products and services, with no corresponding exports. And the indirect economic impact of the war—supply and manpower shortages, lengthened delivery time, reduced competitiveness—also hit the balance of payments. In 1968, two economists estimated that the Vietnam War contributed $3.5 to $4 billion annually to the current accounts deficit, and that without the war, the country would probably have had a current accounts surplus. A Defense Department official disputed the figure, but acknowledged that "the Vietnam War has had a serious adverse effect on the United States trade balance."[17]

One decisive action that presented itself was to find some way to remove the Bretton Woods linchpin, to delink the dollar from gold. Both the Kennedy and Johnson administrations sought innovative ways to reduce the need for non-US central banks to hold dollars as reserve currency. "Roosa bonds," named after Kennedy's Treasury Undersecretary Robert Roosa, were sold in dollars but denominated in foreign currencies, thereby encouraging foreign governments to hold them instead of exchanging them for gold. And many years were spent negotiating and creating "special drawing rights" with the International Monetary Fund, a kind of nation-neutral currency designed for central banks. But these modest steps would slow the gold bleeding, not stop it. A full-scale delinking of gold and the dollar would involve, at a minimum, some kind of drastic controls or moratorium on gold sales between the United States and the world's largest central banks. What had been an uneasy but mostly friendly (except for France) system in which Western European nations and Japan tacitly agreed not to undermine the dollar's central role could quickly spill over into a damaging currency war. Johnson's economic advisers split between those who believed that delinking gold from the dollar was impossible, and those who thought it desirable but couldn't bring themselves to advocate it. To Johnson adviser Francis Bator, the prospect of international revolt was a poker bluff that the United States could nonetheless stare down and defeat. Bator wrote to the president: "The truth is that the present rules of the international money game are stacked against us. If the Europeans force a crisis, our economic strength and real bargaining leverage would soon become very clear to all concerned."[18] But the possible ramifications were too ominous to contemplate; Bator noted in a later essay that one of his colleagues called this the "nuclear war" option.[19]

How preferable, then, to pursue an option that promised cheap and plentiful gold? At precisely the same time that many of Johnson's advisers were contemplating a metaphorical nuclear option for monetary gold, his Treasury Department was confidentially working with congressional leaders to tap the latest technology—some of it literally nuclear—to revolutionize the way that gold was produced. The starry-eyed briefings from the administration's scientists made Joe Barr's 1966 trips to Capitol Hill much cheerier than they'd been the year before. Not only did he have something that made the western congressmen happy, but he bonded with them over forging a secret. Barr knew which members were most likely to support the initiative, and which could be trusted to keep quiet. While the Johnson administration sparred with Congress over seemingly basic issues like passing a tax bill, there was nonetheless consensus between executive and legislative branches to disguise Operation Goldfinger as a broad-based metal-mining program. As Barr wrote to his boss, Treasury Secretary Henry Fowler: "There is general agreement among those I talked to—Mahon, the Interior Subcommittee on Appropriations of the House, and Scoop Jackson—that this program should be wrapped up in a search for all minerals. They advised us (the Treasury and the Administra-

tion) to deny or refuse to comment on any leaks that might orig-
inate and to stick with the cover story of a search for minerals in
short supply in the United States."[20] A push for secrecy also came
from Federal Reserve chairman William McChesney Martin, who
was concerned that "we simply do not know how foreign central
banks would interpret this move."[21]

After all, Goldfinger's anticipated impact was immense. If the
predictions made in 1966 were to come true, the initial investment
of a few million dollars would, in just a few years, look like the
bargain of the century. A sunny Hornig wrote to LBJ in February 1966: "It appears by spending from $10 million to $20 million
per year we stand a good chance of adding several billion dollars to our gold reserves at the present price. With luck it might
be much more." Treasury's general counsel asserted that "The
President's scientific advisers are confident of the success of the
program [and] estimate that new gold reserves valued at up to $10
billion could be expected within five years."[22] That amount—$10
billion—was more than twice the volume of gold then produced
annually worldwide. Goldfinger, therefore, wasn't like discovering some new gold mine—it was like discovering a new planet.
Barr's almost-giddy optimism led him to think that if Goldfinger
yielded genuinely revolutionary scientific gold-mining discoveries, they ought to be shared globally to bolster the world's gold
supply—as if the United States could once more be the red-hot
center of an international gold rush. "If this program is working
out by [1967] we plan to call in geologists from South America,
Africa, and Australia (the principal ore-producing areas) and give
them the results of what we have learned," he wrote to President
Johnson.

Thanks to Barr's lobbying and coordination by Interior Secretary Stewart Udall and Treasury Secretary Fowler, funding
for Operation Goldfinger was discreetly secured. Sticking to the
cover story, Udall submitted in April a request to add $10.3 mil-

lion to his fiscal year 1967 budget "to accelerate programs of the Geological Survey and the Bureau of Mines directed to the discovery, exploration and production technologies of heavy metals in short supply." Shortly thereafter, the Interior Subcommittee of the Senate Appropriations Committee approved the funds, with no hearings involved. To wait until fiscal year 1967, however, would mean largely wasting a year; much of the field work was best done in the summer because of weather and the availability of university personnel. Understandably, the administration wanted to start immediately. But Congress, of course, had appropriated no 1966 funds for Goldfinger's bold adventures. Seeking immediate extra money for Interior risked congressional scrutiny for a project that was supposed to be secret, and at any rate was politically contentious, given strained relations between Congress and the Johnson White House on budget matters.

To jump-start the project, White House officials turned to a curious source of funds: the US Treasury's Exchange Stabilization Fund (ESF). The ESF had been created as part of the Gold Reserve Act of 1934 and was designed to allow the government to intervene in markets to stabilize the value of the dollar. To use the ESF as a path to hunt for obscure gold was a stretch, and Johnson administration officials knew it. Treasury's general counsel Fred B. Smith noted: "A program designed to increase U.S. gold production is, of course, somewhat outside the traditional scope of activities financed from the Fund." All the more reason, then, to keep Operation Goldfinger secret. While Smith declared himself "sure we can legally justify a transfer of funds to Interior for gold research," he acknowledged that "it is possible that the GAO [General Accounting Office] and other critics of the ESF might question the propriety as well as the legality of the transfer." This was not an idle concern. Treasury had drawn fire from the GAO after it had used ESF money in 1964 to purchase a $150,000 house in Tokyo for an American diplomat,[23] leading Smith to note drily, "this is not an especially good time to use the Fund in new and untried areas." Smith proposed a clever bureaucratic fix, by which Treasury would request interdepartmental services—that is, ask the Bureau of Mines and the Geological Survey to "increase our resources to maintain the stability of the dollar"—and reimburse them for their work. And thus did the federal budget allow nearly a million dollars of Treasury money to be used to sniff out gold, with almost no one inside or outside government aware of the details.

In practice, Operation Goldfinger took the form of hundreds of research projects and tens of thousands of collected samples, designed to find gold in places both likely and very unlikely. Like most major projects, public or private, Operation Goldfinger was not created from scratch—it was a mix of recycled research and half-baked ideas that suddenly were given priority. The Roberts Mountains in north central Nevada had long seemed like a promising source of gold, and thus the Heavy Metals Program of the USGS took samples from dozens of areas, looking for surface minerals (such as limestone) known to be associated with gold deposits. Other studies seemed more like long shots. For decades, various scientists had found traces of gold in coal, and so the USGS sifted through coal in dozens of locations in Appalachia and the Midwest. The government even took samples from coal ash and "coal-washing waste products received from various industrial plants." These did not yield gold bonanzas. Similarly, in the 1940s in Czechoslovakia, scientists reported finding gold in the herb *Equisetum palustre*, or marsh horsetail. When government scientists collected twenty-two samples from across the United States, however, they found gold concentrations well below 1 part per million, and concluded, "*Equisetum* would not be useful in prospecting for gold."[24]

Appropriately enough for a plan called Goldfinger, much of the project's early enthusiasm focused on state-of-the-art gadgets. The USGS developed truck-mounted neutron-activation systems, one for detecting silver and one for gold. "It is no longer necessary even to collect a sample, as long as a truck can be driven over the spot that one wants analyzed," boasted a government report.[25] The Bureau of Mines also worked on "a portable X-ray probe that can be lowered into small diameter drill holes" to find gold. James Bond would have been proud.

For Operation Goldfinger, no scientific plan was too obscure to consider: Is there gold in meteorites that hit the Earth? Is there gold in Colorado peat? Is there gold in plants and trees? Is there gold in deer antlers?[26] In almost all cases, government scientists found that the answer was yes—but from those findings it hardly followed that the gold existed in quantities that even approached commercial viability.

An area of exploration that seemed especially fertile was the sea. Just as oil is found underground on land or beneath the seabed, the same geological forces that created gold deposits in, say, California also created them under the ocean floor. In the earlier part of the twentieth century, a German scientist named Fritz Haber had made a convincing case that seawater itself contained traces of gold. The ocean was a natural focus for Hornig, who worked for years on projects including desalination plants and the creation of underwater tunnels. And many of Hornig's counterparts in and out of government were, in this period, increasingly optimistic about deep-sea mining. In 1962, the Marine Diamond Corporation of Cape Town, South Africa, launched a "diamond barge" at the mouth of the Orange River, which ended up extracting 51,000 carats of gem-quality rough diamonds from underwater gravel before it was shipwrecked a year later; by the decade's end, Marine had recovered 1.5 million carats using these barges. Not all of the technological advances were mechanical; the navy also proposed surgically opening a hole in a diver's windpipe and filling his lungs with a special liquid that would allow him to reach depths of 12,000 feet for up to two hours without the need for decompression.[27] "The ocean is big business right now," Hornig declared in the mid-'60s, "and the rate it's going, it's reasonable to expect that it will become an even bigger business in the years ahead."[28]

It was not pure fantasy to think that if diamonds could be mined from the sea, so too could gold; after all, in the 1960s, gold deposits were detected off the shores of Alaska. Preliminary sea-mining for gold became one of the most important components of Operation Goldfinger, and one with which the public could be productively engaged without creating a stir. Not that it was easy; commandeering government ships during the Vietnam War to become twentieth-century *Argos* was a challenge. At the very start of Goldfinger, Treasury tried to get one from the Coast Guard but was rebuffed.[29] Instead, the USGS contracted with the University of Oregon in 1967 to launch the *Yaquina*, a 180-foot-long, 900-ton research vessel, designed to dredge sediment beneath the continental shelf between Coos Bay in Oregon and Eureka in northern California.[30] The project, however, found miniscule amounts of gold.

Operation Goldfinger's ambitions did not stop at US shores. Officials at Treasury and the Geological Survey were excited about a "very promising gold prospect" along the Puruni River in north-central Guyana. In the early part of the twentieth century, a mine there had produced some 40,000 ounces of gold but had been abandoned since 1916. A Geological Survey scientist conducting a study for the Agency for International Development found that some of the mine's veins contained "several ounces of gold per ton . . . they are large and gold-bearing to depths of at least 700 feet." Guyana's regional rival Venezuela also held out hope. This was a pet project for a veteran administration outside adviser with an eccentric bent—Alexander Sachs, who had been an adviser to FDR and was for decades the chief economist at the Wall Street firm Lehman Brothers. Sachs, who was by now in his

70s and lived in Manhattan, had for years been almost a one-man Operation Goldfinger. At least since the early 1960s, Sachs gathered information and contacts in the mining and technology worlds and bombarded Treasury and Federal Reserve officials with elaborate plans to tap the gold resources of Guyana, Venezuela, South Africa, and beyond.

Most administration officials who received Sachs's lengthy, dense memoranda did not consider themselves expert enough to endorse his often utopian plans. Nonetheless, Sachs managed to convince Johnson's highest-level advisers to pursue his ideas. Both Treasury Secretary Fowler and Eugene Rostow, the State Department's undersecretary of political affairs, felt Sachs's proposals were too good to pass up. "I have no way of knowing whether the area of Venezuela under discussion is as promising as Mr. Sachs suspects it to be," Rostow wrote. "But there is evidence of high promise to justify a full feasibility study. . . . I suggest a Public Corporation or Authority established by a Treaty between Venezuela and the United States."[31]

Rostow's suggestion of international cooperation was all the more remarkable because Sachs recommended not merely traditional gold mining, but prying gold out of the Venezuelan ground using nuclear detonations. During the 1960s, many such experiments with underground nuclear explosions were proposed—and some carried out—primarily for mining, drilling, and land-moving purposes, under the auspices of Project Plowshare, a program for the peaceful use of nuclear technology. Plowshare was a particular passion for hydrogen-bomb pioneer Edward Teller, with whom Hornig had worked at Los Alamos Laboratory during the Manhattan Project's construction of the atomic bombs. Teller advocated nonmilitary applications of nuclear energy both for their own remarkable technical achievements and as propaganda, to soften public opposition to nuclear power, which had begun to arise in the late 1950s (some maintain that Plowshare was deliberately designed to woo public opinion and postpone a nuclear morato-rium).[32] In a 1960 article for *Popular Mechanics* Teller asserted that "the dangers from fallout in the weapons-testing program have been greatly exaggerated" and advocated nuclear detonations to acquire oil and to quickly build harbors in places such as Point Hope in northern Alaska.[33] From Plowshare's inception in 1957 to its eventual demise two decades later, dozens of nonmilitary atomic explosions were planned and many were carried out. In July 1962, the then-largest nuclear explosion ever to take place in North America occurred in the Nevada desert. The detonation of a 100-kiloton device moved some twelve million tons of earth and created a crater as deep as a football field and four times as wide. The experiment had no immediate practical application, but many scientists interpreted it as verification for their projections about the size and scope of a blast needed for nuclear-aided land-moving. The projections for negligible radioactive fallout were less accu-rate. As part of the project, thirty beagles were placed in wire cages at distances between 12 and 40 miles from the blast's ground zero, with their mouths taped shut, to test the power of an inhaled radioactive dose. Within 72 hours of the explosion, ten of the dogs died.[34]

The goal of harnessing such massive explosions to mineral mining had not occurred to Alexander Sachs alone. The idea existed in embryonic form years before Goldfinger was hatched, as a way of compensating for the dramatic postwar decline in US copper production. In the late 1950s, the Utah-based Kennecott Copper Corporation purchased a massive, low-grade copper deposit near Safford, Arizona.[35] The company's test drilling indicated that beneath a slab of volcanic rock 500 feet thick lay a 2-billion-ton reserve of ore containing 0.4 percent copper. But the ore could not be reached using conventional explosives, and so Kennecott consid-ered using nuclear explosives to mine it. This could of course not be done without government cooperation, and Kennecott began discussions about such explosions with the AEC in 1963 (other companies involved in mining, including Anaconda and Dow Chemical, made similar queries). By 1965, a feasibility study by Kennecott, the AEC, and the Bureau of Mines was approved, and dubbed Project Sloop. The idea was to explode a 20-kiloton nuclear device 1,200 feet below the ground, then leach the copper out with sulfuric acid. Sloop's projected cost, to be shared between the federal government and Kennecott, was $13 million. Initially these plans were developed secretly, although in October 1967, the AEC held a public meting in Arizona to try and sell the idea to somewhat skeptical residents.

Project Sloop began to generate attention in mining trade journals, local Arizona newspapers, and even *Time* magazine, which led to major obstacles for Kennecott. The second half of 1967 was the most turbulent time in the global copper business since World War II; the Bureau of Mines dubbed it "the year of the strike." In the middle of the year, a large number of copper-mining labor contracts in the United States expired, and the two major unions representing tens of thousands of miners demanded company-wide negotiations with company-wide contracts, thereby greatly expanding the number of mines that would be represented by unions. The industry adamantly resisted, and by midsummer, strikes were rampant across the country and would go on for months; in September, only one copper-smelting facility was operating in the country, representing less than 2 percent of US capacity.[36] Kennecott was one of the strike's biggest targets, and union leaders saw Sloop as an opportunity to argue that using publicly owned nuclear technology to line the coffers of a single private company was wrong.

The Sloop project took on an entirely new dimension when, in early 1968, a member of Congress went public with Sloop details he said he'd obtained from Livermore. Craig Hosmer was a California Republican who served two decades in the House and later became the head of a nuclear industry trade group. Hosmer was almost certainly the most ardent government advocate of the Plowshare program; he continually and unsuccessfully introduced legislation to share Plowshare technology with private companies. He also believed that most or all of the Johnson administration was, in conjunction with various liberal allies, deliberately impeding Plowshare's progress. Denouncing the Budget Bureau, the State Department, and the Arms Control and Disarmament Agency, Hosmer charged that "these people seem to have a paranoiac distrust and abhorrence for Plowshare, which they cannot divorce in their minds from the weapons program."[37]

Given these views, it is unlikely that Hosmer gave the administration advance notice when he revealed that, true to Operation Goldfinger form, Project Sloop's copper-mining goal was partly a cover story for a plan to find gold. "Some of these Plowshare people have begun to seriously investigate the prospect of recovering gold ore in a manner similar to that already studied for recovering another metal currently in short supply, copper." And the early results were good; the AEC had found no technical barriers, according to Hosmer. "It may be possible that gold can be produced in the United States, domestically for less than $10 per ounce, perhaps considerably less . . . not in the 21st century or beyond, but within a decade or less," Hosmer declared, ironically echoing the Goldfinger enthusiasm expressed two years earlier by his Johnson White House foes.[38]

Initially, Hosmer's bombshell got no more notice than the dozens of congressional soliloquies that occur daily. But a week later, the *New York Times* published a business-section story headlined "A-Blasts Studied as Way to Expand U.S. Gold Output," and that got attention in Washington and Livermore. Immediately, an AEC official sent a telex to Livermore indicating that all work involving atomic gold mining should be coordinated with the Bureau of Mines; if Sloop hadn't begun life as an Operation Goldfinger effort, it was about to become one. There were, nonetheless, some tricky questions. One concerned the details of the "in situ" leaching process to bring the gold to the surface; another was whether irradiation would render the gold unusable. After all, a study of Project Sloop's copper application predicted that the resulting metal would be contaminated with ruthenium-106; given that isotope's half-life of one year, the copper would not be suitable for many industrial uses, such as medical equipment. Moreover, since copper is frequently recycled, a government report warned that "slightly radioactive copper will be dispersed into the copper supply of the nation."[39]

A close cousin to the idea of surfacing gold with nuclear detonations was the proposal to create gold using subatomic reactions—another passion of Alexander Sachs. Sachs had assembled a coterie of interested parties and freelance scientists who were keen to get access to government technology to perform the ultimate alchemical experiments: using nuclear energy to turn base metals into gold. And he managed to convince the US treasury secretary to take up his cause. Fowler wrote to both Udall and Atomic Energy Commission chief Glenn Seaborg, touting "well-worked-out and ingenious ideas [Sachs] has advanced concerning the potentiality for extraction of metals by means of nuclear devices." He continued: "Because of the implications of Dr. Sachs's proposal for, among other things, the present vexed international monetary situation, I am extremely anxious that [an] assessment be made—and in the swiftest possible time."[40]

The science being advocated was technically sound. For hundreds of years alchemists suspected that other metals were structurally close enough to gold to be transformed into it, using some elusive external process. Many scientists recognized that the nuclear age had in theory provided the tools. In a 1968 letter that tried to discourage this line of experimentation, Seaborg nonetheless acknowledged "other elements near gold in the periodic table can indeed be transmuted into gold by nuclear reactions." This could be done either in a nuclear reactor or in a particle accelerator. Seaborg himself, in 1980, took part in an experiment at Lawrence Berkeley National Laboratory that created gold almost as a side effect. He and colleagues bombarded foil made from bismuth with high-speed beams containing the nuclei of carbon and neon. Several neutrons were thereby stripped from the bismuth, and the result contained billions of atoms of different gold isotopes. As with so many of Operation Goldfinger's discoveries, however, the problem was the extreme limitation of the atomic scale. Seaborg summed up the problem in a press interview: "It would cost more than one quadrillion dollars per ounce to produce gold by this experiment." [41] The opinions of more sober-minded scientists in and around the Johnson administration prevailed; despite Treasury's eagerness for a subatomic solution to the gold shortage, these proposals were never put into action.

What became of Operation Goldfinger? Most aspects of Goldfinger were kept out of the public and even congressional spotlight, and those that were revealed were rarely presented as part of a broad experimental push for gold. Thus, the decline of the project was similarly piecemeal and opaque. Most of the initial experiments were one-offs and were not funded again after results came in. Individual areas of interest—such as the reopening of a viable gold mine in Cortez, Nevada—showed some success. Other projects were directionally valid over the long term; Guyana and Venezuela, for example, produce substantially more gold today than when Operation Goldfinger was eying them in the late 1960s (although neither is a world leader, and both use no more than conventional explosions to produce gold).

The plans to use nuclear detonation for gold mining never became reality. The original copper rationale for Project Sloop was unable to demonstrate its commercial viability, even with private-sector cooperation. By the early 1970s, most government scientists had scaled back their attempts to use nuclear detonations for earthmoving or mining; opposition from activist scientists and the general population became pronounced, particularly as details of radioactive fallout were made public. Of particular concern was a 1973 test in Rio Blanco, Colorado, in which a nuclear explosion was designed to stimulate natural gas production. A pipe carrying radioactive water to a disposal well sprang a leak, and the Environmental Protection Agency found gas samples from the project with one thousand times the normal background level of radioactivity. A few years later, Colorado voters amended the state constitution to prohibit any nuclear explosions in the state without prior voter approval.[42] Plowshare itself limped along until the Department of Energy was founded in 1977, after which it was defunded.

How seriously did the Johnson administration view Operation Goldfinger, and how seriously should subsequent generations view it? Alas, most of the main participants were deceased by the turn of the twenty-first century. Asked in 2014 for his view of Operation Goldfinger, Francis Bator, an economist who worked in the Johnson administration and closely advised the president on international monetary policy, implied that most of his colleagues did not believe it would ever be a serious solution to the monetary gold shortage. "It was a gimmick. It was a sideshow," he recalled.[43] At best, Bator said, Operation Goldfinger was designed as a show of force, a psychological attempt to ease world markets by hinting that the United States could tap new sources of gold if need be. These efforts might serve to buy some time while the economists and diplomats in the administration could find a palatable way to decouple the dollar from gold. Bator has a point: by 1968, Operation Goldfinger had indeed acquired a propagandistic aspect. For example, the Bureau of Mines made a public announcement in March 1968 about a "major technical breakthrough" that would dramatically increase the amount of gold produced in the United States. The technique, an aqueous chemical treatment allowing more gold to be extracted from carbonaceous ores, was certainly promising, but had only been executed in a Reno research lab. Under the best of circumstances it was years away from any commercial impact.[44]

Yet Bator's view must be balanced against the fact that Operation Goldfinger began its existence in strict secrecy; there is not much point in a show of force that no one knows about. Moreover, there were still men in Treasury, Interior, and Congress advocating Operation Goldfinger's more extreme, nuclear options even after the gold market was suspended in 1968, at which point any Goldfinger propaganda effects had been made largely irrelevant.

It was not, then, Operation Goldfinger's effectiveness (or lack thereof) that determined its ultimate irrelevance; it was, rather, the course of worldwide events. The devaluation of the British pound in late 1967 set off a series of gold-supply crises so threatening to the global economic order that no one around Johnson could afford to spend time thinking about how much gold was contained in deer antlers. By late 1967, Joe Barr would gladly have traded his struggles for the days when congressmen from gold-producing states wanted to harangue him. "In '67 when the British got in all this difficulty, everybody all over the world said, 'I don't want to hold paper money, I want to hold gold,'" Barr later recalled. "We had to meet these commitments, and we were losing gold at an enormous rate. So were all our partners. Everybody was terrified and the markets were just convulsed all through late '67 and early '68. We couldn't pass a tax bill in the United States. The British had devalued. Everybody was just petrified."[45] The long-feared currency crisis had begun.

# How you can Profit from the coming devaluation

### by Harry Browne

# CHAPTER 8

## Dueling Apocalypses

THE PLANES WERE TECHNICALLY called C-141s, but they were best known by their nickname: Starlifters. In the 1960s Starlifters were the largest cargo planes in the world, with the ability to carry a load of more than 60,000 pounds. In 1967, a typical Starlifter sortie was most likely to be carrying troops or supplies to Vietnam, but on November 29 several Starlifters had a purely economic—and confidential—mission that began at Fort Knox, the garrison of gold created by Roosevelt's Treasury Department thirty years before.

Earlier that month, the flailing British government under Labour Prime Minister Harold Wilson had taken the vertiginous step of devaluing the pound, setting off a worldwide rush to buy gold. The once-calming rules of the Gold Pool, established for the London Market in 1961, were no longer enough to match the world's insatiable appetite for gold. In the four days following the pound's devaluation, gold sales were so heavy that the Bank of England could not keep up its daily supply to the private market. On Thursday, November 23—in the United States it was Thanksgiving—the Bank of England secretly "exhausted" its supply of gold.[1] The next morning at 8 a.m.,

Harry Browne's runaway best seller, published in 1970, helped convince hundreds of thousands of Americans that an economic collapse was imminent, and recommended gold as personal financial protection, even though it was not legal for Americans to own.

a Treasury official wrote to Secretary Fowler: "It would not be an overstatement to say that panic reigns in the gold market."[2] For several days, the Bank was forced to come up with creative bureaucratic swaps to fill the demand for gold, while the US Treasury scrambled to figure out a solution.

The solution was none other than the Starlifters. Through the Military Airborne Command—which at times acted as a kind of expensive courier system for various arms of the US government— Treasury arranged for a massive, 214-ton delivery of gold out of Fort Knox. The shipment was so urgent that Treasury Secretary Fowler ordered that the "gold will be delivered from Fort Knox without prior weighing." Each Starlifter shipment was worth $100 million and cost $15,000 to execute; the bill was paid by Treasury— another creative use of the Exchange Stabilization Fund. This was, and still is, the largest known one-time shipment of gold out of the United States. There would be two more shipments of comparable size to the UK over the next few months.

The planes landed at the Royal Air Force base in Mildenhall, which had recently become a hub for US military activity after France, in a quintessential DeGaullian move, quit the military arm of NATO. Mildenhall, appropriately enough, had been in the 1940s the site of a major discovery of precious-metal objects from the Roman Empire. A group of trucks from the Bank of England awaited the plane, along with an escort of police vehicles (the police were armed, unusual for the British police at the time). This convoy carried the hundreds of tons of gold the 71 miles to London, where the gold was loaded into the courtyard of the Bank of England on Threadneedle Street.

Even more than Operation Goldfinger's desperate alchemy, the frantic, gargantuan gold shipments of late 1967 and early 1968 demonstrated a global monetary system whose logic had gone mad. Because the private market for gold overheated and threatened the world's gold supply, the United States, the world's largest holder of gold, had to use its air force to ship hundreds of tons of the metal across a vast ocean—where it was immediately snapped up by the same private market speculators who had provoked the crisis in the first place. This herculean effort was designed to bolster the theoretical value of the dollar, but it produced the opposite effect. It's not merely that the cure was worse than the disease—the medicine was actually making the system sick.

And the crisis was completely predictable—indeed it had been predicted. The US government had known for years that the British pound was vulnerable. As one Treasury official put it: "You've got a major confidence crisis in sterling about every fall on the fall, so to speak, and there was in '64, '65, '66 and then it culminated in '67."[3] President Johnson, whom the British government often solicited for personal meetings and for financial aid, viewed the problem as a lack of fiscal discipline. In a 1965 phone conversation with Federal Reserve chair William McChesney Martin, he compared Britain in his Texan twang to "a reckless boy that goes off and gets drunk and writes checks on his father, and he can honor two or three or four of 'em [then] finally call him in, and tell him, 'Now we've got to work this out.' . . . Time's coming we got to turn him down."[4]

There was a persistent fear that if the pound got too sick its contagion could not be stopped—its devaluation could damage the dollar and inflame the international monetary system. In 1966, the Federal Reserve prepared a contingency study warning of "dire consequences for the international economy" following a drop in the pound's value at between 10 percent and 20 percent. The study, which was widely discussed among Johnson's economic advisers, divided American policy options into three main categories: maintain the status quo; end the universal gold-dollar convertibility but try to maintain the value of the dollar by splitting the public and private markets for gold; or exploit the opportunity to "get the gold and balance of payments monkey off our back."

The pound's devaluation seemed increasingly probable by the spring and summer of 1967, due to three shocks to the British economy.[5] First, the British decision to join the European Common

Market, the precursor to the European Union, seemed likely to create a balance-of-payments deficit and set off a round of speculative bets against the pound. Second, the catastrophic closure of the Suez Canal in the anxious time following the Six-Day War between Arabs and Israelis created substantial delays for British imports. Finally, dock strikes in September created delays on the export side. The days of the British Empire were truly coming to an end, and there were limits to how much the rest of the world could help. Prime Minister Harold Wilson and his chancellor James Callaghan sought, in October and early November, assistance from the United States, IMF, and other quarters, but the billions they sought were not enough to stem off crisis.

By early to mid-November, a sense of resigned inevitability about the pound's demise had set in at the Johnson White House. On the 12th, Treasury Secretary Henry Fowler described to the president a meeting he'd had with a British diplomat: "They [are] at the end of the line, unless they have assurance of substantial long-term credit soon. They may be forced to devalue—perhaps within a week."[6] When the British ambassador requested to see the president on Friday, November 17, Johnson knew what was coming: the British government had been forced to devalue the pound, from $2.80 to the dollar to $2.40. "It was still like hearing that an old friend who has been ill has to undergo a serious operation," Johnson recalled in a memoir. "However much you expect it, the news is still a heavy blow."[7] (Johnson could count himself somewhat fortunate; the IMF received "little more than an hour's notice of [sterling's] devaluation.")[8]

That fall, Federal Reserve official Charles Coombs had taken to describing sterling devaluation and gold markets as "twin time bombs"—if one went off, it would certainly detonate the other. And detonate they did. Immediately upon the announcement of sterling's devaluation, Johnson issued the requisite statement: "I reaffirm unequivocally the pledge of the United States to buy and sell gold to foreign official holders at the existing price of $35 an ounce." But the effort lacked any power over the markets. Over the weekend after the devaluation was announced, multiple nations announced their own devaluations, like falling dominoes: Barbados, Cyprus, Denmark, Hong Kong, Israel, Jamaica, Spain, and New Zealand. In British-controlled Hong Kong, devaluation caused small shops to raise their prices overnight by as much as 25 percent. On the next weekday, Monday, November 20, Japan's stock market experienced its largest one-day drop since World War II. Banks and stock exchanges in Britain remained closed to handle the devaluation aftermath, as did the London gold market. Nonetheless, speculators rushed to buy gold, certain that the devaluation fate that befell Britain and other nations would recur in Washington. Even on the usually tiny private gold markets—chiefly in Zurich and Paris—some $27 million in gold changed hands, many days' worth of normal trading. By Wednesday, with the London market open, the volume of gold traded nearly quadrupled, to $106 million. The next day it reached $142 million—and that was when the Bank of England told the US Treasury that it could no longer back up the market's daily transactions.

Even with the massive Starlifter gold deliveries, there seemed to be no way that the Gold Pool could stay intact. The year 1966 had already proved anxious, and the first ten months of 1967 were worse. On seven separate occasions during that period, Pool members had had to inject payments of $50 million's worth of gold into the system. Making matters worse, France let it be known in late November that it had abandoned the Gold Pool; in fact, it had done so months before, but the timing seemed calculated to weaken the US position. France's withdrawal from the group meant that of every $50 million payment the Pool made, about $30 million came from the United States. The sterling devaluation brought this teetering system to a collapse. In the week preceding devaluation, Gold Pool losses amounted to a heavy $68 million—that is, in a matter of days, the Pool lost more money than any country (other than the United States) had put into the Pool when it was established in 1961. In the week after devaluation, the losses were a staggering $578 million.[9] The London cupboard was bare—every single ounce of gold being sold on the teeming private market was effectively coming straight out of the government coffers of the United States and larger Western European nations.

Even that dire situation did not represent the full extent of the United States' gold exposure. The international jitters that devaluation created gave other countries even more incentive to buy gold directly from the US Treasury, and in late November, an unusually large gold order came from an unexpected source, none other than Algeria. The country barely had a functioning economy, having only recently emerged from a long bloody war of independence from France. It was led by a military "revolutionary council"; its relations with the United States were, as the *New York Times* put it, "cool if not verging on the hostile." Of course, Algeria had as much right as any nation to convert its dollars to gold, but the amount—$150 million—alarmed US government officials.[10] In addition to the sheer size of the order, representing some 4 percent of Algeria's GDP at the time, Johnson administration officials feared that France was covertly pushing Francophone Africa to join its efforts to cash in dollars for US gold.

After a brief calm in early December, the London gold market boiled up again by the middle of the month; between December 11 and 15, the Gold Pool nations lost more than half a billion dollars. The central bankers of nearly all the Gold Pool members let the Federal Reserve know that they were on the brink of abandoning the Pool. The time for decisive action had come. The administration had assembled a balance-of-payments cabinet committee, and its meetings in December 1967 took on an increasing sense of alarm.

In addition, the administration had for weeks been preparing to battle with Capitol Hill on lifting the "gold cover," the requirement that the government had to hold a given amount of gold to prop up the value of its currency. Johnson was skeptical that the budget-hostile Congress would give him what he wanted, especially as he was also trying to push through a "vitally needed tax bill." The cautious Treasury Secretary Fowler believed Congress would cooperate after running through various partial solutions (reducing, say, the gold cover amount from 25 percent to 10 percent). The committee insisted that much more needed to be done, whether Congress liked it or not. It recommended sweeping, unprecedented reductions in money flowing out of the United States, particularly tightening foreign lending, restraining US corporate investment abroad, and reducing foreign aid. These steps were bound to be unpopular. As historian Francis Gavin put it, "For an embattled president entering an election year, this plan was nothing short of political suicide."[11]

Not surprisingly, a frustrated Johnson resisted the plan for as long as he could. The Vietnam War was devouring nearly all of his time and energy. Paying for bombs and napalm was in fact worsening the balance-of-payments crisis, but not to fight the war seemed to Johnson impossible. Through late December, Johnson still perceived gold and the balance of payments as an issue to be worked out by his staff. Moreover, he resented that the thanks the United States got for supporting the world economically and militarily was the imminent threat that its currency would be crushed and its gold reserves wiped out. While his economic advisers grew increasingly anxious through December, Johnson had no initial intention of spending the Christmas holiday huddling with them to deal with the balance of payments. He had committed to attend the December 22 funeral of Australian prime minister Harold Holt, a personal friend and Vietnam ally who had died in a swimming accident. Johnson extended that duty into a 4½-day, 27,000-mile trip that also included a Christmas meeting with Pope Paul VI and, unbeknownst to most of the world, a failed attempt to negotiate peace in Vietnam during meetings in Pakistan, Thailand, and elsewhere.[12]

Johnson was finally moved to public, personal action by a December 22 telegram—he was either in Australia or at the US air base in Korat, Thailand when he received it—from his top domestic aide Joseph Califano. The balance-of-payments gap had widened in the first nine months of 1967, despite improvements in trade; the biggest culprit was net military spending abroad, up more than $500 million. The fourth quarter, however, "threatens to turn the year into a disaster." International speculators on the dollar were a menace that the administration couldn't begin to control. Johnson's advisers, led by Treasury Secretary Fowler, were pushing several remedies: a "border tax adjustment," which would tax imports and subsidize exports by 2 percent or more; a per diem tourist tax of $6 a day on trips abroad; and strong disincentives for US companies to invest abroad.

A clearly agitated Johnson sent back a long response the next day. He lamented Britain's "inept handling" of the pound devaluation. He hated the import tax and predicted that taxing Americans for traveling abroad was "certain to be used by Republicans in an election year—therefore damaging to the president." He sent the committee back to examine options like how best to prevent investment abroad, and to get European nations to pay more for their defense—a not very popular Christmas gift to his staff.

On December 30, the commerce and treasury secretaries flew to the president's private ranch in Johnson City, Texas, along with several top advisers and the majority and minority leaders of the House and Senate. They briefed the president on the bitter medicine he would need to deliver. Many were skeptical that the program could pass Congress, but on New Year's Day, Johnson, speaking from his ranch, issued one of the strangest requests to the American people that any president has ever made. The speech was simultaneously sweeping and contradictory. The president started off by underscoring the interdependence of the global economy: "Your job, the prosperity of your farm or business, depends directly or indirectly on what happens in Europe, Asia, Latin America or Africa." Then in the next breath, he exhorted Americans to cut back their financial ties with the rest of the world.

That morning, the president had signed an executive order transferring to Secretary of Commerce Alexander Trowbridge the authority that the president normally had to regulate foreign investment. These powers would be used to slow and cap most foreign investment. In particular, Johnson said, "new direct investment outflows to countries in continental Western Europe and other developed nations not heavily dependent on our capital will be stopped in 1968." It was, Trowbridge acknowledged, the first time in history that the US government placed mandatory controls on private investments overseas.[13] Banks and financial institutions were also asked to cut back their foreign lending by $500 million.

But by far the most unusual request was that American citizens not leave the Western Hemisphere until 1970 unless they absolutely had to. "It is important to the country," Johnson said, "that every citizen reassess his travel plans and not travel outside of this hemisphere except under the most important, urgent and necessary conditions." Here, too, Johnson's pronouncements seemed contradictory. On the one hand, he presented the travel restrictions as voluntary. "We believe that the most effective action . . . would be for the citizens themselves to realize that their traveling abroad and spending their dollars abroad is damaging their country. If they just have a trip in them that must be made, if they could make it in this hemisphere, or see their own country, it would be very helpful."[14] On the other hand, he explicitly said he'd need authority from Congress: "We do expect that it will be necessary to have certain adjustments made in our present travel policy, and we will ask the Congress to do it."

If it had ever been possible to consider Vietnam as a small, temporary engagement requiring few sacrifices from American civilians, that view was erased by a president making pleas on New Year's Day. Predictably, the travel industry and those whose businesses relied on international travel criticized the measures as "disastrous" and "hysterical."[15] Others mocked the seeming pettiness of the proposals from what was supposed to be the world's most powerful country. In a column for *Newsweek*, economist Milton Friedman—who advocated a "floating" dollar with a value based on its market relationship to other currencies—derided the administration as incompetent and its remedies as risible. "How low we have fallen! The United States, the land of the free, prohibits its businessmen from investing abroad and requests its citizens not to show their faces or open their pocketbooks in foreign ports. . . . Are we wasting so much of our substance on foreign travel that we must be cajoled by our betters to stay home? Total spending on foreign travel in 1967 was less than 1 per cent of total consumer spending."[16]

Allies abroad, however, were largely placated by a coordinated administration lobbying mission. Three State Department officials took Treasury officials and economists on missions to Asia, Australia, Canada, and Western Europe to explain the US plan to address the balance of payments. They found general acceptance— even though allies were anxious about some of the proposed remedies, at least the administration finally seemed committed to do something. Everywhere the delegates flew, however, central bankers and governments asked about removing the gold cover, and insisted that "a successful program depends on our ability to get additional taxes and to cut Government expenditures."[17] And while Congress was not scheduled to return to business for two weeks, leading legislators hailed the president's pronouncements and promised swift action.

The measures announced on New Year's Day were unlikely to reverse the long-term balance-of-payments problem—for that, Johnson would need pointed congressional action, as he laid out in his January 17 State of the Union address. In the meantime, Johnson's advisers set to accomplish as much as they could using executive action alone. For weeks, some of the most powerful figures in the White House debated arcane questions, such as how to define normal business expenses in order to enforce the international travel ban (which would never be enacted anyway).[18] Still, for a few weeks, it seemed as if the pronouncements were working. The demands abroad for US gold subsided and the dollar strengthened in foreign exchange markets. The private gold market returned to some sense of normal, and in the first few days of January the Gold Pool actually took in several millions of dollars.

The White House was grateful to buy time. But the new stability was hardly enough to alleviate the White House gloom, especially in late January as the North Vietnamese attacked scores of South Vietnamese towns in the calamitous Tet Offensive. In early February, British prime minister Harold Wilson visited Washington, primarily to show his skeptical population that he could speak out against America's war in Vietnam. During a private White House session, Johnson showed Wilson a brief analysis that had been prepared for him by Barbara Ward, a prolific economic author and journalist prominent on both sides of the Atlantic. Born in Britain and later knighted as Lady Jackson, her work, much of which dealt with developing nations, had a conspicuous appeal for Johnson. The president once said that Ward's were the only books he read, and said of one of her volumes, "I read it like I do the Bible."

If the Ward memo that Johnson showed Wilson had a biblical aspect, however, it was Old Testament. In the wake of sterling's devaluation and the continued assault on the dollar, Ward warned of a global depression that could effectively destroy the Western capitalist system:

> A situation is brewing up in the world economy with some dangerous overtones of the 1929/31 disaster. If a crisis were to occur, the economic consequences might be so considerable a dislocation of world trade that depression and massive unemployment could appear in Europe and deflation spread quickly to the developing continents. This in turn would have profound political effects. The Russians might scent the long-hoped-for failure of capitalism and revert to

hard-line adventurism and hostility. Despair in the poorer countries would cancel out present disillusion with China and its cultural revolution. The world could tip dangerously away from its present not wholly ineffective "coexistence."

Ward's prophecy seemed only confirmed by the external and internal chaos of early 1968: the Tet Offensive in Vietnam, the resignation of Defense Secretary Robert McNamara, and North Korea's seizure of the USS *Pueblo* and its crew of 83 men, many of whom were beaten and tortured. On February 8, the Federal Reserve Bank of New York announced that the monetary gold stock had dropped $100 million in the previous week and stood at $11.884 billion, the lowest point in thirty years.

And whatever minor peace the New Year's pronouncement and State of the Union address had bought disappeared on February 28, when Senator Jacob Javits lobbed a grenade into the White House's plans. Javits, a liberal New York Republican who indicated that he was reflecting the views of many Wall Street bankers, called for the United States to stop making gold payments to other countries. Without such a measure, he said, "we stand in a very grave economic danger . . . of losing materially the remainder of our gold stock and materially jeopardizing faith and confidence in the American dollar and the ability of the dollar to stand as the standard international unit of currency in the world." The response of the administration to the long-standing balance-of-payments issue, Javits scolded, "has been singularly free of both realism and imagination." The balding avuncular Javits posed on the Senate floor a question that almost no one with insider knowledge had been willing to utter publicly: What happens when the gold stock runs out? Preserving the terms of the Bretton Woods monetary system had shifted from a means to a stable postwar world to an end in itself—but as hundreds of millions of dollars were being flown out of Treasury every month or week, what was the end in sight? The longer the United States put off terminating the dollar-gold convertibility—an action Javits said "is probably inevitable in any case"—the smaller the gold pile to protect would be.

When markets and foreign governments reacted with alarm, the administration appeared to be caught off guard. Yet Javits may have done Johnson's advisers a considerable favor. By this point, many in the White House agreed that the folly of shipping America's gold abroad had to stop, but they were still petrified to take action that could deepen the sense of crisis. Javits's pronouncement, however, was impossible to ignore. It was taken, rightly or wrongly, as a signal of future government policy, which caused Americans to buy gold and silver stocks and investors abroad to snap up bullion at a pace comparable to November's. On Friday, March 1, the Pool lost $90 million in gold trading, and $53 million the following Monday. Pool members signaled that they could not sustain participation much longer. Italy had to buy gold from the United States in January just to cover the amount it lost in trading; Belgium and the Netherlands also looked shaky. Would-be experts were whispering about all kinds of cataclysmic scenarios, some of which echoed Barbara Ward's bleak warnings: South Africa, which had already reduced the amount of gold it made available to the private market, would switch from selling its dominant gold supply in London to Paris; the United States was preparing to make a massive withdrawal from the IMF to cover the gold losses from the pound's devaluation. It was impossible for anyone even to keep track of all the tales moving the markets, much less verify or refute them. "The world is still feeding on each and every rumour that comes its way," lamented *The Economist*.[19]

The rich countries of the West were looking to the United States to solve their shared problems, but a gridlocked Congress in an election year made comprehensive fiscal reform impossible. Some other fix, some rearrangement in gold's relationship to the world's money, would have to do. On March 8, national security adviser Walt Rostow said to the president in a memo: "My own feeling is that the moment of truth is close upon us." Less than a week later, on March 13, with Pool losses for the day around $200 million, Federal Reserve chairman Martin phoned Europe's central bankers and told them the United States might have to close the gold markets. On that day, Vice President Hubert Humphrey wrote to a colleague: "We literally have to frighten people by telling them the sorry facts—the danger to the dollar, the possibility of severe budget cuts, the necessity of financing the war, and the danger of inflation."[20]

That set the stage for one of the most tumultuous days in modern financial history. It began the morning of March 14, when Treasury Secretary Fowler appeared before the Senate Finance Committee. He testified that the constant bleeding of gold "threatens the very preservation of the international monetary system as we know it today." He also revealed that the Federal Reserve was going to hike its discount rate, causing an immediate selloff on the New York stock market; the Dow Jones Industrial Average saw its biggest one-day drop for the year in what was already shaping up as a gloomy quarter for stocks.

A few hours later, the Senate took a vote to lift the gold cover on Federal Reserve notes, thereby freeing up some $10 billion in gold. Failure to pass the bill would almost certainly further crash markets around the globe, yet the acrimonious relationship between Congress and the White House meant that the outcome was far from certain. In February, the House bill removing the gold cover passed by a precarious margin of nine votes. That morning, Senate majority leader Mike Mansfield called Treasury and warned that he wasn't sure he had the votes to pass the bill; there was also a risk that the bill could be delayed or even buried by the amendment process. The day before the Senate vote on the White House bill, another bill nearly passed which would have retained a 12.5 percent gold cover. This measure was especially urged by the westerners who'd been pressuring Treasury and the White House to do something about gold since the beginning of the decade. Colorado's two Republican senators warned of "grave dangers" if the gold cover was removed. Not willing to take any chances, Treasury Secretary Fowler and Federal Reserve chairman Martin paid a highly unusual visit to Senate majority leader Mike Mansfield, hoping to persuade him to push through the House bill with no amendments.

Johnson must have longed for the days of FDR passing financial legislation with near unanimity. Although the bill was presented as an emergency measure, it barely squeaked through the Senate— 39 to 37—a far closer margin than the White House had planned for.[21] More telling than the vote itself was the manner in which the administration's economic reasoning was by turns isolated and rejected. In the final days before the bill's passage, an unusual coalition emerged: conservatives from both parties teamed up with liberal critics of the Vietnam War, presenting the gold-cover bill as a feeble attempt to deal with years of failed spending priorities. Many Republicans and some Democrats echoed Javits's criticism from two weeks earlier;[22] they argued that lifting the gold cover would merely make more gold available to private speculators. George McGovern of South Dakota—his state had a significant gold-mining industry, and he would become the Democratic nominee for president in 1972—typified the connection that congressional liberals made between the gold cover bill and Vietnam spending. Transcripts of executive sessions released in 2010 show that by March 1968, many senators had come to have profound doubts about the viability of the Vietnam War and the truthfulness of the Johnson administration about the war, going back to the Tonkin Gulf incident. To them, the gold-cover bill was a tacit admission that Johnson's foreign adventures had been reckless. "Asking Congress to lift the gold cover is not a cure for the balance of payments; it is a temporary device that will simply further open up our dwindling gold reserves to foreign claimants," McGovern said. "One of the few leverages Congress has left to restore a greater measure of commonsense to American policy is to deny the continuing drain of our gold and to reject the unwise tax increases now being requested to fuel the costs of globalism."[23]

Most Republicans who spoke up agreed. The near-psychic bond that McKinley-era Republicans had felt to gold was almost nowhere on display—it is striking how few Republicans in 1968 proclaimed any fealty to one of the last vestiges of a currency backed by gold. Instead, most took the position that the Johnson administration was doing too little to address fiscal and economic issues that undermined the dollar—such as inflation, the failure to balance the budget, and runaway Vietnam spending. Strom Thurmond, a Republican who'd been a Democrat until 1964, was typical of the opposition: "I cannot believe that removal of the gold cover will restore confidence. In my judgment, it will be interpreted abroad as a sign of weakness—as a sign of our trying to take the easy way out, rather than making the more difficult decision to take the necessary steps to halt the decline in the dollar's purchasing power."

Whether Thurmond's interpretation was correct or not, it was undeniable that, to use the phrase that would catch on in Chicago a few months later, the whole world was watching. While the Senate debated, gold counters at Swiss banks were overwhelmed with orders. A Zurich dealer told a reporter, "The gold buying has reached such proportions that we are not taking any more orders. The physical stamina of my bank employees has reached and now passed permissible limits."[24] Swiss banks closed their gold trading two hours early, just to stay on top of purchase orders. In Paris, a US official cabled to Washington that "mobs" had taken over the Bourse, and 40 tons of gold traded that day in Paris—more than fifty times the average day's volume. In Brussels, dealers simply ran out of gold. Would-be buyers were told they would need to wait three months, with no guarantee of delivery.

At 5:30 pm East Coast time, the Open Market Committee of the Federal Reserve Bank held a hastily scheduled conference call.

The committee's special manager Charles Coombs told the assembled bankers that "the international financial system was moving toward a crisis more dangerous than any since 1931." The committee then authorized a series of changes to its currency swap arrangements, in hopes of preventing a run on the dollar in the next day's foreign exchange markets.

Across the Atlantic, British prime minister Wilson spent the night trying to keep up with the rapid fire of central bank signals, which increased his fear that a new global depression was imminent. At midnight his time, he sent a despairing cable to Johnson, which historians have largely overlooked. In it, he invoked Ward's grim prophecy that Johnson had shared with him: "We must both realise that we may tonight have reached the situation you foresaw when you showed me, in the White House last month, the short document you had received, envisaging a remorseless development of events which could land us back in 1931. At that time you thought it might come through the weakness of sterling. In fact it has come through the scramble for gold."[25] And Wilson's dark night was not yet over. He and his home secretary Roy Jenkins went to Buckingham Palace to see the queen, and at 1 a.m. announced an emergency bank holiday for the next day. At 1:45 a.m. Wilson called a meeting at 10 Downing Street with top economic ministers. They had to manage the fallout that would occur in a few hours, as the world learned that the London gold market would be closed for an indefinite period.

Over the next forty-eight hours the administration reached out to every European government, summoning central bankers to an emergency weekend negotiation in Washington. When embassies abroad reported initial difficulty making contact, Secretary of State Dean Rusk instructed: "You must track down these men at all costs." Every major European economy except France was represented in the hastily assembled meeting in the Federal Reserve Building on Constitution Avenue, as well as representatives from the Fed, Treasury, International Monetary Fund, and Bank of

International Settlements. The ten men in the negotiations collectively controlled some $30 billion in combined gold reserves, or three-quarters of the world's monetary supply. Outside the building, Vietnam War protestors handed dollar bills and apples to reporters and shouted that the United States was spending "$1000 a second to destroy Vietnam."[26]

Every now and then, a crisis atmosphere can be very beneficial; a sense of imminent doom helps focus the minds of sparring principals, and minimizes interference from secondary considerations. In this instance, ten men in a massive conference room—two stories high and sealed like a bank vault—managed to overcome years of squabbling and singlehandedly dismantle the Pool arrangement that had governed the gold market since 1961, as well as mortally wound the Bretton Woods system. Although most elements of the eventual agreement had existed on paper for some time, the pact that emerged was remarkable, given the tight time frame. The Gold Pool would be dissolved but, somewhat surprisingly, the top central banks agreed that the gold they already possessed was sufficient to meet the world's monetary needs. In the future there would be, in noncrisis periods, no need for the world's wealthiest nations to buy and sell gold in private markets. If central banks needed to transfer wealth between themselves, they could still use the gold they had at the rate of $35 an ounce, and if the world required more liquid funds in the whole system, it could use the Special Drawing Rights created with the IMF, the development of which all parties now agreed to accelerate. The arrangement also meant that future gold produced would not be needed to prop up world currencies—it could all go to private investors, and to artistic and industrial use. The US Treasury would no longer buy gold from private sources, nor sell it to licensed artistic or industrial users; those transactions would take place privately. And the private market could do whatever it wanted, since its daily fluctuations would no longer threaten the world's currencies.

The administration was surprised at how cooperative the jittery Europeans were, although skeptical about results. Joseph Barr, who was a few months away from becoming treasury secretary, recalled, "None of us thought the darned thing would work."[27] Two weeks later, on April Fool's Day, the London market reopened and not surprisingly went up, if modestly. By midyear, gold was often trading at more than $40 an ounce. Those who had bought gold in the late '50s and early '60s, expecting some kind of gold-dollar revaluation, had finally been rewarded, although not spectacularly—at least not through 1971 or so.

But the long-term prospects for the hastily agreed-upon gold system were poor. The two-tier plan was, as historian Francis J. Gavin called it, a "fiction" and an "obvious gimmick."[28] Declaring that gold has one value in a given setting and another value in another setting is unsustainable and potentially destabilizing, because it invites speculators to take advantage of the spread between the two. Even Europe's central bankers would be tempted to tap the value in their vaults if the private price of gold rose high enough. Moreover, the world's largest gold producer, South Africa, had a heavy interest in maintaining gold's role in the international monetary system. Since it had never been a member of the Gold Pool to begin with, South Africa did not feel itself bound by any rules, and the two-tier market had no force of law behind it. And so, just a few weeks into the existence of the two-tier gold market, South Africa asked to purchase about $35 million worth of British sterling in exchange for gold, and also requested to sell gold to the IMF. Inside the Treasury Department, officials recognized that there was a "loophole," and South Africa was emerging as a major threat to the two-tier system they had created in crisis.[29]

The failure to shape a more coherent global monetary policy did not stem from a lack of ideas or determination within the Johnson administration. Neither was there insurmountable resistance from most other nations; if anything, the crisis mentality of late 1967 and 1968 created a shared sense of mission among the central bankers and governments whose money mattered most to the world. For all its evident flaws, the two-tier gimmick was one that most major players had an incentive to honor (France, which had incentive to violate it, had by early 1968 lost much of its influence in the international monetary market).

What Johnson could not achieve was the genuine consent of Congress, even within his own party and its historic legislative majorities. The gold-cover legislation limped past the finish line with none of the moral rallying that Roosevelt had once enjoyed. Anything more comprehensive was not even worth proposing. By 1968, the Vietnam War had so distorted the nation's spending and politics that the range of possible financial options had narrowed to a point of near irrelevance. Before the month was out, Johnson would announce his decision not to seek reelection. He famously framed his failure for historian Doris Kearns Goodwin: "I knew from the start that if I left the woman I love—the Great Society—in order to fight that bitch of a war, then I would lose everything. All my programs. All my hopes. All my dreams." The same could be said for any hope for a rational, understandable, and popularly supported policy toward gold and American currency. Johnson's desperate gold strategy proved once again that when America needs to choose between its wars, its sense of foreign supremacy, economic well-being, and gold-backed currency, it's gold that always gives way.

To the world, the two-tier gold system meant that the dollar and not gold was now the mechanism of exchange. To the American nation, it meant that for the first time since the eighteenth century, there was no established relationship between gold and the dollar. There was no fixed price between them, and the market price established daily in London would directly affect almost no one who was obeying the law. There continued to be, from the citizen's point of view, no guaranteed conversion of gold into dollars.

Even when FDR took the United States off the gold standard in the 1930s, there had remained a mandatory quantity of gold sitting in a vault propping up the dollar. With the gold cover now removed, even that abstract relationship was gone.

And for Americans and their money, the unmooring of gold from money led many to seek protection against the falling dollar. Newspaper financial pages in 1968 were filled with anxious analyses of even far-flung investment vehicles, such as autographs and art nouveau objects—which were booming thanks to the aesthetics of psychedelia—but there proved to be few foolproof methods. Investments in metal made some historical sense, but beyond an initial and relatively modest price boost in the spring, it was not immediately clear what would happen to gold—gold's year-end closing price in both 1969 and 1970 would end up dropping more than 5 percent each year—nor how much it mattered, given that it was still illegal for Americans to own gold at home or abroad. Gold's price response to the establishment of the two-tier gold system may have been muted by the fact that, for goldbugs, the end of gold prohibition was the shoe that didn't drop. One gold enthusiast had reasoned that, as soon as the 25 percent gold cover was dropped, "it seemed logical that the legal prohibition to the ownership of gold by US citizens would be removed simultaneously. If our Treasury considers gold worth less than paper, it can scarcely care who owns it."[30] Yet this removal did not occur, and there is scant evidence that the Johnson administration seriously contemplated it.

Investors seeking to protect their assets were left in a kind of limbo. The metal habit retained its allure. Millions of Americans held on to or even actively hoarded the pre-1966 silver coins; with silver trading at more than $2 an ounce in 1968, the old silver dollars, half-dollars, dimes, and quarters were worth substantially more than their face value. For a time banks would take the silver at market value as collateral on loans, but that practice ceased by mid-1968. Silver hoarders were left holding a currency that couldn't be spent at its metallic value and couldn't legally be melted down. Not that some didn't try: Secret Service agents arrested three men in April 1968 in an airplane hangar near Tucson, Arizona, with two tons of silver dimes and quarters and a smelter. Charges against them, however, were thrown out.

No one, including the world's most powerful financial authorities, could say with complete confidence what this new, post–Bretton Woods world would look like. Just as the demonetization of silver in the 1870s had created anger and charges of conspiracy, the idea of currency not backed by metal set off a wave of anxious, even dire predictions. Since the earliest days of gold prohibition under FDR, there had been critics who argued that the continued devaluation of the dollar was a recipe for economic doom—and the 1968 gold crisis increased the volume and urgency of their message. The eternal paper-money doomsayer Franz Pick, for example, found new popularity following the gold crisis—in August 1969 he published a feature-length essay on gold in *Playboy*, a magazine not normally associated with monetary policy. But gold advocates also began to adopt new guises. In some cases, arguments for monetary gold added intellectual heft through association with the Austrian school of economics. In other cases, these views overlapped with the radical conservative, and sometimes conspiratorial, critique of American society offered by, among others, James True Associates in the 1930s and the John Birch Society in the late 1950s. Just as the late 1800s saw a ferment of pamphleteering for and against metallic currency, the mid-1960s to early 1970s saw a blossoming of the "hard money" school into the political and commercial mainstream. Many of the leading figures of the hard-money movement worked or wrote for William F. Buckley's conservative magazine *National Review*. The combination of scholarship, advocacy, and investment advice provided millions of Americans with a framework—however frightening at times—to understand the unprecedented economic and social convulsions around them.

One prominent cornerstone of the hard-money edifice was a brief essay called "Gold and Economic Freedom," which appeared in 1966 in *The Objectivist* newsletter published by the iconic libertarian novelist and philosopher Ayn Rand. The author was Alan Greenspan, the clarinet-playing economist who had become part of Rand's inner circle. The article, which a Greenspan biographer later called "probably his most incendiary essay," was a full-scale attack on government's natural inclination to spend beyond its means. "Deficit spending is simply a scheme for the confiscation of wealth," Greenspan insisted. "Gold stands in the way of this insidious process." These views gained traction at the time, but would become difficult for Greenspan to defend two decades later, when he would take over the Federal Reserve, which props up the largest paper money supply in world history.

The most intellectually fertile work of this era was a sixty-page pamphlet entitled *What Has Government Done to Our Money?*, published in 1964 by the influential economist and historian Murray Rothbard. He offered a sweeping historical view of money, arguing not only that government control of money was a destructive and toxic appropriation of individual freedom, but that any libertarian-conservative vision would be limited in impact unless it tried to remove government's chokehold over money. Part of Rothbard's argument grew out of his study of the "wildcat banking" period of the 1800s, which had resulted in massive bank closings and subsequent economic damage. While many historians had viewed the period as evidence that banking needed to be tightly regulated, Rothbard's study of the period argued that it was a healthy purge of a sick financial system that had been created by government interference.

Government's money monopoly could be replaced, Rothbard argued, with a currency regime of gold (and possibly other metals), in which coins could be privately minted and traded. In situations where physical gold was impractical, gold-warehouse receipts could be used for trade. The free market would handle any issues of fraud and coin degradation that emerged. Although his arguments were logically presented and well documented, Rothbard's rhetoric veered toward the martial. "Government has, step by step, invaded the free market and seized complete control over the monetary system," Rothbard wrote. "The slow but certain seizure of the monetary reins has been used to a) inflate the economy at a pace decided by government; and b) bring about socialistic direction of the entire economy."[31] Rothbard transplanted a scholarly version of Andrew Jackson's absolute rejection of paper money and central banking into a Cold War context, thereby issuing a radical challenge to American conservatives—if you don't advocate the abolition of government-backed money, you are enabling socialism. The effect was explosive; as the economist and investment adviser Mark Skousen wrote, "What *The Communist Manifesto* was to Marxists, Rothbard's *What Has Government Done* was to the hard-money movement."[32]

To Rothbard's revolutionaries, corroboration was everywhere to be seen in the mid-'60s. One devotee was Neil McCaffrey, a *National Review* contributor who left a job in mainstream book publishing in 1964 to publish books through Arlington House and the Conservative Book Club. Many of these were conservative tracts—one successful volume was *Quotations from Chairman Bill: The Best of William F. Buckley, Jr.*—as well as titles that appealed to McCaffrey's passion for jazz and classic movies. McCaffrey began to publish books advocating "hard money" as a reaction to the government removal of silver from nickels and dimes in the mid-1960s. The first two such books were written by William F. Rickenbacker, an investment adviser who was also a senior editor at the *National Review*. Rickenbacker's father was a decorated war pilot who founded Eastern Airlines; William achieved some notoriety in 1960 when he was prosecuted for refusing to fill out a census form, having declared it an illegal search of his home. He published a book called *Wooden Nickels* in 1966. Rickenbacker argued that "future writers . . . will no doubt agree that the event [the removal of silver from quarters and dimes] was one of peculiar importance." In Rickenbacker's view, government meddling with coins had pushed American money off an historic cliff: "For the first time since 1792, we are on a money backed by nothing better than the politician's pledge."[33] This was *before* the 1968 gold crisis; he followed up with a similar volume called *Death of the Dollar* in 1968.

As the decade progressed, there was something ironic about Arlington House's fervor for small government; the company that bought it in 1968, Computer Applications Incorporated, had built its fortune through government contracts from the military and NASA. But Arlington House and its hard-money advocates hit pay dirt when they managed to translate the movement's more abstract ideas into everyday financial realities, with more than a tinge of Chicken Little. The man for the job was Harry Browne, a Tennessee-based investment adviser; if Rothbard was the Marx of hard money, Browne was its Lenin, a tireless synthesizer and proselytizer. Born in New York City, Browne had grown up in Los Angeles, the son of a musician, film composer, and radio personality on the Columbia Broadcasting System. His parents had met at the New York City radio station WABC, and Browne's father wrote and performed 1920s programs such as "The Cellar Knights," which featured two African American janitors, and "Tramp Tramp Tramp," which chronicled hobo life. He was later the producer of the pioneering radio musical-comedy show "The Spike Jones Show." Harry Browne quit junior college after two weeks, noting later that he "couldn't stay awake in class." He tried his hand at editing conservative magazines and then writing a weekly syndicated newspaper column, which ran in dozens of smaller papers in the West and Midwest (regular publishers of Browne's column included the *San Marino (CA) Tribune*, *Lima (OH) News*, and *Pampa (TX) Daily News*).

Browne spent a great deal of time absorbing libertarian and laissez-faire economic thinking—first and foremost Rothbard, whom he said provided "the most important help" for his writing on money. Borrowing from Rothbard, for example, Browne popularized the notion that all paper money—whether it is called "dollar" or "franc" or whatever—should properly be called "money substitute" because it takes the place of the stated equivalent amount of gold, the only "real" money. Under such circumstances, and because only a small amount of gold can be added to the world's usable supply in any given year, any economy that grows at more than about 2 percent a year is guaranteed to produce inflation. From the writer Henry Hazlitt, Browne absorbed the lesson that government officials will often lie or dissemble on crucial issues regarding currency and devaluation.

Browne's intellectual interests took him further afield. He was influenced by a group of entrepreneurial California aerospace engineers who became involved in the insurance and brokerage business, and also founded a school devoted to laissez-faire thought. Although heavily influenced by Austrian theorists such as Ludwig von Mises, they rejected the self-description "libertarian" in favor of the classical sense of "liberal." The spiritual leader of the group was Andrew Galambos, an anarchist whose views were challenged even within libertarian circles. Galambos was a Hungarian émigré who became an astrophysicist planning flight paths for nuclear missiles; he also had a side business selling securities and insurance, and later taught physics at Whittier College. In the early 1960s, Galambos founded a private research and teaching organization called the Free Enterprise Institute, where he taught a political philosophy known as "volitional science."[34] Galambos embraced a view of intellectual property so severe that he prohibited his students from disseminating his ideas; reportedly every time he used the word *liberty* he put a nickel in a jar as a royalty payment to the descendants of Thomas Paine, whom he believed had coined the word.[35] Browne wrote that Galambos "had a profound effect on thousands of individuals who took his courses" and inspired him to write all his books.

Even these eccentrics did not represent the limits of Harry Browne's affinities. Like Galambos, Browne put a value on direct teaching to individuals, on top of his regular newspaper writing. To presumably wealthy clients in Hollywood and Long Beach, California, Browne taught multiday, in-depth seminars with titles such as "The Economics of Freedom" and "The Art of Profitable Living" beginning in about 1966. Through these seminars Browne developed a taste for what would get and hold an audience's attention and tapped into much of the fashionable thinking of the era. For example, Browne was influenced by the embrace of simple, self-reliant living that gained popularity in California in the late '60s, and later would be associated with the environmental movement (epitomized in such works as *The Greening of America*).

But there were also darker strains. Browne, with something of his father's flare for show business, determined that America in the late 1960s had a taste for the apocalyptic. In most respects, Browne's investment outlook during this period was unremarkable, if conservative: stocks and real estate were too tied to the overall health of an unreliable economy, so better to invest in gold and silver, and to protect assets in a Swiss bank account. What distinguished Browne was his insistence not merely that the status quo was untenable, but that economic collapse was imminent—as in a matter of days.

"2 Money Disasters That Could Strike on Saturday (one of them could happen sooner!)" blared the headline on a full-page ad that ran in the *New York Times, Chicago Tribune*, and *Washington Post* in August 1970. Although by this time Browne's Arlington House book *How You Can Profit From the Coming Devaluation* was already selling briskly, such ads were the vehicle by which many mainstream readers were exposed to the book. Browne, the ad promised, "shows you what the effect will be on you, your job or business, your personal finances, your family . . . shows you what *your* plan should be in each crisis—but *always in light of the devaluation that is now inevitable*." Browne's investment plan was mostly practical: he instructed readers on how to convert their money to Swiss francs; on how much of their cash they should keep in silver coins; how and why to buy stocks in gold-mining companies; and similar investment advice. But his severe vision of devaluation and its consequences pushed him to extreme measures; he told people not merely to buy gold, but to bury it in the ground, as he said he did himself.

Moreover, Browne argued repeatedly that every family should have a "retreat"—a place to live, preferably in a rural area, stocked with gold and silver and enough supplies to last a year. (Browne never explained exactly why survivors of an economic apocalypse would find gold and silver advantageous instruments of barter.) In his seminars, Browne often teamed up with Don Stephens, a futurist designer of ecological homes and the author of *The Retreater's Bibliography*, a comprehensive and constantly updated guide to resources for those interested in low-cost and low-impact "retreat" living. *The Retreater's Bibliography* envisioned an economic crisis deeper and more violent than the Great Depression. Major fuel shortages, it said, would require a return to horse-driven agriculture and transportation, and crowds of armed, hungry looters would overtake urban streets with lethal effect. "We have stated a number of times that as much as 85% of urban populations could die in such a time of upheaval with about 10% escaping the cities and as little as 5% staying put and surviving," wrote Don Stephens and his wife Barbie.[36]

For Browne, the retreat was an important part of a defensive investment "program," just as important as the Swiss bank account. Should runaway inflation occur, for example, Browne told his readers that their society would become unrecognizable. "Without a currency, the government cannot operate its schools or police forces or pay tax collectors," Browne explained. "Most likely, all governments in this country—federal, state and local—would collapse."[37] One key to surviving the inevitable crisis, then, was the retreat. "It should be far away from any metropolitan areas,"

Browne advised. "Even rural areas will only be safe if the local residents are largely self-sufficient and individualistic. This part of the program includes anything you might do to give you protection, mobility, and freedom from the chaos and rioting that would accompany runaway inflation." But if readers prepared using Browne's advice, he pledged that they would persevere and "find an opportunity to new wealth."

Browne was certainly dabbling in paranoia. Yet the socioeconomic apocalypse Browne predicted differed only in degree and level of detail from the currency crisis of the government that LBJ, Barbara Ward, Harold Wilson, and many other world leaders feared would take place if dollar-gold convertibility collapsed. And in both scenarios, owning more gold seemed like the best solution—the crucial difference being who gets to hold the gold. In a nation where urban riots, a monetary crisis, and a plummeting stock market—in 1969 the Dow Jones Industrial Average dropped about 15 percent—made the investor class especially anxious, Browne's combination of falling-sky scenarios with hard-money investment advice proved to be a potent formula. Hundreds of thousands of Americans flocked to the message. Browne's book hit the *New York Times* best-seller list in November 1970, representing a bonanza for the author and his upstart publisher Arlington House, which printed at least thirteen editions of Browne's book. Now the gospel of gold was no longer stuck in the provinces of hand-typed newsletters and hotel conference room seminars. Goldbugs of various stripes became minor celebrities; Browne appeared on television and radio talk shows, and mainstream magazines rushed to profile goldbugs.

Bookstores clamored for volumes similar to Browne's, which publishers large and small rushed to provide. Don and Barbie Stephens reported that with Browne's success—he mentioned them in a short bibliography—the "trickle of orders for [*The Retreater's Bibliography*] suddenly became an outburst." An early 1971 book, *Inflation-Proof Your Future*, featured little on gold, but dozens of do's and don'ts on collecting autographs, stamps and coins, Florida swampland, and first editions of Stephen Crane, as well as high-growth stocks. A wordier title the same year was *The Fateful Subversion of the American Economy Consequent on the Gold/Dollar, Trade/Economic and Tax Crises*. In late 1970, Arlington House followed up Browne's hit with *How to Beat Inflation by Using It*, and then in 1972 with *Everything You Need to Know Now About Gold and Silver*. Each chapter of the latter featured an interview with an expert—Harry Browne, Franz Pick, Murray Rothbard, and others. Tellingly, the copyright for the book was owned not by any of the authors, but by the Pacific Coast Coin Exchange, a California-based numismatic trading outfit whose founder, Louis Carabini, wrote the book's introduction (and presumably conducted the interviews). The book was republished several times; a transition was under way, from advising readers to buy gold to out-and-out selling it to them.

The goldbugs of the late '60s and early '70s were numerous and interconnected enough to constitute a movement, one that would increase in influence over the next decade. This didn't mean, however, consensus on all the particulars. Some embraced a conspiratorial/paranoid worldview that was avoided by those chiefly interested in investing. Some believed in using the American electoral system to advance their ideas—Harry Browne, notably, would later run for president as the nominee of the Libertarian Party in 1996 and 2000—while others rejected any association with government. And despite increased popularity, most goldbugs remained well outside mainstream American politics—at least through the mid-1970s. To Rothbard and many of his acolytes, there was no sense in trying to reform institutions like the Federal Reserve Board or the US Mint; government monetary control was intrinsically inflationary, corrupt, and destructive. Similarly, in some crucial ways, it didn't matter to Browne and Rothbard whether the American government defined or didn't define its currency in terms of gold, because in their view gold was the only real money and everything else was a government-created fiction. (Browne would largely abandon the United States in the 1970s; he kept his "retreat" in Canada and moved to Switzerland in 1977 before dying in 2006.) One issue on which all goldbugs could agree, however, was that gold prohibition should end. The metal-heavy investment strategies they favored would function much more efficiently and reach a broader public if not consigned to black markets, backyard bunkers, and secret accounts. Soon enough, they would get their wish.

# CHAPTER 9

○

# This Time for Real

ON SATURDAY, JULY 10, 1971, Undersecretary of Treasury Paul Volcker sat at his office desk, overlooking a sea of disturbing numbers. Volcker was in charge of international monetary affairs, and trouble emerged anywhere he looked. When the Johnson administration had decoupled the dollar from monetary gold in 1968, the hope was that this move would halt or substantially slow the gold drain out of the country's monetary reserves. That failed to happen—instead, US gold stock continued to dwindle. In the second week of May, for example, the United States had lost a steep $400 million worth of gold to Belgium, France, and the Netherlands, causing the US gold supply to hit its lowest level since the 1930s. At best, the demonetization of gold had addressed a symptom without curing the underlying disease: the US balance-of-payments deficit, which Volcker knew could hit $4 billion or even $5 billion that year.

Through the 1960s, foreign official dollar holdings had remained in the range of $13 to $15 billion; as Volcker sat at his desk, the number had soared to more than $24 billion. Germany's central bank, the Bundesbank, alone held more dollars than there was gold in Fort Knox. Even if the world's richest countries could no longer easily exchange their dollars for

On a Sunday night in August 1971, with Congress in recess, Richard Nixon "closed the gold window" by suspending the convertibility of the dollar into gold. His action ceased the run on America's dollar, but led to years of economic turmoil. *Courtesy Richard Nixon Presidential Library and Museum / Byron Schumaker* gold, they were impelled to handle such imbalances through trading on currency exchange markets. And beginning early that May, when Germany sent signals that it was considering letting the value of the mark float on the open market, they began doing so in droves. Huge volumes of dollars began to be traded for German marks, Dutch guilders, and Swiss francs—currencies tied to governments that the international market perceived to be practicing better fiscal discipline than Volcker's.

The result was a disaster for the dollar; between January and June the value of the dollar against currencies of Germany and Switzerland fell by about 4 percent. An IMF economist later wrote: "Never before had the world witnessed a flight out of a key currency of such dimensions."[1] The flood of dollars into Germany's Bundesbank could not be sustained, and on the morning of May 5—having taken in $1 billion in 40 minutes of trading—Germany halted trading in its currency. The deutschmark was now by default a floating currency—it was no longer valued in gold, and the central bank behind it was no longer buying or selling dollars. Smaller countries closely tied to German's economy—Austria, Belgium, Switzerland, and the Netherlands—soon followed suit, amplifying the dollar's weakness. The effects were widely and concretely felt; some American citizens traveling soon found that hotels and airlines would no longer accept dollars as payments, and neither, in places like Switzerland, could they exchange dollars for local currency.

Volcker, a six-foot, seven-inch economist who often appeared in rumpled suits and knew as much about international finance as anyone else in government, had anticipated nearly all of this for months. Yet he had been powerless to prevent it from occurring. Some of the pressure could be relieved by reducing US military spending, but he knew that, as with previous administrations, such cuts were not forthcoming. Another remedy would be to relax the fairly narrow bands in which currencies were allowed to trade against one another, but negotiations on that front were stalled and unlikely to take full effect for two years. Lacking other options,

Volcker strongly considered "closing the gold window" once and for all. Indeed, he and his staff had since the spring of 1971 secretly been preparing contingency plans for removing gold convertibility. Volcker and some other economists believed that separating the value of the dollar from that of gold might cause some pain in the short term, but would have many benefits in the long run. It was far from clear, however, that Volcker's new boss—former Texas governor John Connally had taken the Treasury job in February—would be willing to take such a drastic step. Just a few weeks before, Connally had addressed an IMF gathering, saying, "I want without any arrogance or defiance to make abundantly clear that we are not going to devalue, we are not going to change the price of gold, [and] we are going to control inflation." That seemed unambiguous, although when Volcker questioned his boss about it, Connally replied cryptically: "That's my unalterable position today. I don't know what it will be this summer."

President Richard Nixon might have been even more reluctant, with his reelection vote a mere fifteen months away. The Vietnam War continued to rage with little end in sight, and the public was fed up with it; that spring hundreds of thousands of protestors had descended on Washington, including hundreds of Vietnam veterans who threw their medals over a fence on Capitol Hill. No one could really forecast what would happen to the world economy if most or all of the major currencies were floating with flexible exchange rates. Moreover, Volcker believed that there would be "enormous pressures to increase the gold price once we suspend gold payments," just as had been the case with FDR, again with outcomes that were impossible to forecast with any certainty.

What tipped Volcker's hand that Saturday morning was data on the June trade deficit. Even though the United States had enjoyed a substantial trade surplus in 1970, the June 1971 figure showed a deficit of nearly $600 million. This was precisely the type of fiscal practice for which currency markets had been punishing the United States. And while a deficit in one month or quarter could be reversed, the country was facing the prospect of running its first yearlong trade deficit since 1893, when Grover Cleveland was president. Volcker phoned his Treasury colleague William Dale, a longtime Treasury officer who had also worked for the International Monetary Fund, at home and instructed him to come into the office. Dale, too, was no stranger to the concept that at some point the dollar would need to be separated from gold. As far back as March 1969, he had written Volcker a confidential memo that began, "I have become convinced that gold convertibility of the dollar cannot be maintained indefinitely."[2] When Dale arrived at the office, Volcker asked him what size trade deficit would rock the exchange markets. Dale, fully aware of May's tumult, provided an estimate, and Volcker replied, "you've got it." (And indeed, later that month when the trade deficit figures became public, the already weak dollar went into a multiday slide.) Dale recalled, "He then directed me to do a plan closing the gold window and said, 'This time it's for real.'"[3]

Of course, any plan to close the gold window would need approval from Connally and Nixon, who might well resist a plan that would overturn all international postwar monetary behavior. (And while it could theoretically be done against the will of Federal Reserve chairman Arthur Burns, he would certainly know in advance and would argue strenuously against it.) In contrast to Kennedy's longtime gold obsession or Johnson's rising exacerbation, Nixon most of the time was not even indifferent to the question of gold's relationship to the dollar. White House records of the late spring and early summer of 1971 show almost no presidential interest whatsoever in questions of gold or the currency exchange market. Instead, Nixon spent May, June, and July discussing diplomatic overtures to China; strategic arms talks with the Soviet Union; Middle East negotiations; some domestic economic matters (such as inflation and labor unrest); his reelection campaign and how to influence voters; and, of course, a vendetta against the "conspiracy" of people who leaked the Pentagon Papers, and thus the crucible of the Watergate scandal that would in three years drive him out of office.

It is remarkable, then, that a mere thirty-six days after Volcker told Dale "This time it's for real," the president of the United States would appear in a dark-blue summer suit on prime-time, Sunday night television to declare he had asked the Treasury "to suspend temporarily the convertibility of the dollar into gold or other reserve assets." How did the Nixon White House embrace such a momentous monetary step in such a brief period?

The end of the Bretton Woods system had been foreshadowed by Robert Triffin and others, and was inevitable. Nonetheless, it is surprising that the fateful decision to sever the tie between the dollar and gold would come during Nixon's presidency, particularly toward the end of the first term. At the start of Nixon's presidency, there was "limited support and some strong opposition" to floating the dollar, according to Allan Meltzer's history of the Federal Reserve. During the 1968 presidential campaign, Nixon's top economic adviser Paul McCracken had organized a committee to counsel Nixon on economic matters chaired by Gottfried Haberler, a Harvard professor affiliated with the "Austrian school" of economics, who focused particularly on issues related to international trade. Although the task force explored possibilities for international monetary reform, it argued that tackling domestic inflation ought to be America's highest priority; if that goal could be achieved, other nations could be more readily persuaded to maintain their currencies in a way that would prevent a balance-of-payments crisis.

This became the cornerstone for the early Nixon administration monetary policy widely labeled "benign neglect." Nixon's closest advisers preferred the term *gradualism*, but neglect was an apt description for several reasons. One was that the policies put in place in 1968—the restrictions on international investment, the creation of the two-tier gold market, and the passage of a surtax to help slow inflation and pay for the Vietnam War—actually did improve the country's balance-of-payments situation for a time. Indeed, in 1968, the United States experienced a rare surplus, of $1.6 billion, and again in 1969, of $2.7 billion. So long as the existing system appeared to work, there would be little impetus to change it. Instead, the Haberler task force urged an end to the capital controls that Johnson had established and a focus on making currency exchange rates more flexible.

An equally important, if harder-to-quantify, rationale for "benign neglect" was the low priority that Nixon and his closest advisers assigned to international monetary matters. Economists and officials in the Kennedy and Johnson White House tended to be creatures of a Western monetary consensus: they viewed Western European governments, central banks, and global institutions as vital—if sometimes difficult—partners in a shared project of creating growth and minimizing economic crises. Nixon, who of course inherited the massively debilitating Vietnam War, was mostly focused on conducting foreign policy. To the extent that Nixon and his national security adviser Henry Kissinger had a goal for international monetary policy, it was to minimize interference with carrying out foreign-policy goals. For example, one former Nixon official told the political scientist Joanna Gowa that Nixon "refused even to sanction the continuation of pressure on West Germany to extract foreign-exchange concessions because he valued German-US ties more highly than he did the payments accounts."[4] Vietnam was, not surprisingly, even more off limits; a member of Nixon's Council of Economic Advisers told Gowa, "we didn't like the idea of bringing our troops home or that kind of stuff."

Nixon's White House thus had a limited appetite for dealing with the complex, often frustrating institutions that went along with global currency management. This attitude was epitomized by John Connally, whom Nixon installed at Treasury in February 1971. Connally was a swaggering Texas Democrat who chomped on unlit cigars in meetings; he had been in the black, simonized sedan with John Kennedy on the day he was assassinated in 1963. Unlike his predecessor David Kennedy, Connally had no allegiance to conservative economic ideals. As one of his aides put it, Connally was "not trapped by any theoretical dogma or by position papers he wrote twenty years ago."[5] His independence bordered on irreverence; upon Connally's first visit to the International Monetary Fund, according to an IMF executive, he dubbed it "a museum in which anything that wasn't already stuffed ought to be."[6] In May he made waves more publicly with a speech to an international banking conference in Munich in which he chastised foreign governments for not spending more on their own defense. "No longer does the United States economy dominate the free world," Connally told the group. "No longer can considerations of friendship or need or capacity justify the United States carrying so heavy a share of the common burden."[7] He appeared to relish such global feather-ruffling; he referred to himself as "the bully boy on the manicured playing fields of international finance."

This isn't to say, of course, that Connally took the Treasury seat in 1971 with the goal of ending the dollar's last ties to gold. There is scant evidence that he even considered the issue in his earliest days at Treasury, and at first blush, such a radical proposal could likely have spooked a political creature like Connally. Nixon wooed Connally to cross party lines and join his cabinet after the Democrats gained seats in the House of Representatives in the 1970 election. Connally's appointment was seen as fundamentally political; he was interested in an activist president who could be reelected. A biographer noted that when he was appointed to Treasury, the president's own advisers boasted that Connally was someone who could accomplish an important Republican Party goal: carry Texas for the GOP in 1972. (Hubert Humphrey had won Texas's twenty-five electoral votes—the sixth-largest state at the time—in 1968, but the margin was fewer than 40,000 votes and the state was clearly within Republican grasp.) Also valuable were Connally's general contacts with congressional Democrats. Connally, after all, would soon head up the political organization Democrats for Nixon, and during the summer of 1971, Nixon and his aides discussed with Connally the possibility that they would dump Vice President Spiro Agnew from the 1972 ticket and replace him with Connally.[8]

Indeed, it is impossible to appreciate the economic moves that the Nixon White House made in the summer of 1971 without understanding the heated, and at times surprisingly desperate, political background of those events. The lopsidedness of Nixon's 1972 reelection victory over George McGovern can blind later observers to the fact that only the year before, Nixon's chances of reelection were precarious—and perhaps more important, were perceived internally as precarious. The flirtation with Connolly as vice president represented an administration at war with its own weakness; Nixon had lost faith in his vice president, rarely met with him one-on-one, and considered him a liability on the 1972 reelection ticket. Not long after Nixon left office, one of his advisers observed, "If there had been an election in 1971 Nixon would almost certainly have been defeated."[9] Throughout the first half of 1971, the Harris survey indicated just that—Nixon would have lost to Maine senator Edmund Muskie in April by a margin of 47–39, with 11 percent of voters supporting the segregationist former Alabama governor George Wallace.[10] There were multiple reasons: not only had the president failed to achieve his 1968 campaign promise to bring "an honorable end to the war in Vietnam," he had expanded America's involvement into Cambodia, and the cost of the war in dollars and American lives seemed endless.

But anyone inside the White House asked to name the administration's biggest weakness would have said the economy.[11] While much of the blame for persistently high inflation could be attributed to the Johnson administration's massive and rapid Vietnam buildup, there was little to be gained from asking voters to look backward. The economy fell into a recession in 1970, and even that medicine did not allow Nixon's team, including his handpicked Federal Reserve chairman Arthur Burns, to stem inflation's growth; in the spring of 1971 the inflation rate topped 6 percent for the first time in two decades. A huge amount of Washington's time in 1970 and 1971 was spent debating whether or not the government should freeze wages and prices. This policy was anathema to free-market Republicans, and for a time split Washington's economic minds bitterly. Nixon in particular opposed price controls, even during wartime; he had worked briefly during World War II for the Office of Price Administration and believed price controls to be impractical. George Shultz and Paul McCracken agreed, and through the end of 1970, the very idea invoked the White House's wrath.

Soon, however, Nixon and his advisers felt they had no other choice. Connally, for his part, was untroubled by doctrine, and viewed the idea of wage-and-price controls as a desirable extension of executive muscle. ("If the legislature wants to give you a new power—you take it. Put it in the corner like an old shotgun. You never know when you might need it.")[12] After savings hit a postwar high in early '71, with consumers trying desperately to stave off inflation, Congress in May gave the president the power to impose controls. By June, Nixon's Council of Economic Advisers had decided that a wage-price freeze was necessary.

Simultaneous to this was a debate over whether or not to float the dollar. Volcker was concerned, even fearful, of the consequences of such a move. In March 1971, Volcker drafted a secret memorandum laying out the advantages and disadvantages of four different monetary approaches. Discussing the suspension of gold-dollar convertibility, he worried that other countries would retaliate, by restricting or prohibiting US investment in their economies, erecting higher trade barriers, and driving the dollar further down by increasing the price of gold. There would be no way to stop them, because the US closure of the gold window would leave international institutions like the IMF "helpless and undermined."[13] Still, he argued that resentment from European allies could be mitigated if the suspension were negotiated for months beforehand and presented as part of a coherent and cooperative international effort.

By the spring, two factors began to push Volcker closer to accepting suspending convertibility, regardless of the severity of the world's reaction. One was Germany's floating of the deutschmark, a move that not only increased pressure on the United States but at least theoretically showed that floating the dollar was feasible (the German economy improved somewhat immediately after it floated its currency). The second was a surprise opening presented by Congress. Representative Henry Reuss was a Democrat from Wisconsin who served on the House Banking Committee and had often sparred with Volcker and the administration over gold policy. Reuss particularly opposed the purchases that the United States made from South Africa, arguing that the United States was propping up the apartheid regime. On June 3, Reuss introduced a "sense of Congress" resolution calling on the US government to suspend the dollar's convertibility. Criticizing a monetary system that "unnecessarily cripples itself," Reuss argued that "only by closing the gold window and letting the dollar find a newer and sounder relationship with the yen and other undervalued currencies can we avoid the deterioration of our trading position and a return to trade autarchy."[14] It appears that no vote was ever taken on Reuss's resolution. However, Volcker was given a copy of it and recognized that the resolution represented something new. In March, he'd worried about "an opposition Congress ready, willing and able to frustrate [any dollar devaluation] plan and make political capital of the results."[15] Now, here was a leading congressional Democrat offering—presumably unknowingly—potential political cover for a position that Volcker was beginning to consider inevitable anyway.

Whatever doubts Volcker had about his boss's willingness to embrace a high-risk economic policy overhaul began to recede;

indeed this kind of political jujitsu was Connally's specialty. After all, Connally was already trying to prevail upon the president to accept a strong new economic policy—including the wage-and-price freeze, which Nixon continued to resist through late June— to improve unemployment and inflation. And in part, Connally was engaged in a turf battle against economic advisers within the administration and against Burns. When the pressure from the international money markets eased somewhat in early June, Paul McCracken, who chaired Nixon's Council of Economic Advisers, wrote a memorandum to the president in which he decried the unworkability of the existing system but deemed a floating currency "too uncertain and risky" because it "disrupts the monetary order that has generally prevailed so far."[16] McCracken wanted to convene a large group to follow up on the monetary questions. But Connally, who constantly threatened to resign that spring, shot back, arguing that by law and tradition such decisions should be made by the treasury secretary. Nixon agreed and put Connally in charge. In a stormy meeting with his economic team on June 28 Nixon, tired of endless debates and untraceable press leaks, lowered the boom. There would be, the president asserted, "no more of this crap . . . we need a united front." Economic policy could only function if there were one person in charge, Nixon said, and that person would be Connally.

Effectively, this meant that Volcker could go ahead with the contingency plan he'd drafted earlier in the year. But the decisive argument for Connally was not at its core economic. In mid-July, right around the time that trade deficit numbers converted Volcker to the idea of closing the gold window, Connally read an analysis by a Treasury Department consultant named Edward Bernstein, who had been part of the American team during the Bretton Woods negotiations. Bernstein calculated that a devaluation of the dollar (presumably in the neighborhood of 15 percent) could create 500,000 jobs, the equivalent of shaving 0.5 percent off the politically damaging unemployment rate. Primarily this could be achieved through exports: a lower dollar would make American cars and other manufactured goods more competitive abroad. An economy growing jobs that rapidly would give Nixon a strong advantage going into the 1972 election. An administration colleague said bluntly that Bernstein's "analysis convinced Connally that the devaluation was good politically. Connally always looked at the politics of the economics."[17]

And indeed Connally's perspective was wider still. The suspension of gold convertibility was but one part—and probably not the most important, from a political standpoint—of a dramatic economic package he was assembling for the president's consideration. In terms of short-term economic impact and the likelihood of political support, the wage-price freeze and a surcharge on imports were arguably more attractive. But Connally believed that suspending the gold window would make Nixon look like a leader who embraced decisive, sweeping action.

Assuming he could use that to sell the idea to Nixon himself, Nixon's advisers would fall in line, even if they personally opposed all or some of the proposals Connally was assembling. There was but one obstacle: Federal Reserve chairman Arthur Burns. Burns occupied a peculiar position during the Nixon presidency. On the one hand, his career outside the academy was intertwined with Nixon's; the two men had worked together during the Eisenhower administration, and Nixon wrote in a memoir that Burns had warned him about how the economic trends might affect the 1960 election.[18] Nixon had appointed Burns to the position of Federal Reserve chairman in 1970, and Burns clearly treasured his relationship with Nixon and considered him a valued friend. Nixon did not seem to reciprocate the feeling; in an infamous rant about Jewish domination of the Bureau of Labor Statistics, Nixon said, "There's a Jewish cabal, you know, running through this, working with people like Burns and the rest. And they all—they all only talk to Jews."[19] At the same time, Burns ostensibly asserted the need for the Fed to maintain its independence and integrity. In December of 1970, for example, Burns delivered a speech in Los Angeles in which he supported, however reluctantly, the idea of a board to review wages and prices.[20] The remarks were interpreted as having Nixon's support (and indeed both Nixon and speechwriter William Safire talked to Burns about his speech before it was delivered), but the opposite was true; Nixon was furious that Burns was offering his own policy recommendations. In retaliation for the speech, the White House for a time stopped inviting him to Sunday White House worship services.[21]

It is an understatement to say that the Nixon White House did not value Fed independence, and most historians today portray Burns as a fairly reliable economic ally in the president's reelection.[22] And yet, less than a month before the critical gold window decision was made, Burns was the target of one of the administration's most vicious political attacks outside of the "plumbers" activity associated with Watergate. On July 23, Burns testified before Congress's Joint Economic Committee, venting frustration at an intractable economy. "The rules of economics are not working in quite the way they used to," Burns lamented. "Despite extensive unemployment in our country, wage rate increases have not moderated. Despite much idle industrial capacity, commodity prices continue to rise rapidly." One of the biggest problems, Burns said, was the administration's inability to slow the growth in wages and prices. As long as consumers and businesses believed that prices would continue to grow dramatically, they would hold back on spending and investing, creating a "grave obstacle" to economic recovery.[23]

The idea of the Fed chairman asserting publicly that the administration was unable to improve the economy did not sit well with Nixon and his advisers. In an Oval Office meeting the next day, Nixon debated with aides H. R. Haldeman and John Ehrlichman the most effective way to get back at Burns, whom Nixon painted as conceited, press-hungry, and ungrateful. They loosely agreed that the word should go out in the economic community around

Burns (this, incidentally, was the same day that Nixon erupted about the Jewish dominance in government economic circles) that Burns had fallen afoul of the president. Nixon then presented an idea for a media attack: "Could you get one story leaked through the [Charles] Colson apparatus about Arthur?"[24] He promptly suggested two: one, that the president was considering some equivalent of "court-packing" for the Fed—that is, that the president's advisers were recommending expanding the Federal Reserve's membership. The second was that the president wanted to end the Federal Reserve's independence and bring it inside the executive branch. Nixon explained that a newspaper column questioning the wisdom of Fed independence might "worry Arthur a little." The idea, he added, had come from Connally.

According to Colson's account, there was an added bullet: to attack Burns for promoting wage and price controls while also saying that the salary of the Fed chairman should be increased.[25] Colson says he then instructed an underling to leak Burns's apparent hypocrisy to the *Wall Street Journal*, knowing full well that Burns had recommended a raise only for his successor, not for himself. Sure enough, a *Journal* story soon appeared, reporting that a "furious" president was considering legislation to bring the Federal Reserve under executive control, and quoting an unnamed aide who charged Burns with "hypocrisy" for trying to get his own salary raised by about 50 percent.[26] The president and his top advisers took evident glee in having delivered a blow to Burns. Nixon brought the topic up in several phone calls on July 28: "He's squealing pretty hard." Haldeman said in his diary that the leak "got Arthur pretty upset, as it was intended that it would."[27]

The attack on Burns was especially petty, as it was ostensibly designed to punish him for advocating a policy that the administration was days away from approving anyway. The recession had hit the metal-mining industry particularly hard, and falling production in the nation's mines was a major obstacle to economic recovery. Throughout 1971, the steelworkers' union had used strikes and threatened strikes to great advantage, winning big wage increases for copper and aluminum miners. On August 2, after a strike deadline had passed, the steel industry announced a settlement that would increase wages 30 percent over three years. To pay for it, the steel companies announced that they would raise prices by 8 percent.

This was all the fuel that Connally needed to sell his economic program. The potential damage of the steel agreement was obvious—Connally told the president, "the steel settlement is a hell of an inflationary settlement"—and most of the president's day was taken up with trying to figure out how to react and get his message through. "We've got to grandstand more," he told Shultz and Connally. In addition to wage and price controls for 90–120 days, Connally pitched the reinstitution of an investment tax credit, an insistence on capping federal spending, and the imposition of a 10 percent import quota. The important thing, he stressed, was to take bold action, so that Nixon would appear to be in control of events instead of being controlled by them. The convertibility of the dollar to gold, Connally told Nixon, was something that "we're going to have to stop that at some point. Most people think that $10 billion in gold [reserves] is the point" at which the United States would need to stop convertibility, and "we'll lose a $1 billion in reserves this week . . . I don't think you'll be able to hold [on to gold convertibility] through the election next year." He added that the United States "probably ought to float" the dollar as Germany and Canada were already doing with their currencies. Taken together, Connally insisted, the sweeping package would "stimulate the hell" out of the economy, and he urged the president to "take a position before you are forced to take a position." It would be, Connally said, "as big a coup as your China thing." Different timetables were discussed, from that very week before Congress adjourned to November or December. In his diary entry for that day, Haldeman called Connally's plan "a huge economic breakthrough" and speculated that while Shultz might try to slow the plan down, he would be unlikely to stop it.[28] In a similar Oval Office meeting two days later, Connally became so impassioned that he can be heard on the White House tape thumping the president's desk. When Shultz joined them, he quickly realized that the time for debate had passed. "You have decided to go with this big program, including the gold window and all that?," he said, in a half-question, half-statement.

At this point the president had two main goals: figuring out the right timing to announce his bold new plan, and keeping all leaks out of the press. Any hint of what the administration was planning could easily roil markets. Volcker knew well that his plans were explosive. The briefing book he had prepared for Connally included an entire "Section A" of bogus plans, in case a reporter or other outsider got hold of it; it also contained a "Section C," but no "Section B," to further sow confusion.[29]

In fact, the plan did leak to the press. In early August, syndicated columnist Paul Scott wrote that "it is impossible to exaggerate the gravity of the private discussions now going on here between President Nixon and his economic and financial advisers over the state of the nation's economy." The column referred to Volcker's dollar contingency plan, which "stresses that a controlled devaluation could be brought about by having the Treasury close the so-called 'gold window.' "[30] The premature leak made Connally "very disturbed," and Nixon asked Haldeman—this was the same summer that the "plumbers" later responsible for Watergate were first assembled—to track down who was responsible for the leak.[31]

The Oval Office discussion on August 12 was almost agnostic about which parts of the economic program were necessary so long as the appearance of dramatic action could be conveyed. Steps that could be taken without congressional approval had an obvious advantage; Congress was in summer recess and, by the time it reconvened and scheduled hearings, the administration would have weeks of head start. An import tax, for example, went to the top of the pile, because Shultz and Connally had figured out at least two legal ways to make it happen without legislative action, including invoking the Trading with the Enemy Act that FDR had used. As for closing the gold window, Nixon and his men were uncertain whether it should be presented as temporary or permanent—or indeed whether it should be included at all. Would markets and foreign governments be spooked, as Volcker feared? Or had markets so long suspected the move that it was already priced in, as Shultz argued? Nixon summarized the group's collective ignorance: "Nobody knows what the public reaction will be to the gold window, I mean, because, frankly good God the people that are the experts don't know what the hell it ought to be!"[32] Also unclear was whether each of Connally's proposals carried equal urgency. "I don't think we should do the whole program right now, especially the freeze and the import surcharge," Nixon told Connally. "But if you think shutting the gold window must be done immediately then you can announce it yourself . . . making it sound like a temporary measure, as a prelude to a complete package." They discussed Burns's position and his likely opposition to closing the gold window, but also predicted that he would go along with the decision.

Connally continued to hammer the point that the mechanics of the economic program mattered less than the opportunity to present Nixon as a president who made bold decisions that his predecessors couldn't. This was an especially telling exchange:

> *Connally*: Our problems are basically, to the extent that we have them, right here at home. And when they're solved, your international problems are solved, your international trade problems to a large extent are solved, because it's merely a reflection. It just mirrors your economic strength at home, that's all. . . .
>
> The reason you want this background, in detail along these lines, is to show that we've been deteriorating for twenty-five years—

*Nixon*: Right.
*Connally*: —and that you're the first president that's had the guts—
*Nixon*: Yeah.
*Connally*: —to take this comprehensive—
*Nixon*: Great.
*Connally*: —action.

That very afternoon, the British government requested a $3 billion gold "cover" for all their dollar assets. While the British request didn't itself cause the administration to abandon gold convertibility, it certainly underscored the immediacy and the size of the problem. With less than $10 billion in US gold reserves left—the lowest amount since 1938—fulfilling the request would be highly dangerous. But not fulfilling it could send a panic signal to a key ally.

The time for decision had come; the president and his top advisers relocated to the presidential retreat at Camp David for the weekend. Participants were instructed to pack their bags and not tell anyone—including their wives—where they were going or why. En route to Camp David, Herb Stein from the Council of Economic Advisers told speechwriter William Safire that "this could be the most important weekend in the history of economics since March 4, 1933," when FDR decided to close America's banks. Safire didn't understand what closing the gold window meant, but when he repeated the idea to a Treasury official in the helicopter ride, the man leaned forward, put his head in his hands and whispered "My God!"[33]

Many historians have documented the debate that took place at Camp David August 13–15, and portrayed it as the moment when the decision to close the gold window was made; partly, this is because Safire wrote an engaging account of the weekend. In fact, the plan had almost entirely been approved in advance, with just details and language in need of hammering out. Nixon said while planning the trip, "I personally have pretty much decided what I want to do anyway." The Camp David discussions were, to a large degree, a kind of choreographed stage play, a meeting with a foregone conclusion designed to make participants—chiefly Burns—feel as if they had been consulted (this tactic was common in the Nixon White House). And it may indeed have been the case that Burns had been duped into thinking he had a chance to win the argument. Nonetheless, weeks before—even before the White House smeared him in the press—he had already personally resigned himself to Nixon's railroading of his ostensible independence. In his diary in early July he had written: "I had often noticed RN's love of the imperial manner and its trappings, but now I knew that I would be accepted in the future only if I suppressed my will and yielded completely—even though it was wrong at law and morally—to his authority."[34]

Nixon instructed everyone assembled not to speak to anyone outside the camp for security reasons; "any leak would be treason," Arthur Burns recalled. Probably more than any other attendee, Volcker recognized that a leak could have dramatic market consequences. "Fortunes could be made with this information." (Haldeman quipped: "Exactly how?")

Burns was willing to accept some of the economic program, and thought it could be effective. But he drew the line at ending the dollar's convertibility: "If we close the window . . . we are releasing forces that we need not release." It would amount to "murdering the international monetary system without proposing to put anything in its place." Part of his fear, which Volcker shared, was that other countries would immediately retaliate by increasing the price of gold. Connally, for his part, emphasized the vulnerability of the status quo: "Anybody can topple us—anytime they want—we have left ourselves completely exposed."

As the Friday night discussion came to an end, no formal conclusion had been reached. But at 4:30 Saturday morning, Nixon called Haldeman and told him that he'd made up his mind to close the gold window. All that was left was to determine the timing.

Initially, the group had planned for the president to address the nation on Monday the 16th. But Volcker argued that it was crucial to give international markets as much advance notice as possible. A Sunday night television address would mean interrupting the broadcast of *Bonanza*, one of the most popular programs of the 1960s and early 1970s, although the episode was a summer rerun. The group agreed the risk was worth it.

Nixon worried primarily about how to frame the argument. All the fear and debate about closing the gold window assumed an audience that understood this very complex subject. Yet, as Nixon had pointed out on Thursday, even the experts couldn't agree on what the effects would be—so why bother explaining it at all? Volcker could be dispatched to Europe to soothe his counterparts abroad; what mattered to Nixon was how the domestic audience received the message. As Shultz put it a few years later: "Nixon knew most people wouldn't understand the implications of closing the gold window and wouldn't care about it. Nixon knew he had to make a political statement and that's why he told the people at Camp David not to write a speech for him as he wanted to do it himself." (This was not entirely accurate; Safire was also instructed to draft a version of the speech, but the bulk of the 2,500-word speech did come from Nixon's own pen.) In the helicopter on the way back to Washington, Nixon couldn't help but divulge to Safire: "You know when all of this was cooked up? Connally and me, we had it set sixty days ago."[35]

A relaxed-looking Nixon sat before a camera in front of a blue curtain, wearing a blue suit and tie, with only the collar of his white shirt poking through. His eighteen-minute address gave almost no hint that the international monetary system that had prevailed since the end of World War II was about to be dismantled. Instead, Nixon portrayed the United States as a nation under attack, and the only fair course of action was to fight back. "In the past 7 years, there has been an average of one international monetary crisis every year," Nixon said. "Now who gains from these

crises? Not the workingman; not the investor; not the real producers of wealth. The gainers are the international money speculators. Because they thrive on crises, they help to create them." Then
he laid out the current agenda of these crisis-mongers: "In recent
weeks, the speculators have been waging an all-out war on the
American dollar. The strength of a nation's currency is based on the
strength of that nation's economy—and the American economy is
by far the strongest in the world. Accordingly, I have directed the
Secretary of the Treasury to take the action necessary to defend the
dollar against the speculators. I have directed Secretary Connally
to suspend temporarily the convertibility of the dollar into gold or
other reserve assets, except in amounts and conditions determined
to be in the interest of monetary stability and in the best interests
of the United States."[36]

To refute what he called the "bugaboo" of devaluation, Nixon
made a nakedly patriotic appeal. Yes, if you traveled abroad or
bought a foreign car, your dollar might buy less. But if you were
among the "overwhelming majority of Americans who buy
American-made products in America, your dollar will be worth just
as much tomorrow as it is today." The important lesson that Nixon
imparted to his viewers was that America is strong, and its ability to compete depends on its citizens. "Two hundred years ago a
man wrote in his diary these words: 'Many thinking people believe
America has seen its best days.' That was written in 1775, just before
the American Revolution—the dawn of the most exciting era in
the history of man. And today we hear the echoes of those voices,
preaching a gospel of gloom and defeat, saying the same thing:
'We have seen our best days.' I say, let Americans reply: 'Our best
days lie ahead.'" Nixon reckoned that Americans, offered a choice
between a dollar valued by a chunk of gold and a reassurance about
America's preeminent role in the world, would choose the latter.

The political brilliance of Nixon's plan was evident within hours
of his speech. Most leading Democrats were caught completely off
guard. Especially in the middle of an August recess, few were pre-

pared to take on an issue as complex as closing the gold window, although George McGovern, who would end up as the Democratic nominee the following year, did denounce the speech as "sheer bunk, irrelevancy, and mystery . . . it is a disgrace for a great nation like ours to end in this way the convertibility of the dollar." For the most part, however, Democrats had a sense of victory; they were pleased that Nixon was at last taking on the wage-price freeze they had long advocated. Senate majority leader Mike Mansfield of Montana said: "I'm delighted that [Nixon's] patience has finally run out." There was, as predicted, some confusion in international currency markets, many of which were closed so that they could digest the changes. The dollar would continue to slide against major currencies, but at least in 1971 it was hard to argue that the new policies made matters worse. More important for the White House, domestic market reception was strong: the Dow Jones Industrial Average closed up on Monday by nearly 33 points, or 3.8 percent—its best one-day performance in history to that point. Even the administration's most prominent critics lacked any tangible alternative. "We have proved that we can take violent unilateral action, which may give transitory satisfaction to some," wrote former State Department Undersecretary Eugene Rostow in a stinging *New York Times* op-ed. "But if devaluation was justified, we could have devalued at lesser risk by agreement and not by fiat."[37] Rostow, who just a few years earlier had barely blinked when contemplating putting nuclear bombs underground in a foreign country to blow gold out of the ground, had a justifiable point. Yet by quibbling over details of implementation he was effectively conceding the point: the era of defining the dollar by any amount of gold had ended. While no one could predict the floating future with any precision, neither was anyone with any authority realistically advocating a return.

When FDR initiated gold prohibition in 1933, it was in part because his administration (and Hoover's before him) openly worried about individuals hoarding gold. At various points the Eisenhower, Kennedy, and Johnson administrations also worried about individuals buying and selling gold, usually overseas. By contrast, Nixon's 1971 landmark decision to close the gold window had absolutely nothing to do with whether or not Americans could own or invest in gold. The Nixon administration was trying neither to inhibit nor encourage any particular consumer behavior; indeed, the experience of floating currencies was so unfamiliar that the most experienced authorities in international finance didn't know what to expect. Longtime Federal Reserve official Charles Coombs, for example, stated in a 1967 debate with floating-advocate Milton Friedman that if the dollar were to fully float, he did not believe there would be an exchange market for US currency at all.[38] One searches in vain through memoranda and transcripts for any discussion about creating a private investment market for gold, or even for how floating the dollar might affect the existing private gold market. Not only was it not a motivation, it didn't even appear to be on the radar of the top officials in the White House, Treasury, or Federal Reserve.

This is especially striking because the early 1970s witnessed a booming market for metal investors, which would soon evolve into the modern goldbug investor movement. Its legal foothold took the form of trading in silver coins. When silver was removed from dimes, quarters, and half-dollars in 1965, it became illegal to export or melt down the pre-1965 silver coins. For several years, this policy frustrated those who collected or hoarded the coins; rising silver commodity prices—silver traded well above $2 an ounce in 1968—gave the coins a much higher metallic value than face value. By 1969, however, very few silver coins remained in common circulation, and silver prices had begun to fall. That spring, Nixon's Treasury Department lifted the prohibition against melting down the coins.

This jump-started a market in buying and selling silver coins. Demand became widespread and sophisticated enough that, in April 1971, the New York Mercantile Exchange began trading silver coin futures contracts. But silver enthusiasts did not need the "official" market, thanks to a burgeoning cottage industry of coin traders; between 1972 and 1973, some twenty coin exchanges began doing business in California alone. An exchange's standard offering was a bag of pre-1965 coins with a face value of $1,000, but with silver content that exceeded that. The granddaddy of the coin exchanges was Pacific Coast Coin Exchange (PCCE); between 1970 and 1974, PCCE sold $1 billion in coin contracts to approximately 25,000 investors. The firm, which later was named Monex International, was founded by Louis Carabini, a coin dealer in Newport Beach, California. Carabini and PCCE had close ties to many of the writers and thinkers offering policy and investment ideas around gold and silver through the publisher Arlington House. Harry Browne's bestseller *How You Can Profit from the Coming Devaluation*, for example, gave readers PCCE's address and called the firm "well acquainted with the silver market and the inflationary problems of today." Browne particularly suggested PCCE to readers looking to tap the silver commodity market, in which PCCE would lend money for a portion of the purchase price of silver coins. In 1972, Carabini edited his own volume for Arlington House, *Everything You Need to Know Now About Gold and Silver*, which featured interviews with Harry Browne, Franz Pick, Murray Rothbard, and others.

It turned out that the ties between Carabini and the burgeoning goldbug movement were more than ideological; the Arlington House books were explicitly used to drum up business for his company. An investigation by the Securities and Exchange Commission revealed that Browne actually held the title of director of marketing for PCCE and received about $100,000 in commissions from the company between 1970 and 1974. Specifically, according to the SEC, the company paid Browne "a commission for investors attracted to PCCE from reading Browne's books." Browne had not bothered to share this information with his many readers. (Franz Pick, too, was prominently featured in PCCE's advertising, although the SEC's summary of its litigation does not mention Pick.)

But if the SEC complaint made Arlington House look like it was deceiving readers by dressing up a sales pitch as independent analysis, it was far more damning about PCCE and the coin market itself. First, the SEC portrayed PCCE as preying on consumers who weren't positioned to make good judgments. The complaint criticized PCCE's "polished, hard-sell fraudulent promotional and marketing campaign . . . directed at attracting large numbers of small and unsophisticated investors with little understanding and experience in such investments."[39]

Second, the agency asserted that PCCE was lying about what it offered. PCCE, the agency said, almost never actually sold physical coins to its investors. PCCE's advertisements listed depositories ("in California, Florida, New York, Texas, Utah & Canada") in which investors' silver coins were supposedly stored. In fact, the SEC claimed, PCCE owned no depositories and in most cases never purchased the silver coins it touted to investors. In this manner, PCCE was able to sell more "coins" to investors than were likely to have been available anywhere. "I believe that more silver coins have been sold than were ever produced," a money market executive told the *New York Times* in 1974, when the New York State attorney general obtained an injunction against PCCE for committing what he called "colossal fraud" against New York residents.[40] Instead of selling coins, PCCE, the SEC charged, commingled investor funds with its own funds used for general operations and investments. PCCE may have made futures and options purchases in the silver market, but its investors had no rights or title to those investments.

Most PCCE investors had bought their fictional coins on margin—that is, they paid a percentage of the coins' face value (plus commission and fees) and would either pay the rest over time, or through profits that their investment made. According to the SEC, the latter scenario effectively never occurred. If customers asked to sell their own coins, they would typically be forced to sell at a price dictated only by PCCE; at times, the complaint said, PCCE "refuses to accept sell orders." Moreover, the SEC charged that the managers used investor funds to make questionable purchases that were never disclosed—including a private jet, a gold mine, and a cattle business—and that company officers took personal loans from investors' funds. The SEC stopped short of calling PCCE a Ponzi scheme, but one legal scholar concluded that "a between-the-lines reading of the allegations indicates that a Ponzi probably existed."[41] Carabini settled the case with the SEC without admitting wrongdoing and pledged to avoid future violations of securities law (a pledge he would have difficulty fulfilling).

If any of this unscrupulous behavior slowed down the enthusiasm or momentum of the goldbugs, however, it was hard to see. If PCCE was shelling out tens of thousands of dollars to Browne for referrals, it was because Browne dominated bookstores throughout 1974 with his follow-up book, *You Can Profit From a Monetary Crisis*. In it Browne hit his familiar themes, although with a slightly less apocalyptic tone. He noted that, even though the calamitous prophecies of his 1970 book had not come to pass, investors who took his advice would still have fared far better than those who put their money into blue-chip stocks. He touted PCCE as a place to buy gold and silver coins, saying, "I've had numerous dealings with it and have never had reason to complain."

Not that Browne promised easy times ahead. He continued to predict "a more difficult depression than that of the 1930s." He also still advocated a well-stocked retreat in case life in much of America became untenable, although he acknowledged that such ideas "have an air of paranoia and cultism about them." But he also offered practical instructions and price charts for those who wished to purchase gold coins legally—which was clearly a growing population—by declaring their investments to have "numismatic purposes."[42] Americans, whether responding to Browne's grim scenarios or his investment advice, devoured the message.

The book entered the *New York Times* best-seller list in February 1974, hit number 1 in April after ten weeks, and stayed on the list until November—a total of thirty-nine weeks, putting Browne at or near the top of a rarefied camp of personal finance authors (including Sylvia Porter and "Adam Smith" and very few others) whose reach could rival the nation's best-known novelists and personalities. It was remarkable that Browne could marshal such a vast audience at a time when most Americans could not legally purchase gold for investments. But of course Browne, PCCE, and everyone around them were anticipating the payoff when, at long last, Americans could.

# CHAPTER 10

## Legal at Last

THE RITUAL IS as long-standing as it is typically fruitless: on the first day of the session, a member of Congress proposes a slew of bills that set out a fresh legislative agenda. The actual chances of the bills becoming law, particularly if the legislator's party is in the minority, are on that optimistic and delicate day beside the point. In this tradition, on January 3, 1973, Representative Philip Crane, Republican of Illinois, introduced HR 435, a two-sentence bill designed "to permit American citizens to hold gold."[1] With equal hope and enthusiasm, on the same day of bill-packing, Crane also threw in bills to provide tax deductions for private school payments and to increase penalties for certain narcotics crimes.

By all rights, Crane's gold bill should have met the quiet fate of its many predecessors. On multiple occasions since gold prohibition began in 1933, various members of Congress had proposed legislation—more or less symbolically—designed to restore the legal right of Americans to own gold. Harold Johnson, for example, who was elected to Congress in 1958 from the northern California district that included the historic Sutter's Mill site, introduced a gold legalization bill on the first day he served in the House.

Just days after Richard Nixon resigned in 1974, newly installed president Gerald Ford signed a bill allowing Americans once again to buy and sell gold as an investment. His action was little noticed at the time, but would eventually create a robust domestic market in gold as an investment. *Courtesy Gerald R. Ford Presidential Library*

Howard Buffett's quixotic bills dated to the 1940s, though he was focused more on restoring a gold standard than in restoring gold ownership as an investment. Crane himself had introduced a similar bill in 1970, shortly after he arrived in Congress, but he had been unable to persuade Banking Committee chairman Wright Patman to schedule hearings, and so the bill died.

These efforts had always been extreme long shots, the monetary equivalent of betting on a 50–1 filly at the Kentucky Derby, particularly when the Bretton Woods system was intact. The Treasury Department fought fiercely through the 1950s and 1960s to maintain the prohibition against individual gold ownership, and was never going to approve a law that, from its perspective, would unnecessarily damage the US economy and international monetary system. Indeed, in a global economy where national borders mattered less every day, gold ownership was incompatible with a stable dollar exchangeable for a fixed amount of gold. Had Americans been able to participate freely in the private gold market run-up in the fall of 1960 detailed in chapter 6, for example, the US government would almost certainly have exhausted the gold that was legally required to shore up the dollar. American investors would have snapped up gold in London and other private markets, thereby raising the price and creating more panicked sales, all the while sending dollars outside the United States that would be redeemable for the shrinking volume of gold held in US reserves. (Presumably, the US government could simply have opened its "gold window" to American individuals and organizations and achieved the same calamitous result more quickly.)

After August 1971, however, some members of Congress like Crane could see an opening. Creating a private US market for gold was never a stated part of the Nixon White House's intentions when the gold window closed. Nonetheless, some kind of market was a logical and relatively straightforward consequence of that 1971 policy. With a dollar no longer automatically redeemable anywhere in the world for a fixed amount of gold, the private gold market's fluctuations would—within reasonable limits—not obviously harm the US economy. Not surprisingly, the end of gold-dollar convertibility caused the price of gold to shoot far higher than had been the case when the Bretton Woods regime was in place. Shortly after Nixon made his announcement, the price of gold on the private market went up to $43.40 an ounce; in 1972, a year later, it had soared to $70 an ounce.

Prices like that ripened conditions for a return to gold ownership. In the beginning of 1973, at least five bills in addition to Crane's were introduced into Congress with a goal of allowing Americans to buy, hold, and sell gold as an investment, and several others would aid the domestic gold-mining industry. Principally these came from Republicans, although some were sponsored by Democrats, like Harold Johnson, whose states had strong mining interests.

And yet, despite an apparent groundswell toward gold legalization, Congress on the whole tried to sidestep the issue, addressing it directly only when forced. The House scheduled no hearings on gold legalization per se; the Senate took the lead on gold inadvertently; and the White House paid so little attention to the legislation's signing that it almost seemed it was trying to keep a secret. As a result, the press shrugged, and a good portion of Washington's institutions seemed to think they might be able to kill the gold initiative before citizens actually began buying and selling bullion and coins.

Crane was a figure from the far right of the Republican Party. He had worked on Barry Goldwater's quixotic 1964 presidential campaign, and before the 1970s came to an end he would launch his own presidential bid. Like many free-market conservatives in the 1970s, Crane viewed gold ownership as a simple case of individual liberty—the difference was that he believed he could change the laws. Crane had for years been chipping away at the House leadership's—and the Nixon administration's—opposition to gold ownership laws, by slipping small text packets into official law.[2]

In the spring of 1972, after the gold window had closed, Congress passed the Par Value Modification Act, which officially devalued the dollar by about 8.5 percent. Although the dollar could no longer be exchanged for gold, the act redefined the value of the dollar from 1/35 an ounce of gold to 1/38, as had been agreed among the world's largest economies in the December 1971 "Smithsonian Agreement." Through his persistence, Crane had managed to get some language allowing eventual gold ownership tacked on to the bill, even though it was later stripped off by Banking Committee chair Wright Patman. Another legislative opportunity arose in the spring of 1973, when the dollar was being devalued yet again (to $42.22 for an ounce of gold). For this Par Value bill, Crane coordinated his effort with Idaho's newly elected senator James McClure, and actually managed to get into the final law some clauses that reversed forty years of gold prohibition—but which would take effect only when the president determined that the "elimination of regulations on private ownership of gold will not adversely affect the United States' international monetary position." This was a legislative victory for Crane and his allies, but almost entirely a theoretical one. Still, it gave a slice of confidence that there was sufficient congressional will to legalize gold at a date that Congress could fix, instead of waiting on the executive branch to decide.

At the time, the executive branch had higher priorities; and there were, after all, many difficult-to-answer questions about the restoration of an investment gold market in the United States. Would Americans rush to buy the long-forbidden metal? If so, would they flood the market—and what effect would that have, at home and abroad? For his part, Crane downplayed the impact on average investors. "I don't think it would have that great effect because the majority of persons are not in a position to make major purchases," he told a newspaper reporter. "And many would not, because of the lack of familiarity with that type of investment."[3] This perspective was interesting because Crane himself was an investor in gold coins, owning both historic American gold coins as well as Austrian krones and Mexican pesos.[4]

Perhaps Crane was trying to tamp down potential objections to his bill. But Crane and many of his allies, on Capitol Hill and beyond, did not view gold ownership primarily as an issue of choosing one investment over another. It was an assertion of fundamental American individual rights, rights that took precedence over any goal of any government. Crane's office drew on some of the same ideological sources that had informed Harry Browne's best-selling books, who treated gold as a literal instrument of human liberty. To make their point, Crane's staff sought to insert into the *Congressional Record* the text of Alan Greenspan's essay "Gold and Economic Freedom" that had been published in Ayn Rand's newsletter *The Objectivist* in 1966, which linked a ban on gold ownership to the "shabby secret" of welfare-state spending. Ayn Rand personally gave a Crane staffer, who was also her longtime fan, permission to reproduce Greenspan's article.[5]

Creating a new American gold market raised, however, several intriguing and thorny issues that could not be resolved by appeals to abstract libertarian ideals. For one: while the US gold supply had been shrinking since the 1950s, it nonetheless remained the largest owner of gold in the world by far. Was it fair for the US government to participate in the same gold-trading market as, say, a civilian trying to buy a few gold coins as a long-term investment or inflation hedge? While the government couldn't necessarily control the gold market at all times by buying or selling, it could certainly influence the price of gold, especially if it collaborated with other large gold-holders, such as the central banks of other nations— an advantage clearly not possessed by the average investor. At the same time, if the United States didn't put some of its gold holdings into the private market, it could easily be perceived as trying to undermine the private market. Crane's eventual bill was sophisticated enough to include rules for government participation, but of course these provisions were likely moot so long as Treasury opposed a public gold market in its entirety.

Further complicating the idea of a private American gold market was the still volatile world economy, in which gold continued to play a vital role. Just because the administration had declared a temporary separation of dollar-gold convertibility in 1971 did not, after all, guarantee that it would stay unstuck. Forceful players, at home and abroad, often seemed to ache for a return to the seductive stability of the Bretton Woods system or some similar gold-exchange standard. Federal Reserve chairman Arthur Burns, for one, never seemed in the 1970s to truly accept the desirability or permanence of going off the gold standard. In September 1971, he compiled a list of all the retaliatory measures that various countries had taken against the United States since the August 15 announcement. He presented them to Nixon and Treasury Secretary Connally with a warning that "a postponement of serious efforts to rebuild international monetary order would probably lead to a wave of protectionism and restrictions of all kinds, and that [the president] was taking a chance of ushering in an era of growing restrictionism, trade wars, currency wars, and the like."[6] This threat was partially resolved by the "Smithsonian Agreement" at the end of that year, which devalued the dollar and established new exchange rate bands.

Even then, however, the post–Bretton Woods system was far from locked in. After all, the major economies of the world could hardly be faulted for wanting a global monetary order based on something else than the dollar—because the dollar, in the doldrums of the early and mid-1970s, was a disaster. The devaluation by 8.5 percent in late 1971 changed next to nothing, and the Nixon administration was forced to devalue the dollar again, by 10 percent, in early 1973. This led *Time* magazine to scold: "Once upon a very recent time, only a banana republic would devalue its money twice within 14 months."[7]

The terminal weakness of the dollar hindered Washington's ability to dictate monetary terms to Western Europe, which had its own sets of problems and priorities. While Germany and Britain had adopted an attitude of disappointed resignation to the end of Bretton Woods, France's president Georges Pompidou remained as committed as his hero Charles de Gaulle to an international gold standard. Through the late summer and fall of 1973, secret talks took place in which European governments discussed trading gold among themselves at a price that approached the private market rate (at the time, close to $100 an ounce). This might well have magically increased the holdings of many European central bankers, who "seem anxious to be able to write up the value of the gold in their reserves from the current official $42.22 price."[8] George Shultz, who by then had become treasury secretary, warned of a major threat from European officials who "see the proposed move as enhancing the probability that gold will work its way back into the center of the international monetary system, and facilitate a French-European vision of a new monetary policy." One compromise that Shultz and others in the administration came up with was: let monetary authorities sell gold into private markets at prevailing rates, but allow buying from any other source to take place only at the official rate.

Washington's leading financial officials continued to see the gold supply as so fraught with risk that they opposed even seemingly innocent introductions of gold into the American market. Throughout the early 1970s, Americans were gearing up for official and unofficial celebrations of the country's "bicentennial" (the official date being July 4, 1976, the two hundredth anniversary of the signing of the Declaration of Independence). Many members of Congress favored the idea of commemorating the event with specially minted gold coins. The Fed and Treasury got to play the wet blanket role. The frequently grumpy Treasury Undersecretary Paul Volcker argued that even commemorative gold coins would send the wrong signal internationally: "Congressional action requiring the minting of gold coins would be particularly unfortunate," Volcker wrote to Congress. "The issuance of gold coins by the U.S. Government would be viewed abroad as an attempt to reemphasize the monetary importance of gold."[9] As they did so often on such matters, Volcker and the Fed got their way. The law that passed authorized a special bicentennial design for 1976-dated dollar, half-dollar, and quarter-dollar coins, as well as some special commemorative coins struck in silver—but conspicuously no gold coins.

The standoff with several dozen members of Congress on one side, and the administration and Federal Reserve on the other, might never have been resolved without Watergate, a defining event that hung over the capital like a black-funnel tornado for more than two years. Had the Watergate scandal somehow evaporated in late 1973 or early 1974, it is far from clear that the Nixon administration would have accepted gold legalization on anything resembling an imminent timetable, if ever. After all, Fed chair Burns never changed his position and held out hope that some version of a pre-1971 gold standard could be restored. Yes, pressure for gold legalization was building in Congress, but the Nixon White House was ever-resourceful in finding ways to thwart legislative intent. Nixon himself never showed any interest in the question of gold ownership and, without someone making a forceful counterargument, would likely have been persuaded that such a step needlessly risked the progress he thought for a time he'd made with the economy, to say nothing of international relations.

What changed was the position of treasury secretary. By early 1974, Shultz was limping along in his job, clearly adrift and miserable. He told friends that he had tried to resign twice, including once in a handwritten letter to the president, only to be rebuffed by the men cautiously running the besieged White House, who said that the timing was unacceptable.[10] When he finally was allowed to leave, he chose his deputy William Simon to replace him—not Nixon's first choice, but others had declined to accept the position, and there were not a lot of prominent volunteers to join a doomed administration. Simon was the first treasury secretary since the early '60s to have a Wall Street background, having worked in the government bonds division of Salomon Brothers. Unlike the pragmatists Connally and Shultz, Simon was a fervent believer in a free market; his memoir published in 1978 featured a preface from Milton Friedman and a foreword by F. A. Hayek.

In Simon's view, the combination of individual demand to invest in gold and growing congressional pressure meant that it was time for Treasury to drop its long-standing objection to gold ownership. That spring, Simon declared that restrictions on American gold ownership "are repugnant to me." He asked that Congress have "sufficient faith" to leave the timing of its removal to the president, rather than legislate a specific date, and also hinted that such a decision was mere months away.[11]

Congress, in the meantime, was finding its own way to gold ownership, albeit in a remarkably roundabout manner. Crane's and McClure's bills on gold legalization would likely have languished in obscurity if not for an unforeseen glitch in a policy area most people would not associate with gold ownership—foreign aid. The World Bank was one of the leading global institutions created by the Bretton Woods agreement, designed to provide loans to underdeveloped nations. A few years into the Bank's existence, it became clear, particularly to several of the world's poorest countries, that some otherwise desirable loans created balance-of-payments issues for the receiving nations. In response, the Bank created in 1960 the International Development Association (IDA), widely known as the Bank's "soft-loan window." The IDA made loans similar to the Bank's—for projects in transportation, electric power plants, dams, and education—but they were specifically aimed at the very poorest nations and charged only nominal interest.

For more than a decade the IDA enjoyed reliable, if lukewarm, support on Capitol Hill. But by early 1974, the landscape had shifted considerably. Several big changes included the worldwide oil crisis, notably the OPEC embargo that had begun in 1973, and the war between India and Pakistan in 1971; at the time, IDA assistance amounted to some 30 percent of all aid that India received annually. On top of the seemingly endless Vietnam War and rampant inflation in the United States, these developments left many Americans and their representatives feeling that the country would do better to spend its development dollars on its own weak economy. (Real household income sank about 5 percent between mid-1973 and early 1974, one of the fastest drops in modern US history.)[12] An influential Texan congressman summarized the view of many peers: "I am not going to vote to increase our commitments at a time when we cannot take care of folks at home, when the dollar has been under heavy pressure, when the national debt has increased by about one-fifth in the last four years and when we are going in debt this year by another $15 billion."[13]

In January, with the Nixon White House stymied by Watergate, the House rejected an IDA funding bill by a significant margin: 248–155. Nearly all Republicans voted against it, despite the White House's support—but they were joined by many liberal Democrats, who had tired of spending money on countries like India that, however needy, seemed to have enough money to fund wars. Robert McNamara, president of the World Bank, decried the House vote as "an unmitigated disaster for hundreds of millions of people in the poorest nations of the world."[14]

The Nixon administration was unpleasantly surprised by the vote. Foreign aid was part of the international chess game, and the White House was not happy to lose a battle unexpectedly, especially because the House's rejection scuttled a multinational agreement the administration had completed months before. Shultz and Kissinger issued a statement calling the vote "a major setback to our efforts of cooperation and to the ability of the United States to provide leadership in a world where there is an increasingly serious tendency for nations to believe that their best interest lies in going it alone." They scrambled to find a way to boost support for the IDA bill, and were willing to work with House and Senate Democratic leaders to find it. The answer was to win over some of the Republican opponents of the IDA bill by merging it with Crane and McClure's measure to reverse gold prohibition.

In the Senate, then, McClure's amendment for gold legalization was tacked onto the IDA bill—with White House support—in hopes of getting senators who were otherwise skeptical of foreign aid to support the bill. The floor debate, which took place over two sessions before and after Congress's Memorial Day recess, veered widely. In the period since the House had rejected the IDA bill, India had exploded a nuclear weapon, which made IDA aid to that country even harder to accept. Senator Harry Byrd argued that foreign aid would simply "permit countries like India to use her own resources to develop a weapon that could plunge this country into chaos."

On the other side were senators who were clearly attracted to the idea of restoring gold ownership to Americans. Pete Dominick, Republican of Colorado, called the United States "the only country whose citizens are not entitled to own gold." (This was not accurate, although restrictions against gold ownership dating from the Depression/World War II era were easing.) "When we do not have any gold convertibility in our dollar, it makes no sense to treat gold any differently than we would treat any other raw material."

The bill passed by a roll call vote 55–27. That strong margin gave Treasury Secretary Simon plenty of leverage with which to pressure Burns. "I continue to feel that it is imperative that a comprehensive decision be reached this week on the U.S. position regarding gold," he wrote to Burns the following day.[15] Burns had expressed a fear that, with the Europeans still trying to maneuver to find a way to restore an official price of gold, opening up the private market to US citizens could damage the US position. Simon cautioned Burns that sentiment in the House made it "most unlikely" that gold ownership could be postponed beyond year's end, and urged him to find a way to make peace with what was coming.

Cynical observers might have perceived some tactical brilliance in pairing a bill that many would reluctantly support but few actively wanted—IDA authorization—with a bill that many actively wanted: gold ownership. There was also a hint of hypocrisy in linking foreign aid expenditures—arguably the very type of big government spending that gold advocates opposed—to a bill that relegalized gold ownership. On the floor of Congress, few bothered to actually examine the economic impact of gold ownership. One exception was California's Thomas Rees: "What worries me about the ownership of gold is that a lot of innocent people will be buying gold, and I think they are going to lose their shirt. The speculators will eat them up." More common were those who decried the way the issues had been awkwardly molded together. Henry Gonzalez of Texas, who had introduced the original IDA authorization bill that the House rejected, now cried foul: "The authors of this bill hope that everyone will have his eyes blinded by gold, and that gold will be the subject of debate, and that nobody will pause and ask about that other little thing, the billion and a half for IDA." He continued: "These issues are wholly unrelated, and there is not one reason on the Earth or in heaven that they should be joined."[16]

Some conservative Republicans, too, had trouble accepting the improbable merger of issues. Those who had opposed the IDA authorization back in January were no happier with foreign aid in July. Maryland's Robert Bauman, a founder of the conservative campus group Young Americans for Freedom, addressed his ideological allies directly: "You are trading off your principles totally without any gain. You are making a great mistake. If this bill and other bills like it pass, we all will need our gold because our money will be worthless."[17] Bill Ketchum of California asked Crane bluntly: "Would it not occur to the gentleman that in this field perhaps a little bribery is at stake here?" Crane replied: "I would not call it bribery. I would call it exactly what politics is all about, frankly, the art of compromise."

Bribery or compromise, the resolution passed the House by a vote of 225–140. The roll call vote was about as topsy-turvy as a House vote gets. Liberal Democrats who normally would have supported foreign aid voted against the bill—but so did Jack Kemp, a conservative Republican who would soon become synonymous with gold politics. The whole effort nearly came to a halt over a tiny but significant difference in language between the House and Senate versions. On July 25, the Senate appeared to clear the bill, through a voice vote and with no discussion about differences with the House bill. There was, arguably, some ambiguity over whether the House version of the bill might have left loopholes that a president could use to reinstate a ban on gold ownership. McClure then maneuvered to invalidate the earlier Senate vote and add an amendment. Senator Hubert Humphrey then tried to hold the bill up in late July. The details were hammered out, and the final bill cleared both houses. But the drama had yet to end: The bill still needed to be signed by the president—and where was the president?

On August 2, the chief executive clerk at the White House received S 2665 for the president's approval, and asked the Office of Management and Budget for "reports and recommendations" from various departments about whether or not the president should sign or veto the bill. (Presumably the OMB director Roy Ash was not involved; he had recused himself from gold policy, apparently because he was an investor in gold stocks.)[18] These reports dribbled in over the next several days. In his typical go-slow manner, Federal Reserve chairman Burns was fearful of moving ahead. "There are significant risks—unsettlement in financial markets, pressure on the dollar in exchange markets—associated with allowing private ownership of gold at this time," Burns warned. "I therefore believe that the portion of the bill referring to gold regulation is unfortunate," Burns wrote, and recommended monitoring market reaction closely and possibly repealing this part of the bill.[19] Treasury Secretary Simon expressed the idiosyncratic and rather dire view that the language in the statute might "be interpreted as prohibiting all regulation of gold transactions, even when such regulation is applicable to other commodities and does not single out gold." Simon insisted that "the President must have the same authority to regulate gold as he has to regulate other commodities—and that this might be especially important in an emergency situation." Nonetheless, Simon did not formally oppose signing the bill.

The griping within the administration was not limited to those whose views had been officially sought. Herb Stein from the Council of Economic Advisers admonished a Treasury official for not having set up a meeting to discuss the pending gold legislation. He was aghast that the president was not being presented with more pessimistic views. For one, he said, "There are people who will think that the sale of gold is the dissipation of our last patrimony."[20] He also pointed out that "we don't have the foggiest idea of the amount of additional gold American citizens will want."

All of this was wasted verbiage, as it is doubtful that President Nixon ever laid eyes on any of these comments. On August 8, Nixon announced to the world what he had been discussing with confidants for days: that he would resign the presidency, effective the next day. This threw supporters and critics of the IDA/gold bill into confusion—had Nixon signed the bill into law before announcing he was stepping down? In the chaos and secrecy surrounding the White House, for a time no one in Congress knew; "eventually, it was determined that he had not."[21]

It fell to freshly installed president Gerald Ford—as of this day, the only American president who was never elected by the nation's voters—to sign the IDA/gold bill into Public Law 93-373 on August

14; it was, in fact, Ford's first signing of a bill into law. There was next to no pageantry or pomp about the event. A signing statement drafted for Nixon didn't mention the bill's gold provision at all. The White House press office—perhaps distracted by the continued whirl of events around Nixon, his aides, and Congress, or perhaps fearful of the delicate politics around the bill—also did not trumpet the newly restored right of Americans to buy and sell gold. In the noon press briefing that day, White House press secretary Jerry terHorst announced that the president had met with his national security team; he had met with the Soviet ambassador; and he had planned meetings later in the day with the Egyptian foreign minister as well as various American mayors and governors. At no point did he mention that Ford had signed into law a bill allowing Americans to own gold for the first time since FDR's presidency— and neither did any reporter ask about it.[22] Accordingly, the news coverage the following day was muted. The *New York Times*, for example, did not publish a staff-written story the next day about Ford's approval of the bill, relying instead on a dispatch from the Reuters wire service. Each of the three network news broadcasts devoted a segment to it: ABC's and NBC's were ten seconds long, and CBS's was twenty seconds long. Reactions from various markets were largely ambiguous, and given the turmoil in the world at the time—the chance that Nixon and other top aides would be indicted, the looming oil crisis, American inflation, and a coup d'etat in Cyprus followed by a Turkish invasion—it would have been close to impossible to pinpoint an exact reaction to the end of gold prohibition. One exception was the stock market: on the day that Ford signed the gold legalization bill into law, the Dow Jones Industrial Average, for the fifth consecutive day, declined and hit a four-year low—which made the rally in gold-mining companies stand out even more.

Throughout Congress's gyrations, the private American gold market was preparing itself for a bonanza. During the first half of 1974, as gold continued to trade at more than $100 an ounce, US citizens were traveling north to Canada to buy gold wafers as small as 25 grams.[23] Each purchaser had to sign an affidavit declaring that the purchase "does not in any way contravene the gold regulations of the U.S. Treasury Department," but in truth, the government had ceased to enforce the law in any systematic way for small purchases. By early August, even before Ford signed the bill into law, four of the largest commodity-futures exchanges had announced their plans to begin trading gold-futures contracts as soon as the ban was officially lifted. Prior to this, the only gold-futures market in the world was in Winnipeg. At least one Wall Street broker, Samuel Weiss, sought and received permission to trade gold bars in various sizes through the New York Stock Exchange (NYSE), on which he would charge a 6 percent markup over a given day's spot price—dramatically less than coin dealers charged. "This is a chance for the average person to buy gold in quantities he can afford without having to go into the numismatic market and pay much higher prices," Weiss told the press.[24]

All this preparation assumed, of course, that trading would begin on December 31, as the law stipulated. This assumption was not universally shared. As late as November 1974, with the gold legalization start date as authorized by Congress a month away, the Ford White House considered putting on the brakes.[25] There were many reluctances, some obscure, but the main one was the fear of "downward pressure on the dollar in the exchange markets, since all the gold for private investment will need to come from imports."[26] This is a remarkable sentiment, implying that allowing Americans to own gold as an investment would effectively undo one of the presumed advantages of Nixon going off the gold standard more than three years before. From this point of view (attributed to Arthur Burns), the ease of international trading created a free market in gold which in turn meant that the value of the dollar was threatened no matter what its relationship to gold—fixed or floating. Whether or not one accepts the idea, it's also a compelling reminder that, in the mid-1970s, almost any public

policy idea—from deficit spending to foreign aid—could be effectively attacked if plausibly presented as fanning the inflation fires.

The question of the government's role in the gold market—not
addressed in the final version of the law that Congress passed—
continued to vex officials. Part of Burns's objection seemed to arise
from a sense of philosophical consistency: "I would be inclined to
oppose at this time any effort to maintain an 'orderly market' via
sales or auctions out of the Treasury gold stock. The primary argument that has been used by proponents of private ownership is that
a prohibition on U.S. citizens' purchases and sales is an infringe-
ment of their rights and freedoms. Treasury sales of gold could be
viewed as undercutting this philosophy." Perhaps more troubling
was the idea that once Treasury was in the market, it might be hard
to get out: "Moreover, once some Treasury sales had been made,
it might be difficult to resist pressures for further intervention in
the future—either to support the price or to keep it from rising.
All in all, it would seem better to let the market find its own level
and bear the costs of any speculative excesses that might manifest
themselves at the outset."[27]

And if experts addressing one another behind the scenes had
trouble settling the question of the government's relationship to
gold, among the general public it was downright peculiar. Ever
since gold prohibition had begun in the 1930s, the public had been
fascinated by the store of gold in Fort Knox, Kentucky. Although
it was not the largest stockpile of government gold in the United
States, the degree of military security around the gold developed
into legendary proportions. Two men were needed to unlock com-
binations to the main vault, neither one knowing the other combination; if a blowtorch were to touch the main part of the vault, the
chamber would be flooded with poisonous gas, supposedly stron-
ger than any gas mask; etc. The mythologizing of Fort Knox probably climaxed with the 1964 James Bond movie *Goldfinger*, which
featured an elaborate plot to penetrate Fort Knox's security and
irradiate its gold (this modified the plot of the Ian Fleming novel,

in which Goldfinger and his gang attempt to steal all the gold). *Goldfinger* was the highest-grossing movie in the United States in 1964; some theaters stayed open around the clock to accommodate viewer demand.

Perhaps by coincidence, at around the same time that Congress was moving to allow individuals to buy and sell gold, rumors began to circulate that Fort Knox was missing all or some of its gold. Such theories had been pushed at least since the early 1960s by the John Birch Society and other fringe groups. But by 1974, at least part of the fringe had moved into the political mainstream. In 1973, a man named Peter David Beter published *Conspiracy Against the Dollar*, a book in many ways aligned with Harry Browne and other "hard money" titles of the time, but with a more conspiratorial edge and a particular animus against the Rockefeller family. In 1974, Beter charged that the government had drained Fort Knox of much of its gold and sold it to David Rockefeller. Victor Harkin, the civil servant in charge of Fort Knox's gold, dismissed Beter's charges as "the remarks of an idiot."[28]

The vagueness of Beter's accusations made them difficult to prove or disprove. It was true, for example, that hundreds of tons of gold were shipped out of Fort Knox to Great Britain in late 1967 and early 1968 (see chapter 8). But there's no way of knowing if those shipments were what Beter was referring to; nor is there any reason to think that the shipments weren't accounted for in Treasury's books (though certainly Treasury did not try to draw attention to the sizable gold drain). While no mainstream media organizations gave the Fort Knox story noticeable attention, the tale spread through unorthodox channels, including the tabloid *National Tattler* and a popular Dallas radio host.

It was Congress that brought Beter's loose charges into the official record. That summer, Crane directly confronted Treasury Secretary Simon with the idea that Fort Knox gold had been depleted. With Watergate secrecy dragging government credibility to a modern low, Simon responded with a dose of transparency, suggesting that a congressional visit and a government audit would be in order. In September, Crane and several conservative colleagues—including onetime John Birch Society officer John Rousselot—took an unprecedented tour through Fort Knox. US Mint Director Mary Brooks opened a vault door to "oohs" and "aahs," while members of Congress sized up bullion bars with tape measures. Treasury insisted that no gold had left the facility in three years, and the members declared themselves satisfied that the rumors were baseless.

For a time, anyway. It is usually hard to know how such rumors get started, and harder still to know their motivations. Certainly in the waning months of gold prohibition, it appeared that some people perceived a financial advantage in fudging the facts. Even after the September inspection, for example, House conservatives would not let go of the idea that Fort Knox gold was not all it seemed. Three days before Treasury's first scheduled gold sale in January 1975, Congressman John Conlan of California (who had been part of the September delegation) sent Simon an urgent telex message calling for "immediate postponement for 30 days of the U.S. government gold sale." The reason, Conlan explained, was that "financial experts" were advising him that the Fort Knox audit "may show government holdings of pure-delivery gold are substantially below the 24-million ounces treasurer [sic] officials originally announced were among U.S. stocks."[29] (The audit, when released in February, showed nothing of the kind, although skepticism about Fort Knox's holdings never fully disappeared.)[30]

In the end, President Ford and Treasury Secretary Simon rejected the idea of stalling, and the government also made a commitment to sell 2 million ounces of its gold holdings. The beginning of legal gold trading prompted President Ford to make perhaps his only public remark about gold ownership. On December 31, the day that the gold markets reopened in America, Ford was skiing in

Vail, Colorado (he and his wife had bought a condominium there a few years earlier, during a time when Vail was not a common destination for those outside Colorado). The president, dressed in a blue ski parka and blue pants and carrying skis over his shoulder, was on his way to the chairlifts that morning when the press peppered him with a few light questions. "You gonna buy any gold, Mr. President?" a reporter asked. Ford's brief reply: "No, I'm not a speculator."[31]

And in the early days of legal gold ownership, many seemed to share Ford's indifference. Despite all the buildup; despite all the assertion of gold ownership as a fundamental American right; and despite the tens of thousands of Americans who had snapped up Harry Browne's books, the market for bullion and gold futures met with a lackluster reception. During the entire first day of trading, the Wall Street firm Merrill Lynch took exactly one gold order—for 20 ounces. Samuel Weiss, who'd arranged with the NYSE to trade gold even before the law had been signed, told the New York Times that first day: "There is no gold rush. It's the biggest dud I've seen in my entire life."[32]

One consequence of the convoluted way in which gold legalization came about is that Congress hadn't bothered to address the tax question, and states reached different conclusions. California's state tax code, for example, specifically exempted from taxation any sales of gold coins or bullion over $1,000. New York, New Jersey, and Pennsylvania all found ways to adopt the opposite view, while in Florida, it took years of litigation before the matter was settled.[33] In the early days of gold trading, it was thus impossible for many Americans to get reliable advice on the tax consequences of a gold investment.

As 1975 wore on, the American demand for gold took on a form that few had anticipated. The appetite for buying and storing physical gold was modest; gold bullion in particular held little appeal for the American investor. But gold legalization did create a strong market for gold futures—that is, a contract to buy gold at some future date at an agreed-upon price. By late July, about 500 tons' worth of gold, worth about $2.5 billion, had traded in futures contracts since the beginning of the year, making US gold futures the largest gold market in the world.[34] (By 1977, the volume of gold futures contracts would soar to more than $15 billion.) It is plausible that Americans found this method of gold investing less risky or more convenient or both. However, if the goal was to hedge against inflation it was, by midyear, a disappointment for many investors; the price of gold had dropped about 10 percent since the first futures contracts began trading in January, while inflation continued to rise to dangerous levels. All the mystical and historic properties of gold as a storage of value could not change the fact that anything traded as a commodity will rise and fall in value.

Of course, it could also be argued that the gold market in 1975 was not exactly open and fair. The role of the federal government—and by extension, the role of Western central banks and the IMF—in the gold market was never resolved to universal satisfaction (and never will be). The law Ford signed did not stipulate what role, if any, Treasury or the Federal Reserve was to play in the gold market. Although in theory the government ought to have been agnostic on the price of gold, in practice there were powerful reasons to see its price remain stable at a relatively low level. In the broadest sense, the US government remained committed to reducing the global monetary role of gold, and a higher price could push other nations to deviate from that goal. Still, the logic of this position was elusive, even to some financial experts. In a December 1974 meeting in Martinique between high-level French and American officials, French president Valery Giscard d'Estaing, who had twice been his country's finance minister, asked Ford and his aides: "Your people in Treasury are violently opposed to monetizing gold. Why? Five years ago it was protecting the dollar, but now it is floating." William Simon's response was less than illuminating: "The concern is that if everyone raised the price and kept it at the center of the system, it would make the system more vulnerable."[35]

More concretely, a higher gold price would benefit the two largest producers—South Africa and the Soviet Union—each of which, the United States feared, could create market distortions that were best avoided.[36] To keep the gold price low, then, the US government began to sell gold into the private market. (The gold sales also had the effect of easing the trade balance deficit, because gold sales to foreign entities counted as exports.) The administration committed in advance to selling 2 million ounces of gold once the US gold market began in January 1975; it could not, however, command the price it wanted (above $153 an ounce) and ended up selling less than half of the amount up for auction.[37] The irony was deep and wrenching. For decades, the United States had vigilantly guarded its gold supply against any market development that would force it to ship the metal overseas. Now, at last, when it was ready to sell, the government couldn't find enough buyers at the right price. Subsequent auctions, beginning in mid-1975, were for smaller piles of gold. But Arthur Burns's prediction came true—having started out as a participant in the gold market, the US government found it impossible to get out.

In a tremendous coincidence of supply and demand, the market was about to explode for the perfect gold vehicle: the Krugerrand. The Krugerrand is the widest-circulating gold coin in human history; some 50 million have been minted as of this writing. It represents a world-class marketing triumph for the government and gold-mining industry of South Africa. The Krugerrand features on its face the likeness of Paul Kruger, a Boer nationalist who became a four-time president of the Republic of South Africa toward the end of the nineteenth century; on the reverse is a springbok, the national symbol of South Africa. Each coin contains exactly one troy ounce of fine gold (it is 11 parts gold to one part copper, which adds durability to the metal), making its value extremely simple to calculate at any time. Since production began in the late 1960s, the coin has always had legal-tender status in South Africa, but it has no monetary value stamped on it and was never intended for use in commercial trade.[38] Rather, the legal-tender status allowed other countries to import the coins without paying the import duties that would be tacked onto a commemorative coin or medal.

When gold trading became legal in the United States, the Krugerrand was already the largest-circulating gold coin in the world, with the United Kingdom as its largest external market. But that was about to change, and quickly. In the fall of 1975, Intergold—the marketing arm of South Africa's Chamber of Mines—hired the New York advertising agency Doyle Dane Bernbach to create a campaign to sell the Krugerrand to Americans. The ads focused on two basic ideas: gold is a smart thing to have as part of an overall investment portfolio; and the Krugerrand is the best way to own pure gold. The campaign began with an eleven-week test beginning in October, with newspaper ads in Los Angeles and Philadelphia, and newspaper ads plus television spots in Houston. The target audience was men between the ages of 25 and 54.[39] The television spot featured a man walking toward a cube meant to represent all the gold that has ever been mined in the history of mankind—a mere 18 yards on each side. "It's rare," intones a voiceover. "It's precious. And there's less new gold to be mined each year. You can own one ounce of that precious gold with every South African Krugerrand." To make action very simple, the spot provided a national, toll-free 800-number that viewers could call to get more information and be directed to a gold dealer in their area.

The results were startling. Prior to the ad campaign, American familiarity with the Krugerrand was at or close to zero. During the period that the ads were running, fully half of all Krugerrands sold in the United States were in those three markets. A single Houston bank reported selling 1,600 Krugerrands during the test period. In 1976 the campaign was extended to include $4 million of ads across twenty-five markets. In January 1978, South Africa sold 669,000 Krugerrands—more than triple the number sold the previous January, and the majority of these were sold in the United States. By the time 1978 came to a close, more than 6 million coins had sold for the year, nearly doubling the previous year's sales. By this time, the US government had decided that it needed to get in on the one-ounce gold coin action. Jim Leach in the House and Jesse Helms in the Senate worked to get Treasury to mint and distribute one-ounce commemorative gold coins featuring American heroes like Mark Twain and Willa Cather. And with the market price of gold over $300 an ounce in early 1979, many of the earliest Krugerrand buyers in the United States had been handsomely rewarded.

The ease with which Americans could buy Krugerrands seemed to carry a potent cultural symbolism beyond a mere investment tool. In the 1981 novel *Rabbit Is Rich*, John Updike treated Krugerrands like a psychological aphrodisiac, a symbol of America's newfound wealth and even virility. His hero Rabbit Angstrom buys a stack of Krugerrands and surprises his otherwise sexually estranged wife with them in the bedroom. He strews Krugerrands on the bedspread and places coins on her naked body as they carnally roll in gold like some X-rated version of Scrooge McDuck.

Increasing Americans' awareness of South African gold, however, carried a darker side. South Africa since 1948 had been run as an apartheid regime, in which a white ruling minority denied voting and other basic rights to a large black majority. There was no country of comparable size with such a vast racial divide, and as far back as 1950, the United Nations had begun a series of increasingly harsh criticisms and attempts to isolate the South African government. In late 1968, for example, the UN General Assembly approved a resolution urging all states to suspend any cultural, educational, or sports ties to South Africa. And in the mid-1970s, the South African government's oppression appeared to be worsening. Protests in the Soweto township in June 1976 turned violent, and the police shot and killed hundreds of protestors, nearly all of them high school students.

Although the sins of apartheid were probably not major concerns for Americans buying Krugerrands, South Africa's gold industry was directly linked to its segregation practices.[40] On a symbolic level, Soweto and other townships surrounding Johannesburg owed their very existence to the gold mines nearby. In the mid-1970s, the South African mining industry employed about 380,000 workers, of whom approximately 90 percent were black. Those workers were paid an average of $124 a month, about one-fifth of what white South Africans were paid. And gold exports were absolutely vital to the apartheid government's operations: in 1976 gold exports earned the country more than $2.7 billion, representing 40 percent of its foreign trade total. Congress had concluded at least as far back as the late 1960s that without gold exports, the South African state would experience "massive deflation and domestic industrial dislocation."[41] Indeed, South Africa's role as the world's largest gold-mining state had raised political issues in the past. When, for example, the Nixon administration cut a deal in 1970 allowing the IMF to buy gold from South Africa, Congressman Henry Reuss of Wisconsin criticized the arrangement for "institutionalizing South Africa as a supplier of gold."

Nonetheless, most American official criticisms of South Africa's gold from the era when Americans couldn't buy it focused more on potential abuse of South Africa's gold market power than on its ties to a systematically racist state. The antiapartheid movement in the United States in 1977 was relatively small, but beginning to show considerable organizing power. Krugerrands made a highly visible target, and the more they sold, the bigger the target became. One obvious bit of activist ammunition was that Paul Kruger had written in his memoir: "The black man had to be taught that he came second and that he belongs to the inferior class that must obey."

The largest local TV stations in the country—the three television channels in New York City that were owned and operated by the major networks, WABC-TV, WCBS-TV, and WNBC-TV—responded to local pressure by ceasing to broadcast the Krugerrand ads. On October 13, 1977, the Massachusetts State House of Representatives officially condemned the ads and the sale of Krugerrands. City councils in Chicago, Dayton, Denver, and San Antonio passed resolutions denouncing the ads. In several cities, activists used the TV spots' 800-number against them—they would call the number to get a local gold dealer's address, and then set up a protest outside. These protests had genuine impact: at the end of 1977, Merrill Lynch, the nation's largest brokerage firm, announced that it would stop selling Krugerrands; it had been the target of well-organized protests in Los Angeles and elsewhere. In the eyes of millions, buying a Krugerrand had come to mean endorsing an unjust racist government that propped itself up by brutalizing its own citizens. An editorial in the *Berkshire Eagle* concluded harshly: "The security sought by the investor in South African gold—which might in any case be less secure than imagined due to the fluctuating world price of gold—is bought at the expense of a majority whose only security is the peace of the grave."[42]

It seemed impossible that America's Krugerrand party could go on forever. Just three years after Crane's gold-ownership bill had become law in the most unlikely way, on the opposite side of the Capitol Hill aisle, several Democrats began introducing ambitious bills of their own, focused on trade with South Africa and the Krugerrand at the head of the line. As early as October 1977, Massachusetts congressman Edward Markey introduced the South African Trade Limitation Act, which would "prohibit the importation of articles manufactured or produced by labor whose wages are differentiated on the basis of race." Congressman Stephen Solarz of Brooklyn, New York, said that prior to offering his specific ban on Krugerrand sales in the United States in 1980, he took seriously the idea that a ban might end up harming South African miners. Solarz wrote in a memoir that he consulted Cyril Ramaphosa, a prominent antiapartheid lawyer who created a miners' union.[43] According to Solarz, Ramaphosa "made it clear that exerting pressure on the South African government to abandon apartheid was essential, even if this meant that some of his union's members would lose their jobs."

The decades-long effort to open the world's gold market to American citizens had finally succeeded. Accompanying it, though, came the world's complicated, often hostile politics; Krugerrands would end up illegal again in a few short years. And what did not occur, in the years immediately following gold legalization, is economic prosperity. Whatever it might accomplish, the right to buy and sell gold did not restore the dollar, or bring about the reductions in inflation that Nixon and Ford both promised, or create jobs; in 1975, the unemployment rate soared above 8 percent for the first time since the Depression. By the late 1970s, Philip Crane, Jesse Helms, Ronald Reagan, and legions of brokers and dealers would try to sell Americans on the idea that gold could cure those ills—if only we made it the basis of our money again.

# CHAPTER 11

## Goldbugs in Power

IT WAS THE FINAL DAY of the Senate's session of the 94th Congress—Friday, October 1, 1976. It being a presidential election year, President Ford that day was soon heading off on a six-day campaign tour, after meeting with the French foreign minister as well as several high-ranking Soviet officials. The House had already wrapped up its business and many members had already left town.

And the Senate was hoping to do the same, but there was at least one bill that seemed stuck, if not outright doomed, keeping the senators and staff there until after midnight. Ever since the world's largest economies had adopted a system of floating currencies, the International Monetary Fund had been operating under an outdated set of rules, particularly regarding its use of gold in international transactions. The bill before the Senate would update the rules, in line with an agreement that had been hammered out among the IMF's largest members in a Jamaica meeting earlier in the year.[1] This seemed like a straightforward and sufficiently popular plan; the Ford administration was pushing the bill hard, and the House had passed its version back in July by a better than 2-to-1 margin.

But in the Senate, the IMF bill nearly died. Senators on both the right and left were intent on hold-

Encouraged by the brisk sales of South African Krugerrands, the United States began minting and selling its own gold coins in 1986. They quickly became the best-selling gold coin in the country and added to the strong comeback of the US gold-mining industry.

ing up the bill to make broader political points. Banking Committee chair William Proxmire, a liberal Wisconsin Democrat, wanted
to add provisions that would have made it illegal for American
companies to participate in the Arab boycott of Israel. And Jesse
Helms, a North Carolina Republican, wanted to put additional constraints on the IMF's use of gold, as well as to restore that relic that
nearly derailed FDR's gold plan more than forty years before: the
gold clause in contracts. During the long period of gold prohibition, contracts that pegged the value of payments to gold—once
common—were not practical and were effectively outlawed. But
with gold now legal for Americans to own and decoupled from the
dollar, Helms and many others argued that there was no longer
any valid reason to keep people from drawing up "gold clause" contracts (including in bond issues or rental/loan agreements). Such
contracts had potential appeal to creditors, who could be assured
that they would not be paid back over time with dollars worth far
less than when the contract was signed. In the mid- and late 1970s,
with inflation rates sometimes crossing into double digits, that was
far from a theoretical concern.

Howard Segermark, who worked for Helms as an economic
counsel, was standing on the Senate floor when a page approached
him. There was a phone call in the cloakroom from the Treasury
Department, from someone wanting to speak to Senator Helms.
Did Segermark want to take the call? Segermark had only been
working for Helms for a few months and was unsure of procedure,
but decided he should. When he picked up the phone, on the other
end was an irate Treasury Secretary William Simon. "His language was very coarse," Segermark recalled.[2] "Every other word
was 'shit' and 'fuck,'" Simon was in a bind. He was scheduled to
travel to Manila in a few days for the annual meeting of the IMF
and World Bank board of directors, and he did not relish the idea of
showing up empty-handed. Simon tried to apply pressure: he said
he was being personally embarrassed, and moreover the United
States was being embarrassed, by the Senate holdup of the IMF bill.

Segermark listed Helms's conditions for support. "He said 'Explain to me what the gold clause is.'" Segermark did, and Simon said he wouldn't stand in the way of restoring the gold clause. This was a victory for Helms, but an empty one: it was too late to amend the House bill to include a gold clause because the session had closed; any gold-clause legislation would have to wait for the 95th Congress. In addition, there was a reasonable chance that Ford would lose the election in a month, in which case Simon would no longer be Treasury Secretary, and the theoretical victory would evaporate. Thinking quickly, Segermark told Simon that if the election went to Jimmy Carter, Simon should include in his instructions to his successor that Treasury should support the restoration of gold clauses in contracts. Simon said that he would and remarkably, according to Segermark, "he kept his word."

It is a trademark tale of Jesse Helms politics. To most of the public, Helms, the Republican senator from North Carolina for thirty years, was and is known as a "righteous warrior" for causes championed by social conservatives: opposition to abortion, affirmative action, women's rights, and gay rights, and support for prayer in public schools. He also fought tirelessly for anti-Communist regimes abroad. His legislative maneuvers—threats of filibusters; holding up seemingly routine judicial and diplomatic appointments to make a political point—gave headaches to several presidents, especially Jimmy Carter and Bill Clinton, and earned him the nickname "Senator No." Helms's uncompromising politics could at times be awkward even for those who broadly agreed with him, such as his efforts to prevent the federal government from creating a holiday honoring Martin Luther King Jr., whom Helms labeled a Communist.

Far less well known is that in the 1970s, Helms proved himself highly effective in garnering support for laws to increase gold's influence in America's economic life. To this day, even Helms's biographers and official champions almost always overlook his gold advocacy.[3] Such omissions are striking, because the economically tumultuous late 1970s and early 1980s represent a kind of high-water mark for the gold-standard movement in post-FDR America, at least in terms of its actual viability to change monetary policy (as opposed, say, to political popularity). As inflation and unemployment ravaged the nation, and as annual budget deficits began to routinely top $100 billion, many politicians on the right wing of the Republican Party continued to push gold as an economic fix. Tens of thousands of Americans now owned gold, and much of the political rhetoric extolling gold ownership as a form of freedom transferred over to a gold-based monetary system (even if, in theory and in practice, these were very different animals). And the politicians preaching the power of gold were no longer on the margins. Ronald Reagan's rise to power in 1980 corresponded with a wave of West Coast, mostly Republican politicians—such as Golden Rooster defense lawyer turned Nevada statesman Paul Laxalt—who deliberately mixed gold advocacy with a broader lower-tax, smaller-government agenda. In some cases, these legislators had close ties to mining interests, such as Steven Symms of Idaho. Symms bought silver futures while serving on a House subcommittee overseeing the Commodity Futures Trading Commission, which many saw as a conflict of interest (which he denied), and would later serve on the board of directors of a gold mining company.

The Gold Commission that Helms was able to pass through Congress was the most protracted and serious public effort the federal government has undertaken since the Roosevelt administration to assess gold's monetary role. And by the late '80s, Alan Greenspan—a disciple of Ayn Rand—was chairman of the Federal Reserve Board. At no point in postwar America have so many highly placed officials been so well disposed to restoring a gold monetary system as in the 1980s.

And Helms certainly laid the groundwork. Although his attachment to gold was largely an extension of his deeply held beliefs in a free-market economy, Helms had grown up in Monroe, North Carolina, the epicenter of the nineteenth century Carolina Gold Rush. As a teenager during the Depression, he'd seen desperate men return to the Carolina mines in hopes of prying a living out of the ground. Helms took office in 1973 and quickly began working on gold advocacy, albeit in some unlikely-seeming areas. The gold-clause legislation was something he inherited from congressional allies. It began life with a law professor's 1975 opinion article in the *Wall Street Journal* which made the case to restore gold clauses.[4] The article cast the argument in terms of ultimate freedom for individuals. "If the dominant political philosophy holds that government is omnipotent—that it can grant, withhold or withdraw its citizens' rights whenever it wishes, for any reason or for no reason at all; that it can exterminate its unwilling young men in declared or undeclared wars or force the productive to support the indigent—then it has the power to outlaw Gold Clauses. On the other hand, if the dominant political philosophy holds that government power is limited, that its citizens' rights are inalienable, that its proper function is to protect life, liberty, and property, then, but only then, will Gold Clauses be secure."

Within a few weeks, Representative Phil Crane, who had hit legislative pay dirt the year before with gold ownership, introduced a bill "to remove all obstacles to the use of gold clauses." As with so many such sweeping bills, it was referred to the House Banking Committee and ignored. In early 1976, Helms—guided by Segermark—wrote to Fed chair Arthur Burns and Treasury Secretary William Simon to inquire about their views on gold clauses. Simon's opposition was reflexive and absolute; Treasury in general objected to any move that would increase the monetary role of gold. Burns said that he might personally have no objection to gold clauses but that the Federal Reserve board would likely be "split" on the matter.

Helms was characteristically undaunted. On June 14, 1976, he introduced a Senate resolution similar to Crane's. His rationale was straightforward: "When Congress restored the freedom of Americans to own gold, it neglected to restore the freedom to enter into contracts which require payment in gold or dollars measured in gold. It is time this oversight is rectified."

Despite the seeming simplicity, Helms's proposed law raised at least two practical questions. The first was: Did anyone really want to use gold-clause contracts? The wheels of commerce had not exactly ground to a halt after Congress negated gold-clause contracts, or when the Court upheld their abrogation; businesses both inside and outside the United States found ways to adapt. And yet, for some American businesses trying to cope with a continually weakening dollar, gold-clause contracts could appear attractive. Chief among these were shipping and grain companies who exported their items abroad; between the changing value of commodities and the fluctuating exchange values of currencies, they could be hammered even by a contract that was fulfilled on its terms. Another possible application of the bill would be for companies to issue investment bonds indexed to gold; in industries that are especially sensitive to changes in interest rates, such as utilities, this was potentially useful. Even so, there wasn't exactly a clamor from the American business community to restore gold-clause contracts; demand for them was "mostly anecdotal," according to Segermark. Instead, Helms viewed the gold-clause bill as one of several steps that America could take on the way to returning to a gold standard.

The second, more arcane question was: Could the law be applied retroactively? That is, if legal obstacles to gold-clause contracts were formally removed, would the parties to gold-clause contracts signed before 1934, which had been voided by Congress and the Supreme Court, now have a case that the contract was enforceable? This was a multibillion-dollar can of worms that even some goldbugs, let alone members of Congress, were not eager to open. As noted in chapter 5, the value of bonds with gold clauses in the United States—including security bonds, state and municipal bonds, and corporate and real estate bonds—at the time of the congressional ban was estimated at more than $100 billion, of which $40 billion was ostensibly wiped out by dollar depreciation. Although few were actually debating the Helms proposal, it raised in principle the same dilemma that the Roosevelt administration and the Supreme Court had faced, except in reverse. Helms, hoping to pass his resolution but not wanting to alienate goldbug absolutists, added a fudging amendment to his resolution two months after its introduction, to the effect that it "intended to stand neutral with regard to the enforceability of gold clause obligations issued in the past."

Helms worked hard to secure support for a bill that was on almost no one else's agenda. He sought and received support from no less an economic authority than Milton Friedman, the renowned free-market theorist who won the Nobel Prize in economics that year. The economist expressed "strong support for your measure and the hope that you are successful in achieving its passage this year." Friedman continued: "I believe the prohibition on the use of gold clauses in contracts was never justified, should not have been adopted in 1934 and certainly has no place whatsoever today now that gold no longer has any significant relation to our monetary system."[5] For his part, Helms saw a grander agenda, a clarion call for restraining government spending and a weapon to help slay the big government spending that many conservatives complained about in the 1970s but often found it impossible to stem. "In my mind, use of gold-clause contracts will be a clear warning that people are tired of irresponsible Government monetary and fiscal policies," Helms said. "If gold clauses begin to be widely used, it will be time for Government to restore integrity to the dollar."[6]

Sweet-sounding arguments, however, would not suffice to push through a bill that most legislators could barely describe if they were aware of it at all—even if Treasury stuck to its bargain not to

oppose the bill. And so, just as Crane had done with the gold legalization bill in 1974, Helms found a legislative vehicle on which his
proposal could hitch a ride. It was a thoroughly boring bill, little
more than a bit of government housekeeping. Going back at least
to the days of Andrew Jackson, there has been an American uneas-
iness with the idea of letting the federal government run banks, or
even allowing the government to use the banking system in order
to make money. Through 1977, the federal government maintained
accounts in the twelve Federal Reserve banks and some 14,000 commercial banks across the country; the latter neither paid interest
nor charged fees for maintaining the accounts. This system served
a variety of purposes, one of which was to store the withholding
tax that employers took from employee paychecks. Treasury had
no legal authority to collect interest on these funds—banks could
use the money interest-free for up to ten days—and, as a result, was
losing $260 million to $300 million a year.

Closing this loophole in 1977 was one of the least controversial
actions that Congress has ever taken; in April, the bill passed the
House by a vote of 384–0. The ever-savvy Helms could see that
the Senate wanted just as badly to pass its own version, and so
he managed to attach some amendments, despite their tangen-
tial connection to the main legislation. Two amendments tough-
ened the requirements for US and IMF participation in foreign aid
programs—and another made gold-based contracts legal again.[7]
There was some excitement in financial circles about the return
of gold clauses; one commodity market analyst told the *New York
Times* that the bill represented "a sleeping giant that has come to
the front so rapidly no one can fully understand the implications."
Alas, the giant mostly kept dozing. Although Treasury stayed
true to its promise not to oppose the bill, its regulations kept most
people from wanting to use gold contracts at all. Treasury's interpretation of gold contracts was that if, because of a change in the
value of a dollar, a creditor is paid in gold for an amount over
the dollar value of the contract, that difference constitutes a capi-

tal gain, and is taxed. And so even though Americans could now legally use gold clauses in contracts as of 1977, almost no one did, then or now.

Helms's victory for gold contracts was but a prelude to a better-known work: the creation of a Gold Commission, which began deliberations in 1981. While Reagan's more pragmatic advisers succeeded in preventing him from making too many public statements about a gold standard, they were very effective behind the scenes. With the exception of Barry Goldwater in 1964, it is reasonable to say that the postwar Republican Party platforms reached further and further to the center-left on economic matters. But in 1980 that changed; Reagan's economic team included a strongly pro-gold team: New York congressman Jack Kemp, Michigan congressman David Stockman, and supply-side economic consultant Jude Wanniski. Just before the New Hampshire Republican primary, Reagan recorded a television ad in which he advocated a return to the gold standard (although he requested that it not be broadcast, apparently on the advice of Milton Friedman). Still, Reagan's gold team managed to insert a plank into the 1980 Republican Party platform saying that "one of the most urgent tasks in the period ahead will be the restoration of a dependable monetary standard—that is, an end to inflation."[8] The passage read like the monetary reform that dare not speak its name, but those paying attention understood it to mean a gold standard, and it rallied goldbugs to Reagan's cause. The announcement of the Gold Commission just a few weeks into the Reagan presidency felt like a reward for the goldbug support and a legitimization of their views.

For all the identification, however, between Reagan and gold, the law that created the Gold Commission was actually passed by a House and Senate controlled by Democrats, and signed into law in October 1980 by Democrat Jimmy Carter one month before he lost reelection. This did not, of course, occur because the Democrats were keen to evaluate, in the statute's phrase, "the policy of the United States Government concerning the role of gold in domestic and international systems." The law was passed in roughly the same way that the return of gold ownership in 1974 had been—a persistent Republican legislator (Helms) with some vocal allies found a way to create a Gold Commission by tacking it onto a bill that Democrats wanted to pass, as a condition for his support.

Like the IDA bill in 1974 that returned gold ownership to Americans, re-upping of America's commitment to the International Monetary Fund was a vital goal for official Washington—and Helms knew it. When an IMF authorization bill came before Congress in 1980 with an increase in the amount the United States would have to pay, Congress had moved to the right, and even some liberal Democrats began to question whether the money was worth it. After all, 1980 was a presidential election year, and excessive government spending was a powerful issue for the Republican Party; moreover, the IMF had few natural supporters among the general public, even if Treasury and official Washington considered it vital. The National Taxpayers Union, a conservative lobbying group, took on the IMF authorization bill as a rallying cause. Helms sensed that there was political power to be gained by threatening to block the bill. In June of that year, he added an amendment to the bill to create a commission to study "the role of gold in domestic and international monetary systems." The Democrats calculated that support from Helms and his political allies was more important than whatever political loss a gold commission might cost—and so the Gold Commission was born, although it would not begin its proceedings until the summer of 1981.

To describe the Commission as undisciplined is an understatement. At the outset, chairman Donald Regan announced that the Commission hearings would be held in secret; "I don't want to see my quotes spread through the newspapers," the feisty former Merrill Lynch chairman grumbled. Apparently, no record exists of the Commission's first meeting on July 16.[9] The secrecy decision was

particularly offensive to those commissioners who wanted publicity for the gold cause, and after much complaint and an astrin-
gent attack from syndicated columnists Evans and Novak, Regan
relented and opened the Commission's doors. Gold-standard advocates nonetheless never lost the sense that the deck was stacked
against them from the beginning, and in some sense they were
right. To get the legislation passed, the Commission had to be
bipartisan; all the Democrats opposed a gold standard and most
of the Republicans were more inclined to monetarism than metal.
Anna J. Schwartz, Milton Friedman's vital coauthor, implied that
the Commission existed not to be a blueprint for genuine reform,
but almost entirely for political show. And that was not merely
because the Commission's Democrats were not going to accept
a restored gold standard. "I think one of the serious hurdles to
a really sympathetic investigation of what a gold standard could
achieve was the fact that the Reagan Administration never signaled that it was interested in having that kind of investigation by
the Commission," Schwartz later said. Schwartz noted that Reagan's own economic advisers appointed to the Commission—Jerry
Jordan, who had worked in the Federal Reserve Bank of St. Louis,
and Reagan's head of the Council of Economic Advisers, Murray
Weidenbaum—"never really expressed any views that either supported or opposed a gold standard." It was probably inevitable that
a genuine consensus on what seemed to be the central issue—
should the United States return to a gold standard?—was going to
be impossible.

As a result, the Commission's hearings and final report became
a forum for symbolic pet causes of the Reagan '80s, some of them
obscure even to economists, and took on the atmosphere of an
open casting call. Many of the statements the Commission gathered
were plucked from the catalogues of long-standing gold-standard
advocates, including Henry Holzer and Murray Rothbard. Some
were thoughtful comments from economists who, while sympathetic to the goals that a gold standard might try to achieve,

nonetheless sternly warned that the remedy was wrong. One such example was conservative economist Allan Meltzer's "Epistle to the Gold Commissioners," which began: "The gold standard is an idea whose time is past—long past." Meltzer continued: "Advocates of a return to the gold standard offer their nostrum as a means of stabilizing prices but offer few details about how this goal would be reached. All that we are usually told is that the gold standard is a 'supply-side' solution, a radical change that will reduce interest rates, stabilize prices and eliminate the summer's excess supply of zucchini. None of these claims is true."[10] Others were more exotic; among those who submitted statements to the Commission was Lyndon Larouche, the gadfly political figure whose views on monetary policy expressed the apocalyptic tone that defined early 1980s economic malaise. "Since approximately October 1981," Larouche wrote, "the economy of the United States has entered the beginning phase of a new world depression."[11] One of the Commission's members, Republican congressman Chalmers P. Wylie, called the group—in its own report, on the first page of the introduction—a "runaway" Commission and lamented that "many, many hours were spent debating issues which were extraneous to the Congressional assignment."[12]

There was little doubt that the late 1970s saw increased interest in restoring a gold standard, thanks to the political ascendance of figures like Reagan and Alan Greenspan; the growing goldbug movement; the prolonged instability in the US and global economy; and the plethora of Krugerrand sales. But increased popularity is no guarantee of effectiveness. Under the spotlight of Commission hearings, it quickly became evident that there was more than one idea of what a "gold standard" means, and opinions divided sharply on whether such a thing had ever actually existed. After the Commission's first (four-hour) hearing, chairman Regan proclaimed: "We can't even agree on the historical facts."[13]

At one end of the Commission's spectrum was Ron Paul, a Texas doctor who launched a political career as a response to Nixon closing the gold window in 1971, and was elected to the House of Representatives in 1978. Paul took the position that the only genuine gold standard was one in which the US monetary system was based on gold coins. This would involve turning the clock back not to the 1930s, but closer to the 1830s. In an echo of Murray Rothbard's 1964 manifesto (see chapter 8), Paul wanted to "repeal the privilege of banks to create money" by removing the legal-tender laws, outlawing paper money, and allowing anyone who wished to mint gold coins that would become the sole basis for day-to-day commerce. Such a system was often referred to as a "gold coin standard," and no other commissioner shared Paul's enthusiasm for it.[14]

Closest to Paul's point of view were two commissioners from the private sector, Lewis Lehrman and Arthur Costamagna. Lehrman was a drugstore executive who later ran for governor of New York State as the Republican nominee. He was a close follower of the French economist and DeGaulle adviser Jacques Rueff. Lehrman's desire for a dollar convertible to gold seemed less ideologically motivated than Paul's; Lehrman instead believed that a convertible currency was necessary to stabilize that era's damaging inflation and force interest rates to their most effective level. He called for a new international monetary conference "under the leadership of the United States, with the goal of establishing a true gold standard, one which would rule out the special privilege of <u>official</u> reserve currencies and thus remedy the most profound defect of the Bretton Woods exchange-rate regime."[15] Unfortunately for Lehrman, there was scant evidence in 1981 that the financial leadership of any major economy wanted such a system; even the long-standing French desire for an international gold standard had cooled by the late 1970s. As for Costamagna, an attorney who had worked with Reagan in California, Anna J. Schwartz, the economist who served as the Commission's executive director, later wrote that "his sole concern for the present was to provide the market with U.S.-minted bullion coins."

This unlikely trio did not come close to swaying the Commission to accept a reform of the monetary system with gold at its heart. The Commission failed even to produce a parade of expert witnesses who genuinely advocated a full return to a gold standard. In the two hearings devoted to the role of gold in domestic and international monetary systems, twenty-three witnesses testified—and only two argued in favor of a return to a traditional gold standard. One of them should have carried a great deal of weight: the economist Arthur Laffer, who was one of the most influential voices among Reagan's supply-side advisers. He drafted a detailed plan for returning the country to a gold standard, but with a provision to protect US gold reserves from either being depleted or building up too high, to the point where they would be more than 175 percent of a stated target reserve. If such triggers were hit, Laffer's plan called for a "gold holiday," during which the official price of gold would be recalculated. Laffer pointed out that the gold market could be subject to sudden variations, such as a brand new discovery of gold. "When there is a disturbance in the gold market, I don't want to see the whole economy suffer inflation or deflation because of some change in that market." But as repeatedly happened during the Gold Commission's life, the people who were most passionate and knowledgeable on the topic of a gold standard were the ones who found it hardest to forge a consensus. Ron Paul would not accept Laffer's plan, arguing that it would preserve the ability of the Federal Reserve and Congress to "abuse the monetary system." Paul told Laffer: "This may actually be worse than what we had before."

The Commission delved deeply into a variety of such proposals, only to determine that they would be wildly impractical to implement. For starters, at what price should dollar-gold convertibility be restored? The stakes were very high, as the Commission report summarized: "An incorrect price might lead to a huge inflow of gold and inflation if it were too high, a huge outflow and economic contraction if it were too low." (Both Britain and France had experienced versions of these problems when their currencies "reentered" gold convertibility decades before.) But how should the "correct" price be determined? Economists could try to back-calculate the loss of purchasing power since the dollar had last been devalued at $42.22 an ounce; or take some average of market-trading prices for a given period before restoring convertibility; or divide the dollar value of the gross national product of the world by the amount of gold in the world—all of these suggestions, and more, were debated. Depending on the formula, the value of gold might be $50 an ounce—or $3,500 an ounce.

As if that issue weren't complex enough, the ability of Americans to own gold as an investment had, by 1981, created political pressure over gold's price that at least some commissioners had to consider. That is, many of the plans being offered seemed highly likely to produce a fall in the market value of gold, which at the time of the Commission's hearings was north of $400 an ounce and had been higher in 1980. Lehrman's 1980 paper on the topic, for example, not only implied this downward effect, but put it forward as a goal. The hundreds of thousands of Americans who by then had purchased Krugerrands or similar gold-investment vehicles may or may not have been politically sympathetic to the idea of a gold standard. But presumably few of them would be cheering for a policy change that would make their gold investment worth less.

Then there was the issue of other countries. Given the unlikelihood of getting the rest of the world to cooperate with a gold standard, restoring the dollar-gold convertibility raised serious questions of enforcement. What would prevent outside individuals or institutions from using American proxies to trade dollars for gold? Presumably, US citizens buying gold would have to sign oaths that they were not making purchases on behalf of foreign entities. That measure would probably have to be combined with reinstating the legal restrictions against importing or exporting gold. And, as the Commission's report acknowledged, "In both cases, an enforcement army of inspectors would appear to be needed."[16] For

298 | ONE NATION UNDER GOLD

those hoping to promote gold as an instrument of free markets and human liberty, capital controls and gold-snooping Treasury agents represented unwanted steps backward.

The closest thing to monetary gold that a majority of commissioners would accept was an agreement that the United States should get back into the business of minting gold coins. But even here, there was a disagreement over the ultimate goal. Should the United States try to create a gold coin that would compete as an investment vehicle comparable to the Krugerrand? Or was the objective to get Americans accustomed to using gold coins as daily money? In which case, should the coins be designed for commercial transactions and given legal-tender status, to restore the United States to a nineteenth-century metallic money basis? Or was the most important goal, from a macroeconomic point of view, to use the coins to anchor the value of the dollar to a physical amount of gold?

From his purist's perch, Helms was disappointed by the failure of the Commission he'd created to take a hard stand in favor of a return to the gold standard. In a letter to the *Wall Street Journal*, Helms wrote: "As a longtime friend and supporter of President Reagan, I am sorry that his advisers—and the Gold Commission—have not been more attentive to the 1980 Republican platform with respect to monetary reform. The people deserve better than a continuation of monetary disorder."[17]

Monetary disorder, however, was not exclusive to those who disagreed with Helms. The Gold Commission exposed an undeniable rift in the "Reaganomic" coalition of conservatives, populists, Wall Street titans, and independent financial experts. There was an uneasy relationship between the ideal of a gold standard, the role that gold would play in the day-to-day running of the world's largest economy, and the state of American politics. The Reagan administration and many of its top economic advisers keenly appreciated that the idea of a gold standard had a powerful appeal to the modern-day Republican Party. In addition to all of gold's traditional atavistic lure, it was an easily understood and potent symbol of many of the messages of modern Republican politics. A gold standard had come to be a political shorthand for lower government spending, a balanced budget, and a reliance on market forces—and by extension a mistrust of government and its institutions.

But the power of gold's symbolism was capable of outstripping what the metal could actually do. This was a place and a time when symbolism and political reality became jumbled. Modern conservatives hold Ronald Reagan in the highest regard, and for many of them the emblematic weight that Reagan tried to lend to a gold standard reinforces that reverence. Nonetheless, the fact remains that Reagan's key cabinet members, Donald Regan and George Shultz, were never disposed to actually bringing about gold-based monetary reform. The president's economic advisers were no friendlier to the idea. In his diary in June 1981, Reagan wrote of a meeting with his economic advisory council: "Art Laffer dropped a grenade on his colleagues when he said we weren't going to solve the fiscal program until we returned to convertibility of money for gold. I would like to have heard the discussion among those economists after I left."[18] Decades after the Commission rejected a return to a gold standard, Reagan economic adviser Weidenbaum said he viewed his role on the Commission as a "damage-limitation function or the avoidance of economic harm."[19]

Even Alan Greenspan was not able to square his once-fervent theoretical belief in a gold standard with the responsibilities of power, much to the disappointment of goldbugs. Here, after all, was a true friend and disciple of Ayn Rand, a man whose 1966 essay in her newsletter had ignited followers with its absolutist stand on a gold basis for money and its swipes at excessive government spending. But during his 1987 Senate confirmation hearings to become chairman of the Federal Reserve, Greenspan had to climb down from Randian idealism to a position more befitting the steward of the world's largest economy. Asked by Banking Committee chairman William Proxmire if, as Fed chair, he would make a return to the gold standard a "top priority," Greenspan gave a response very much in line with the Gold Commission's conclusions about infeasibility. "Under the conditions of the nineteenth century the gold standard probably worked more effectively than critics assert today, and if the key conditions could be replicated we might be well served by such a standard," Greenspan said. "However, considering the huge block of currently outstanding dollar claims in world markets, fixing the price of gold by central bank intervention seems out of reach."[20]

It is nonetheless short-sighted to dismiss the Gold Commission as unsuccessful. The Gold Commission succeeded in its support for a program of US government-minted gold medallions and coins. To most Americans, this might seem like merely a matter for coin collectors. But the US gold coin program also played at least two important political roles: it lent legitimacy to gold advocates within American politics, mostly among Republicans, and it helped the American gold industry to reposition itself against the gold giant South Africa. The US Treasury had begun selling gold medallions in 1980 via the US Post Office, but demand for them had been well below Treasury's target sales of one million ounces a year. In the spring of 1983, less than a year after the Commission released its report, Treasury switched the marketing effort to a private-sector firm with deep experience in the gold market: J. Aron & Company, a division of the investment bank Goldman Sachs. (Conveniently, J. Aron's chairman Herb Coyne had served as one of the gold panel's commissioners.)

To a degree, the motivation was for the US gold industry to cash in on the demand for investment gold coins that the Krugerrand had demonstrated. After all, in 1979, the Canadian government introduced its one-ounce Maple Leaf coin, which within a few years displaced the Krugerrand as top-selling gold coin in North America. And in this sense, the pro-gold forces in the United

States had a valuable ally in the form of the antiapartheid movement which, by the mid-'80s, had been tremendously effective in targeting the Krugerrand. Organized on college campuses and in churches, the movement's economic goals had close support from a handful of Democratic members of Congress, notably Stephen Solarz of Brooklyn, who used his seat on the House Foreign Affairs Committee to put pressure on South Africa's apartheid government. In 1983, Solarz added a measure to the authorization of the State Department's budget that required US companies doing business in South Africa to adhere to a set of equal-opportunity labor practices, and also prohibited the importing of Krugerrands. US sales of the South African coins had remained reasonably strong, subject to fluctuations in the broader gold market.

The Reagan administration opposed most congressional antiapartheid measures, in part because it viewed the uninterrupted flow of South African gold as vital to the global economy, and in part because South Africa president P. W. Botha threatened retaliation in the form of cutting off exports to the United States of chromium which, he said, could threaten a million jobs in the United States. But protests throughout the United States got larger and more vociferous. In Boston in late 1984, antiapartheid activists specifically targeted Deak Perera, the largest precious-metal trader in the country, and demanded that the company stop selling Krugerrands until apartheid was ended; some occupied the office until they were arrested. By 1985 legislative sentiment against apartheid was too powerful for the Reagan administration to stop. That summer, both houses of Congress passed, by veto-proof majorities, bills to impose economic sanctions against South Africa. The version of the bill in the Republican-controlled Senate (SB 995), however, was weaker, and would have delayed by two years any consideration of banning Krugerrand imports.

It seemed obvious that a major break in the economic relationship between the United States and South Africa was going to occur—the questions were when and how profound. As the inev-

itability of antiapartheid action sank in, many in Congress and in
the administration began to realize that, at least where gold was
concerned, South Africa could move from being an ally to a competitor. Tacked onto the Senate bill, for example, was an amendment authorizing the US government to mint its own coin to
compete with the Krugerrand. In the meantime, President Reagan
issued an executive order declaring a national emergency because
"the policies and actions of the Government of South Africa constitute an unusual and extraordinary threat to the foreign policy and
economy of the United States."[21] Reagan deliberately singled out
the country's signature coin: "The Krugerrand is perceived in the
Congress as an important symbol of apartheid. This view is widely
shared by the US public. I am directing this prohibition in recogni-
tion of these public and congressional sentiments." Among other
measures, the order authorized the government to seek out the
views of other GATT nations about a ban on Krugerrand imports,
and directed Treasury "to conduct a study to be completed within
sixty days regarding the feasibility of minting and issuing gold
coins with a view toward expeditiously seeking legislative authority to accomplish the goal of issuing such coins."

That same year, Congress authorized Treasury to mint gold
coins in face-value denominations between $5 and $50, the first
general circulation gold coins in the United States for more than
half a century—and the gold in the coins was required to come
from sources within the United States. Known as the "American
gold eagle" series, they became available in 1986 and began to sell
in numbers that rivaled the early US sales of Krugerrands.


The issue of South Africa's gold continued to haunt American pol-
icymakers, and led even prominent Republicans to advocate ideas
that in the 1960s and 1970s would have been unthinkable. In the
summer of 1986, for example, the Senate Foreign Relations Committee overwhelmingly passed a bill to impose a variety of sanc-

tions against South Africa, from denying landing rights to South African aircraft to cutting off imports of South African coal and uranium. But one provision, offered by the committee's chairman Richard Lugar, authorized the president to sell off large quantities of gold, in order to suppress the price of gold and thereby hurt South Africa's economy. The idea, a Lugar aide told the press, had come from an editorial in *The Economist* magazine. The magazine reckoned that there was just under a billion ounces of gold held in the vaults of the world's central banks, more than a quarter of which was in the United States. The mere announcement that the government would begin selling gold on a specific date would, *The Economist* asserted, "make a large cut in South Africa's earnings within one hour, because private hoarders from Bombay to Brittany would be rushing to sell their gold at crashing prices before the central-bank selling began."[22]

The changes implied here were profound. During the postwar period the very idea of the United States selling off gold in any significant quantity would have been laughed off the table; no prominent Democrat or Republican would have proposed it. Now, the idea of a gold selloff was not only coming from a senior senator, but a Republican who wanted to use gold sales to drive down the market price in order to punish a long-standing ally of the United States. On top of that, he borrowed the idea from a magazine that made its argument in the name of free markets!

Reflected in Lugar's proposal was a tremendous shift that had taken place in the global gold market. Throughout the 1970s and early 1980s, the United States (and the global economy) needed South Africa's gold—an important reason why the United States was relatively late to cut economic ties to the apartheid regime. But beginning in the early 1980s, the American gold industry began a boom that rivaled, and by many measures surpassed, the California-Colorado gold rushes of the 1840s and 1850s. Between 1980 and 1990, US gold production shot up more than 500 percent, to some 300 metric tons per year, and continued to grow. As a result, some in the United States began to look at South Africa as less of a vital ally and more of a competitor. The US-minted gold coins captured the rivalry starkly, and contributed modestly to the domestic revival of the industry—Congress made certain to guarantee that the metal in them had to be mined in the United States.

Improved technology, too, was a factor. Some of the mining processes touted by Operation Goldfinger's architects in the 1960s (minus the nuclear explosives and the particle-accelerator alchemy) had indeed proven effective. Mines that had been abandoned in the early twentieth century were given new life through expanding a procedure that allowed the metal to be extracted from ore that had previously been considered to have marginal gold content. The process involves pulverizing the ore into a very fine powder, and then soaking it in liquid cyanide, which changes the gold chemically. A carbon electrode is then inserted into the solution. Most of the gold will stick to it and can then be melted off. Beginning in 1965 at the Carlin mine in Nevada operated by the Newmont Mining Corporation, this technique was used to produce bars from gold that, in its ore form, could not be seen, even with a microscope. As a consequence, massive amounts of ore had to be used— three tons to produce a single ounce of gold.[23] The increasing use of these massive "open-pit" mines was a major contributor to the '80s gold boom, although they brought with them considerable environmental damage.

It was reasonable to expect that, once Krugerrands and other affordable, easily traded gold investment vehicles became the standard way for Americans to invest in gold, the type of fraud in the gold trade that government authorities found in the 1970s with the rise of coin exchanges would subside. Yet the opposite seems to have occurred. More Americans interested in buying more gold meant more shady dealers and a larger potential group of consumers to bilk. The most prominent and spectacular fraud was the International Gold Bullion Exchange (IGBE). It had started as a jewelry store in Fort Lauderdale, Florida, run by two brothers, James and William Alderdice, both of whom were legally blind from early childhood. They took advantage of legal gold ownership to build their business at breakneck speed. In 1983, after just three years in business, they had annual sales of nearly $100 million, 1,000 employees, and branch offices in Dallas and Los Angeles; they claimed to be the largest gold and silver dealer in the United States. In advertisements ("Profit from the '80s Gold Rush!") in the *New York Times* and the *Wall Street Journal* and on television, IGBE touted gold at discount prices.

Gold experts were puzzled. When *Forbes* magazine asked veteran gold traders how IGBE could make a profit by selling gold at or below market price, the responses ranged from "It's impossible!" to "If you find out how they do it, let me know."[24] One major catch was that customers had to wait several months for delivery; in the interim, the Alderdice brothers had access to the money they'd been paid and would wait for dips in the market to get metal at a price below what their clients had paid. Across the country, IGBE customers began complaining, starting in 1982, that the deliveries never came at all. A Connecticut church lost $278,000 that had been intended as an investment to build a new chapel. A 52-year-old divorced woman living in a trailer home in Texas lost $46,000, telling a magazine: "I'm in a terrible financial bind. I sent them my life savings, but evidently they are a bunch of crooks."[25]

Some 25,000 would-be gold and silver buyers were defrauded. The attorney general of Florida descended, the company declared bankruptcy, and the brothers were arrested and charged with fraud. When a court-appointed attorney opened the vault in the company's Fort Lauderdale office, he found wooden blocks that had been painted to look like gold. While the brothers were initially in prison, they met a man who ended up living with them when they got out on bail; that man, James Doyle, stabbed William to death with a kitchen knife in 1984 and was convicted of third-degree murder. In a bizarre coda to the case, a judge granted James Alderice the right to try to pay off IGBE creditors by digging for gold in a mine off the shore of Alaska.

Another company engaged in a widespread rip-off was the Bullion Reserve of North America. In radio ads (which happened to catch the attention of the New York State attorney general) the company boasted that it held title to some $60 million in gold that was stored in a mountain vault in Utah that was supposedly also used by the Mormon Church. The chairman had no background in metals trading, and he liked to spend lavishly; he bought a Maserati and leased a Lear jet monthly. He paid for his $500,000 divorce settlement with company checks.[26] Bullion Reserve went to great lengths to project an image of integrity. It enlisted the endorsement of Jerome Smith, an established metal-market analyst who published a best-selling book in 1980 called *The Coming Currency Collapse.* "I say unequivocally and without hesitation that you can trust Bullion Reserve of North America completely and without reservation," Smith wrote in a letter to 90,000 precious-metal investors. "I put my name and reputation—and my future—on the line in saying this." Bullion Reserve paid Smith $5,000 to write the letter and had promised him another $27,000 for additional letters. Before any further batches had been mailed, the company had filed for bankruptcy. The Utah storage vault contained no more than $1 million worth of gold. The chairman of the company committed suicide by running a hose from the exhaust pipe of a motorcycle into a sauna in his home in Venice, California. Between the two firms, more than $100 million in investments from tens of thousands of customers evaporated.

Is there something intrinsic to trading gold that lends itself to fraudulent activity more than, say, trading pork-belly futures? Some law enforcement officials, novelists, and psychologically inclined economists have hinted as much, although the question is impossible to answer definitively. Part of the apparent rise in gold fraud in the 1980s may have been due to lax enforcement and

confused lines of regulatory jurisdiction—familiar culprits in economic busts from Black Friday to the mortgage-backed securities
crisis that triggered the Great Recession of the twenty-first century.
A law review article from the mid-1980s labeled precious-metal
trading "the last frontier of unregulated investment."[27] The SEC
had long taken the position that precious metals were not securities and thus did not fall under its domain. The Commodity and
Futures Trading Commission (CFTC) had jurisdiction over some
gold-selling arrangements, but not others, and couldn't begin to
take on the hundreds of thousands of transactions that gold legalization had enabled. The CFTC had been powerless during the late
'70s attempted takeover of the silver market by the Hunt brothers,[28]
and showed little more promise in taking on the "boiler room"
operations that were dominating the precious-metals market. In
a Senate hearing, William Roth was blunt: "Frankly, during this
time, the principal enforcement agency, the CFTC, has been seriously outgunned by its opposition. The CFTC, with its roughly 25
lawyers and 10 investigators charged with protecting the public, the
investing public, has been no match—no match—for the avalanche
of schemes."[29] Many argued that the laissez-faire advocates running
the executive branch preferred an agency that didn't interfere with
futures markets. In a news story noting that the Reagan administration had invited the Chicago-based commodity exchanges to
take a leading role in naming the CFTC chair and all of its commissioners, the Wall Street Journal said that the "commodities watchdog
is often more like a friendly puppy."[30]

When fraud is sufficiently brazen and widespread, it can interfere with markets anyway by making consumers wary to participate. A Senate investigation took testimony from convicted
commodity fraudsters who described boiler-room operations in
which the company had no expectation that any customer would
ever make a profit. The volume and prominence of these scandals
at times affected the price of gold, and created what one metals
trade journal called a "black eye" for the industry. Trade groups

began proposing an insurance system for gold coins and bullion that would guarantee delivery within sixty days of purchase.[31] These were unwelcome developments for those who argued that the gold market represented a culmination of human freedom. For tens of thousands of fleeced consumers, Senator Roth's description of a "floating crap game" seemed more apt.

In addition, even though the entire record of the Gold Commission made it clear that the Reagan administration had no genuine interest in actually restoring a gold standard, the publicity that the Commission generated for a gold standard did coincide with the early stages of a shift in the economic thinking of some prominent Republicans. Through the Nixon and Ford administrations, the economic policies of the twentieth-century Republican Party were broadly aligned with the interests of America's elite class, as defined by Wall Street and the executives of big business. National Republicans could generally be relied on to support a balanced budget; to be skeptical of government spending, particularly on antipoverty or similar social programs, and regulation; to seek minimal influence of organized labor; and to fear inflation more than unemployment. Establishment Republicans were usually content to give key economic positions to corporate CEOs or banking/ brokerage executives. Conservative criticism about the wisdom of mainstream Republican economic thinking was largely confined to elements of the "Old Right"—including some, like Howard Buffett, associated with Taft and isolationism—and outsider groups like the John Birch Society.

The "Reagan Revolution" changed this perspective, by adding and institutionalizing a populist element to conservative economic thought. The most prominent member of the team who wanted to move forward with the gold standard was Kemp. Although Kemp's participation in Republican politics dates as far back as his football career in the 1960s, he does not appear to have embraced gold as a pet political cause in the beginning of his congressional tenure— not in the way that he embraced, say, tax cuts. As noted in chapter

10, Kemp voted against the 1974 bill that restored legal gold ownership. A few years later, Kemp seemed to warm to the gold cause. In 1979, when introducing the landmark Kemp-Roth tax-cut bill, Kemp said that the United States needed to return to "a monetary standard of some fixed value behind the currency," presumably referring to a gold standard. A Kemp biography cites his greater passion that same year. In a 1979 Marriott Hotel hallway encounter between Kemp and future congressman Dan Coats, Kemp pulled a gold coin out of his pocket and shouted, "We'll never be back where we need to be as a country until we get back on the gold standard!"[32]

But the issue really began to gain traction for Kemp after Reagan took office in 1981. His supply-side colleagues who'd taken positions within the administration had largely sided with the monetarists, leaving Kemp and his allies fearful that the official medicine would not be strong enough to fix the country's ailing economy. Kemp, according to columnists Evans and Novak, began pressing the gold-standard issue at a Republican gathering in May of that year, to broad indifference. But once the House passed his tax-cut legislation in late July, Kemp's advisers urged him to become a kind of gold-standard-bearer, a role he accepted that fall. There were others within the GOP who supported the gold standard, including Phil Crane. But none would attain the same political prominence as Kemp, who became the party's vice-presidential nominee in 1996 without ever moving publicly away from his gold-standard position.[33] And even if, in practice, a Republican president was wary of implementing a gold standard, the party recognized that it made good politics. The 1984 Republican platform was more explicit than before: "The Gold Standard may be a useful mechanism for realizing the Federal Reserve's determination to adopt monetary policies needed to sustain price stability." Yet to this day, even if they are as popular as ever with a segment of Americans, these remain earnest words on paper.

# CHAPTER 12

## God, Gold, and Guns

THERE ARE THREE economic scenarios scrawled on a portable chalkboard on the Fox News Channel studio set: Recession, Depression, and Collapse. Standing in front of it is the host Glenn Beck, being filmed live. He is dressed conservatively in a dark suit and yellow tie but clearly as agitated as any street protestor. The date is November 23, 2009, and the United States is officially but imperceptibly no longer in a recession; a huge percentage of Americans remain out of work, bankruptcies continue to mount, and the once-mighty auto industry is struggling even after a multibillion-dollar government bailout. To tens of millions of Americans, the psychic pain of the "Great Recession"—with the meltdown of the stock and housing markets that began in the fall of 2008—is all too present, and none of the scenarios Beck is discussing would seem out of the question.

On this particular day, Beck is giving a potted course in personal finance, which could easily have been cribbed from Harry Browne's books from thirty-five years before. In the case of a return to recession, Beck advises his audience to "get out of debt and save." Politicians, he says, "will never tell you to do this, because they need you to spend money to keep the

In the twenty-first century, a return to a gold standard, despite its impracticality, has become part of a populist mistrust of technocratic elites. In a 2011 congressional hearing, Republican congressman Ron Paul asked Federal Reserve chair Ben Bernanke if gold is money. *Getty Images / Chip Somodevilla* economy going." In the case of a depression, Beck recalls earlier generations' habit of stockpiling food: "If you're going to the store, and there's one can of soup, and it's on sale, get two." But if the American economy were to collapse, Beck says his audience will need to rely on "the three G's," which he defines as God, Gold, and Guns.

To millions of regular Fox News Channel viewers, the advice to buy gold was unexceptional. Fox had become a regular fount of economic gloom, all or most of which its hosts readily blamed on the Obama administration. The month before, Beck had asked his audience, "Are we facing the end of the almighty dollar?" He stood at a table and moved stacks of coins from one side of a table with several miniature flags of the world, to the other side with a US flag, to represent the movement of gold in the early to mid-twentieth century. Alas, "you"—the viewer—have no gold, only a small stack of dollars which, Beck said, had lost 29 percent of their value in the previous seven years. The clear solution, as Beck evinced in an interview with management consultant David Buckner, was to "invest in things that are friendly to inflation," which meant real estate and gold. This was something of a false choice. The once-booming real estate market, Fox viewers knew, had imploded the year before and showed few signs of recovering soon—or maybe ever. Moreover, Buckner noted, real estate might rise in value, but if interest rates got too high, no one would be able to buy—and that left gold.

The constant advice to buy gold as a protective investment might also have sounded familiar to Beck's viewers because it was echoed in the many advertisements that supported Beck's daily television broadcast and radio show, as well as many other Fox News programs, including those hosted by former Republican presidential candidates Mike Huckabee and Fred Thompson. Buying gold and buying into the Republican Party message were at this point intertwined; indeed, buy-gold messages had become practically nonstop on Beck's show. A campaign had begun earlier that year to persuade corporations to stop advertising on Beck's program after the host declared that President Obama has "a deep-seated hatred for white people or the white culture." The campaign had, by the fall of 2009, been highly effective; major companies including Wal-Mart, CVS, and Best Buy pulled out from Beck's program. As a result, some of the most loyal advertisers remaining on Beck's program were precious-metal sellers, including Discount Gold Brokers, ITM Trading, and Goldline International. The last firm had a particularly strong relationship with Beck. The talk-show host promoted Goldline as "a top-notch organization" and "the people that I trust," endorsements that the company frequently promoted. Beck brought Goldline president Mark Albarian onto his radio program to talk about how high the price of gold might go.

To Beck's critics, the blurred lines between Goldline as an advertiser and gold being pushed as an investment in Beck's programs transformed Beck into a paid spokesman for the gold company. (In 2009, Fox, concerned that Beck was violating Fox's rule against paid product endorsements by on-air talent, sought "clarification" about Beck's role at Goldline. Although the Goldline site actually did identify Beck as a "paid spokesman," Beck's representative responded, and Goldline confirmed, that Beck had never actually received any separate fees for speaking on Goldline's behalf. Goldline subsequently changed Beck's online designation from "paid spokesman" to "radio sponsor.")[1]

Representative Anthony Weiner, a New York City congressman who served on a consumer protection subcommittee and would soon disgrace himself in a digital sex scandal, accused Beck and other on-air hosts of "shilling for Goldline." These hosts, Weiner charged, "are either the worst financial advisors around or knowingly lying to their loyal viewers." According to Weiner's investigation, the average markup on coins sold by Goldline was 90 percent above the coin's value if melted, and in one case 208 percent higher. In addition, Weiner charged that Goldline tacked on fees for storage, shipping, and reselling that effectively made it impossible for anyone buying a Goldline coin to earn any money on the investment unless the market price of gold doubled.[2] Weiner's investigation had been guided by a 2006 incident in which a Missouri state authority had fined Goldline and forced the firm to return the investment of a consumer the state said had been illegally provided with investment advice. Evidently, little had changed in the retail gold market since the SEC had tried to crack down on Pacific Coast Coin Exchange in the 1970s.

Weiner's charges became more resonant when, in 2011, a California consumer protection unit charged Goldline with criminal theft and fraud. The city attorney of Santa Monica, where Goldline is based, maintained that Goldline used "bait and switch" tactics that pressured consumers into buying overpriced gold coins instead of gold bullion. Among the tactics Goldline deployed, according to the criminal complaint, was to stoke fear about a potential government heist of gold bullion. Part of the Goldline pitch was to invoke Roosevelt's gold prohibition of 1933. That is, salespeople were trained to make "customers fear . . . government confiscation of bullion and to tell customers that the overpriced coins were exempt from such confiscation."

Although Goldline initially refuted the charges, the company agreed in February 2012 to an injunction that required it to refund up to $4.5 million to past customers and set aside $800,000 for restitution of future claims. In one of the most bizarrely specific constraints about how a commercial entity is allowed to discuss history, the Santa Monica City Attorney's office wrote specific scripts for how the company could represent the 1930s to existing and potential customers. For example, Goldline is allowed to say that "for more than a generation, Americans were banned from owning certain quantities of gold coins and bars." But only if a customer wants more details is the company permitted to discuss Roosevelt's actions toward gold, and it must avoid the word *confiscation* and note that gold owners were reimbursed at the then-prevailing price.

While the characters and specific charges had changed, the

entire episode followed a historical pattern that had begun even before gold again became legal to own: a doomsday-scenario sales pitch; an overly cozy relationship with a popular media figure; and an investigation that uncovers irregularity and fraud in the selling of gold. The consistency of the fraudulent gold investment pitch is striking, and grows out of the fact that gold as an investment is a peculiar market animal. One of the properties that makes gold attractive to many of its admirers is that it cannot be physically destroyed. This indestructibility guarantees that the overall supply of gold on Earth cannot be lower tomorrow than it is today (unless someone were to shoot the gold into space). On the contrary, the supply is constantly increasing; typically, the supply of usable gold on the planet increases by 1 to 3 percent per year. Demand is more complicated; approximately 20 percent of all the world's gold is currently tied up with central banks and not readily available for the private market. Gold trading by central banks is carefully orchestrated and often secret, so as to prevent undue marketplace shocks. And therefore, the only normal way for the value of any particular cache of gold to increase is for private-market demand to increase. Usually, gold market prices rise when people think the economy is weak or weakening (lots of people want to buy gold, because they fear that other assets will stagnate or lose value), and fall when the economy is strong or optimism is rising (lots of people want to sell gold, because they believe other assets will yield a better return). At least since the days of Harry Browne, predicting economic disaster has been a useful way to try and stoke the market for gold and drive up the value of existing gold owners' investments. For the 1970s, it was runaway inflation that was supposed to bring about economic collapse; for the 2010s, it is runaway government debt— those selling gold offer it as a solution to any and all economic ills, just as free silver advocates did for their preferred metal in the late nineteenth century.

In the context of Fox News, gold advocacy served a political function at least as important as its economic function—peddling gold as a solution to a bad economy meant blaming the government (and especially the Obama administration) for the state of the economy. The fact that most people in the government opposed the idea of a gold standard only seemed to confirm their irresponsibility! And if Goldline was prohibited from telling Americans that their gold might be insecure, there were others happy to fill the gap. The Swiss-born economist and noted gloom-monger Marc Faber, a frequent guest on CNBC, said in 2012: "If I were an American, I would store [gold] outside the U.S., because in the U.S., it is not completely unlikely that they will eventually take it away."

Judging by the price of gold, however, the arguments in favor of gold worked pretty well in the first decade of the twenty-first century. Many American gold owners also believe that the United States today would be better off if it returned to a currency tied to gold, both because it would back up the US dollar with something of genuine value, and because it would enforce fiscal discipline on a government addicted to the creation of seemingly unlimited debt with a single computer keystroke.

One might have predicted that when the United States (and nearly every major economy) weaned its currency from gold in the early 1970s, the grip that the precious metal has on the American psyche would loosen. If anything, the opposite has occurred. Much of America seems locked in a permanent nostalgic infatuation with gold. The Gold Commission of the 1980s may have failed to restore gold to the center of the American monetary system. Yet the arguments that gold-standard advocates made to the Commission live on in political rhetoric, as do the people who made them. Former congressman Ron Paul, the Commission's most outspoken goldbug, ran for president in 2008 and 2012 and made a gold standard part of his personal crusade. Although he failed to rally a large number of Republican primary voters, he nonetheless used his various platforms to score points for gold however he could. In a July 2011 congressional hearing, Paul grilled the long-suffering Federal Reserve chairman Ben Bernanke (a fellow Republican who'd nonetheless caught much flak from the American right for his Fed policy). Paul asked Bernanke directly: "Do you think gold is money?" When Bernanke asserted that it was simply a precious metal, Paul went on to ask why central banks held it in reserve, instead of diamonds.

While Bernanke and his fellow technocrats may have seen this as little more than an eye-rolling exercise, the exchange electrified supporters of Paul and gold across the Internet. Web video versions have been viewed hundreds of thousands of times, and social media outlets such as Reddit and Twitter crackled with partisan examinations of the argument's finer points.

In the twenty-first century Republican Party, arguing for gold makes effective politics. During the 2012 Republican presidential primaries, for example, a majority of the candidates, including Ron Paul and former House Speaker Newt Gingrich, said that if elected they would either restore the country to a gold standard, or seriously consider it. One important exception was the eventual nominee, Mitt Romney; nonetheless, the 2012 Republican platform reflected the consensus view. The platform alluded to the Gold Commission from 1981, designed to "consider the feasibility of a metallic basis for U.S. currency." While that Commission rejected the idea of a gold standard, the 2012 Republicans said, "we propose a similar commission to investigate possible ways to set a fixed value for the dollar."[3] In 2016, GOP presidential candidate Ted Cruz pushed for a gold standard, echoing the view of one of his largest financial backers, while the nominee Donald Trump gave an interview to GQ magazine in which he said: "Bringing back the gold standard would be very hard to do, but, boy, would it be wonderful. We'd have a standard on which to base our money."[4] And the 2016 Republican platform repeated the same "fixed value" language as 2012's.

There was little likely harm in including such a plank in the Republican platform, and at least some potential political benefit.

For millions of Americans in the twenty-first century, gold has become simultaneously an article of economic faith and a political cause. It has been fueled by the deepest recession since the Great Depression and the often achingly weak economic recovery that followed. Polls of likely Republican voters in the 2012 primaries in at least three states found majorities strongly or somewhat favoring it.[5] And a national poll of all voters in 2011 found 44 percent favoring it.[6] That same poll found that juicing the question a bit yielded an even more dramatic result. Asked if they would "favor or oppose returning to a Gold Standard if you knew it would reduce the power of bankers and political leaders to steer the economy," those in favor increased to 57 percent versus only 19 percent opposed.

The reliability of such polling is certainly open to argument. Nonetheless, it is striking that in no other modern nation are citizens hotly debating whether or not to tie their currency to a precious metal—or to any physical entity at all. The backdrop, of course, is a nationwide sagging confidence in nearly every institution that once defined American life. The presidency, churches and organized religions, big business, labor, Congress, banks, the medical profession, the Supreme Court—all of them inspire less confidence in the second decade of the twenty-first century than they did in the 1970s, which itself was not America's most optimistic decade.[7] In the age of Obama, older white Americans felt particularly detached from the nation's traditional centers of power and economic growth; the long-standing manufacturing job base of their youth and the pensions that came with it had in many places disappeared. Their anger fueled the rise of the Tea Party, which made itself felt in the 2010 elections. Indeed, Obama had famously (and to some, offensively) observed in 2008 that in small midwestern towns, when jobs had gone and wages had fallen, "they cling to guns or religion or antipathy toward people who aren't like them or anti-immigrant sentiment or anti-trade sentiment as a way to explain their frustrations." Politically, this group was also sympathetic to Glenn Beck and the third "G" in his doomsday scenario—gold.

Of course, as gold-standard Republicans discovered in the 1980s, what makes for passionate politics does not readily translate into policy. The obstacles to actually restoring a gold standard are enormous—so enormous that the sincerity of those arguing for it must be questioned. For starters, gold-standard advocates can't agree on what system they want. This difficulty was very much on display during the Gold Commission hearings in the early 1980s. For some purists, the only acceptable monetary standard is best labeled *free-market money* or a *gold-coin standard*—that is, a system in which gold is the physical basis for American money; in which legal-tender laws would be removed and paper money would be outlawed; and anyone who wished could mint gold coins that would function as day-to-day currency.

A more practical version would be a *gold bullion standard*, in which the dollar would be defined as a fixed amount of gold, but gold itself would not circulate as currency. This was roughly the system that obtained during the Bretton Woods system, in which the value of the world's major currencies was defined in relationship to gold and, within very narrow ranges, in relationship to one another. However, with the crucial exception of the US dollar, currencies were not truly convertible to gold; instead, the US dollar functioned as the peg and the reserve currency for other nations. Although such a system would probably be easier to establish than other forms of a gold standard, essentially no one today argues for it. Most of the world recognizes that the system broke down when global economic development outgrew it, and for American gold-standard advocates it would not achieve the fiscal spending constraints they usually advocate.

One further level of abstraction from an absolute gold-coin standard would be a system in which paper currency is "backed" or "covered" by a defined quantity and purity of gold; this has been the case at various points in US history, as recently as the late 1960s. One putative anti-inflationary virtue of such a system is that it limits how much paper currency the government can print. Twenty-first-century American gold-standard advocates, however, tend toward purism and would be unlikely to support such a system unless the paper currency were genuinely convertible into gold.

Even assuming that American gold-standard advocates could agree on a system, it's nearly impossible to imagine a desirable political scenario under which the system would be imposed. For better or worse, big, groundbreaking monetary changes are almost always timed due to crises, not careful and inclusive debate, and they are often badly executed. As this book has repeatedly demonstrated, novel monetary strategies are devised in secret, rushed through Congress or enacted outside of Congress, and justified with war or other emergencies. The Supreme Court decisions that result—from the legal-tender cases through the gold-clause cases—are widely acknowledged to be among the worst argued and worst handled cases in the country's history, in part because it is so difficult to square straight constitutional interpretation with economic and political necessity.

And in those rare instances when the issue is deliberately studied and intensely debated a strict, populist view of the gold standard has tended to lose. The 1980s Gold Commission is the most recent, and probably the most thorough, currency discussion the nation has ever had, under some of the most favorable political circumstances that goldbugs could hope for—and it roundly rejected a gold standard. The founding of the Federal Reserve system in 1913, often cited by today's gold populists as a kind of original sin, was also an example of a policy that had been studied for decades—it, too, rejected a pure gold standard. For better or worse, today's gold populists have failed to make the political case for their system at the very moments when they might have succeeded. That problem may be intrinsic to the task of trying to turn monetary policy backward. Kenneth Dam, University of Chicago law professor who worked in the Reagan and George W. Bush administrations, has noted: "The case for a gold standard is most appealing when inflation is rampant but, paradoxically, rapid inflation makes a gold standard impracticable."[8]

Moreover, existing governmental and financial institutions have powerful, almost intractable reasons for sticking with the monetary status quo—notably, the ability to fight and pay for war. One of the most appealing ideas behind American support for gold-backed money is this: if you make the government stick to money backed up in gold, you actually remove both the ability and the temptation for Congress and the Federal Reserve to screw the economy up. As former Kansas City Fed chairman and onetime Republican presidential contender Herman Cain wrote in a 2012 *Wall Street Journal* op-ed: "Gold is kryptonite to big-spending politicians. It is to the moochers and looters in big government what sunlight and garlic are to vampires."[9]

For all its obvious appeal, this argument has repeatedly been trampled by war. It is remarkable to consider that more than 150 years after the end of the US Civil War, there remain critics who say that Lincoln's decision to issue "greenbacks"—paper money not backed by any metal—was a violation so great that allowing secession to proceed would have been more constitutionally sound than finding a way to raise money to fight to protect the Union. Such views may contain a perverse intellectual consistency, but very little realism. If the Constitution gives the government the power to declare and fight wars, it surely follows that the government has the right to raise money for that purpose. Every major war (and several minor ones) that the United States has fought since then has required some kind of deficit spending or debt acquisition that would be extremely difficult under a strict form of gold standard. That hardly means that imposing a gold standard would make wars or war spending impossible—merely that it would force the future Lincolns and Roosevelts and LBJs to find clever and debatably legal ways around its restrictions. A good analogy is the balanced budget amendment. Many American conservatives argue that adding such an amendment to the US Constitution would rein in spending; as evidence of its viability they point to the dozens of individual states that have such amendments. But the argument demolishes itself—such amendments rarely restrain states from exercising the spending authority that they truly believe they want and can politically get away with. The amendments simply force governors and legislatures to use gimmicks and runarounds.

A similar point is that financial institutions, notably the Federal Reserve, will fight to protect their ability to mitigate recessions. This is almost literally a twenty-first-century dividing line between technocratic opinion and gold populism. Technocrats argue that the very existence of a central bank was required a little more than a century ago because the Panics of 1893 and 1907 demonstrated how powerless a fragmented banking system and Treasury was. In this view, the Great Depression was also either created or accelerated by a Federal Reserve system that did not or could not avail itself of necessary tools.[10] Most of America's financial leaders regard returning to a gold standard as a dangerous road to the past.

Assuming, however, that all the political and institutional obstacles to a gold standard could be overcome, that still wouldn't solve the supply problem that has stymied every previous attempt to peg monetary value to gold. Quite simply, there will never be enough gold in the world to support the US economy at its current size. Any form of the gold standard in the United States, from the founding of the Republic through Bretton Woods, has been accompanied by a fear that the gold supply was insufficient—a fear that repeatedly spilled over into crisis. In the late nineteenth century, Treasury's gold dwindled to the point where it had to be bailed out by J. P. Morgan. Sixty years later, even with the country having amassed the largest stockpile of gold in human history, the same scenario repeated itself, with multiple gold bailouts coming from the International Monetary Fund in the late 1950s and in 1960.

Even granting that gold provided a salutary monetary standard in the agrarian nineteenth century, the growth of the US and world economies has far outstripped the amount of gold available to conduct daily business, leaving aside the tremendous impracticality of doing so. The Roosevelt White House acknowledged this in the 1935 gold-clause case arguments; thirty years later, a congressional committee reiterated the point: "There is not enough gold in the world to permit its being used as an international medium of exchange, for actual transactions between private traders, simply because there is so much more business than there is gold."[11]

A related question is how a return to the gold standard would affect the market price of gold. The massive amount of cash and other Treasury securities in existence would need to be backed up by gold owned by the US government. In 2012, when Republican candidates suggested a commission to study a return to the gold standard, the commodities analysis group Capital Economics pointed out that the monetary base of the United States was about $2.56 trillion, and that the amount of gold in US reserves was about 262 million ounces. That would give the gold in US vaults an implied value of about $10,000 an ounce, or approximately 5 times the market price of gold in mid-2012. That might make current holders of gold ecstatic, but it could also have drastic economic consequences for people across the world.

Of course, an explosion like that wouldn't happen overnight, and it would also be possible to reserve only a fraction of the country's currency against gold—as was the case throughout the twentieth century until the connection was dissolved altogether. But even that action could be construed by gold-standard purists as undue government influence, because who would get to decide that fraction and thereby determine an "official" price of gold? In practice, it could only be the federal government and the US Federal Reserve, in conjunction with the world's other major, gold-holding central banks—precisely the kind of elite control over currency that gold-standard advocates have long opposed. The economic stakes of getting such a calibration "wrong" would be very high, and inevitably would create winners and losers, depending on what assets existing investors currently held and whether the new price would revalue those assets up or down. In a very important sense, the essence of fixing the price of a currency to a chunk of gold means there is never a "right" time or right rate at which to do it. The author and financial adviser James Rickards, who favors a role for gold in the international monetary system, has written: "To have a gold standard today that was nondeflationary, you'd have to have a price between $10,000 an ounce and $50,000 an ounce depending on which assumptions you want to make about the choice of money supply, the percentage of gold backing, and the specific countries that would be included in the new system."[12] Needless to say, the difference between $10,000 an ounce and $50,000 an ounce is vast, and the consequences of one price versus another could be catastrophic.

Also unclear in such a scenario is whether the official price of gold as established by a renewed gold-dollar link would apply to the world's private gold market. That is, if the gold-dollar ratio were fixed at the price of the time of this writing—about $1,200 an ounce on the spot market—would that price be enforced by central bank action on the private gold market? Such price containment would be immeasurably harder than it was in the 1950s and 1960s. Alternatively, the new price could be applied only to government transactions, as was the case after 1968, and the private market left to its own devices. In neither instance, as administrations from Eisenhower on can attest, is the record of stability encouraging.

Supply and volatility problems are two major reasons why today, most of the world doesn't want a gold standard. As of this writing, not a single major economy anywhere in the world defines its currency in terms of gold or any precious metal. Indeed, the trend in recent decades has been in the opposite direction. Switzerland was the last major economy to remove the gold standard, through a 1999 referendum that took effect the following year. In 2014, a populist/right movement managed to get a new referendum before voters that would have increased the amount of gold the Swiss National Bank needed to back up the franc; voters rejected it by nearly 4 to 1.

As in the United States, the governments and central banks of the world long ago determined that their interests are better served without tying money to gold. It is true, as Rickards notes, that many countries continue to stockpile gold in what he labels a "shadow gold standard."[13] That is nonetheless a far cry from an actual gold standard, and China's recent history of managing the value of its currency suggests that it might well have reasons to resist a return to an international fixed standard. To get China, Japan, Russia, India, Brazil, and the larger economies of Europe (some of which use the euro, some of which don't) on board with a new gold standard would require an international lobbying effort larger and more complex than Bretton Woods, and without, at the moment, the kind of urgency and consensus that existed in the waning days of World War II. The issue isn't simply whether the United States should adopt a monetary system based on a popularity contest. Rather, the realities of the twenty-first-century economy mean that trade is as genuinely global as it has ever been. And it is not merely a question of the billions of dollars of trade in goods and services between the United States and other countries, all of which could be affected by a switch to a gold standard. Trillions of dollars of foreign-exchange transactions take place every day, with the large majority of them denominated in dollars.[14]

The alternative would be for the United States to impose a gold standard on its own. This seems destined to lead to outcomes at odds with the stated goals of gold-standard advocates. If the United States reopened the gold window, what would prevent a repeat of the balance-of-payments crisis that began in the 1950s and was only resolved by shutting the window? Any country or combination of countries—including China, Russia under Vladimir Putin, or an even more antagonistic regime—could in theory threaten the monetary system of a gold-standard United States by exchanging dollars and dollar-backed securities for gold. Just as Stalin's idea of "socialism in one country" proved unworkable, a gold standard in one country would over time undermine itself. The economist Michael Bordo, who has published numerous papers and books on the gold standard, recognized this decades ago: "One country alone on the gold standard would likely find its monetary gold stock and hence its money supply subject to persistent shocks from factors beyond its control."[15] Whatever weaknesses the current international currency system may have, the use of interest rates and exchange rates as feedback mechanisms to adjust currency valuations tends to prevent most major currencies from experiencing the shocks that were common during the gold-exchange standard of Bretton Woods (and indeed caused that system to be abandoned).

The sheer infeasibility of a twenty-first-century gold standard is a chief reason why almost no mainstream economists advocate a return to a gold standard. This was perhaps the most striking feature of the Gold Commission in the early 1980s. The Commission literally could not find enough supportive, presentable economists to populate a single hearing. The more careful ones who did, such as Arthur Laffer, believed that the system had to be protected from the vagaries of any commodity market. Those hedges, in turn, were not acceptable to the politicians (represented in this instance by Ron Paul) for whom the gold standard was a kind of measure of political purity.

There are some respected economists and financial figures who argue that the gold standard in economic history was superior to other monetary systems. The British economist Susan Strange wrote in 1988: "Never since then has there been so long a period of financial stability, both in the credit system and in the relations of major trading currencies."[16] In 1981, the Federal Reserve Bank of Saint Louis published a paper that concluded: "Economic performance in the United States and the United Kingdom was superior under the classical gold standard to that of the subsequent period of managed fiduciary money."[17]

Of course this period included one of the worst economic episodes in US history—the panic of 1893. And even accepting that judgment on its own terms, many systems that worked reasonably well in the nineteenth century are not necessarily appropriate for the twenty-first. When you ask economic experts today, you get a uniform opinion (which is hardly the norm in economics): returning the United States to a gold standard, regardless of whatever theoretical merits it might have, would be bad for American jobs and for price stability. Of forty economists teaching at America's most prestigious universities—including many who've advised or worked in Republican administrations—exactly zero responded favorably to a gold-standard question asked in 2012.[18] Austan Goolsbee, the former chairman of Barack Obama's Council of Economic Advisers, responded: "Eesh. Has it come to this?" And Richard Thaler, an economist at the University of Chicago, asked, "Why tie to gold? Why not '82 Bordeaux?"

Beyond their belief that a gold standard would hurt the economy, technocrats see the entire enterprise as silly, as premodern, echoing John Maynard Keynes's description of gold money as a "barbarous relic." Today, massive amounts of money change hands instantaneously; maintaining that velocity and flexibility is vital in a globally integrated economy. By contrast, even if you're only using gold as a currency's reserve, it's bulky, heavy, and impractical to transfer. Just a few decades ago, if, say, France wanted to buy gold from the US Federal Reserve, the idea of actually shipping bullion overseas was expensive and unthinkable. Instead, bars of gold would literally be moved from one part of a vault to another, via forklift. Today's technocrats share the view of Robert

Triffin, an economist who in the late 1950s predicted that the Bretton Woods version of a gold standard could not sustain itself, and commented: "Nobody could ever have conceived of a more absurd waste of human resources than to dig gold in distant corners of the earth for the sole purpose of transporting it and re-burying it immediately afterwards in other deep holes, especially excavated to receive it and heavily guarded to protect it."

Even F. A. Hayek, the Nobelist free-market economist and social philosopher who died in 1992 and whose theories of currency competition inspired many modern American gold-standard advocates, came to believe that the system was unworkable. "I sympathize with the people who would like to return to the gold standard. I wish it were possible," he said in a 1984 interview.[19] "I am personally convinced it cannot be done for two reasons: The gold standard presupposes certain dogmatic beliefs which cannot be rationally justified, and our present generation is not prepared to readopt beliefs which were old traditions and have been discredited. But even more serious, I believe that any attempt to return to gold will lead to such fluctuations in the value of gold that it will break down."

On a pragmatic political level, it almost doesn't matter if the majority of economists are "wrong." A return to a gold standard requires a huge change in public behavior, and a wholesale disruption of the multitrillion-dollar international economy. Such momentous decisions will be made only by some combination of the executive branch, Congress, and the Federal Reserve Board. No responsible democratically elected federal government is going to undertake such a massive project against the advice of the established financial and economic community—the risk, both economic and political, is simply too high. The mere airing of oddball views on gold made many Republicans in the mid-1980s aghast at the direction that gold seemed to be driving the party. Jim Leach, an Iowa Republican elected to the House in 1977 who would serve for thirty years, said in 1984: "We're very close in the Republican

Party to endorsing the gold standard. That's nuts. Somebody's got to tell the world, or it's going to happen."[20]

And yet, what seemed "nuts" to a Republican in 1984 has today effectively become party doctrine, at least at the presidential level. The rise of populism within the GOP in recent decades has a parallel in the form of gold populism. Gold populism not only rejects the technical expertise offered by the Federal Reserve and the economic establishment—it flips it on its head. Gold populists argue that supposed economic expertise is one of the sources of the problem—indeed, it may be the biggest source of the problem. To gold populists, the authorized alternative to a metal-backed currency is fiat currency that too easily creates accumulating mountains of debt in the United States and abroad. Sooner or later, they surmise, that debt will collapse on itself, and an international monetary reckoning will occur. The winners on that day, they say, will be the ones holding the most gold. Thus far, twenty-first-century history has provided these advocates with plenty of evidence—from the Great Recession to the Greek crisis to the British vote to leave Europe—that the day is nigh. Because even the most powerful and best-run political and financial institutions are unlikely to ever prevent future shocks like the Great Recession, that argument will always find adherents.

Visions of an economic apocalypse can be very effective political tools, even if the apocalypse never occurs, as William Jennings Bryan and LBJ both knew. Similarly, it does not seem much of an exaggeration to say that arguments for the gold standard today have more value as political expression than they do as an actual political program. After all, if Reagan and Greenspan couldn't or didn't want to accomplish a return to a gold standard at a time when interest rates, inflation, and unemployment rates were at crisis levels, it is next to impossible to imagine another president, Congress, and Federal Reserve pulling the task off, especially because official inflation in the United States since the late 1980s has not been the massive problem it was during the Nixon-Ford-Carter years. As a consequence, the question of returning to a gold standard has taken on the characteristics of marginalized populism; it's attractive for some voters to hear, but almost no person in political power actually wants to bring it about. Indeed, gold populists may get more leverage from the idea of a gold standard than from its actually occurring. (A comparable idea on the other side of today's political spectrum might be abortion rights; if abortions were readily obtainable throughout the country, the Left and the Democratic Party would lose one of the most effective organizing and fundraising tools in their arsenal.) In this regard, today's gold populists are not so different from the silverites of the William Jennings Bryan era (except for the chosen metal). Bryan's economic ideas, too, were generally dismissed by orthodox economists and financiers, but to use today's parlance, they certainly "stirred up the base."

It remains an open question as to how powerful a political force today's gold populism is—in part because the political agenda is vague or unattainable, and in part because the ultimate size of the movement is hard to gauge. Listening to today's gold populists, it can be difficult to distinguish between the sales pitch for buying gold and the arguments for gold-backed currency; it seems likely that some of that confusion is a deliberate blurring of passions, and that a portion of the public does indeed want both. Yet a gold-backed currency may not be in gold owners' best interest. Roughly speaking, the use of gold as a monetary instrument runs at odds with its use as a personal investment. That is, if the dollar were fixed to a defined amount of gold, then the dollar value of gold would not appreciate in an amount that makes gold an attractive investment to holders of dollars. (It would also not depreciate very much, but during normal economic times most investors seek a return beyond mere value protection.)

Somewhat surprisingly, there are few reliable statistics on how many Americans own gold as an investment (presumably in coin or bullion form). Certainly a notable proportion of the country believes that gold makes a good investment. As noted in the introduction, significant percentages of Americans have told pollsters that they consider gold to be the best, or among the best, long-term investments. This is a very different question than how many Americans actually own gold. At various points in America's history, that question has either been close to irrelevant (because, for example, in the nineteenth century the vast majority of Americans could not afford to invest in any assets beyond those that kept them alive) or a non sequitur (because, for example, from 1933 to 1975 it was not legal for Americans to own gold as an investment). Even today, although gold ownership is reasonably common, one is forced to estimate. In 2015, the US Mint sold about $1.2 billion worth of American Eagle and American Buffalo gold coins.[21] That represents a fresh supply every year of hundreds of thousands of gold coins, and many Americans also purchase gold bullion and gold coins from other countries. Market vagaries, however, make it difficult to extrapolate from that figure how many Americans are buying: some individuals may purchase large quantities of coins, and there is no easy way to track secondary coin markets, the number of non-Americans buying gold in the United States, etc.

The World Gold Council, which gathers and disseminates mountains of statistics about gold, says it can provide no estimate for the number of Americans who own gold as an investment.[22] Metals Focus, a London-based precious-metals consultant, says that it has no figures it can release, but allows that it has "seen market research" that confirms an estimate I provided that fewer than 10 percent of American adults own gold as an investment.[23] A detailed 2010 poll designed to elicit the views of Americans sympathetic to the Tea Party found that 5 percent of those who viewed the Tea Party favorably said that they had purchased gold coins or bars in the preceding twelve months (unfortunately, the poll did not report a result for the same question from the general population).[24] Many of the newsletters and consultants that advise people to buy precious metals use a figure of between 1 and 3 percent of the American population owning precious metals.

These estimates mean that somewhere between 2.5 and 25 million Americans own gold as an investment. That range is wide enough to make any concrete analysis difficult, though it seems fair to say that at no point in American history have more Americans owned gold as an investment than they do in the twenty-first century. Even at the smaller end of that range, the gold constituency in America is large enough to be a political force of some size, despite the enormous obstacles in reestablishing a link between gold and the dollar.

Populism, after all, is neither defeated by obstacles nor undone by paradox. Populism is a mobile fixation, propelled forward by a promise to restore the past, no matter how unattainable or indeed fictional that past may be. Those who advocate returning national currency to a gold standard have massive hurdles in front of them, but they have certainly not given up. They have moved their battles to other arenas where they might have a better chance of victory— such as technological innovation and local government.

One of the most dramatic monetary developments of the twenty-first century has been the rise in the use of digital currencies, and the innovative infrastructures that support them. On the one hand, Bitcoin and other forms of digital currency represent the opposite of a gold-based money standard: not only does the Bitcoin contain no intrinsic value, it doesn't even physically exist. On the other hand, Bitcoin attracts some of the same people who are interested in a gold standard because it is not dependent on government or a central bank. Both systems derive value from relative scarcity; the total number of bitcoins that can be "mined" is preset at 21 million, and while the amount of gold is more open-ended, the metal is scarce and new supply can only be produced by mining and refining; typically the world increases its gold supply by 1–3 percent a year. Moreover, the "blockchain"—a kind of widely accessible digital ledger of transactions—that enables Bitcoin provides what some have argued is a promising method for tracking digital transactions backed by gold.[25] One putative advantage of such a system is that it relies merely on consensus; as long as gold can be legally obtained and owned, there are no obvious laws against such a system.

Of course, those Americans who believe that gold confiscation is a possible threat would have little trouble imagining government interference with a private, gold-backed currency. As some of these twenty-first-century argonauts have discovered, monetary systems that are created outside of governmental authority are almost automatically magnets for illegal behavior, regardless of what their investors may have intended. As far back as 1996, a prominent Florida-based company called E-gold began offering a digital currency backed by $20 million in physical gold; by 2002 the company had amassed a customer base of over 1 million people in one hundred countries.[26] However, the company found itself on the wrong side of a regulatory redefinition and was charged in 2008 with illegal money transferring. Its assets were seized and its cofounder was placed under six-month house arrest.

Others have tried to bring the battle over metal-backed money to the state level, where populist voices often get a more favorable hearing. In March 2011, Utah became the first state to pass a law altering its definition of "legal tender" to include silver and gold. The law recognized silver and gold coins issued by the federal government as legal tender, and removed certain state taxes from their transfer. The bill was laden with the symbolism of mining days old and new. It was drafted by Larry Hilton, chairman of the Utah Precious Metals Association and also a Tea Party activist; when the governor signed it into law, a local real estate financier named Wayne Palmer handed a set of commemorative gold and silver coins to the state as a gift. Here, too, the line between populist energy and illegal activity is not always clearly drawn; less than a year later, the SEC charged Palmer with running a Ponzi scheme that defrauded investors of tens of millions of dollars.[27]

Aside from some limited tax benefits for individuals, the impact in Utah has been minimal. A gold coin issued by the US Mint might have a metallic value of over a thousand dollars, but it could only be spent at its face value of, say, $50. The law thus makes it legal to spend gold in ways that no one would. One Utah insider said: "If somebody is stupid enough that they want to buy a Snickers bar at 7-Eleven with a gold coin worth thousands of dollars, they will be able to do that."

Nonetheless, "sound money" legislation has become a popular trend in state government in recent years. Legislators in Missouri and South Carolina introduced sound money bills in 2012, though neither one actually became law. In 2013, the governors of Louisiana and Texas within a week of each other signed nearly identical bills to exempt gold and silver coin and bullion transactions from state sales taxes. Similar legislation was introduced in Arizona, Colorado, Tennessee, and several other states.

The spate of bills was not accidental. The American Legislative Exchange Council (ALEC) is a network of conservative state legislators that drafts and distributes model legislation on a wide variety of issues. ALEC and other groups attempted to replicate the Utah law in more than a dozen states; one group even drafted a "constitutional tender" bill template and encouraged gold-standard fans to send it to friendly legislators.

The motives and rationales behind such efforts are as mixed as their success. At a minimum, they want to call attention to weaknesses in the Federal Reserve system of paper money. The freshman Republican legislator in Utah who introduced that state's bill did not support a return to a gold standard, however. And to governors, some of the bills looked politically attractive because conservative voters presumably would like to hear that taxes were eliminated on anything, especially precious-metal transactions. (After gold-and-silver bills became law in Louisiana and Texas, both states' governors went on to run for president in 2016, although neither one made it to the actual primary voting stage.) Even here, though, success was not uniform. Arizona's conservative governor

Jan Brewer vetoed a Utah-like bill in 2013, calling it "vague" and citing uncertainty over its tax implications.

By 2013, the price of gold had already begun to fall, and with it, seemingly, the momentum for this type of state legislation. But the passion for gold continued in other forms. In 2015, Texas passed a law authorizing it to build the nation's only state-run gold bullion depository. The idea is that any resident or business in Texas, or any precious-metal investor in the world, could open an account to store gold in the depository. Then, at least according to some visions for the project, they could be issued checks or credit cards that draw on the bullion. The state representative who introduced the bill said: "I would like to see this all come together so we become a commodities hub for the continent."[28]

Texas may or may not succeed in becoming a continental gold hub. The point is that the fullness of America's relationship with gold far transcends the question of restoring gold money, nationally or locally. We cannot get enough of the metal; after India and China, two countries with populations of over a billion people, the United States is the largest consumer of gold in the world. Consider that for forty years in the twentieth century through the 1970s, the United States Treasury minted no gold coins at all. Today, the US Mint is the largest producer of gold and silver bullion coins in the world. In 2015, Treasury reported that demand was so high that the mint at West Point was operating in three shifts a day, seven days a week, and paying workers overtime to make American Eagle coins. After a slump during the Great Recession, American sales of gold jewelry rose for several quarters in a row. The United States is the fourth-largest gold producer in the world, having surpassed long-time rival South Africa; while down somewhat from a peak in the late 1990s, the 210 metric tons produced in 2014 represents a higher level than for nearly all of American history.

Of course, there are downsides to this gold fixation. The most pressing problem the American gold-mining industry faces in the twenty-first century is not, strictly speaking, financial—it is environmental. The open-pit cyanide-leaching techniques that helped restore the industry beginning in the 1980s are remarkably productive but require tremendous effort and hazard. In the average open-pit mine, operators must unearth three tons of ore to produce enough ore for a single wedding band. The rest of the ore becomes a mound of chemically toxic waste.[29]

And, as with other areas of American society, there are moments when gold fever spills over into potentially violent conflict. In 2015, owners of a Montana gold mine who were being cited by a federal agency arranged for an armed local militia to stand guard and prohibit access to the mine and surrounding public lands. It did not lead to actual armed confrontation, but served as a reminder that "God, Guns, and Gold" is a potentially combustible formula in a country as armed as America.

What is striking about these gold debates, sales pitches, fraudulent schemes, eruptions, and political posturing is that they endure almost as much as the metal itself. Consider how distant so much of our country's political and economic history feels from today's world. The overwhelming majority of Americans are not today publicly wondering whether banks should exist, as was the case in the Andrew Jackson era, or whether silver should be freely coined and legal tender, as in the age of Bryan. Getting rid of paper currency—a serious political stance in the middle of the nineteenth century—would have few more serious proponents in a truly open national debate than would a flat earth. The International Monetary Fund and World Bank have vociferous critics on all sides of the political spectrum, but you won't find an audience to watch presidential debates about them, and no serious American politician today offers a vision of a global economy that lacks such institutions—they are a widely accepted feature of the financial landscape.

Yet two hundred years after the discovery of gold within the United States, we are still fighting about it. If anything, gold has become a more widespread political and economic force today than during much of the last century. For millions, gold is the repository of hope in something eternal, a protector of liberty, combined with a promise of wealth. It is an unquestioned safe haven and a connection to a past that is deeply American and beyond American. To millions of others, it is a hopeless artifact, a damaging delusion, an environmental blight. The arguments and rhetoric may be inverted, borrowed, riddled with misleading claims or made in bad faith—but they are strikingly similar to those made by our grandparents and great grandparents. Even as we disagree on positions, the metal keeps finding ways to assert itself into our political imagination. Americans are united, as we are divided, by our passions about gold.

# ACKNOWLEDGMENTS

A book of this scope requires considerable collaboration, both direct and indirect. My most frequent content collaborators have been the librarians and archivists who guided me through mountains of ore to find the golden nuggets. Many, including those at the New York Public Library and Columbia University Library, have done so anonymously. But especially helpful were Jennifer Cuddeback and Alexis Percle at the LBJ Library, Diane Shaw at Lafayette College, Valoise Armstrong at the Eisenhower Library, and Andrea Faling at the Nebraska Historical Society.

Over the course of four years I deployed a small army of researchers—including Zoe Carpenter, Douglas Grant, Sarah Miller, Bartie Scott, Christian Wallace, and Mauro Whiteman—whose contributions to this book have been indispensable.

Many friends and allies generously reviewed and commented on portions of the manuscript prior to publication. My thanks for this aid go to Liza Featherstone, Martin Hipsky, Michael Kazin, Richard Panek, Anya Schiffrin, Jack Shafer, Paul Smalera, Joseph Stiglitz, Bernhard Warner, and Julian Zelizer.

Writing a book while holding a full-time job is greatly aided by supportive bosses. I am fortunate to have had two—Chrystia Freeland at Reuters and Eric Schurenberg at *Inc.*—while working on this project.

The team at Liveright and Norton has been spectacular throughout. Robert Weil is an outstanding, erudite editor whose style and insights are reflected on every page. Marie Pantojan patiently helped me through the editing process; Gary Von Euer and Don Rifkin provided a careful and insightful copyedit; and Steve Attardo gave the book its handsome look. My agent, the intrepid Chris Calhoun, championed the project when it was purely theoretical and pushed me to write a compelling proposal.

My deepest thanks go to my family—Erinn and Henry. This book took many weekend afternoons in the library and quite a few nights away on research trips. I am exceedingly grateful for their patience and support.

# NOTES

## Abbreviations

DDEL    Dwight David Eisenhower Library, Abilene, Kansas
FDRL    Franklin Delano Roosevelt Library, Hyde Park, New York
*FRUS*   Foreign Relations of the United States
GFL     Gerald Ford Library, Ann Arbor, Michigan
LC      Library of Congress, Washington, DC
LBJL    Lyndon Baines Johnson Library, Austin, Texas
NARA    National Archives and Record Administration, College Park, Maryland

## Introduction

1. James K. Polk: "Fourth Annual Message," December 5, 1848, Gerhard Peters and John T. Woolley, *The American Presidency Project*, http://www.presidency.ucsb.edu/ws/?pid=29489.

2. "Mineral Wealth of California," *Albany Argus*, reprinted in *Pittsfield Sun*, December 7, 1848.

3. "California," *The American Review*, no. 16 (April 1849): 335.

4. James Rawls and Walton Bean, *California: An Interpretive History* (Boston: McGraw Hill, 2011), 113.

5. In Switzerland, a group of gold-standard advocates managed in 2014 to get a nation-wide referendum on increasing the gold reserves backing up the Swiss franc from 7 percent to 20 percent. The proposal was roundly rejected; 78 percent voted against it.

6. Peter Blakewell, "Gold and the Discovery of America," in *Gold in History, Geology and Culture: Collected Essays* (Raleigh, NC: North Carolina Department of Cultural Resources, 2001), 83.

7. Fletcher Melvin Green, "Gold Mining: A Forgotten Industry of Ante-Bellum North Carolina," *The North Carolina Historical Review* 14, no. 1 (January 1937): 3.

8. Gallup Poll Social Series: Economy and Personal Finance. Interviews conducted April 3–6, 2014.

9. "A Man Who Is Not Going to California," *New York Herald*, February 19, 1849, 1.

## Chapter 1: El Dorado Comes True

1. George Washington to Burwell Bassett, April 22, 1879, in *The Writings of George Washington from the Original Manuscript*, 14:432. The biographer's estimate is in Paul Leland Haworth, *George Washington: Farmer* (Indianapolis: Bobbs-Merrill, 1915), 286.

2. *John Sherman's Recollections of Forty Years in the House, Senate and Cabinet: An Autobiography* (Chicago: Werner, 1895), 254.

3. *Sherman's Recollections*, 254.

4. A thorough examination of the benefits and drawbacks of free banking can be found in Arthur J. Rolnick and Warren E. Weber, "Free Banking, Wildcat Banks and Shinplasters," *Federal Reserve Bank of Minneapolis Quarterly Review* 6, no. 3 (Fall 1982): 10–19.

5. The most thorough account of Jefferson's views on currency takes this quotation as its title; Donald F. Swanson, in *The Virginia Magazine of History and Biography* 101, no. 1 (January 1933), 37–52.

6. Drew McCoy, *The Elusive Republic: Political Economy in Jeffersonian America* (Chapel Hill: University of North Carolina Press, 1980), 138.

7. Ebenezer Smith Thomas, *Reminiscences of the Last Sixty-five Years* (Hartford: The Author, 1840), 2:84–85.

8. An excellent account of Jackson's slow strangulation of the Second Bank of the United States can be found in Robert V. Remini, *Andrew Jackson and the Bank War* (New York: W. W. Norton, 1967).

9. Davis Rich Dewey, *Financial History of the United States* (New York: Longmans and Green, 1903), 100.

10. Bray Hammond provides a pointed discussion of the American obsession with "purity" around banking and government in *Sovereignty and an Empty Purse: Banks and Politics in the Civil War* (Princeton, NJ: Princeton University Press, 1970), 22ff.

11. For an exhaustive account of Jackson's pet bank strategy, see Harry N. Scheiber, "The Pet Banks in Jacksonian Politics and Finance, 1833–1841," *The Journal of Economic History* 23, no. 2 (June 1963): 196–214.

12. Jackson to Van Buren, January 3, 1834, Van Buren Papers, LC. Cited in Remini, *Andrew Jackson and the Bank War*, 154–155.

13. The relationship between the banking wars of the 1830s and the economic slump that ensued is hotly debated. While many historians have linked Jackson's banking policy to the later boom and crises, Peter Temin forcefully argues in *The Jacksonian Economy* (New York: W. W. Norton, 1969) that the economy was largely driven by factors beyond Jackson's control. And regardless of cause, Murray Rothbard maintains that the "1839–1843 contraction was healthful for the economy in liquidating unsound investments, debts, and banks, including the pernicious Bank of the United States." *A History of Money and Banking in the United States Before the Twentieth Century* (Auburn, AL: Ludwig von Mises Institute, 2002), 103.

14. Address delivered in Fort Wayne, Indiana, October 11, 1865, Hugh McCulloch, *Addresses, speeches, lectures and letters upon various subjects* (Washington, DC: W. H. Lepley, 1891), 49.

15. Abraham P. Nasatir, "The French Consulate in California, 1843–1856, The Moeren-haut Documents," *California Historical Society Quarterly* 13, no. 1 (March 1934): 66.

16. S. M. McDowell to family, probably early 1853, cited in Malcolm J. Rohrbough, *Days of Gold: The California Gold Rush and the American Nation* (Berkeley: University of California Press, 1997), 213.

17. Richard Walker's essay "Another Round of Globalization in San Francisco" contains a wealth of data about the effects of the gold rush on San Francisco's economy: *Urban Geography* 17 (1996): 60–94.

18. Official Report on the Gold Mines, Colonel Richard Barnes Mason to Brigadier-General R. Jones, August 17, 1848, available at http://sfmuseum.org/hist6/masonrpt.html.

19. "The Gold Mine," *The Californian*, August 14, 1848. This editorial is accessible through the California Digital Newspaper Collection.

20. The gold rush presented a fascinating alternative and challenge to what we often think of as the "natural" system of private property in the United States. So long as placer mining was prevalent, vast tracts of bountiful land legally belonged to no one but the person who could lay a claim first. Neither the state nor any private actor could intervene—a system in marked contrast to the development of property in Europe and the eastern part of the United States. By the 1870s, a state legal framework arose that would change that situation, but not before a powerful squatter's rights movement had asserted itself. See Henry George, *Progress and Poverty* (New York: Robert Schalkenbach Foundation, 1942), 385–386; and Donald J. Pisani, "The Squatter and Natural Law in Nineteenth-Century America," *Agricultural History* 81, no. 4 (Fall 2007): 443–463.

21. Robert F. Heizer, *The Other Californians: Prejudice and Discrimination under Spain, Mexico, and the United States to 1920* (Berkeley: University of California Press, 1977), 155–156. See also John Soennichesen, *The Chinese Exclusion Act of 1882* (Santa Barbara, CA: Greenwood Press, 2011).

22. Charles N. Alpers, Michael P. Hunerlach, Jason T. May, and Roger L. Hothem, "Mercury Contamination from Historical Gold Mining in California," United States Geological Survey, 2005. http://pubs.usgs.gov/fs/2005/3014/.

23. H. W. Brands, *The Age of Gold* (New York: Doubleday, 2002), 442.

24. Details of the development of the Panama route are in John Walton Caughey, *The California Gold Rush* (Berkeley: University of California Press, 1948), ch. 4.

25. Banking figures compiled from *Banker's Magazine*, in William G. Sumner, *A History of Banking in All the Leading Nations* (New York: Journal of Commerce and Commercial Bulletin, 1896), 456.

26. The international economic effects of the Gold Rush are discussed in Gerald D. Nash, "A Veritable Revolution: The Global Economic Significance of the California Gold Rush," in *A Golden State: Mining and Economic Development in Gold Rush California*, ed. James T. Rawls and Richard J. Orsi (Berkeley: University of California Press, 1999), 276–292.

27. A thorough compilation of the details of the *Central America* sinking and aftermath is contained in E. Merton Coulter, "The Loss of the Steamship *Central America*, in 1857," *The Georgia Historical Quarterly* 54, no. 4 (Winter 1970): 453–492.

28. Albert J. Churella, *The Pennsylvania Railroad, Volume 1: Building an Empire, 1846–1917* (Philadelphia: University of Pennsylvania Press, 2012), 192.

29. The causes of the 1857 Panic remain much debated. However, a thorough account of its unfolding is given in James L. Huston, *The Panic of 1857 and the Coming of the Civil War* (Baton Rouge: Louisiana State University Press, 1999), ch. 2.

30. W. P. Tatham to Messrs. Baring Brothers & Co., October 12, 1857, cited in Austin E. Hutcheson, "Philadelphia and the Panic of 1857," *Pennsylvania History* 3, no. 3 (July 1936): 182–194.

31. *Sherman's Recollections,* 251.

32. "Will the Federal Government Be Financially Successful?," *The Economist*, August 24, 1861, 927.

33. Many bankers and members of Congress in 1862 maintained that the adoption of greenbacks was more expedient than it was absolutely necessary—that even if heavy taxes and unusually high interest rates on loans were necessary to fund the war, those were nonetheless preferable to the adoption of a paper currency with questionable constitutional legitimacy. Some economists and historians have held to this view, including Wesley Clair Mitchell in *A History of the Greenbacks* (Chicago: University of Chicago Press, 1903). Nathaniel Stephenson, in *Abraham Lincoln and the Union* (New Haven: Yale University Press, 1920), asserts as a "common" estimate that the use of paper money added $600 million to the cost of the war. Others maintain that many of the late nineteenth- and early twentieth-century historians of the greenback period had hard-money biases.

34. An 1886 account from Donn Piatt, an author and onetime Lincoln ally, offered an unsourced, undated conversation between Lincoln and Chase in which Chase insists that paper money is not constitutional, and Lincoln replies: "I will violate the Constitution if necessary to save the Union." As Stephen Sawyer and William J. Novak have written, this is "now thought a false tale." Other accounts emphasize a letter—ostensibly written in 1864 but not publicly circulated until the 1880s—in which Lincoln credited a friend, Colonel E. D. Taylor, with being "the father of the present greenback." But the authenticity of the letter is dubious, and its content is irrelevant: the letter credits Taylor with suggesting a paper money system to Lincoln during a meeting "on or about the 16th" of January 1862. By that time, Spaulding's legal-tender bill had already been drafted, reported to committee, debated in the House Ways and Means Committee, and circulated to heads of the nation's largest banks. In his book *Lincoln's War* (New York: Random House, 2004), Geoffrey Perret places the meeting between Taylor and Lincoln in the summer of 1862, which makes even less sense, given that the law creating legal-tender paper money passed in February.

35. Davis Rich Dewey, *Financial History of the United States* (New York: Longmans, Green, 1903), 284.

36. Pendleton, quoted in Elbridge Gerry Spaulding, *History of the Legal Tender Money Issued During the Great Rebellion* (Buffalo: Express Printing Company, 1869), 44.

37. Mitchell, *A History of the Greenbacks,* 59.

38. Representative Clement Vallindigham, quoted in Spaulding, *History of the Legal Tender Money,* 53.

39. Hammond, *Sovereignty and an Empty Purse,* 227.

*Chapter 2: A Crash, a Clash, and a "Crime"*

1. My version of the events leading up to Black Friday relies on several sources, all of which are dependent upon the House inquiry *Investigation into the Causes of the Gold Panic*, 41st Congress, 2nd session, report no. 31 (Washington, DC: Government Printing Office, 1870). The most thorough standalone book is by Kenneth D. Ackerman, *The Gold Ring: Jim Fisk, Jay Gould, and Black Friday 1869* (New York: Dodd, Mead, 1988). Other information has been gleaned from Maury Klein, *The Life and Legend of Jay Gould* (Baltimore: Johns Hopkins Press, 1986); W. A. Swanberg, *Jim Fisk: The Career of an Improbable Rascal* (New York: Scribner's, 1959); and William McFeely, *Grant: A Biography* (New York: W. W. Norton, 1981), 319–331.

2. *Report of the Secretary of the Treasury on the State of the Finances for the Year 1865* (Washington, DC: Government Printing Office, 1865), 4.

3. Grant's 1869 inaugural address can be found at http://avalon.law.yale.edu/19th_century/grant1.asp.

4. *Investigation into the Causes of the Gold Panic*, 152–153.

5. An in-depth discussion of postwar banking challenges in the South can be found in George L. Anderson, "The South and Problems of Post–Civil War Finance," *The Journal of Southern History* 9, no. 2 (May 1943): 181–195.

6. *The Journal of the Joint Committee of Fifteen on Reconstruction*, ed. Benjamin B. Kendrick (New York: Columbia University Press, 1914), 283.

7. "Financial Policy of the Administration," *New York Times*, August 25, 1869.

8. The early September letter from Grant to Boutwell feels like a hot pistol emitting no smoke. It appears to have been sent; Boutwell testified before Congress that he received the letter and acted on it by September 4. Yet to the best of my knowledge, no record of the letter's text exists anywhere. Boutwell told Congress that he believed the letter to be in his residence in Groton; Congress, in an otherwise sweeping investigation, does not appear to have demanded to see it. Inquiries at relevant archives have been similarly unproductive.

9. Robert Sobel, *The Big Board: A History of the New York Stock Market* (New York: Free Press, 1965), 93.

10. Joseph M. Cormack, "The Legal Tender Cases: A Drama of American Legal and Financial History," *Virginia Law Review* 16, no 2 (December 1929), 140.

11. "Legal Tenders," *New York Times*, February 8, 1870.

12. *Hepburn v. Griswold*, 75 U.S. 603 (1869).

13. See, for example, Richard Timberlake, *Constitutional Money: A Review of the Supreme Court's Monetary Decisions* (New York: Cambridge University Press, 2013), ch. 12 and 13.

14. Sidney Ratner adduced evidence, including from Boutwell's memoir, and concluded that "it seems highly probable" that Grant knew the content of the Court's decision before appointing two judges who had supported the constitutionality of greenbacks in lower court decisions. "Was the Supreme Court Packed by President Grant?" *Political Science Quarterly* 50, no. 3 (September 1935): 343–358.

15. Charles Fairman, *Mister Justice Miller and the Supreme Court, 1862–1890* (Cambridge, MA: Harvard University Press, 1939), 170.

16. Charles Evans Hughes, *The Supreme Court of the United States* (New York: Columbia University Press, 1966), 50.

17. The act did allow for a "trade dollar," heavier than the old silver dollars, to be used for transactions outside the United States, primarily in China. The economist Paul M. O'Leary made a case that the omission of the silver was intentional, although he rests responsibility not with any member of Congress but with Henry Richard Linderman, a former director of the Philadelphia Mint, who had a hand in drafting the 1873 legislation. See "The Scene of the Crime of 1873 Revisited: A Note," *Journal of Political Economy* 68, no. 4 (August 1960): 388–392. There is no question that Linderman did not favor minting a silver dollar. However, O'Leary's argument is somewhat undermined by the fact that the original 1870 Treasury draft of the legislation—on which Linderman worked, as O'Leary argues—did in fact include a provision for a regular silver dollar. Only days later was this removed when the bill was actually introduced into Congress; later still, an amendment included the heavier trade dollar. See *History of the Coinage Act of 1873* (Washington, DC: Government Printing Office, 1900). Linderman is also the culprit in Samuel DeCanio's groundbreaking article "Populism, Paranoia, and the Politics of Free Silver," *Studies in American Political Development* 25 (April 2011): 1–26. DeCanio elicits substantial evidence that Linderman was in fact bribed by William Ralston, president of The Bank of California, both to craft the legislation and to ensure its passage. Ralston's influence apparently also included some legislators, including Nevada senator William Stewart, who later came out vehemently against the "crime." DeCanio further developed the bribery thesis in his book *Democracy and the Origins of the American Regulatory State* (New Haven, CT: Yale University Press, 2015).

18. The mystery of how the Coinage Act became so reviled continued to intrigue historians and economists more than a century later. Milton Friedman published a useful and thought-provoking paper entitled "The Crime of 1873" (Hoover Institution, Working Paper No. E-89-12, April 1989), from which some of this account is drawn. One person who did notice the bill's silver demonetization and recommended against it was James Ross Snowden, a former treasurer of the Mint. He told Sherman he found the change "unadvisable," although even he did not envision the silver dollar commonly circulating as currency. See *History of the Coinage Act of 1873*, 85.

19. "How the Silver Question Effects the Working of Silver Mines," *Idaho Statesman*, August 31, 1876.

20. Ewing gave a lengthy speech, "On Resumption, Contraction, Free Banking," which was reproduced in *The Ohio Democrat*, September 6, 1877.

21. Ernest Seyd to Samuel Hooper, February 17, 1872, reproduced in *History of the Coinage Act of 1873*, 131–148.

22. Mining Stock Association to Senator William Stewart, published in the *Nevada State Journal*, February 8, 1890, cited in Paul Barnett, *Agricultural History* 38, no. 3 (July 1964): 178–179.

23. Richard Bensel, *Passion and Preferences: William Jennings Bryan and the 1896 Democratic National Convention* (New York: Cambridge University Press, 2008), 14.

24. Sobel, *The Big Board*, 135.

25. Margaret Good Myers et al., *The New York Money Market: Origins and Development*, 291, cited in Milton Friedman and Anna Schwartz, *A Monetary History of the United States* (Princeton, NJ: Princeton University Press, 1963), 107n26.

26. The gold reserve figures come from Sobel, *The Big Board*, 138.

27. See "Discussion in the Senate," *New York Times*, February 1, 1895. In addition, there is some question as to whether the $100 million figure had the full force of law. It was included in a bank charter statute passed in 1882. See Alexander D. Noyes, "The Treasury Reserve and the Bond Syndicate," *Political Science Quarterly* 10, no. 4 (December 1895): 573–602.

28. Charles Hoffmann, "The Depression of the Nineties," *The Journal of Economic History* 16, no. 2 (June 1956): 137–164.

29. "Starving in the Arid Lands," *New York Times*, November 12, 1893.

30. Grover Cleveland, *Presidential Problems* (New York: The Century Co., 1904), 152.

31. See, for example, H. W. Brands, "Upside-Down Bailout," History Net, June 3, 2010, http://www.historynet.com/upside-down-bailout.htm.

32. Alyn Brodsky, *Grover Cleveland: A Study in Character* (New York: St. Martin's Press, 2000), 363.

33. According to a contemporary account from a financial journalist, a coffee importer was able to undersell the Morgan bond syndicate slightly and began filling its orders by withdrawing gold from Treasury, worth more than $30 million. See Alexander D. Noyes, "The Treasury Reserve and the Bond Syndicate," *Political Science Quarterly* 10, no. 4 (December 1895): 600–601.

## Chapter 3: The Dangers of the Yellow Brick Road

1. Gerald Ford was born, and lived for a few weeks, in Omaha, Nebraska, but he was never elected president.

2. Richard Franklin Bensel constructed a useful state-by-state chart in his fascinating book *Passion and Preferences: William Jennings Bryan and the 1896 Democratic National Convention* (New York: Cambridge University Press, 2008), 29–30. This chapter draws on his work, as well as R. Hal Williams, *Realigning America: McKinley, Bryan and the Remarkable Election of 1896* (Lawrence: University Press of Kansas, 2010); Michael Kazin, *A Godly Hero: The Life of William Jennings Bryan* (New York: Alfred A. Knopf, 2006); and Karl Rove, *The Triumph of William McKinley: Why the Election of 1896 Still Matters* (New York: Simon and Schuster, 2015).

3. "Ohio Democrats: The State Convention Declares for Free Coinage," *Philadelphia Inquirer*, June 25, 1896.

4. The issue of anti-Semitism among Bryan's followers has been hotly contested for decades. Oscar Handlin drew explicit connections between anti-Rothschild and anti-Shylock material distributed by Populists in the 1890s and the Christian symbolism in Bryan's convention speech in "American Views of the Jew at the Opening of the Twentieth Century," *Publications of the American Jewish Historical Society* 40, no. 4 (June 1951): 323–344. Richard Hofstadter focused on some of the darker aspects of Progressivism and populism in *The Age of Reform* (New York: Vintage Books, 1955). In *The Tarnished Dream* (Westport, CT: Greenwood

Press, 1979), Michael Dobkowski gives a detailed discussion (pp. 170–208) of how Populist imagery incorporated existing stereotypes about Jews as moneylenders. Norman Pollock marshaled a defense of Bryan and others in "The Myth of Popular Anti-Semitism," *The American Historical Review* 68, no. 1 (October 1962): 76–80.

5. Hill quoted in "The Presidential Campaign," *Public Opinion* 21 (July 16, 1896), 70.
6. Hofstadter, *Age of Reform*, 5–6.
7. "Republican Comment on the Chicago Convention," *Public Opinion* 21 (July 16, 1896), 77.
8. *Memoirs of William Jennings Bryan* (Philadelphia: J. C. Winston, 1925), 115.
9. "The Convention and Candidate," *Minneapolis Tribune*, July 11, 1896, 6. The sentence about suicide does not appear in the edition of the paper digitized by the Minnesota Historical Society. However, it is quoted in the news digest magazine *Public Opinion* 21 (July 16, 1896): 77. It is possible that it appeared in some but not all of the paper's four daily editions.
10. A. Scott Berg, *Wilson* (New York: G. P. Putnam's Sons, 2013), 129.
11. James Livingston details the politics and meaning of the "sound money" campaign in *Origins of the Federal Reserve System: Money, Class and Corporate Capitalism 1890–1913* (Ithaca, NY: Cornell University Press, 1989), 88ff.
12. Ken Coates, from the introduction to the reprinted edition of E. Tappan Adney, *The Klondike Stampede* (New York: Harper, 1899), xvi–xvii.
13. Gold stock figures come from Friedman and Schwartz, *A Monetary History of the United States*, 141.
14. Roberts's speech was reproduced in part in "Financial Law's Results," *New York Times*, May 18, 1900.
15. Henry M. Littlefield, "The Wizard of Oz: Parable on Populism," *American Quarterly* 16, no. 1 (Spring 1964): 50.
16. See, for example, Hugh Rockoff, "The 'Wizard of Oz' as a Monetary Allegory," *The Journal of Political Economy* 98, no. 4 (August 1990): 739–760.
17. Robert F. Bruner and Sean D. Carr, *The Panic of 1907: Lessons Learned from the Market's Perfect Storm* (Hoboken, NJ: John Wiley & Sons, 2007), 14.
18. "Biggest Gold Cargo Landed From Liner," *New York Times*, November 9, 1907.
19. James Parthemos, "The Federal Reserve Act of 1913 in the Stream of U.S. Monetary History," Federal Reserve Bank of Richmond, *Economic Review*, July/August 1988, 25.
20. Carter Glass, quoted in Gerald T. Dunne, *A Christmas Present for the President* (St. Louis: Federal Reserve Bank, 1984), 7.
21. Speech of Hon. Elihu Root, The Banking and Currency Bill, December 13, 1913, 24.
22. Fifth Annual Report of the Federal Reserve Board (Washington, DC: Government Printing Office, 1919), 35.
23. Barry Eichengreen and Peter Temin, "The Gold Standard and the Great Depression," *Contemporary European History* 9, no. 2 (July 2000): 184–185.
24. Although it is little recalled today, the Federal Reserve actually did engage in a large, unprecedented campaign to improve conditions through market operations. The Glass-Steagall legislation passed in February 1932 (not to be confused with the identically titled legislation, passed two years later, that broke up big banks) gave

the Fed the authority to buy government securities with gold, thereby freeing up the metal for commercial purposes. In mid-April, for example, the Fed bought over $100 million of securities in this manner. But after a few months, the Fed simply gave up, for reasons that economists have debated for decades.

25. Stabilization of Commodity Prices: Hearings Before the Subcommittee of the Committee on Banking and Currency, House of Representatives, 72nd Congress, 1st session, on H.R. 10517 for Increasing and Stabilizing the Price Level of Commodities, and for Other Purposes, Parts 1–2, p. 492.

26. Theodore G. Joslin, *Hoover Off the Record* (Garden City, NY: Doubleday, Doran & Company, 1935), 170ff. "Hours" is almost certainly an exaggeration.

## Chapter 4: FDR Bids Good-bye to Gold

1. Theodore G. Joslin, *Hoover Off the Record* (Garden City, NY: Doubleday, Doran & Company, 1935), 171.

2. George Warren's diaries can be found in his collected papers at the Cornell University Library. I am indebted to Eric Rauchway's *The Money Makers: How Roosevelt and Keynes Ended the Depression, Defeated Fascism, and Secured a Prosperous Peace* (New York: Basic Books, 2015), chapter 2, for its clear account of FDR's first weekend, based in part on Warren's Washington visit. Not all historians agree on the decisiveness of Warren's influence. Thomas Ferguson, for example, points to the influence of a business interest group—representing Standard Oil and Sears Roebuck, among others—called the Committee for the Nation, that supported FDR's 1932 campaign and urged moving off gold. See *Golden Rule: The Investment Theory of Party Competition and the Logic of Money-Driven Political Systems* (Chicago: University of Chicago Press, 1995), 149–150. Ferguson also points to the influence of Rene Léon, a securities and exchange expert who corresponded with FDR. Elliot A. Rosen, in his book *Roosevelt, The Great Depression and the Economics of Recovery* (Charlottesville: University of Virginia Press, 2005) says that Léon had, as early as January 1933, pointed both Raymond Moley and FDR to the possibility of using the Trading With the Enemy Act to take the country off the gold standard. See 246n5.

3. Ben S. Bernanke, "The Macroeconomics of the Great Depression: A Comparative Approach," *Journal of Money, Credit and Banking* 27, no. 1 (February 1995): 4.

4. A detailed account of Hoover and his advisers' discussions of using the Trading With the Enemy Act for peacetime banking purposes can be found in Raymond Moley, *The First New Deal* (New York: Harcourt, Brace & World, 1966), 157–160. Some of that account relies on Francis Gloyd Awalt, "Recollections of the Banking Crisis of 1933," *The Business History Review* 43, no. 3 (Autumn 1969): 347–371.

5. FDR press conference #13, April 19, 1933. FDR press conferences are archived at the FRDL and online at http://www.fdrlibrary.marist.edu/archives/collections/franklin/?p=collections/findingaid&id=508.

6. The draft legislation is reproduced as document 6 in *Documentary History of the FDR Presidency*, ed. George McJimsey (Bethesda, MD: University Publications of America, 2001), 3:33ff.

7. This account comes from a letter dated March 16, 1966, from former Fed staffer

Walter Wyatt to Raymond Moley, and is quoted extensively in Moley's *The First New Deal*, 176.

8. Walter Wyatt, oral history, Rare Book and Manuscript Library, Columbia University Library, 86.

9. George Harrison to Arthur Ballantine, March 24, 1933; George Harrison to William Woodin, April 17, 1933. George Leslie Harrison Papers on the Federal Reserve System, Box 24, Rare Book and Manuscript Library, Columbia University Library, New York, New York.

10. Moley, *The First New Deal*, 154.

11. *Congressional Record*, 73rd Congress, 1st session, 76.

12. Moley, *After Seven Years* (New York: Harper & Brothers, 1939), 152.

13. Hoover used the figure $1.4 billion in hoarded money during a news conference on February 5, 1932. It is unclear how that amount was calculated. Official statistics from the Federal Reserve for January 1932 show $120 million in gold coin and $850 million in gold certificates in circulation (*Banking and Monetary Statistics*, 1914–1941, part 1, p. 412). The remainder could have reflected the $399 million in silver coins and certificates in circulation, or perhaps an estimate for nonmonetary gold in the form of gold bars and bullion, or the fact that the Federal Reserve retroactively changed the way it computed the value of gold.

14. Central bank gold reserve figures can be found in the *Federal Reserve Bulletin*, October 1932, 647.

15. Herbert Hoover, "White House Statement About the Conference on the Hoarding of Currency," February 6, 1932, online at Gerhard Peters and John T. Woolley, *The American Presidency Project*, http://www.presidency.ucsb.edu/ws/?pid=23366.

16. Joslin, *Hoover Off the Record*, 170ff.

17. Herbert Hoover, "Address at the Lincoln Day Dinner in New York City," February 13, 1933, online at Gerhard Peters and John T. Woolley, *The American Presidency Project*, http://www.presidency.ucsb.edu/ws/?pid=23427.

18. File memorandum of White House letter to Gloria Bedrosian, April 7, 1933, Franklin D. Roosevelt Papers as President, Gold Hoarding file, FDRL.

19. Memorandum for the Attorney General, "Gold Hoarding Prosecutions," December 5, 1933. Franklin D. Roosevelt Papers as President, Henry Morgenthau Jr. Collection, Box 110, Gold file, FDRL. A detailed discussion of the case against Campbell, including the judge's mixed rulings, can be found in Henry Mark Holzer, "How Americans Lost Their Right to Own Gold and Became Criminals in the Process," monograph no. 35, Committee for Monetary Research and Education, Inc., December 1981, 12–15.

20. "Small Gold Hoard Will Be Ignored," *New York Times*, May 5, 1933. The senator was Charles Thomas, a Democrat from Colorado. His daughter Edith was later investigated for hoarding a larger amount of gold.

21. "President's Order Will Be Quick Means to Reach Hoarders, Declares Cummings," *New York Times*, August 30, 1933.

22. *Selected Papers of Homer Cummings, Attorney General of the United States 1933–1939*, ed. Carl Brent Swisher (New York: Charles Scribner's Sons, 1939), 101–105.

23. See chart, "Kinds of Money In Circulation," *Federal Reserve Bulletin*, August 1934, 517.

24. *Banking and Monetary Statistics, 1914–1941*, part 1, p. 522; *Annual Report of the Board of Governors of the Federal Reserve System, 1934*, 67n2.

25. Friedman and Schwartz, *A Monetary History of the United States*, 464n45.

26. Moley, *The First New Deal*, 302. The quotation has been attributed both to FDR's Wall Street ally James Warburg and to budget director Lewis Douglas.

27. *Congressional Record*, May 23, 1933.

28. Elmus Wicker, "Roosevelt's 1933 Monetary Experiment," *The Journal of American History* 57, no. 4 (March 1971): 864.

29. James Chace, *Acheson* (New York: Simon & Schuster, 1998), 65.

30. "See No Move to Cut Dollar," *New York Times*, August 30, 1933.

31. Diaries of Henry Morgenthau, vol. 00 (Farm Credit Diary), November 4, 1933, 96, http://www.fdrlibrary.marist.edu/archives/collections/franklin/?p=collections/findingaid&id=535&q=&rootcontentid=188897#id188897.

32. Minutes of meeting, executive committee of New York Fed, November 2, 1933, George Harrison papers, Box 23, Columbia University, New York, New York.

33. Salant oral history in *The Making of the New Deal: The Insiders Speak*, ed. Katie Louchheim (Cambridge, MA: Harvard University Press, 1983), 271.

34. Kenneth D. Garbade, *Birth of a Market: The U.S. Treasury Securities Market from the Great War to the Great Depression* (Cambridge, MA: MIT Press, 2012), 237–242.

35. Arthur M. Schlesinger Jr., *The Coming of the New Deal: 1933–1935* (vol. 2 of *The Age of Roosevelt*), reprint ed. (New York: Houghton Mifflin Harcourt, 2003), 240.

36. Diaries of Henry Morgenthau, October 29, 1933, 88.

37. Letter to E. M. House, November 21, 1933. *F.D.R.: His Personal Letters*, ed. Elliott Roosevelt (New York: Duell, Sloan and Pearce, 1950), 373.

38. Will Rogers, "Complete Heads or Tails of the Gold Problem," 1934, reprinted in *Will Rogers' Weekly Article*, vol. 6, *The Roosevelt Years*, ed. Steven K. Gragert (Stillwater: University of Oklahoma Press, 1982), 78–80.

39. For concision purposes I have omitted discussion of the Silver Purchase Act of 1934, which paralleled the government purchase of gold. An account of the politics behind its passage can be found in Allan Seymour Everest, *Morgenthau, The New Deal and Silver: A Story of Pressure Politics* (New York: King's Crown Press, 1950).

40. See, in particular, Charles W. Miller, *The Automobile Gold Rushes and Depression Era Mining* (Moscow: University of Idaho Press, 1998).

41. Robinson Newcomb, Charles White Merrill, and O. E. Kiessling, *Employment and Income from Gold Placering by Hand Methods, 1935–37* (Philadelphia: U.S. Bureau of Mines and U.S. Works Projects Administration, June 1940).

42. An account of Hoover's and Warburg's efforts can be found in Rosen, *Roosevelt, The Great Depression and the Economics of Recovery*, ch. 4.

43. The most complete account of True and his activities is by Donald Strong, *Organized Anti-Semitism in America: The Rise of Group Prejudice During the Decade 1930–40* (Westport, CT: Greenwood Press, 1979), 124–128. This is a reprint of a pamphlet published in 1941 by the American Council on Public Affairs.

Chapter 5: The Arsenal of Gold

1. Robert Jackson, *That Man: An Insider's Portrait of Franklin D. Roosevelt* (New York: Oxford University Press, 2003), 59. There is one significant discrepancy in Jackson's account of the January 10 discussion. He says that he told the president that evening about Sidney Ratner's article "Was the Supreme Court Packed by President Grant?" *Political Science Quarterly* 35, no. 3 (September 1935): 343–358. However, given the publication date of that article and the fact that in its first paragraph it makes reference to several events that took place after January, two possibilities suggest themselves: Jackson had seen an early draft of Ratner's article or, more probably, Jackson conflated his chronology and thought the article came out before the conversation. It seems unlikely, however, that Jackson would have made up the incident entirely, especially because Harold Ickes's diary also notes that Roosevelt discussed court packing with him as well on January 10.

2. *The Secret Diary of Harold L. Ickes* (New York: Simon and Schuster, 1953), 273–274. See also William Leuchtenburg's account in "The Origins of Franklin D. Roosevelt's 'Court-Packing' Plan," *The Supreme Court Review* (1966): 347–400. Leuchtenberg omits the role of Jackson and Ratner, but his article was published decades before Jackson's lost memoir, for which Leuchtenburg wrote a preface.

3. *Bronson v. Rodes* 74 U.S. 229 (1868).

4. Marian McKenna, *Franklin Roosevelt and the Great Constitutional War: The Court-Packing Crisis of 1937* (New York: Fordham University Press, 2002), 49.

5. Roy L. Garis, "The Gold Clause," *Annals of the American Academy of Political and Social Science* (January 1933): 221.

6. James Truslow Adams, "The Gold Clause Would Probably Be Upheld by the Supreme Court," *Barron's*, August 22, 1932.

7. H.R. 14604, 72nd Congress, 2nd session, introduced by Rep. Ed Campbell.

8. "Fourth Section of Analysis of Proposal for Devaluation of the Dollar (draft)," February 8, 1933. Papers of Alexander Sachs, Container 98, Gold Clause file, FDRL.

9. Senate report no. 99, 73rd Cong., 1st sess., reprinted in *Federal Reserve Bulletin*, vol. 6 (June 1933).

10. "Senate Repeals the Gold Clause," *New York Times*, June 4, 1933.

11. Excerpts from Cummings's oral argument can be found in *Selected Papers of Homer Cummings, Attorney General of the United States 1933–1939*, ed. Carl Brent Swisher (New York: Charles Scribner's Sons, 1939), 112–120.

12. "Hughes Assails Repudiation of Gold Payment," *Chicago Daily Tribune*, January 11, 1935.

13. "Justices Quiz Lawyers on Gold Clause," *Chicago Daily Tribune*, January 10, 1935.

14. Melvin I. Urofsky, "The Brandeis-Frankfurter Conversations," *The Supreme Court Review*, vol. 1985 (1985): 337.

15. "Capital Debates Gold Issue; Justices Confer for 5 Hours," *New York Times*, January 13, 1935.

16. "Talk of Packing the High Court if Gold Case Loses," *Chicago Tribune*, January 13, 1935.

17. Diaries of Henry Morgenthau, January 14, 1935, 3:98.

18. Memorandum prepared by Parker Gilbert, January 17, 1935, reproduced in Diaries of Henry Morgenthau, 3:146–151.

19. Diaries of Henry Morgenthau, January 21, 1935, 3:190.

20. For example, the *New York Times* wrote: "In the financial circles in New York yesterday it was understood that while the SEC has not formally considered a closing of the stock exchanges in the event of an adverse decision on the gold clause by the Supreme Court, it was prepared to do so." "SEC, With Power to Close Stock Exchanges, Is Ready to Do So on Adverse Gold Decision," February 2, 1935.

21. Alexander Sachs to Marvin H. McIntyre, January 31, 1935, Alexander Sachs collection, Box 98, Gold Clause file, FDRL.

22. Franklin Roosevelt, "Proposed Statement: Gold Clauses," February 18, 1935, Speech file microfilm, FDRL.

23. *Perry v. United States*, 294 U.S. 330 (1935).

24. Walter Lippman, "Today and Tomorrow," *Los Angeles Times*, February 20, 1935. See also David Glick, "Conditional Strategic Retreat: The Court's Concession in the 1935 Gold Clause Cases," *The Journal of Politics* 71, no. 3 (July 2009): 800–816. An excellent account of the administration's struggles with the gold-clause cases can be found in Jeff Shesol, *Supreme Power* (New York: W. W. Norton, 2010), ch. 6.

25. McReynolds's tirade was not recorded anywhere. Newspaper accounts vary slightly in their wording. "Constitution Gone, Says M'Reynolds," *New York Times*, February 19, 1935.

26. Roosevelt to Joseph P. Kennedy, February 19, 1935, in *F.D.R.: His Personal Letters, 1928–1945*, ed. Elliott Roosevelt (New York: Duell Sloan and Pearce, 1948–1950), 1:455.

27. "Roosevelt's monetary inflation bore bitter fruit. It increased credit when no one wanted to borrow and improved America's foreign trade position when all too few wanted American products. At best, domestic prices stabilized rather than rose. Debtors and small producers were not benefited. Neither was large wealth penalized; just horrified. Adversely, the almost halved dollar raised the tariff by nearly 50 percent (by the change in the rate of exchange) and thus helped bolster a wall of economic nationalism." Paul K. Conkin, *FDR and the Origins of the Welfare State* (New York: Thomas Y. Crowell, 1967), 44–45.

28. Allan H. Meltzer, *A History of the Federal Reserve, Volume 1, 1913–1951* (Chicago: University of Chicago, 2003), 504ff.

29. Winston Churchill, *Their Finest Hour* (Boston: Houghton Mifflin, 1949), 2:573–574.

30. There are several detailed accounts of how the Bretton Woods agreements came to be. One is in Rauchway's *The Money Makers*, from chapter 10 onward. Another is in Benn Steil, *The Battle of Bretton Woods: John Maynard Keynes, Harry Dexter White, and the Making of a New World Order* (Princeton, NJ: Princeton University Press, 2013).

31. Robert W. Oliver, *Bretton Woods: A Retrospective Essay* (Santa Monica, CA: California Seminar on International Security and Foreign Policy, 1985).

32. Republican Party Platform, 1952.

33. Francis H. Brownell, *Hard Money* (Washington, DC: US Government Printing Office. 1944), 13.

34. 79th Congress, 1st session, H.R. 629, May 30, 1945. *Report from the Committee on*

*Banking and Currency to Accompany H.R. 3314*, Minority Views of Hon. Frederick C. Smith and Hon. Howard H. Buffett, 111–120.

35. "McCarran Asks Free Market Again in Gold," *Reno Evening Gazette*, May 6, 1949.

36. "Fort Knox Gold Hoard Can Lead to Ruin, Says Buffett," *Omaha World-Herald*, March 24, 1949.

37. 80th Congress, 2nd session, H.R. 5031.

38. *United States Treasury Department Provisional Regulations Issued Under the Gold Reserve Act of 1934*, January 30 and 31, 1934, section 19.

39. US Treasury Department Mint Service to Lillie Mae Hubbard, October 16, 1934, http://credo.library.umass.edu/view/pageturn/mums312-b072-i237/#page/1/mode/1up.

40. Ernest Buffett produced thousands of stickers reading "I AM AGAINST THE THIRD TERM" and sold them, not for profit, to individuals and organizations that ordered them in 1940. This campaign is recalled in Bill Buffett, *Foods You Will Enjoy: The Story of Buffett's Store* (self-published book, 2008), 119–121.

41. "'Goldbacks' Back," *Sunday (Omaha) World-Herald Magazine*, August 29, 1948.

42. Treasury natural gold estimates come from *Minerals Yearbook 1950* (Washington, DC: US Bureau of Mines), 561.

43. Truman press conference, July 22, 1948, http://www.presidency.ucsb.edu/ws/index.php?pid=12965.

44. "Searls Unites With M'Carran in Gold Fight," *Nevada Mining Journal*, May 20, 1949.

45. 81st Congress, 1st session, Hearings Before the Committee on Banking and Currency on S. 13 and S. 286, May 5th and 6th, 1949. Searls's testimony is on 79–94.

46. Howard Buffett, *Washington Report*, May 8, 1952, Nebraska State Historical Society.

47. Michael Bowen, *The Roots of Modern Conservatism: Dewey, Taft and the Battle for the Soul of the Republican Party* (Chapel Hill: University of North Carolina Press, 2011), 6.

48. Robert A. Taft to Winthrop Aldrich, July 5, 1944, *The Papers of Robert A. Taft: 1939–1944* (Kent, OH: Kent State University Press, 2001), 567.

## Chapter 6: Out of Balance

1. "The London Gold Market," *Quarterly Bulletin*, Bank of England, March 1964.

2. Minutes of Meeting in Secretary Anderson's Office at 2 p.m. Wednesday, December 7, 1960, Julian Baird Papers, Minnesota Historical Society, Box 1.

3. Theodore G. Sorensen, *Kennedy* (New York: Harper & Row, 1965), 408.

4. "Week's Gold Loss Biggest Since '31," *New York Times*, September 23, 1960, 41. In 1947 and 1959, quota payments to the International Monetary Fund entailed larger gold outflows, but the one in September 1960 was the largest in a "normal" week since 1931. Moreover, the gold outflow to the IMF in 1959 was effectively reversed, as discussed later in this chapter.

5. Charles A. Coombs, *The Arena of International Finance* (New York: John Wiley & Sons, 1976), 54.

6. Ibid., 59.

7. Meeting with the president, Regarding Recent Developments in the London Gold

Market, October 25, 1960, *FRUS*, 1958–1960, Foreign Economic Policy, vol. 4, document 56.

8. See, for example, various memoranda from Julian Baird and Robert Anderson to the Nixon campaign, October 1960, Julian Baird Papers, Minnesota Historical Society, Box 1.

9. Remarks of Senator John F. Kennedy, New Fieldhouse, Moline, IL, October 24, 1960.

10. "Text of Eisenhower's Address to Republican Leaders in Philadelphia," *New York Times*, October 29, 1960.

11. Anderson to president, 11/9/60, DDE Diary Series, Box 54, DDEL.

12. Memorandum of Conference with President Eisenhower, November 15, 1960, *FRUS*, 1958–1960, Foreign Economic Policy, vol. 4, document 58.

13. 338th Meeting of the National Security Council, October 2, 1957, Box 9, NSC Series, Dwight D. Eisenhower: Papers as President, DDEL.

14. *FRUS*, 1958–1960, vol. 4, document 57.

15. Minutes of Meeting in Secretary Anderson's Office at 2 p.m. Wednesday, December 7, 1960, Julian Baird Papers, Minnesota Historical Society, Box 1.

16. The exact reasons why the IMF sold gold to the United States during the Eisenhower years are debatable. Officially, in 1956 the IMF expressed a need to strengthen its internal financial resources; the Fund constantly ran operational deficits in its early years. And thus it sold $200 million in gold to the United States, with a right of repurchase, and invested the funds in US dollar securities. See, for further explanation, the IMF report "Factors Relating to Burden-Sharing in the Fund," EBS/85/126, May 14, 1985, 8–9. But of course, that goal could have been accomplished in any number of ways. Moreover, there was no indication when the initial 1956 transaction took place that supplemental sales would be necessary, and when a second sale occurred in 1959, an IMF Board director admitted that the Fund had a surplus, and thus "it would not be legally possible for the Fund to sell gold to the United States in order to replenish its supply of dollars." (See *FRUS* Foreign Relations, 1958–1960, vol. 4, document 47.) And the November 1960 sale was clearly initiated by US Treasury officials who were panicked by the balance-of-payments crisis. It's worth noting that the IMF did buy the gold back in the early 1970s.

17. My discussion of the early formation of the London Gold Pool relies in part on *International Economic Relations of the Western World 1959–1971*, vol. 2, ch. 3 (New York: Oxford University Press, 1976), and in part on Coombs, *The Arena of International Finance*.

18. Coombs, *The Arena of International Finance*, 32.

19. "Impatience at a Stern Voice," *Wall Street Journal*, December 2, 1960.

20. "Plugging a Gold Leak," *New York Times*, January 16, 1961.

21. Background Memo for Anderson-Dillon Conference, undated, from Horace Busby to Senator Johnson, LBJL, Vice Presidential Security Files, Box 9, Notebook on NATO 1960, document 39.

22. Report on Survey of Items of Jewelry and Other Objects Containing Large Amounts of Gold, August 22, 1961, General Records of the Department of Treasury, Office of Gold and Silver Operations, Gold Subject File, 1933–1974, Box 12, NARA.

23. Robert Triffin, *Gold and the Dollar Crisis* (New Haven: Yale University Press, 1960), 52.

24. Many of the details of Franz Pick's life and philosophy are taken from John Kobler, "The Black Marketeers' Best Friend," *Saturday Evening Post*, May 2, 1953. See also Tom Bethell, "Crazy as a Gold Bug," *New York*, February 4, 1980.

25. "Ex-Chief of Toronto Exchange Suspended in Mining Stock Deal," *New York Times*, November 15, 1957.

26. Assistant U.S. Attorney Grenville Garside, quoted in United Press International story, May 24, 1962.

27. Thomas Wolfe to Bruce MacLaury, September 14, 1970, General Records of the Department of Treasury, Office of Gold and Silver Operations, Gold Subject File, 1933–1974, Box 28, NARA.

28. William H. Brett, Director of the Mint, to John M. Laxalt, April 9, 1958.

29. Details of Polk's biography and art work can be found in *F-F-F-Frank Polk: An Uncommonly Frank Autobiography* (Flagstaff, AZ: Northland Press, 1978).

30. Laxalt's biographical details come from Richard L. Spees, "Paul Laxalt: Man of Political Independence," in *The Maverick Spirit: Building the New Nevada* (Reno: University of Nevada Press, 1999), 166–193.

31. U.S. District Court for the District of Nevada, Civil no. 1502, *United States of America v. One Solid Object In Form of a Rooster*, Reporter's Transcript of Proceedings, 2:220, 225–226.

### Chapter 7: Operation Goldfinger

1. During the Cold War, tremendous energy and resources were devoted to estimating the level of Soviet gold production and gold reserves; production estimates in the early 1960s ranged widely, anywhere from $300 million to $700 million. Significant quantities were sold regularly in Western markets, from which estimates were made. In 1964, however, the CIA provided a far lower estimate—below $200 million—causing some other institutions to change their guesses. See Keith Bush, "Soviet Gold Production and Reserves Reconsidered," *Soviet Studies* 17, no. 4 (April 1966): 490–493.

2. *Minerals Yearbook 1966* (Washington, DC: US Bureau of Mines), 80.

3. Bartlett made this comment during a hearing on March 15, 1962, before the Senate Subcommittee on Minerals, Materials and Fuels of Interior and Insular Affairs.

4. Ernest Gruening et al. to the President, August 30, 1965, White House Central File, Subject Files on Finance, Box 54, LBJL.

5. Sorenson, *Kennedy*, 408; Ball oral history interview #2 (July 9, 1971), LBJL, 19.

6. Oral History Transcript, C. Douglas Dillon, AC 74-12, Interview 1, p. 7, LBJL.

7. Conversation between President John F. Kennedy, William McChesney Martin Chairman of the Federal Reserve, and Theodore Sorensen—August 16, 1962, 5:50–6:32 p.m., tape 13, President's Office Files, JFKL.

8. Johnson quote to Dirksen, March 1965, cited in Francis J. Gavin, *Gold, Dollars & Power: The Politics of International Monetary Relations 1958–1971* (Chapel Hill: University of North Carolina Press, 2004), 117.

9. John F. Kennedy, "Address and Question and Answer Period at the Economic Club of New York," December 14, 1962, online at Gerhard Peters and John T. Woolley, *The American Presidency Project*, http://www.presidency.ucsb.edu/ws/?pid=9057.

10. Joseph W. Barr, Oral History, Interview 2, January 16, 1970, p. 23, LBJL.

11. William B. Dale, Memorandum to Paul Volcker, March 10, 1969, Volcker files, NARA.

12. 456th Meeting of the NSC, October 31, 1960, Whitman File, NSC Records, DDEL, *FRUS 1958–1960*, vol. 4, document 266. I have been unable to verify the facts of Anderson's assertion, but if he was falsely claiming that the Italian government had drained the US gold supply, this only underscores the degree of the White House's fear.

13. A detailed discussion of the burgeoning industrial uses of gold can be found in ch. 14 of Ray Vicker's *The Realms of Gold* (London: Robert Hale, 1975), 223–225.

14. *Thirty-Sixth Annual Report*, Bank for International Settlements (Basle, 1966), 33–34.

15. *International Monetary Fund Annual Report*, 1966, 114.

16. "First Major Change Made in Coin System," in *CQ Almanac 1965*, 21st ed. (Washington, DC: Congressional Quarterly, 1966), 882–886, http://library.cqpress.com/cqalmanac/cqal65-1258091.

17. The exchange took place in the pages of *The Review of Economics and Statistics*. See L. Dudley and Peter Passell, "The War in Vietnam and the United States Balance of Payments," November 1968, followed by Douglas Bohi's response in November 1969.

18. Memorandum from the president's Deputy Special Assistant for National Security Affairs (Bator) to President Johnson, July 6, 1966, LBJL, National Security File, Balance of Payments, vol. 3 [1 of 2], Box 2.

19. Bator's essay was a comment on Richard N. Cooper, "Foreign Economic Policy in the 1960s: An Enduring Legacy," in *Economic Events, Ideas, and Policies: The 1960s and After* (Washington, DC: Brookings Institution Press, 2000), 139–176.

20. Memorandum to the Secretary, April 4, 1966, Subject: Operation Goldfinger, LBJL, Fowler papers, Box 88.

21. Memorandum for the President, April 6, 1966, from Henry Fowler and Charles L. Schultze, LBJL, Fowler papers, Box 88.

22. Memorandum to the Secretary, March 24, 1966, from Fred B. Smith, LBJL, Fowler papers, Box 88.

23. The diplomat in question was Robert Pelikan, the financial attaché to the American Embassy in Tokyo. The 1965 GAO report was an embarrassment for Treasury and the Johnson Administration; it noted that the Tokyo house featured "gold-plated bathroom fixtures and a glass display case for jewelry." See "Special Treasury Fund Challenged by GAO," *Washington Post*, August 1, 1965.

24. *U.S. Geological Survey Heavy Metals Program Progress Report 1968—Field Studies*, Geological Survey Circular 621 (Washington, DC, 1969), 106.

25. *The Investment in Natural Resource Science and Technology: A Special Report*, United States Department of the Interior, 83.

26. A summary of Goldfinger projects can be found in *U.S. Geological Survey Heavy Metals Program Progress Report 1968—Topical Studies*, Geological Survey Circular

622 (Washington, DC, 1969). See also *Gold in Meteorites and in the Earth's Crust*, Geological Survey Circular 603 (Washington, DC, 1968).

27. John E. Bardach, *Harvest of the Sea* (New York: Harper & Row, 1968), 77.

28. Hornig quoted in Robert Rienow, "Manifesto for the Sea," *American Behavioral Scientist* 11, no. 6 (July–August 1968).

29. Memorandum from J. P. Hendrick to Fred B. Smith, March 28, 1966, LBJL, Fowler papers, Box 88.

30. "Vessel to Explore Floor of the Pacific for Precious Metal," *New York Times*, March 6, 1967.

31. Memorandum to the Treasury Secretary from Eugene V. Rostow, "Reflections on our recent talks with Alexander Sachs," March 12, 1968, LBJL, Fowler papers, Box 88.

32. Plowshare's propagandistic origins are explored in Trevor Findlay, *Nuclear Dynamite: The Peaceful Nuclear Explosions Fiasco* (Sydney: Brassey's Australia, 1990).

33. Edward Teller, "We're Going to Work Miracles," *Popular Mechanics*, March 1960, 100.

34. A thorough account of the Sedan detonation and the subsequent controversy over radioactive fallout can be found in chapter 4 of Scott Kirsch's *Proving Grounds: Project Plowshare and the Unrealized Dream of Nuclear Earthmoving* (New Brunswick, NJ: Rutgers University Press, 2005). See also Philip L. Fradkin, *Fallout* (Tucson: University of Arizona Press, 1989), 135–136.

35. The AEC and Livermore produced a booklet called *Sloop: A Study of the Feasibility of Fracturing Copper Ore Bodies with Nuclear Explosives* (Springfield, VA, 1967), but it does not cover the project's intersection with gold mining. By far the most comprehensive secondary account of Project Sloop I have found is a study produced for the Department of Energy, *The Off-Site Plowshare and Vela Uniform Programs: Assessing Potential Environmental Liabilities through an Examination of Proposed Nuclear Projects, High Explosive Experiments, and High Explosive Construction Activities* (vol. 2 of 3), Desert Research Institute, Las Vegas, 2011, section 4.37.

36. *Minerals Yearbook 1967*, U.S. Bureau of Mines, 446.

37. Remarks of Rep. Craig Hosmer, Symposium on the Public Health Aspects of Peaceful Nuclear Explosives, Las Vegas, Nevada, April 8, 1969.

38. *Congressional Record—House*, February 21, 1968, 3690–3691.

39. *Nuclear Dynamite*, 184. See also Gulf Universities Research Consortium, *Peaceful Nuclear Explosion Activity Projections for Arms Control Planning* (Galveston: The Consortium, 1975), 129.

40. Fowler's identical letters to Seaborg and Udall are dated March 25, 1968, and located in the Fowler papers, Box 88, Operation Goldfinger file, LBJL.

41. The technical findings from Seaborg and his colleagues are in "Energy Dependence of $^{209}$Bi Fragmentation in Relativistic Nuclear Collisions," *Physical Review C* (March 1981): 1044–1046. A useful summary of the experiment in layman's terms can be found in "Fact or Fiction? Lead Can Be Turned Into Gold," *Scientific American*, January 31, 2014. Seaborg's comment was to the Associated Press, March 22, 1980.

42. A detailed account of the Rio Blanco explosion can be found in Frank Kreith's and Catherine Wrenn's *The Nuclear Impact* (Boulder, CO: Westview Press, 1976).

43. Telephone interview with the author, December 15, 2014.

44. See, for example, "New Gold Recovery Process Tested," *Washington Post*, March 28, 1968.

45. Joseph W. Barr Oral History Interview II, 1/16/70, by Joe B. Frantz, LBJL, 8.

### Chapter 8: Dueling Apocalypses

1. Federal Open Market Committee meeting, November 27, 1967, 6.

2. T. P. Nelson to Secretary Fowler, "Gold and Exchange Market Developments, November 23–24," November 24, 1967. Fowler papers, Box 83, Gold: September 1967 file, LBJL.

3. Frederick Deming Oral History, tape 2, p. 18, LBJL.

4. Johnson phone call with William McChesney Martin, August 5, 1965, conversation WH6508.02, audio accessible at http://millercenter.org/scripps/archive/presidentialrecordings/johnson/1965/08_1965.

5. This account relies on the memoirs of Harold Wilson and others, as well as Arran Hamilton, "Beyond the Sterling Devaluation: The Gold Crisis of March 1968," *Contemporary European History* 17, no. 1 (February 2008): 73–95.

6. Memorandum from Secretary of the Treasury Fowler to President Johnson, November 12, 1967, LBJL, National Security File, NSC History, Gold Crisis, November '67–March '68, Box 54.

7. Lyndon Johnson, *The Vantage Point* (New York: Holt, Rinehart and Winston, 1971), 315.

8. Sir Alec Cairncross, *Sterling in Decline: The Devaluations of 1931, 1949 and 1967*, 2nd. ed. (New York: Palgrave Macmillan, 2003), 191.

9. The Gold Pool loss figures come from Federal Open Market Committee meeting minutes, November 27, 1967, 3.

10. When the Algerian gold sale was reported in the press, the amount was put at "more than $100 million"; *New York Times*, December 11, 1967. Minutes from the Federal Reserve Open Market Committee put the figure at $150 million.

11. Francis J. Gavin, *Gold, Dollars & Power: The Politics of International Monetary Relations 1958–1971* (Chapel Hill: University of North Carolina Press, 2004), 3. A detailed account of the often acrimonious debates leading the committee to recommend capital controls is in James E. Anderson and Jared E. Hazleton, *Managing Macroeconomic Policy: The Johnson Presidency* (Austin: University of Texas Press, 1986), 197ff.

12. The remarkable itinerary of Johnson's December 1967 trip is recalled in Sid David, "When LBJ Took a Flying Leap at Peace," *Washington Post*, December 24, 2007.

13. Trowbridge's remark is in "No 'Basic Change'—Controls First for U.S.—No Time Limit Set for Their Duration," *New York Times*, January 2, 1968.

14. The President's News Conference at the LBJ Ranch, January 1, 1968, *The Johnson Presidential Press Conferences* (New York: Earl M. Coleman Enterprises: 1978), 2:881–888.

15. "Travelers and Agents Dismayed by Johnson's Call for Cutbacks," *New York Times*, January 2, 1968.

16. Milton Friedman, "The Price of the Dollar," *Newsweek*, January 29, 1968, 72.

17. Report on Our European Balance of Payments Trip, January 7, 1968, Papers of Francis M. Bator, "B/P—Katzenbach & Deming, January 1968," Box 17, LBJL.

18. See, for example, Benjamin Read, "Memorandum for Mr. Walt W. Rostow," January 29, 1968, in Papers of Anthony Solomon, Box 22, Folder 4 (Balance of Payments Program 1), LBJL.

19. "The Latest Gold Rush," *The Economist*, March 9, 1968, 58.

20. Humphrey to Barefoot Sanders, March 13, 1968, Papers of Barefoot Sanders, Box 29, Tax Bill 1/68–3/68 file, LBJL. Cited in Julian E. Zelizer, *The Fierce Urgency of Now: Lyndon Johnson, Congress, and the Battle for the Great Society* (New York: Penguin Press, 2015), 287–288.

21. Nearly a quarter of the Senate did not cast a vote on the gold cover legislation. Several senators "paired" their votes—a yea combining with a nay and agreeing not to formally vote—and nine Democrats (including Ted and Bobby Kennedy and Walter Mondale) acknowledged support but did not cast votes.

22. Javits, however, voted with the administration on the gold cover legislation.

23. *Congressional Record—Senate*, March 12, 1968, 6162–6163.

24. "Swiss Bankers Close Counters Early, But Say Gold Orders Continue Rise," *Washington Post*, March 15, 1968.

25. Cable from Harold Wilson to President Johnson, March 14, 1968, Papers of Francis M. Bator, "Gold Crisis, March 13–16, 1968, FMB Washington Trip," Box 10, LBJL.

26. "10 at Washington Parley Seek to Solve Gold Crisis," *New York Times*, March 17, 1968.

27. Joseph W. Barr Oral History Interview II, 1/16/70, by Joe B. Frantz, LBJL, 11.

28. Francis Gavin has done at least as much archival work on the March 1968 gold crisis as any other scholar. These quotes come from chapter 7 of *Gold, Dollars & Power*. I have relied on his work throughout this chapter as a supplement to my own archival research. Another valuable source is Robert M. Collins, "The Economic Crisis of 1968 and the Waning of the 'American Century,'" *The American Historical Review* 101, no. 2 (April 1996): 396–422; however, some important Johnson material has come to light since Collins's article was published.

29. T. P. Nelson, "Memorandum for the Secretary," June 14, 1968, Papers of Henry Fowler, Box 83, "Domestic Economy: Gold" Folder, LBJL.

30. Robert A. Gilbert, *Gold Mining Shares: An Institutional Study* (New York: Investors' Press, 1968), 16.

31. Murray Rothbard, *What Has Government Done to Our Money?* 4th ed. (Auburn, AL: Ludwig von Mises Institute, 1990), 88–89.

32. See Skousen's essay "Murray Rothbard as Investment Advisor" in *Man, Economy and Liberty: Essays in Honor of Murray N. Rothbard*, ed. Walter Block and Llewellyn H. Rockwell Jr. (Auburn, AL: Ludwig von Mises Institute, 2007).

33. William F. Rickenbacker, *Wooden Nickels or, the Decline and Fall of Silver Coins* (New Rochelle, NY: Arlington House, 1966), 9, 156–157.

34. As of this writing, the Free Enterprise Institute still exists as a collection of online study material. Its Web site is at http://www.fei-ajg.com/index.html#aboutFEI.

35. Brian Doherty gives a succinct account of Galambos's influence and eccentricities in *Radicals for Capitalism: A Freewheeling History of the Modern American Libertarian Movement* (New York: Public Affairs, 2007), 323–326. A firsthand recollection from his close associate Alvin Lowi Jr. is in Walter Block, *I Chose Liberty: Autobiographies of Contemporary Libertarians* (Auburn, AL: Ludwig von Mises Institute, 2011), 200–205. The story about Galambos's putting money in a jar every time he said the word *liberty* comes from Jerome Tuccille, *It Usually Begins With Ayn Rand* (San Francisco: Fox & Wilkes, 1971), 62. Harry Browne's warts-and-all portrait of "Andrew Galambos—the Unknown Libertarian" was published in *Liberty*, November 1997.

36. Don and Barbie Stephens, *The Survivor's Primer & Updated Retreater's Bibliography* (Glendale, CA: Stephens Printing, 1976), 11.

37. Harry Browne, *How You Can Profit from the Coming Devaluation* (New Rochelle, NY: Arlington House, 1970), 85–86.

## Chapter 9: This Time for Real

1. Onno de Beaufort Wijnholds, *Gold, the Dollar and Watergate* (New York: Palgrave Macmillan, 2015), 88–89.

2. Memorandum, "Limited Gold Convertibility in a Cooperative Framework," William B. Dale to Paul Volcker, March 10, 1969, Record Group 56, Department of the Treasury office for the undersecretary of monetary affairs, Box 11, Folder "Gold," NARA.

3. Dale was interviewed by Thomas Forbord and cited in his 1980 Harvard PhD dissertation, "The Abandonment of Bretton Woods: The Political Economy of U.S. International Monetary Policy," 244.

4. The unnamed official was interviewed by Joanne Gowa for her valuable account *Closing the Gold Window: Domestic Politics and the End of Bretton Woods* (Ithaca, NY: Cornell University Press, 1983), 69.

5. Charles Ashman, *Connally: The Adventures of Big Bad John* (New York: William Morrow, 1974), 207–208.

6. Charles A. Coombs, *The Arena of International Finance* (New York: John Wiley & Sons, 1976), 219. Coombs's clashes with Connally make him perhaps a biased observer; still, Connally objectively exhibited disdain for international monetary niceties on many occasions.

7. Connally's speech "Mutual Responsibility for Maintaining a Stable Monetary System" was published in the *Department of State Bulletin*, July 12, 1971.

8. Nixon's first discussion with Connally about joining him on the 1972 presidential ticket appears to have been on July 19, 1971; see Haldeman's entry for that day in *The Haldeman Diaries: Inside the Nixon White House* (New York: Putnam, 1994).

9. Hendrik Houthakker, "The Breakdown of Bretton Woods," in *Economic Advice and Executive Policy: Recommendations from Past Members of the Council of Economic Advisers*, ed. Werner Sichel (New York: Praeger, 1978).

10. Louis Harris, "Muskie Still Leading Nixon," *Chicago Tribune*, July 19, 1971.

11. I have relied throughout this chapter on Allen Matusow's comprehensive book *Nixon's Economy: Booms, Busts, Dollars and Votes* (Lawrence: University Press of Kansas, 1998).

12. James Reston Jr., *The Lone Star: The Life of John Connally* (New York: Harper & Row, 1989), 396. Reston's source was Jim Smith, who lobbied Congress for Treasury in the early 1970s.

13. "Contingency Planning: Options for the International Monetary Problem," March 14, 1971. Papers of Paul Volcker, New York Federal Reserve, Box 0108477, 57–58.

14. "Shift on Monetary Set-Up Is Proposed in the House," *New York Times*, June 4, 1971.

15. Volcker, "Contingency Planning," 52.

16. *FRUS, 1969–1976*, vol. 3, document 157.

17. Thomas Forbord, "The Abandonment of Bretton Woods: The Political Economy of U.S. International Monetary Policy" (PhD diss., Harvard University, 1980), 249.

18. Richard Nixon, *Six Crises* (New York: Touchstone, 1990), 309–310.

19. Nixon conversation 545-1, July 24, 1971.

20. "The Basis for Lasting Prosperity," address in the Pepperdine College Great Issue Series at the Beverly Hilton Hotel, Los Angeles, December 7, 1970, https://fraser .stlouisfed.org/title/?id=449#!7961, accessed on September 6, 2015.

21. Bob Woodward, *The Last of the President's Men* (New York: Simon and Schuster, 2015), 74.

22. See, for example, Burton A. Abrams, "How Richard Nixon Pressured Arthur Burns: Evidence from the Nixon Tapes," *The Journal of Economic Perspectives* 20, no. 4 (Fall 2006): 177–188. Abrams asserts bluntly: "Richard Nixon demanded and Arthur Burns supplied an expansionary monetary policy and a growing economy in the run-up to the 1972 election."

23. Statement by Arthur F. Burns, Chairman, Board of Governors of the Federal Reserve System, before the Joint Economic Committee, July 23, 1971, 2–3.

24. Nixon conversation 545-3.

25. Charles Colson, *Born Again* (Old Tappan, NJ: Chosen Books, 1976), 62–63. Colson's account of the spring and summer of 1971 seems at best garbled. For example, he says he attended the July 24 meeting in which Nixon recommended that Colson plant negative stories about Burns; the White House tape shows otherwise. Burns wrote in his diary that in 1974, Colson told him about a plot to smear Burns hatched on the presidential yacht *Sequoia*, with Colson, Haldeman, Caspar Weinberger, and others in attendance. However, Colson's book places the *Sequoia* trip in May, too early to have been retaliating for Burns's July testimony. Nonetheless, Colson's account of leaking the story to the *Journal* is credible.

26. "White House Hints It Plans Attack on Reserve Board's Independence," *Wall Street Journal*, July 29, 1971.

27. *Haldeman Diaries*, 332.

28. Ibid., 335–336.

29. The details about Volcker's plans come from William Silber, *Volcker: The Triumph of Persistence* (New York: Bloomsbury Press, 2012), 82.

30. Paul Scott, "Devaluation of Dollar Seen As a Possibility," *Lebanon Daily News*, August 6, 1971, 17.

31. *Haldeman Diaries*, August 9, 1971. Nixon and Haldeman thought presidential adviser Pete Peterson was behind the leak.

32. Transcript of Executive Office Building tape, August 12, 1971, in *The Nixon Tapes: 1971–1972*, ed. Douglas Brinkley and Luke Nichter (Boston: Houghton Mifflin Harcourt, 2014), conversations 562-6.

33. Safire wrote one of the first eyewitness accounts of the Camp David weekend in *Before the Fall: An Inside View of the Pre-Watergate White House* (New York: Da Capo Press, 1975), 509–528. Haldeman's recollections were published in his *Diaries*. Another useful, if secondhand, account of the meeting is Henry Brandon's *The Retreat of American Power* (New York: Doubleday, 1973).

34. *Inside the Nixon Administration: The Secret Diary of Arthur Burns, 1969–1974*, ed. Robert Ferrell (Lawrence: University Press of Kansas, 2010), entry for July 8, 1971, 47–48.

35. *Before the Fall*, 527.

36. Richard Nixon, Address to the Nation Outlining a New Economic Policy: "The Challenge of Peace," August 15, 1971.

37. Eugene Rostow, "Devaluation by Agreement, Not Fiat," *New York Times*, September 5, 1971.

38. Coombs made his comment in a debate with Milton Friedman, reproduced in *The Balance of Payments: Free Versus Fixed Exchange Rates* (Washington, DC: American Enterprise Institute, 1967), 185.

39. Securities and Exchange Commission Litigation Release No. 6638, December 12, 1974.

40. " 'Colossal' Fraud in Coins Reported," *New York Times*, July 11, 1974.

41. James C. Treadway Jr., "SEC Enforcement Techniques: Expanding and Exotic Forms of Ancillary Relief," *Washington & Lee Law Review* 32 (1975): 649.

42. Harry Browne, *You Can Profit from a Monetary Crisis* (New York: Macmillan, 1974), 5, 142, 240.

### Chapter 10: Legal at Last

1. 93rd Congress, 1st session, H.R. 435.

2. I am grateful here for the concise but detailed summary provided by Edwin J. Feulner Jr., "How the Gold Bill Was Passed," *Euromoney*, November 1974, pp. 47–48.

3. "Bill Seeks Legal Gold Ownership," *Chicago Tribune*, June 7, 1971.

4. Crane's gold coin collection was revealed in Jack Anderson's *Washington Post* column "Washington Merry-Go-Round," January 6, 1975.

5. See the interview with former Crane aide Ken MacKenzie in *100 Voices: An Oral History of Ayn Rand* (New York: Penguin, 2010), "1970s" section.

6. *Inside the Nixon Administration: The Secret Diary of Arthur Burns, 1969–1974*, ed. Robert Ferrell (Lawrence: University Press of Kansas, 2010), September 10, 1971 entry, 55.

7. "The Winners and Losers from Devaluation," *Time*, February 26, 1973.

8. Memorandum for the President, FG 56, George Shultz papers, Box 6, file "Gold Sales," NARA.

9. Treasury Undersecretary Paul Volcker to Wright Patman, chairman, House Banking and Currency Committee, July 13, 1973.

10. See, for example, *Secret Diary of Arthur Burns*, March 17, 1974 entry, 121–122.

11. Department of the Treasury News Release, WS-27, June 11, 1974.

12. Federal Open Market Committee meeting, Memorandum of Discussion, January 20–21, 1975.

13. George Mahon, quoted in "Congress Rejects, then Approves IDA Funds," *CQ Almanac 1974*, 30th ed., 517–519.

14. "House Curb on Aid 'Disaster' for Poor, McNamara Says," *New York Times*, January 25, 1974.

15. Treasury Secretary William Simon to Federal Reserve chair Arthur Burns, *FRUS*, vol. 31, document 65. The letter is undated, but it refers to the Senate vote as "yesterday," implying that it was sent on May 30.

16. *Congressional Record—House*, July 2, 1974, 22008.

17. *Congressional Record—House*, July 2, 1974, 22003.

18. See *FRUS*, vol. 31, Document 68. Also, Burns wrote in his diary for April 4, 1974, that Shultz had told him that Ash "is heavily involved in gold stocks." Ash and a business partner owned a ranch in Nevada that would later be sold to Newmont Mining and help that company dramatically improve its gold production in the 1980s. See Water Guzzardi Jr., "The Huge Find in Roy Ash's Backyard," *Fortune*, December 27, 1982, 48–65.

19. Arthur Burns to William Skidmore, August 9, 1974. White House Records Office: Legislation Case Files, Box 1, "8/14/74 S2665 US Contribution to the International Development Association" file, GRFL.

20. *FRUS*, vol. 31, document 71.

21. Feulner, "How the Gold Bill Was Passed," 48.

22. Transcripts of terHorst's press briefings are in Box 1 of the Ron Nessen file, GFL. The one for August 14 can be found online at http://www.fordlibrarymuseum.gov/library/document/0151/1671247.pdf. TerHorst lasted as press secretary only a month; he resigned in protest over Ford's pardon of Nixon.

23. "Gold Rush Beginning at Canadian Banks," *New York Times*, March 2, 1974.

24. "Big Board Approves Gold-Bar Sales Plan," *New York Times*, August 5, 1974.

25. Ford, like his immediate predecessor, displayed little interest in the generic question of whether or not individuals ought to be able to purchase and own gold. His aides were clearly driving the policy. In mid-November, Ford sent a handwritten note to Treasury Secretary Simon: "What are we doing + when on the gold purchase + sale matter?," prompting Simon to brief the president again on the matter. President's Handwriting File, Subject File, Box 19, Finance—Gold, GRFL.

26. Memorandum From Secretary of the Treasury Simon to President Ford, November 18, 1974. *FRUS*, 1969–1976, vol. 31, document 77.

27. *FRUS*, Foreign Economic Policy, 1973–1976, vol. 31, document 76.

28. Harkin comment in "There's Gold in Fort Knox," *Los Angeles Times*, September 24, 1974.

29. A copy of Conlan's telex message is in the William Simon papers at Lafayette College in Easton, Pennsylvania, Series 3B, Drawer 23, Folder 1, "Gold." A stamp indicates that Simon saw the message.

30. *Accountability and Physical Controls of the Gold Bullion Reserves*, FOD-75-10, U.S. Government Accountability Office, February 10, 1975. Well into the twenty-first century, there are goldbugs who insist that the members of Congress and the GAO were duped into mistaking fake gold bars for real ones, or that the actual weight of the bars was not as reported.

31. Pool Report on Ford's Morning Skiing, December 31, 1974, White House Press Releases, Box 6, GFL.

32. "Gold Sales Find Scant Response from U.S. Buyers," *New York Times*, January 1, 1975.

33. The conflicting state approaches are described in Neal S. Solomon and Linda D. Healy, "State Attempts to Tax Sales of Gold Coin and Bullion in the United States: The Constitutional Implications," *Boston College International and Comparative Law Review* (1982), 297–344.

34. "The Biggest Gold Market: Futures," *New York Times*, August 12, 1975.

35. *FRUS*, vol. 31, document 80.

36. Of course, another perspective was possible. A rising gold price could also coax the Soviet Union into selling its gold reserves—as did happen in the 1980s—which could be seen as a strategic gain for the United States.

37. See "Big Boom in a Barbarous Relic," *Time*, February 26, 1979; and "U.S. Finds Few Gold Buyers; Accepts Bids of $153 to $185," *New York Times*, January 7, 1975.

38. Details about the Krugerrand come from *A Comprehensive Guide to the Krugerrand*, a pamphlet published by the bullion dealership organization GoldCore in 2013.

39. "Business Briefly," *Broadcasting*, July 12, 1976, 9.

40. A very useful summary of antiapartheid activists targeting Krugerrand advertising is by Barbara Demick, "An Ounce of Love?" *More*, December 1977, 25.

41. "The Pedigreed Gold System: A Good System—Why Spoil It?" Report on the Subcommittee on International Exchange and Payments of the Joint Economic Committee, Congress of the United States, December 1969, 5.

42. "An ounce of apartheid," *Berkshire Eagle*, December 10, 1977.

43. Stephen J. Solarz, *Journeys to War and Peace* (Waltham, MA: Brandeis University Press, 2011), 82–83. Solarz's timetable is difficult to resolve. He says he introduced the legislation in 1980; congressional records show him introducing a curb on South African investments (though nothing about the Krugerrand) in 1978. He says he talked to Ramaphosa about the bill before introducing it in 1980, but Ramaphosa did not actually form a miners' union until 1982. These discrepancies do not seem to negate the overall thrust of Solarz's claim that he took seriously the relationship between US gold purchases, apartheid, and the livelihood of South African miners.

*Chapter 11: Goldbugs in Power*

1. For an exhaustive background on the Jamaica settlement, see Tom de Vries, "Jamaica, or the Non-Reform of the International Monetary System," *Foreign Affairs*, April 1, 1976.
2. Telephone interview with the author, December 15, 2015.
3. Even historians and biographers tend to overlook Helms's advocacy for gold causes. The otherwise comprehensive 643-page biography of Helms, *Righteous Warrior: Jesse Helms and the Rise of Modern Conservatism* (New York: St. Martin's Press, 2008), for example, never mentions Helms's gold legislation efforts and achievements.
4. Henry Mark Holzer, "Can We Restore the Gold Clause?" *Wall Street Journal*, March 17, 1975. For the chronology of legislation around gold clause contracts, I am grateful to Holzer's monograph *The Gold Clause* (Highlands Ranch, CO: Madison Press, 2014).
5. Milton Friedman to Senator Jesse Helms, July 30, 1976. Submitted into *Congressional Record* 122, part 25, September 28, 1976, 32956.
6. "Washington & Business: The U.S. Gold-Clause Legislation," *New York Times*, October 20, 1977.
7. A year earlier, when Helms had tried but failed to get similar amendments attached to the bill readjusting the rules of the IMF and World Bank, he relayed his views on the topic in Senate report 94-1295, Amendment of the Bretton Woods Agreements Act and Other International Monetary Matters, September 22, 1976, 27ff. Ironically, a few years later Helms's allies in the Reagan administration did not make Helms any happier. Despite Reagan's initial hostility to IMF reauthorization, his administration came around to supporting it in 1982 to help stave off widespread default from debtor countries, including Argentina and Mexico. To pass that legislation, Reagan had to turn to Democrats in Congress for support.
8. "Reagan Advisers Tout a Return to Gold Standard," *Washington Post*, July 31, 1980.
9. "Enemies of Gold," *Washington Post*, August 5, 1981.
10. *Report to the Congress of the Commission on the Role of Gold in the Domestic and International Monetary Systems* (Washington, DC: March 1982), 2.
11. "An Urgent Return to the American System," letter from Lyndon Larouche, January 8, 1982, in *Report*, 2:449.
12. *Report to the Congress of the Commission on the Role of Gold in the Domestic and International Monetary Systems*, 1.
13. "Gold Panel Off to Slow Start," *New York Times*, September 19, 1981.
14. My account of the Gold Commission's hearings and internal dynamics is deeply indebted to Anna Schwartz's 1987 essay "Reflections on the Gold Commission Report," a chapter in her monograph *Money in Historical Perspective* (Chicago: University of Chicago Press, 1987), part of a series by the National Bureau of Economic Research.
15. Lehrman wrote an essay in January 1980 called "Monetary Policy, the Federal Reserve System, and Gold," which was distributed as a research paper by the investment bank Morgan Stanley.
16. *Report to the Congress of the Commission on the Role of Gold in the Domestic and International Monetary Systems*, 140.

17. "Fiscal Nostrums for Monetary Ills," letter to the editor, *Wall Street Journal*, April 22, 1982.

18. *The Reagan Diaries*, vol. 1, ed. Douglas Brinkley (New York: HarperCollins, 2007), June 11, 1981 entry.

19. Murray Weidenbaum, *Advising Reagan: Making Economic Policy, 1981–82: A Memoir* (St. Louis: Washington University in St. Louis, 2005), 26.

20. Nomination of Alan Greenspan: Hearing Before the Committee on Banking, Housing, and Urban Affairs, United States Senate, 100th Congress, 1st session, July 21, 1987, 61.

21. Executive Order 12532 Prohibiting Trade and Certain Other Transactions Involving South Africa, September 9, 1985.

22. "Go for Gold," *The Economist*, July 19, 1986, 11.

23. Details about the development of heap leaching at Carlin can be found in Jack Morris, *Going For Gold: The History of Newmont Mining Corporation* (Tuscaloosa: University of Alabama Press, 2010), ix–xiv.

24. "The Will Rogers Method," *Forbes*, July 19, 1982, 42.

25. "Fool's Gold," *Time*, May 9, 1983.

26. Details of Bullion Reserve's excesses can be found in the Senate testimony of his ex-wife, who was also working for the company. *Commodity Investment Fraud II: Hearings Before the Permanent Subcommittee on Governmental Affairs, United States Senate*, 98th Congress, 2nd session (Washington: U.S. General Printing Office, 1984), 56ff.

27. David J. Gilberg, "Precious Metals Trading: The Last Frontier of Unregulated Investment," *Washington and Lee Law Review* 41, no. 3, 943–991.

28. For details of how the Hunt brothers were able to stay steps ahead of the CFTC, see Stephen Fay, *Beyond Greed* (New York: Viking Press, 1982).

29. Hearings Before the Permanent Subcommittee on Investigations of the Committee on Governmental Affairs, United States Senate, 97th Congress, 2nd session, February 23, 1982, 1–2.

30. "Futures Imperfect: Puppylike Watchdog Irks Some but Pleases Commodities Industry," *Wall Street Journal*, August 2, 1984.

31. "Insurance Plan for Dealers Planned: Gold, Silver Bullion, Coins." *American Metal Market*, November 29, 1984.

32. Fred Barnes and Morton Kondracke, *Jack Kemp: The Bleeding-Heart Conservative Who Changed America* (New York: Sentinel, 2015), 81.

33. It is fair to say that the Dole-Kemp ticket and the Republican Party in 1996 did not emphasize a gold standard. But as late as June of that year, Kemp urged the next president to "reinstate the dollar/gold link that was broken in 1971." See Jack Kemp, "A Bipartisan Economic Agenda," *Wall Street Journal*, June 18, 1996.

### Chapter 12: God, Gold, and Guns

1. John Carney, "Glenn Beck's Gold Endorsement Goes Too Far For Fox," *Business Insider*, December 8, 2009, http://www.businessinsider.com/glenn-becks-gold-endorsement-goes-too-far-for-fox-2009-12; Bill Carter, "Glenn Beck's Gold Deal

Raising Questions at Fox," *New York Times*, December 13, 2009, http://www
.nytimes.com/2009/12/14/business/media/14beck.html?_r=1.

2. "As Seen on TV: An Investigation of Goldline International," report presented by Congressman Anthony D. Weiner, May 17, 2010. Available at http://
www.avaresearch.com/files/20100527200653.pdf.

3. Republican Platform 2012, p. 4.

4. Zachary Mider, "What Kind of Man Spends Millions to Elect Ted Cruz?" *Bloomberg
Politics*, January 20, 2016; "Donald Trump Weighs in on Marijuana, Hillary Clinton, and Man Buns," https://thescene.com/watch/gq/donald-trump-weighs-in-on-
marijuana-hillary-clinton-and-man-buns.

5. Polls done for the advocacy group American Principles in Action showed majorities of Republican voters in Iowa, New Hampshire, and South Carolina favoring a
return to a gold standard. The polls were conducted by Polling Co., Inc. It should
be noted that these polls were not widely released to the public and were conducted on behalf of an organization that seeks to restore a gold standard, and so
they should be read with a degree of skepticism. Nonetheless, their findings for
Republican voters are not out of line with the national poll (see next note) or the
behavior of Republican candidates in the 2012 race.

6. "Public Has Mixed Views of Return to Gold Standard," *Rasmussen Reports*, October
21, 2011. The survey questioned 1,000 likely voters on October 18 and 19, 2011, and
had a margin of error of +/− 3 percent.

7. See "Confidence in Institutions/Gallup Historical Trends," http://www.gallup
.com/poll/1597/confidence-institutions.aspx.

8. Kenneth Dam, *The University of Chicago Law Review* 50, no. 2, Fiftieth Anniversary
Issue (Spring 1983): 504–532.

9. Herman Cain, "We Need a Dollar as Good as Gold," *Wall Street Journal*, May
13, 2012.

10. The argument that gold-backed money hindered the US response to the Depres-
sion is most prominently associated with Barry Eichengreen, *Golden Fetters: The
Gold Standard and the Great Depression, 1919–1939* (New York: Oxford University
Press, 1996).

11. 89th Congress, 1st session, H.R. 702, Committee on Government Operations, July
30, 1965.

12. James Rickards, *The New Case for Gold* (New York: Portfolio, 2016), 131.

13. Ibid., 52ff.

14. Bureau of International Settlements, 2013 survey.

15. Michael D. Bordo, "The Classical Gold Standard: Some Lessons for Today," *Review
(Federal Reserve Bank of St. Louis)*, May 1981, 16.

16. Susan Strange, *States and Markets* (New York: St. Martin's Press, 1994), 97.

17. Bordo, "The Classical Gold Standard," 2.

18. Chicago Booth School, IGM Forum, January 12, 2012, http://www.igmchicago
.org/igm-economic-experts-panel/poll-results?SurveyID=SV_cw1nNUYOXSAKwrq.

19. James U. Blanchard III, "Exclusive Interview with F. A. Hayek," *CATO Policy Report*,
May/June 1984.

20. David Shribman and Dennis Farney, "Survival Strategy Plotted: GOP Moderates Are on the Outside," *Wall Street Journal*, August 22, 1984.

21. *United States Mint Annual Report 2015*, 6.

22. Peter Tulupman, corporate communications, World Gold Council, email to author, March 5, 2016.

23. Neil Meader, Metals Focus, email to author, March 10, 2016.

24. *New York Times*/CBS News Poll: National Survey of Tea Party Supporters. The poll was taken April 5–12, 2010, with 1,580 total respondents, of whom 881 were identified as Tea Party supporters. The poll had a margin of error of ±3 percent but higher for subgroups, making the 5 percent figure for gold buyers statistically questionable.

25. See, for example, Thorsten Polleit, "How the Blockchain and Gold Can Work Together," *Mises Daily*, February 1, 2016, https://mises.org/library/how-blockchain-and-gold-can-work-together.

26. Kyle Chayka, "How Digital Currencies Led to the Biggest Money Laundering Case Ever," *Pacific Standard*, February 5, 2014, http://www.psmag.com/business-economics/digital-currencies-led-biggest-money-laundering-case-ever-bitcoin-74083.

27. "SEC Wins Case Against Ponzi Schemer in Utah." U.S. Securities and Exchange Commission, Litigation Release No. 23419, December 4, 2015, *Securities and Exchange Commission v. National Note of Utah and Wayne L. Palmer*, https://www.sec.gov/litigation/litreleases/2015/lr23419.htm.

28. "In Bullion Depository, Supporters See Golden Opportunity," *Texas Tribune*, July 3, 2015.

29. *Encyclopedia of American Business History*, "Mining Industry," 278.

# INDEX

Note: Page numbers in *italics* refer to illustrations. Page numbers after 340 refer to notes.

# ABOUT THE AUTHOR

———————————————○———————————————

James Ledbetter is the editor of *Inc.* magazine and Inc.com. He was previously the opinion editor of Reuters and has also worked on staff at *Slate, Time,* and the *Village Voice.* He is the author or editor of five previous books including, most recently, *Unwarranted Influence: Dwight D. Eisenhower and the Military-Industrial Complex.* His writings on politics, business, and media have been published in *The New Yorker,* the *New York Times,* the *Washington Post, Quartz, American Prospect, Industry Standard, Mother Jones,* the *Nation, New Republic,* and dozens of other publications. He lives in New York City with his wife and son.